Vivien Leigh

Hugo Vickers

HAMISH HAMILTON LTD
Published by the Penguin Group
27 Wrights Lane, London W8 5TZ, England

Viking Penguin, Inc., 40 West 23rd Street, New York, New York 10010, U.S.A.
Penguin Books Australia ltd., Ringwood, Victoria, Australia
Penguin Books Canada, Ltd., 2801 John Street, Markham, Ontario, Canada L3R 1B4
Penguin Books, (N.Z.) Ltd., 182-190 Wairau Road, Auckland 10, New Zealand
Penguin Books Ltd., Registered Offices: Harmondsworth, Middlesex, England

First published in Great Britain 1988 by
Hamish Hamilton Ltd.

1 3 5 7 9 10 8 6 4 2

British Library Cataloguing in Publication Data

Vickers, Hugo, 1951 –
Vivien Leigh: a biography
1. Great Britain. Acting. Leigh, Vivien, (1913-67)
Biographies
1. Title
792'.028'0924

ISBN (10 Digit): 0-9725951-3-9
(13 Digit): 978-0-9725951-3-1

Printed in the USA

Acknowledgments

The author is grateful for the publisher's permission to quote extracts from the following books:

Confessions of an Actor by Laurence Olivier, Weidenfeld & Nicolson
The Noël Coward Diaries edited by Sheridan Morley and Graham Payn, Weidenfeld and Nicolson
Sir Larry by Thomas Kiernan, Sidgwick & Jackson

Contents

HARTLEY

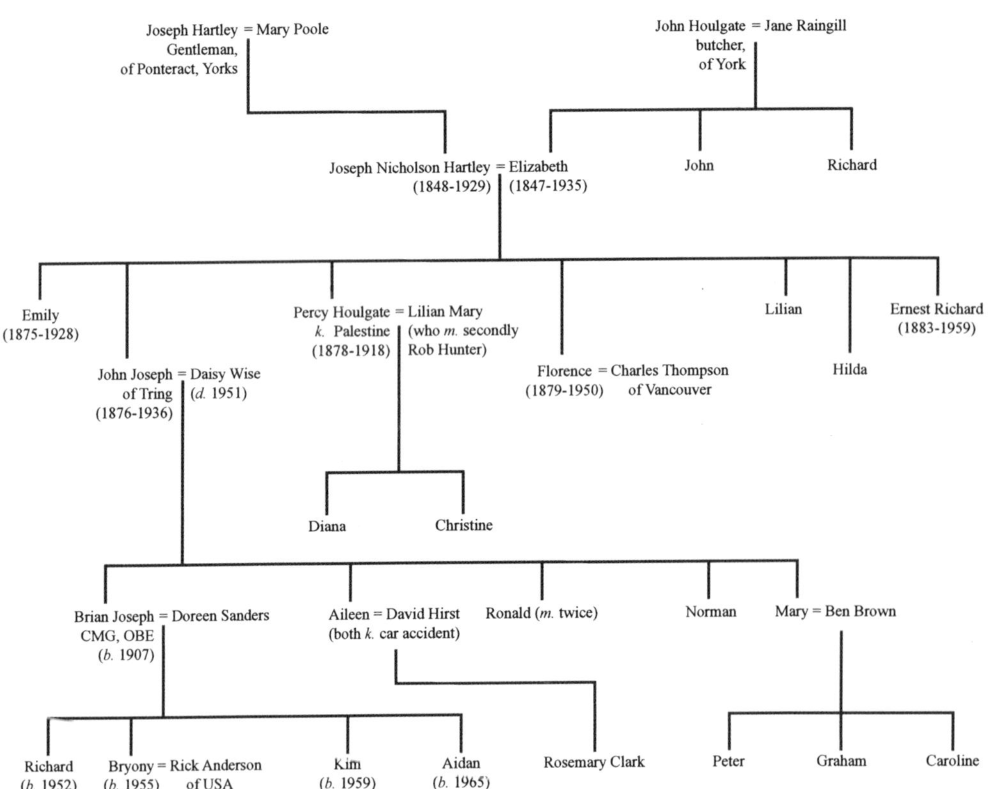
Joseph Hartley = Mary Poole
Gentleman,
of Ponteract, Yorks
John Houlgate = Jane Raingill
butcher,
of York
Joseph Nicholson Hartley = Elizabeth
(1848-1929) (1847-1935)
John
Richard
Emily
(1875-1928)
Percy Houlgate = Lilian Mary
k. Palestine (who m. secondly
(1878-1918) Rob Hunter)
Lilian
Ernest Richard
(1883-1959)
John Joseph = Daisy Wise
of Tring (d. 1951)
(1876-1936)
Florence = Charles Thompson
(1879-1950) of Vancouver
Hilda
Diana
Christine
Brian Joseph = Doreen Sanders
CMG, OBE
(b. 1907)
Aileen = David Hirst
(both k. car accident)
Ronald (m. twice)
Norman
Mary = Ben Brown
Richard
(b. 1952)
Bryony = Rick Anderson
(b. 1955) of USA
Kim
(b. 1959)
Aidan
(b. 1965)
Rosemary Clark
Peter
Graham
Caroline

YACKJEE

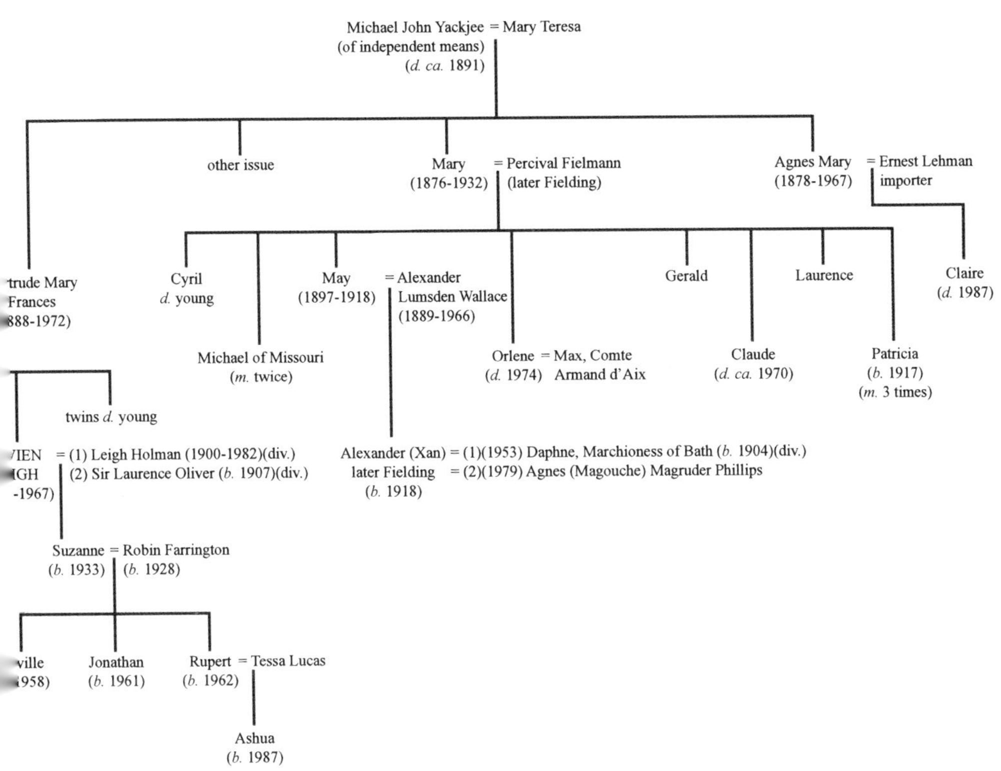

Michael John Yackjee = Mary Teresa
(of independent means)
(d. ca. 1891)
other issue
Mary (1876-1932) = Percival Fielmann (later Fielding)
Agnes Mary (1878-1967) = Ernest Lehman importer
trude Mary Frances 888-1972)
Cyril d. young
Michael of Missouri (m. twice)
May (1897-1918) = Alexander Lumsden Wallace (1889-1966)
Orlene (d. 1974) = Max, Comte Armand d'Aix
Gerald
Claude (d. ca. 1970)
Laurence
Patricia (b. 1917) (m. 3 times)
Claire (d. 1987)
twins d. young
/IEN IGH -1967) = (1) Leigh Holman (1900-1982)(div.)
(2) Sir Laurence Oliver (b. 1907)(div.)
Alexander (Xan) later Fielding (b. 1918) = (1)(1953) Daphne, Marchioness of Bath (b. 1904)(div.)
= (2)(1979) Agnes (Magouche) Magruder Phillips
Suzanne (b. 1933) = Robin Farrington (b. 1928)
ville 958)
Jonathan (b. 1961)
Rupert (b. 1962) = Tessa Lucas
Ashua (b. 1987)

To my Aunt,

Joan Vickers

With Love

List of Illustrations

VIVIEN LEIGH

Hugo Vickers

VIVIEN LEIGH

Prologue

I began to write this book with one thought in mind – that Vivien Leigh was almost certainly more interesting than hitherto presented. The filmography (Hollywood) approach did not seem a satisfactory one in her case – with endless details of contracts and studio rows, none of which interested her very much. Nor was she merely a romantic star, nor, equally, some kind of maniac. One technique applied to her was to present her climbing up one side of a hill as a rising star only to descend the other as a manic depressive. Clearly it was more complicated than that. Inevitably a considerable mythology surrounded her. The only way to unravel this was to start again at the beginning, question every fact presented, find out who her parents were, where they came from, and what they were like, and take it from there. I applied the same kind of research that is necessary for any subject, first and foremost going on location. Admittedly I was lucky that the sixth grave I examined in the first churchyard I found in Bridlington contained a family of Hartleys, who subsequently proved to be Vivien's grandparents. Another character who had remained hitherto an ill-defined one was Leigh Holman, her first husband and consistently her best friend through life. Here, too, I was lucky in being allowed access to the diaries of the late Oswald Frewen. He first met Leigh in 1924, then Vivien in 1932 and Olivier in 1936. Friends to them all, he was an invaluable first-hand witness of their lives for over thirty years, most particularly in the late 1930s.

One of the joys of researching the life of an actress who was also a film star was the chance to watch a great number of videos in the cause of research. I have always favored the technique of letting the subject of a book speak for himself, primariy through letters, but also in interviews given over the years.

Vivien's daughter, Suzanne Farrington, generously made available a considerable number of family papers. These included all the letters that Vivien wrote Leigh Holman between 1932 and 1967, the diaries of Vivien's mother, Gertrude Hartley, from 1920 to 1972, the letters from friends which Mrs. Hartley kept, and the albums of press-cuttings and photographs compiled (and frequently annotated) by Mrs. Hartley.

Among these papers were a number of letters written by Vivien to her parents and to her daughter, and similar letters from Laurence Olivier, Leigh Holman, and John Merivale. There were theatre programs and all the letters of sympathy received by Mrs. Hartley at the time of Vivien's death.

John Merivale also preserved a considerable collection of letters from and about Vivien. He kindly gave me access to these and also to ten fascinating boxes of sterolist slides, taken by himself and by Vivien in the 1960s, some of which are reproduced in this book.

Further letters from Vivien were loaned by Maxine Audley, Jane Pauling (Mrs. David Glass), Mercia Swinburne (Mrs. George Relph), Rosemary Geddes, and Sunny Lash. I located six letters from Vivien to Bernard Berenson in the Harvard Center for Italian Renaissance Studies at Villa I Tatti, near Florence.

As Cecil Beaton's literary executor, I was in the fortunate position of being able to give myself unrestricted access to his papers (now at St. John's College, Cambridge). There is a considerable amount of material about the Oliviers in his papers and unpublished diaries, some of which I recalled from my earlier research. I also spent a profitable morning in the Warner Bros. Archives at the University of Southern California in Los Angeles. These contained material relating to the films *A Streetcar Named Desire* and *The Roman Spring of Mrs. Stone*.

My first debt of gratitude for help in my research is to Peter Hiley, who ran L.O.P. Productions from 1949 to 1962, was Vivien's executor from the start, and sent me on many enjoyable missions to see Vivien's friends. He was also unfailingly helpful in giving me clues to follow and in answering questions.

Suzanne Farrington has also been extremely generous, not only in giving me access to the papers, but also in answering many complicated questions, and introducing me to further key sources who had known her mother since her early days. I particularly enjoyed my two visits to Zeals, which was originally her father's home.

John Merivale was most generous with his time. I had almost weekly interviews with him between November 1986 and May 1987, and returned many times to ask him about new pieces of information that arose. There was an added bonus to my visits to Jack in being able to talk to his wife, Dinah Sheridan.

I also greatly enjoyed my two visits to The Sheephouse by kind permission of Mrs. Oswald Frewen. I spent long hours there transcribing passages from the meticulously kept diary of the late Oswald Frewen. I am also grateful to Jonathan Frewen for his advice concerning the Frewens and for allowing me to reproduce two photographs from his great-uncle's collection. And I am grateful to Frances McGlennon who helped me see the diaries, and who was so hospitable during my visits.

I am also particularly grateful to Maxine Audley and Leo Maguire, David Conville, and Michael Denison and Dulcie Gray for their considerable help throughout my research; to Michael Redington for lending me all the letters he wrote on the Old Vic Tour of Australia and New Zealand in 1948-49; and to Nora Swinburne for allowing me access to the unpublished memoirs of her husband, the late Esmond Knight.

I felt that, whereas the big stars had spoken or written about Vivien in the past, her fellow actors and actresses had been somewhat neglected. It is my experience that the occasional spear-holder has more time to observe the leading lady than does the leading man, who is often more concerned with his own part. Having thought that I would find myself traveling far afield, it seemed a good omen that the majority of sources dwelt within the Royal Borough of Kensington and Chelsea, meaning that I could park with impunity outside their houses. However, I did pay two visits to New York and one to Hollywood, and I wrote part of this book while staying at the Locanda di San Vigilio on Lake Garda, a favorite haunt of the Oliviers.

I did not meet Lord Olivier. The only time our paths crossed was at the ballet at Covent Garden in January 1986, shortly after I began work on this book. I opened a door and he came through it, looking rather like a country schoolmaster. He muttered 'Thank you,' and went on his way. I don't think anybody else recognized him, but I did because he was in my thoughts. Then, the day before I finished the book, he appeared again, a frail, bearded figure sitting in the actors' church, St. Paul's Covent Garden at the memorial service for Ginette Spanier. It was extraordinary to see him there, accompanied by the son of his first marriage and the son of his last.

I am grateful to Hon. Richard Olivier, who gave me permission to reproduce segments from Lord Olivier's letters to Vivien after the first publication of this book.

I am grateful to John Julius Norwich for permission to quote from Lady Diana Cooper's letters. There is a list of books consulted in the bibliography. However, I relied heavily on Alan Dent's *Vivien Leigh: A Bouquet*, Lord Olivier's *Confessions of an Actor,* Felix Barker's *The Oliviers*, Thomas Kiernan's *Sir Larry*, and *The Noël Coward Diaries*.

I would also like to thank the following for their help with this book, either in interviews or in answering specific questions or in generally assisting me with my research: Mr. Leith Adams, Mr. Derek Adkins, Mr. Larry Adler, Miss Melissa Allen, the late Hon. Mrs. Pandora Astor, Mr. Stephen August, Monsieur Jean-Pierre Aumont, Mr. H. W. Austin, the Countess of Avon, Mr. Frith Banbury, Mrs. Iris Banham-Lee, Mr. John Barnard, Dr. Richard Beadle, Mr. Robert Becker, Mrs. Amanda Claire Beech, Colonel Philip Beeman, the Earl of Bessborough, Mrs. David Birkin (Miss Judy Campbell), Surgeon Vice Admiral Sir Eric Bradbury, Mrs. Emma Brash, Miss Coral Browne, Mr. Tony Butler, *Bridlington Free Press* (ed. Arthur Porter), Mrs. Mary Sykes Cahan, Miss Jane Carmichael, Mr. Charles Castle, Mr. William Chappell, Miss Diana Churchill, Hon. Colin Clark, Mr. Edward Close-Smith, Mrs. Enid Collett, Hon. Artemis Cooper, the late Lady Diana Cooper, Mr. Desmond Corcoran, the Lord Cottesloe, Mrs. John Counsell (Mary Kerridge), Miss Elizabeth Counsell, Mr. Marlin Peck Cruse, Mrs. Cyril Cusack, Mr. Allan Davis, Mrs. Lucinda Ballard Dietz, Mr. David Dodimead, the Rev. Anthony P. Dolan, Mr. and Mrs. Patrick Donnell, Mrs. Doreen Dor, Miss Fabia Drake, the Rev. Walter Drumm, Mrs. Sheila Egerton, Air Vice Marshal John Elton, Miss Ellen Exum, Mr. Robin Farrington, Mr. Xan Fielding, Mr. Alastair Forbes, Mr. Michael Forgacs, Sr. & Sra. Massimo Freccia, Mrs. Ashley Gabriel, Princess George Galitzine, Mr. James V. Gardiner, Mrs. Jane Glass, Mr and Mrs. John Gliddon, Miss Rumer Godden, Miss Daisy Goguel, Mr. Milton Goldman, Marshal of the RAF Sir John Grandy, Sir

Alec Guinness, Mr. Stanley Hall, the late Hamish Hamilton, Mrs. Hamish Hamilton, Miss Emma Hardy, Mr. Robert Hardy, Mrs. Sally Hardy, Miss Radie Harris, Mrs. Brian Hartley, Mr. Peter Hartley, Sir Anthony Havelock-Allan, Mr. Charles Higham, Mr.William Hiley, Mr. David Hinton, Mr. Philip Hoare, Mrs. John Hodges, Mr. Anthony Holden, the Lord Holderness, Mrs. Roshan Horobin, the late Eileen Hose, Miss Sally Ann Howes, the Lord Jenkins of Putney, Mr. Garson Kanin, Miss Julie Kavanagh, Lady Kelvedon, Miss Barbara Ker-Seymer, Mr. Charles Kidd, the late Esmond Knight, Mrs. Esmond Knight (Miss Nora Swinburne), Dr. Ann Marie Koller, Mr. Robert Lacey, the Viscountess Lambert, Lord Lambton, the late Baroness Lane-Fox, Mrs. Sunny Lash, Princess Nina Lobanov, Miss Moira Lister, Mr. and Mrs. John McCorquodale, Miss Elspeth March, Laura, Duchess of Marlborough, Mr. Hugh Martin, Mrs. Frances Martin, Mrs. Dido Merwin, Lady Alexandra Metcalfe, Mrs. J. H. Methold, Mgr. Frederick Miles, Mr. and Mrs. Hugh Montgomery-Massingberd, Mr. and Mrs. Terence Morgan, Mr. Roy Moseley, Mr. William Mostyn-Owen, Mr. Charlie Nickols, Miss Lucy Norton, Mrs. Anne Norwich, the Viscount Norwich, Lady Nutting, Mr. John Pearson, Mr. John Perry, Mrs. Tanis Phillips, Mr. Bill Poole, Miss E.R. Poyzer, Mr. Peter Reid, Mrs. George Relph (Mercia Swinburne), Lady Richardson, Mr. M. S. Robinson, Mr. William Roerick, Mr. Toby Rowland, Lt. Commander John Rusher, RN, Mr. Martin Russell, Miss Dorothy Safian, Miss Philippa Salisbury, Mrs. Irene Selznick, Mr. Jeffrey Selznick, Mrs. Lydia Seton, Miss Athene Seyler, Commander W. F. Skelton, RN, the late Ginette Spanier, Christina Stephenson, Mrs. Hester St. John Ives, Mr. David Stern, Mrs. Summerscale (Jay Wilson), Dr. Fiorella Superbi, Mrs. Joyce Sykes, Mrs. Irina Baronova-Tennant, Miss Elizabeth Thomson, the late Ian Thomson, Mr. Michael Thornton, Mrs. Anne Tovey, Hon. Mrs. Tritton (Georgina Ward), Mr. Graham Turner, Mrs. Diana Vreeland, Mr. David Weguelin, Mrs. Peter Wehrli, Commandant Paul-Louis Weiller, Mr. Peter Willes, Mr. Dick Wordley, Mr. Peter Wyngarde; and my sister, Imogen Vickers for exploring Campbeltown for me.

I would also like to thank my publishers, Christopher Sinclair-Stevenson and Ray Roberts for their continual help, guidance, and encouragement, and my agent Gillon Aitken for his continued protection. Above all I am grateful to Louise Corrigan, who not only collated and coordinated the research and typed and retyped the manuscript with effortless efficiency, but also took a keen interest in the development of the book and offered valuable advice at all times. Without her help this book would not have been finished by the twenty-first anniversary of Vivien's death.

Hugo Vickers
8 July 1988

P.S. A great number of my sources have died since 1988. I have not added 'the late' in front of their names. For this edition I would like to thank Scott Baber, Henry Beers, Richard Jay Hutto, Gary Pulliam, and Joni Woolf of Indigo Publishing Group. I am glad to have been offered the chance to make a few amendments to the text, though I have not made substantial changes.

H.V.
March 2009

Introduction

She had a mind that left most people behind. Most of us simply don't keep our minds in diamond-cutting gear all the time. We get lazy. We watch the snooker on television or whatever. We suffer by it and make foolish remarks – engage our mouths without making sure our minds are in gear. We say all sorts of trivialities and inanities which we really don't work out. And we get through life like that. It's one of the cushions that we just need. Vivien didn't do that. Vivien's mind was just like a diamond drill. I suppose that must have been the reverse side of the mentally depressive coin.

– Colin Clark

One of the most astonishing things about Vivien was her energy, which is probably the secret of her life. Certainly the secret of acting. You can't act without energy, even if you are acting a dull man, an old dying man. You've got to have energy to push that out. And she had energy from the moment she woke up till she went to bed – very late.

– David Dodimead

She was enormously helpful about acting. I remember during the New York *Duel of Angels* asking Peter Wyngarde about a problem with something and he said: "Go and ask her. She knows."

She taught me so much, her appreciation, her taste in colors. She wanted to see everything that was good and going. And she was very cross if things weren't good.

She was a wonderful mixer. She had no sense of religion, color, creed, class. She was wonderfully liberal. She thought I was funny. I think that's what really held us together. She loved to laugh and I could make her laugh.

– John Merivale

VIVIEN LEIGH

She had the kind of festiveness and longing to make everything an occasion that people usually have more when they're quite young. I never thought of Vivien as a fabulous star. Vivien never acted as though she was.

– Lucinda Ballard Dietz

She was a star in the real meaning of the word, in that she spread light on everybody. She gave an incredible endorsement of what stardom was about. She knew how to run a company. She knew everything about everybody's life. If anyone's parent or lover was ill there would be flowers. She was kept well informed – a star in the right way.

The Oliviers brought speech to the English stage. Vivien was visual and Larry was oral. She learned about 'the word' from him. She had such intelligence, beauty, and style. She never left the stage-door unless impeccably dressed. She was always amusing. And she was honest, totally and utterly honest. She was a woman, and yet always somehow a child.

– Peter Wyngarde

The reason the relationship succeeded so well professionally was because Larry helped Vivien in every way to realize her ambition to become an outstanding stage actress. She could have had no better tutor, nor a more unselfish co-star when they acted together in the great plays when they toured in England, America, and Australia. Later when Vivien was established (as a star of the theatre in her own right), Larry wanted to pursue his own career and to play the great male roles, many of which do not provide great opportunities for female stars.

– Sir Anthony Havelock-Allan

I first met her when I was filming *Anna Karenina.* She had been ill so her contract limited her time on the set to between eleven and four. Every time she stepped onto the set the telephone would ring and it would be Larry checking she was all right. Then at four he'd ring again to make sure she didn't work any longer. I was seventeen and thought it very romantic.

She always made you feel that you were the most important person in her life. Apart from her great physical beauty, she was the kindest of friends with the most beautiful manners. You don't get that in the theatre today. You didn't get it then.

– Sally Ann Howes

Alan Webb said to me that if you found yourself naked with Vivien in the Sahara Desert with absolutely nothing, twenty-four hours later you would be coming out in a Rolls-Royce, covered in minks and drinking champagne.

– David Conville

When she was good, she was very, very good, but when she was bad, she was *awful!*

– Maxine Audley

Chapter 1
Not a Sleepy Baby

> *A garden, with the sloping lawn and azaleas and lilies growing, and cuckoos and birds flying around, looking down to this river right down there and then right up at an angle, forty miles away, this glittering rampart of the Himalayan hills, right across the sky, glistening blue and gold and silver. Wonderful place – marvelous place to be born in.*
>
> Esmond Knight to the author, 11 February 1987

"I was born in one of the most romantic places in the world – Darjeeling," wrote Vivien Leigh, "although I have only confused impressions of its beauty, and of the gaiety of life there..."[1] The summer outpost of Darleeling, within sight of Mount Everest and Kanchenjunga, does indeed seem to provide the perfect setting for Vivien's birth. She came into the world at Shannon Lodge, soon after sundown on Guy Fawkes Day, 5 November 1913. For weeks before, her mother had trusted the Indian superstition that, if she gazed at Kanchenjunga, a beautiful child would be born. Nor was Mrs. Hartley to be disappointed in Vivian Mary,* dubbed by Gladys Cooper "the prettiest Guy every born."[2]

Due to the mythomania of Hollywood producers and others, a number of

*Vivian changed to Vivien in 1935. She was Vivian Leigh for a short phase, but became Vivien Leigh at the time of *The Mask of Virtue*. For simplicity it will be Vivien throughout this book.

conflicting stories have grown up about the origins of Vivien's parents. Just before the shooting of *Gone with the Wind,* David O. Selznick informed Ed Sullivan: "Scarlett O'Hara's parents were French and Irish. Identically, Miss Leigh's parents are French and Irish."[3] There was no truth in this. Her father came from Yorkshire, a county that contains a great number of Hartleys. In the middle of the nineteenth century Joseph Hartley, a gentleman, was living in Pontefract, a mid-Yorkshire town, thirteen miles southeast of Leeds. Later, before 1874, he made his home in Selby. His son, Joseph Nicholson Hartley, who was born in Pontefract on 18 June 1848, served for forty years as an administrator in the Civil Service, first as a Collector for the Inland Revenue and later as a Collector of Customs and Excise. At the age of twenty-five on 9 June 1874, he married Elizabeth Houlgate, a girl six months older than he. Elizabeth came from a family of butchers. Her father, John Houlgate, was a butcher, living at 17 Shambles, York. Both her brothers, John and Richard, maintained the family business, living side by side at 17 and 18 Shambles.

J.N. Hartley, who was evidently "greatly esteemed by all the officials with whom he came in contact,"[4] moved about England and Ireland in the course of his career. He had seven children. The eldest two, Emily and John Joseph* (a customs man like his father, he later lived in Tring), were born in Sunderland in 1875 and 1876. Next came Percy Houlgate born in 1878 (who was killed in Palestine in 1918); then Florence, born in 1879 who married a Canadian, Charlie Thompson, and went to live in Vancouver; two unmarried sisters, Lilian and Hilda, and finally Ernest Richard, born on the island of Islay (where there are a number of distilleries) on 19 February 1883.

Joseph Nicholson Hartley retired from Civil Service in 1910 and, four years later, went to live in Bridlington. Ernest's parents spent their last years at 14 Belgrave Square, just off South Marine Parade, and quite near the harbor. A neighbor remembered Vivien's grandparents from her childhood:

> I recall Mr. and Mrs. Hartley as being old fashioned and Victorian-type in the way they dressed. Both were slightly below average height, Mr. Hartley being a trifle shorter than his wife, and he had a white beard. Mrs. Hartley was a prim little figure and wore black and a bonnet when she

*His eldest son, Brian Hartley, CMG, OBE (1907 - 92) was Oxfam's Consultant in East Africa and a world expert on camels.

> went to church – not to Emmanuel which is just at the end of Belgrave Road, but they always walked two miles to Priory Church which is very historical and situated in what is called the Old Town.[5]

Bridlington is a slightly depressing resort, full of bed and breakfasts, beach huts, and donkey-rides, and old folk and young families, trying to enjoy their escape from the daily round on two fine curving beaches. Beautiful sailing boats are still the most attractive feature of the sweeping bay. One of the dramatic happenings of the nineteenth century was the great gale of 1871 when a fleet of ships were wrecked and the lifeboat "smashed to matchwood"[6] with most of its crew drowned. The dead sailors lie in the churchyard of the fine Priory Church whose northwest tower is a conspicuous landmark. And today Joseph and Elizabeth Hartley also lie within the shadow of that church.

The stolid middle-class life of Yorkshire offered little to the youngest son, Ernest Hartley, and so, influenced by the tales of Rudyard Kipling, a fellow Yorkshireman, he set off to seek his fortune in India. He arrived in 1905, aged twenty-two, and was employed as a junior exchange broker in the firm of Pigott, Chapman and Co. of 5, Royal Exchange Road, Calcutta. As a young man he was described as "invariably effervescing with fun."[7] India was rich with opportunity for those who survived the diseases that killed so many. Equally, the cemeteries of India are filled with adventurers who succumbed to typhoid and cholera. Ernest Hartley was lucky. He prospered and was able to enjoy amateur theatricals, cricket, polo, and breeding racehorses.

Ernest's new friends had enjoyed a better start in life than he. Arthur George Macpherson came from a long line of Indian Army officers. Geoffrey Martin, whose family were to be an important influence on Vivien, went to India because he, too, had to earn his living. There was also Jack Thomson whose life became intimately woven with that of Ernest and his wife.

In those days Calcutta had to rely on itself for entertainment. The Calcutta Dramatic Society produced about three plays a year. Ernest and Arthur George Macpherson starred in Conan Doyle's story about a deadly snake, *The Speckled Band*, and, recalled a friend, "What a handsome pair they were."[8] Another time Ernest gave a fine character performance as jury foreman, rendered in a more than acceptable Devon accent. He appeared as 'The Bad Wolf' in a satirical pantomime, and at the end of the Great War in 1918 he took the part of Warren Hastings.

His love of horses provided an enjoyable outdoor life and involved him in due course in a number of ceremonial occasions with the Light Horse, such as the arrival of the Prince of Wales in Calcutta in 1921. Years later, his racing activities reached their peak when his horse, Kilbuck (at odds of 100-1), came in ninth out of twelve of the forty-three horses that completed the Grand National course in March 1931, and subsequently won at Fontwell Park in April 1932 and at Wetherby that May.

Ernest himself was a jovial fellow who greatly enjoyed making a lot of money and spending it on good living. Geoffrey Martin's daughter, Frances, usually known as Mills, recalled:

> He was marvelous to have fun with. He had a histrionic ability to relate terrible Irish jokes. I can see him now standing there with his bandy legs. He enjoyed his fishing and golfing and spending money in flashy hotels. He was 'hail fellow well met,' but very much a fair weather friend. Vivien certainly inherited any histrionic ability from him.[9]

It has invariably been stated that Ernest's wife, Gertrude Yackjee, was also born in Yorkshire, but this is incorrect. Her only link with Yorkshire came with Ernest. Gertrude's passport reveals that she was born in Darjeeling on 5 December 1888.

Gertrude Mary Frances was the youngest of the large family of Michael John Yackjee, a man of independent means. She used to say that her maternal grandparents were called Robinson and had left Ireland because of religious difficulties following the union of a Catholic and a Protestant. They had sailed to India but were killed in the Indian Mutiny of 1857, leaving her mother an orphan cared for by nuns. Mr. Yackjee had arrived and spied her in the orphanage. He decided to make her his bride. He died about 1891 when Gertrude was two years old. Most who recall the Hartleys in India remember that Mrs. Hartley had Armenian blood, believing that this explained Vivien's dark Eastern beauty.

Gertrude had a sister called Mary, born about 1876, who married Percival

Fielmann, a box-wallah, who later changed his name to Fielding. One of Mary's daughter's, May, married Alexander Wallace and died at Ootacamund in 1918, giving birth to the travel writer, Xan Fielding. Because he was only a year younger than his aunt Patricia, Xan was raised for years in the belief that he was the son of his grandparents. He believed his grandmother might have been half-caste Parsi Indian. One of his aunts, Orlene, was very dark, and both Gertrude and Vivien had tight hair that crinkled easily. If the half-caste theory is true, it explains why so little information has been forthcoming. Both the pure Indians and the British in India looked down on the half-castes. Thus, such origins were invariably disguised. The name Yackjee was sometimes changed to Yackje, or they used the inherited maternal name of Robinson, though this does not appear on Gertrude's marriage certificate.

It also draws an interesting parallel with the film star, Merle Oberon, whose career ran side by side with Vivien's. She was the daughter of a railway engineer from Darlington, County Durham and a Eurasian girl, with a part-Maori background. Merle Oberon pretended throughout her life that she had been born in Hobart, Tasmania, whereas in fact she was born in Bombay in February 1911.

Gertrude herself had a fair, peach-like skin, which encouraged many in the belief that she was Irish. As a young woman she was extremely beautiful – many people say more so than Vivien. Rumer Godden remembered her 'beautiful dark auburn hair and magnificent blue eyes."[10] Her early life in India was no less enjoyable than Ernest's. A friend, Jeanie Tayler, reminisced about "Mary's astonishing house and parties," of a first ride in a motor car owned by a German who wanted to marry Gertrude, and of a man called Harper who loved her "for many years."[11] Gertrude met Ernest in Calcutta. One evening Geoffrey Martin and Ernest were being driven in the latter's car. Geoffrey asked Ernest, "Who is the girl in the front?" he replied evasively, "It's the chauffeur's sister."[12]

When Ernest announced that he wanted to marry Gertrude it caused a considerable stir in Calcutta, as Geoffrey Martin's son, Hugh, recalled:

> Ernest was told that he must expect social ostracism if the marriage went ahead. He was, I believe, required to resign from the Bengal Club and the Saturday Club.* My father

*The Saturday Club was immensely exclusive, the Bengal Club less so.

> stood up for Ernest, and in a short while the social climate changed. Ernest's good humor and charm, combined with Gertrude's good looks and vivacity, made them a popular couple in the 'best circles' of European society of Calcutta of the time.[13]

In 1911 Gertrude sailed to London in *City of Sperta* in order to marry Ernest in his fatherland. She settled at 198 Holland Park in Kensington, with her mother, Mary Teresa Yackjee. She and Ernest were married at the Catholic Church of Our Lady of Victories in Kensington High Street on 9 April 1912. They returned to India on the Anchor Line's *Maidan*. During their brief absdence, they had missed the celebrated Delhi Durbar visit of King George V and Queen Mary.

In those days, Calcutta was reached by train from Bombay, through beautiful fertile countryside. From the windows, monkeys, camels, and elephants could be seen by the track. Calcutta was the Imperial capital where the Viceroy lived, where the Commander-in-Chief was stationed, the center of the Government of India, the Legislative Assembly, and of all the officials who worked for them. But in the Durbah ceremony the King announced that Delhi would be the new capital, so that in effect Calcutta would be demoted to Provincial capital.

By and large this was a successful plan, reversing the ill-effects of Curzon's policy of partition in Bengal, but it was met by "implacable opposition"[14] from the British commercial community, who resented the loss of prestige. The Viceroy, Lord Hardinge of Penshurst, was denounced as a villain in the Calcutta press.

Prestige was all that Calcutta lost. There were no material disadvantages, yet on his 1912-13 visit to India, E.M. Forster did not bother to go there, having been advised that "there is nothing to see in Calcutta except people and the tapirs in the Zoo."[15] There was, however, a fine golf course and race course (on which it was more refreshing to ride in the early evening than before a day's work). High season was Christmas when the All-India Polo Championship Tournament was held. These were the days of big game hunting, the bagging of tigers, and hunting of bears – days when Lord Hardinge could still describe pig sticking as "that exhilarating sport."[16] When Ernest went hunting, he was accompanied by five white friends and eighteen

Indian bearers. They played polo in jodhpurs and wide-brimmed solar topees, and relaxed in club rooms, lined with bottles. Ernest's early photographs show men with rifles and happy-go-lucky faces, and later, when the early motor cars appeared, the men sat lazily on their bonnets, their legs hanging over the sides. Meanwhile Gertrude developed a life-long passion for golf.

Calcutta itself remained old-fashioned. When the dancer Maud Allan visited the city, the Europeans protested that her performance and style of dress might offend the Indians. As it happened she so modified both that "even the Europeans considered them dull and uninteresting."[17]

It was traditional in summertime to leave over-heated Calcutta for one of the cooler hill-stations. Thus in the summer of 1913 the Hartleys set off for Darjeeling. A big train took them to the foot of the Himalayas and they then transferred to a smaller one, reminiscent of those seen in amusement parks. The last stage of the journey was steep. A coolie sprinkled sand onto the rails to help its grip and gradually it made its day-long climb, the first- and second-class compartments comfortable and roomy, the third-class filled with Indians (some seated on the window ledges), children, hens, and luggage crammed into every possible corner.

The Hartleys settled at Shannon Lodge, a two-storeyed house with a wide-sloping roof, set in its own wooded grounds. Sometimes they went to look at the Buddhists at prayer on top of Observatory Hill. At other times they were content to gaze down on the wooden homes perched at random amongst the tree-encrusted hills. The monsoons washed Bengal, and Ernest was able to return to Calcutta, but he rejoined his wife in time for the birth of Vivien, their only child to survive.*

Vivien was born a Catholic, of a strict Catholic mother. She soon displayed the restless energy that would always be part of her nature, so much so that Gertrude worried about the short hours she slept. The doctor assured her there was nothing wrong, but that she was "not a sleepy baby." Laurence Olivier always felt this would be a good title for a book about Vivien.

It is likely that Vivien would soon have been sent home to England, but nine months after her birth war broke out between Britain and Germany.

Ernest was soon in khaki (with chain-mail epaulets and solar topee), putting his horsemanship to good use in the Indian Cavalry. First, he was stationed at Meerut, where, in 1915, a Mahratta anarchist succeeded in

*Later, Gertrude had twins that lived no longer than a week.

breaking the lines of the 12th Cavalry, bearing ten loaded bombs, before his arrest. Vivien and her mother lodged at Mussoorie, and Vivien had a brown pony to ride.

In 1917 Ernest was transferred to the military station at Bangalore, where he trained remounts for Mesopotamia. His wife and daughter took refuge at Ootacamund. At first, Vivien was cared for by an Indian amah, but later a Catholic nanny, Miss Holden, was imported. There is evidence of one occasion on which Vivien performed in public, at the age of three-and-a-half. They were back at Mussoorie, where they met the Godden sisters, the children of Anglo-Indians based at Gulmarg, the hill-station of Kashmir. Jon and Rumer Godden recalled:

> In Coonoor Nancy was chosen to dance *Tom, Tom the Piper's Son* in a charity matinée opposite a bewitching little girl, Vivien Leigh, then Vivian Hartley, as Bo-Peep. The rest of us danced too, but in the rut. Rose was Little Jumping Joan; Fa, who was up on short leave, called her little Thumping Thoan and it was true she shook the stage.[18]

Rumer Godden remembered Vivien as "a most enchanting little girl with wonderful coloring."[19] She also recalled that another girl had been destined for the role of Bo-Peep, but when the organizers saw Vivien, she was instantly allotted the part, the cause of considerable jealousy. The guest of honor was Lady Willingdon, wife of the Governor of Madras. Not long after this, when Vivien's mother was enacting the Bible story of Daniel in the Lion's Den, Vivien played the lion and ruined the story by biting her mother in the leg.

In later years, Vivien claimed that she was not lonely like other only children because of her mother, "who was blessed with an imagination that could turn ordinary, everyday happenings into an exciting adventure, and make you feel that there was always something wonderful waiting just around the corner."[20] Her mother encouraged her to read. She shared her father's love of Kipling, and other favorites were Hans Christian Anderson, Lewis Carroll, and Charles Kingsley. She also enjoyed Greek mythology. All these combine elements of fantasy with cruel reality.

When the war ended in 1918, the Hartley family returned to a spacious house in Calcutta, 18 Alipore South, and Ernest became senior partner of Pigott, Chapman. He prospered and would continue to do so during the decade he remained in India.

For all its romance, India left little mark on Vivien herself. In 1953, when making the ill-fated film, *Elephant Walk,* with Peter Finch in Ceylon, she revealed that she was terrified of the black eyes of the natives, and always had been. But there was an imperious, commanding side to her nature which often came to those brought up in a household of Indian servants. She heard her mother giving commands that she expected to be obeyed. At least one theatrical dresser in later life felt himself similarly treated.

Vivien was taken back to England at the age of six in 1920 on the *City of Baroda* and, though she longed to rejoin her parents, she did not return to India until 1964.

Chapter 2
The Convent

Protestants always have morbid ideas about nuns...
Antonia White, *Frost in May*

The City of Baroda docked at Tilbury on a cold, wet Easter Monday, 5 April 1920. The Hartleys, Vivien, and Miss Holden arrived in London the next day and stayed at the Carlton Hotel. They were there for four days and one of their excitements was to be reunited with another of Ernest's partners, Jack Thomson, who was staying at the Charing Cross Hotel.

John Lambert Thomson, known as Tommy, arrived on the scene with a good story to tell – a man had been murdered in the room next door to him at his hotel.

Tommy was a much-loved friend of both the Hartleys and an important influence in their lives until his tragic early death in 1938. His nephew, Ian Thomson, described him as "a confirmed bachelor with a life-long love for Gertrude Hartley."[1] He continued:

> He was a wonderful fellow, in the eyes of a teenage boy. He had enough money, being a bachelor, to do all the things I thought were wonderful like big game fishing (salmon and trout), shooting, sailing, etc. He was a charming chap with a 'way' with women as they say, as have all the Thomsons! He also had 'hollow legs.'[2]

Gertrude Hartley told Tommy's niece, Elizabeth, that Tommy was 'the love of her life,"[3] though she added that in those days it would have been unthinkable to do anything about it. The Hartleys and Tommy either traveled as a threesome, or Ernest and Tommy went fishing together, or Ernest entrusted Gertrude to Tommy's care and they traveled together. Mills Martin recalled: "He was completely attached to them. He was part of the Hartley family."[4] The precise nature of the arrangement is unclear, but Mrs. Martin recalled her father stating somewhat uncharacteristically on one occasion: "When Tommy wants a woman he knows where to find one."[5] The most important aspect of the situation was that Ernest, Tommy, and Gertrude were all perfectly happy about it, and remained so.

The Thomson family came from Campbeltown in Scotland and Tommy was born in nearby Islay. Campbeltown itself was grey and dour. Machrihanish, about five miles away, was equally remote but more beautiful with a handsome golf course, which was a constant lure for the Hartleys. Otherwise they all went to Ireland to fish in Waterville. Liz Thomson could never understand how Gertrude could prefer 'Uncle Jack' to the powerful, handsome Ernest, a larger than life figure. To the young Thomsons, Vivien's father was a considerable raconteur "with a great ability to tell a story and act it out."[6] He held his youthful audiences rapt for hours. They found Gertrude "a very self-assured and competent woman and as such she had enough confidence in herself not to be in the slightest bit bitchy."[7]

Gertrude was also a staunchly loyal friend with a strong character and considerable resolve in adversity. She had great organizing skill, and was in no sense scatty. Mills Martin liked her but noted: "She had no sense of humor – not one spark, and she was completely urban."[8]

The Hartleys stayed in England until 22 October, and Vivien met her grandparents in Bridlington for the first time in the course of a three-day visit. On 20 September the Hartleys took Vivien to a show and the next day deposited her at the Convent of the Sacred Heart at Roehampton. Mrs. Hartley visited her there several times, finding her "very sad indeed;"[9] on 10 October she took her to the zoo. Then Mrs. Hartley sailed back to India. Vivien would not see her parents for sixteen months.

Vivien was educated at the Convent of the Sacred Heart for most of the next eight years, but, though her parents were away, she was not wholly bereft of relatives to visit her. Nevertheless, the absence of parents made her more remote and at times more demonstrative. It was important to make friends for the holidays, to establish a character of her own. The actress Dulcie Gray, whose parents lived in Kuala Lumpur, thought that the absence of parents had caused many to turn towards a life of performing, citing Margot Fonteyn and Googie Withers:

> While you are at school, you become a clown or an entertainer because it's your passport to have somebody love you, to take notice of you.[10]

Sir Alec Guinness remembered that an actress friend of his, who had attended the same convent, recalled that Vivien was looked down on because her parents were 'in trade' in India. He thought this a most unlikely role for her, given her later sophistication.[11]

Antonia White's novel, *Frost in May*, is a fictional account of life at the Convent of the Sacred Heart, based on her own experiences there between 1908 and 1914. Published in 1933 (and read that year by Vivien), the book painted a grim portrait of the exigencies of Catholic life. At its most exaggerated, the Reverend Mother told the school of the shining example of a true Catholic's spirit: Molly had had problems with her veil and a short-sighted nun had put a safety-pin through Molly's ear when helping her. This was endured by Molly as symbolic of the Lord's wearing of the Crown of Thorns:

> I am sure Molly received a very wonderful grace at her First Communion and I should like to think that anyone here had such beautiful, unselfish devotion as that. She might have gone about all day with that pin through her ear, if she had not fainted at breakfast.[12]

According to Elizabeth Bowen, the convent of the Five Wounds at Lippington, the fictional recreation of the Convent of the Sacred Heart, was "presented with cool exactness."[13] Formerly an eighteenth century country house, a faintly secular air still hung around some of its rooms, each of which was named after a particular saint. There was rigid discipline in which personal friendships between the girls were discouraged, letters home were read and censored, and desks were searched for 'offensive' literature and personal possessions. Each girl was encouraged to examine her conscience daily and to mortify the senses by such acts as putting salt on rhubarb. Good Catholics were urged to dwell "constantly in the spiritual presence of death"[14] and St. Teresa was quoted as having exclaimed at each striking of the hour: "An hour nearer to death. An hour nearer to heaven or hell."[15] Elizabeth Bowen concluded: "As a school Lippington does, of course, run counter to the whole trend of English liberal education; to the detached mind this is in itself fascinating. The child-psychologist will be outraged by the Lippington attitude to sex and class."[16]

Another feature of Lippington life and certainly of the Convent of the Sacred Heart was that old girls of the school never quite shook off its influence. Vivien was not, however, the archetypal convent girl, nor did she feel such bonds of loyalty. She was by no means the traditional entrant, not having come from one of the austerely grand pre-Reformation Catholic families, but from the exotic background of India, which caused the other girls to invest her with an aura of some romance.

Very much younger than the other children, she was shown special favors by the nuns. A little white kitten would never have been allowed to be a bedtime companion in Antonia White's novel, and Vivien was the only child extended this privilege. From early on she showed poise, self-containment, and the ability to sustain a private existence. She welcomed the structure of religious life (years later she wrote to her sister-in-law that she sometimes wished she had held on to her early zest), and she adopted manic neatness in folding clothes. Vivien's mother prepared the stipulated wardrobe for her daughter – sixteen frocks (six embroidered, four colored, three morning, three lace), eight pairs of socks, fourteen petticoats, two slips for lace frocks, two cotton night gowns, and eight pairs of warm stockings.

Vivien was once sent salmon by her father from Ireland and immediately offered to share this with her friend, Patsy Quinn, who was not enjoying her somewhat stodgy school whiting. Her father also sent her a huge doll in a box from India. There was considerable excitement when it arrived, but tears when it was opened to reveal the doll's head was broken. Other girls also noticed that Vivien was always better dressed, wearing silk stockings and gold bracelets, before submitting to the regulation school uniform. In a competition Vivien was once voted the prettiest girl in the school. One friend, Maureen O'Sullivan,* recalled that she seldom cried or sulked and that she was considered fun without being a goody-goody. "She was everything you would long to be. We would play silly games – who would you like to be if you could be someone else? Most of us wrote – Vivian Hartley."[17]

Vivien's early education at the Convent was not exceptional. She very much disliked mathematics: "I always found them quite impossible and don't think I've really felt the loss of never understanding what they were all about,"[18] she wrote in 1944. Later still she commented:

> I can scarcely remember when I first thought of going on the stage, because it was such an accepted fact of my childhood. I never even imagined myself in any other career, and as I was fortunate enough to have understanding parents all my education and early life were shaped to that end. So instead of being harassed over the weakness of my mathematics – apparent to this day – I was allowed to specialize in history, literature, and music, and to study language abroad.[19]

Her first excursions onto the stage took place at the Sacred Heart and were not especially successful. The part of Fairy Mustardseed in *A Midsummer Night's Dream* was followed by that of Miranda in *The Tempest.* Alas, her shrill voice did not reach beyond the front row and she stumbled over ill-remembered lines. Bridget Boland, the child producer, taught her a sound lesson by hitting her over the head (off-stage) with a candlestick. Vivien much enjoyed dancing and took ballet lessons after seeing *Where the Rainbow Ends*. She was once discovered gazing attentively at some trees reflected in the water of the school lake, observing a balletic quality in their gentle swaying. She studied the violin, played the cello in the school orchestra, and became proficient at the piano (later choosing a piano as her luxury on Roy Plomley's radio program, *Desert Island Discs*).[20]

When Mrs. Hartley was in England she paid frequent visits to Vivien at the Convent. She came in March 1922, and again in April 1923, sailing to

*Later famous as a Hollywood actress, and the mother of Mia Farrow. Thus mother-in-law of Frank Sinatra and André Previn.

France, and then flying (for the first time ever) with Tommy from Paris to Croydon. Easter was spent at Bridlington, and Vivien was taken on a day trip to Scarborough with Mrs. Hartley and Ernest's sisters, Lilian and Emily. Tommy took mother and daughter to see *Brighter London* in April and to *So This Is London* in June. In September Vivien accompanied her mother to Nice, Monte Carlo, and Cannes.

Mrs. Hartley was again in England in 1924, and then, in 1925, made a long and well-recorded trip home from Bombay in the company of Tommy. They traveled to Aden, Port Said, and Cairo, and Gertrude had several rows with her companion. "Tommy horrid,"[21] she noted on 17 March. Then, after a stay at the Grand Hotel in Venice,they arrived in Lugano where Mrs. Hartley underwent an operation, which made her "very sad,"[22] the first of a series over the next years, seemingly of a gynecological nature, involving much bleeding and pain. Tommy was with her, keeping her room at Dr. Herinan's Clinica San Rocco filled with flowers. At 3:30 a.m. on 30 March she wrote: "I want Ernest and Vivian…desperately lonely. Tommy is a pet."[23] Presently she was up and about, dancing and playing golf (ever her favorite pastime). She went to Paris mainly to shop and then flew to London, finding Vivien with her paternal aunt Lilian. In May she took Vivien to Virginia Water one day and to a 'bad show' at the Coliseum the next. She called at the convent to discuss Vivien's progress on 19 May and found her "looking beautiful and in a most amusing mood."[24]

Vivien was free for her summer holiday on 22 July. They went to Bridlington, Weybridge, Frinton-on-Sea, London, Bath, and Teignmouth, and Tommy was seldom far away. Before returning to Calcutta, Mrs. Hartley took Vivien to see *Beginner's Luck*, which they thought excellent.

In letters home Vivien confessed that she had been caught interrupting in class and had forfeited part of her half-term holiday. Mother Brace-Hall told her "the other day that she hoped I had *tribulation* – she said it would do me a lot of good and she said that my best friends wished I had it. So I said that you and Daddy jolly well didn't. So she laughed."[25] Vivien admitted that she had not been very good, but was enjoying Egyptian history: "I simply love it."[26]

Vivien also reported that she had taken her music exam at the Royal Academy of Music, "the most unearthly place – at first you went into a thing that looked like an office with a lot of cooks rushing about."[27] The examiner had expected them all in the morning and was therefore in bad humor at this late hour of the day. However, Vivien did well and achieved a Primary Division Pass in the 'School' Examination.

Vivien's interest in the theatre extended to seeing George Robey sixteen times in *Round in Fifty* at the Hippodrome, writing later: "It was the delight of my youth and the curse of my elders."[28] Once during a holiday in the Lake District she rejoiced to find him in the same hotel:

> When I discovered him seated at a table in the dining-room of our hotel, prosaically putting away a big plate of eggs and bacon, I could not take my eyes off him. In the end my unblinking stare caught the attention of his wife, Blanche Littler,* who was sitting by him, and she nudged his arm, looked in my direction, and whispered something. He turned and favored me with a broad smile and almost took my breath away, and a moment later – oh, joy of joys – the two of them stopped at our table on their way out of the room! I was so overcome with emotion that I could only murmur: 'I adore you.'[29]

Vivien was rewarded with no less than ten photographs of her favorite star, and he was her hero for life.

More foreign travel came in 1926, this time with both her parents. Aunt Lilian brought Vivien to Lugano on Easter Day, for two and a half weeks. Mrs. Hartley was in London all summer, and there was a holiday in Scotland with her parents and the ever-present Tommy. Ernest left for India on 9 September, and the next evening Tommy and Gertrude dined à deux at the Café de Paris: "topping night,"[30] she wrote. Tommy and Gertrude then took Vivien to Devon for a week. Gertrude then sailed back to India.

Vivien remained at the Convent of the Sacred Heart until the summer of 1928, taking in another Easter holiday in the South of France and Paris with her parents and Tommy.

Various friends have testified about Vivien's behavior at the convent. Jane Pauling, later Mrs. David Glass, was at first annoyed that Vivien was

*Blanche Littler married George Robey in 1938.

allowed a kitten, while she was forbidden her favorite rag-doll. However, a firm friendship was forged. She recalled:

> Vivien, Maureen O'Sullivan, Rosemary O'Malley Keyes, and I were such a nuisance at school games that we were relegated to the bottom of the garden with worn-out racquets and told to get on with it, which we did with relish.[31]

> Patsy Quinn, later Viscountess Lambert, described her looks: So tiny and delicately made, with wonderful large blue eyes and chestnut wavy hair nearly to her waist – the tiny retroussé nose, and the only complexion I have ever seen that really *was* like a peach, almost downy as a peach is.[31]

Even at that young age, Lady Lambert could pay tribute to her generosity and her thoughtfulness in the selection of presents she knew the recipient would cherish. And she confirmed that Vivien already "showed signs of the weakness of her chest when we were in the convent."[32]

Another friend, who hid behind the veil of anonymity, gave a more disturbing account to Laurence Olivier's biographer, Thomas Kiernan. She told him:

> Vivien would get along fine for a few weeks, a few months – be perfectly normal and friendly and involved in her activities. Then suddenly, a complete turnaround. Sometimes it would last only a few hours, other times a day or more. But when it happened, we'd see a completely different girl – moody, silent, petulant, rude, often hysterical. None of us understood it, not even the schoolmistresses.[33]

On the other hand, Mills Martin, with whom Vivien spent part of her holidays at Teignmouth in Devon, firmly discounted any form of congenital manic depression, nor thought her by nature a tragedienne. Furthermore, she recalled:

> Vivien was never schoolgirlish or gawky. I can't remember a time when she wasn't quite lovely. She made me feel like granite compared to this little polished marble beauty. She

was not classically beautiful. Her hands were too big, her feet were too big, she had a funny little mouth. Yet she had this extraordinary star quality and emanated something that other people didn't.[34]

Chapter 3
The Grand Tour

I was sent successively to schools in France, Italy and Bavaria, and this erratic education was a great help afterwards.

Vivien Leigh in an interview,
What Success has Taught Me

Vivien's parents returned to India on 18 October 1928, and then left Calcutta for good on 2 March 1929 after a series of farewell dinner parties. Tommy accompanied them on their journey to Marseilles.

The later Indian years had been good for Ernest. After the First World War, he had succeeded Geoffrey Martin as senior partner in Pigott, Chapman. He enjoyed Calcutta life to the full. One retiring member of Pigott, Chapman wrote to Gertrude in 1922:

> No one could possibly have had a better burra-sahib, nor, if you won't think me impertinent for saying so, a nicer burra-mem, and this means more in a a place like Calcutta than many people realize.[1]

Another friend, Gerald E. Kingston, recalled: "the gloriously happy times which I had in your house and in every place where we ever may have forgathered."[2]

Over the years much has been written of Ernest's marital infidelities. He was attracted by and attractive to a number of beautiful women. Gertrude told John Merivale that she had once given a dinner party at which every couple included a wife who had at one time been Ernest's mistress. Vivien told Radie Harris that she always knew when he was having an affair because he would buy her bracelets.

Gertrude Hartley also had admirers beside Tommy. In February 1923 Henry Musgrave pressed his suit from the sanctity of the United Services Club. He had met her at a dance and sent her roses, explaining that he had to do it and he had awoken that morning "surrounded by that delightful atmosphere imparted by you."[3] The next day he wrote again saying: "Nothing worth having can be obtained unless you fight for it." He urged her to join him for a game of golf at Tollygunge "any afternoon this or next week or ever." He promised to drive her down and "return you safely afterwards to your reckless gambling husband on his return from the office."[4] This time he sent her two eggs, destined for his breakfast. He remained in contact for some years, pleading from the Fowey Hotel in Cornwall: "I expect you will give me a dance when you do return and if you have not forgotten all about me as you always do, and so ruin my life."[5]

Then there was Maurice Stern, the Managing Director of M. & B. Stern, the Liverpool-based cotton brokers. He was dubbed 'Mamma's cotton beau' by Vivien, and, like other admirers, was a provider of lunches and dinners in London, her occasional dancing partner into the small hours, and on friendly terms with Ernest. He remained a constant friend. He met Gertrude at Dinard in 1925 and was amused that the man at the Casino would not admit her into the Baccarat rooms because children were not allowed, and Gertrude was then thirty-seven.

In the late 1950s, Laurence Olivier asked Ernest and Gertrude: "Is there such a thing as a happy marriage?" and Gertrude replied: "Yes, we are."[6] Between them, Ernest and Gertrude had found a way of living which was workable and practicable and which in no way offended society. And, by and large, they remained on good terms (with one notable lapse in the late 1940s).

Ernest was one of many who suffered badly in the Wall Street Crash of October 1929. At first he was able to settle in Biarritz and show very little interest in work. But, by the time Vivien's schooling was completed, the easy life was over and the family were relying on the kindness of the

Martins, who loaned them a bungalow in Devon. Lady Lambert remembered Tommy and Ernest "getting rather squiffy of an evening and adding up their losses on the Stock Exchange in India."[7] Ian Thomson, Tommy's nephew, recalled:

> I was always led to believe that he [Tommy] got out of the firm with his money intact before the crash, whereas poor old Ernest did not.[8]

There was another reason for coming closer to home. Ernest's parents had suffered a tragedy with the loss of their eldest daughter, Emily. In 1929 both parents were eighty-one years old. Joseph Nicholson Hartley was suffering from "an illness of several months' duration, which was borne with patience and fortitude,"[9] more specifically general sclerosis and sarcoma of the right upper jaw. On 24 November Joseph Nicholson Hartley died of a cerebral thrombosis. Ernest's mother lived on at Bridlington until 1935, dying at the age of eighty-seven.

Shortly before the final winter in India, Mrs. Hartley had taken Vivien to a sister convent of the Sacred Heart at San Remo, where she remained until the following summer of 1929. She had already attended school at Dinard, though this can have been no more than a short holiday course. Vivien had an aptitude for languages and spoke good French. It was hoped that San Remo would perfect this and add some Italian.

Vivien already knew the French Riviera from summer holidays. San Remo is the capital of the Italian Riviera, near the border with the South of France. In the winter it is scented with carnations, jasmine, narcissi, and mimosa, but in later life Vivien recalled primarily the peonies the girls picked to scatter at the feet of the priests as they processed on the Feast of Corpus Christi. The old town, full of winding streets, alleys, and stairways, overlooked the sea and the convent stood near the twelfth-century church of San Siro. Vivien was in her most religious phase, never missing early mass, but she was also beginning to show signs of rebellion. Vivien was caught describing the Reverend Mother in a line drawing of a cat.

Vivien celebrated her fifteenth birthday at the convent. She was now fast developing from a slightly chubby-faced girl into a more languid, angular teenager, her eyes taking on the melting green beauty that would lead to her later stardom. Vivien endured six months' separation from her parents, who arrived by boat from India on 28 March. The next day, Good Friday, Vivien rejoined them in Marseilles, and they shared a fortnight's Easter holiday. The summer term meant bathing, but the mode of dress was a black one-piece suit, buttoned to the neck with long sleeves and calico shirts attached. Vivien was not at all sad to say farewell to convent life in June.

That summer was spent in Ireland, at Aasleagh, where Ernest liked to fish the Erriff. Later the Hartleys and Vivien spent a week in Bridlington with Ernest's widowed mother. Meanwhile they settled in Biarritz, where Mrs. Hartley began to take an interest in the world of beauty products.

On 27 September 1929 Vivien went to Paris to spend a term at Mlle. Manilève's finishing school, the Villa Sainte-Monique at Auteuil. The school consisted of three classes: very good, moderate, and beginners. There were about twenty-four girls in all.

Mlle. Manilève's own history was extraordinary. Brought up in a chateau in Auvergne, her father had gambled away his money. She brought herself and her brother up and was the first woman to achieve a baccalauareat in France. At one time she and her mother had but one pair of shoes between them. She had taught French at a girls' school in England called St. Monica's at Burgh Heath, where she was remembered as an attractive, kind teacher.

The Villa Sainte-Monique contained not only girls from English families, but also Jewish girls, South Africans, and Australians, as well as one or two from the Convent of the Sacred Heart at Roehampton. The purpose of the school was to teach French – language and literature – and to send them out into the world with a good marriage set firmly in their sights. Mlle. Manilève was not intellectual, but the girls had to work hard.

One of the pupils was Betty Harbord, later Mrs. John Hodges (Superintendent of the WRNS). She recalled:

> Vivien was not sixteen until 5 November that winter and was the youngest in the school. And she looked like a little girl compared to the rest of us – quite petite. She spoke excellent French. We had a *cour de danse* each Saturday night when Mademoiselle's friends would come for a soirée and play bridge and their sons came to be our dancing partners – young men from St. Cyr University, etc. The

> first time the girls would be assembled in the grand salon talking nervously in French to the young men who were equally shy. Suddenly they all turned round – Vivien had come into the room, in a short simple little dress when all the rest of us had long ones, and no make-up. The rest of us were deserted and all the boys excused themselves to go and ask Vivien to dance. She hadn't said anything…She had that charisma.[10]

Being smarter than most of the others (described by Betty Harbord as 'big beefy girls'), Vivien was naturally chosen to be the heroine of the school play at Christmas, wearing a Marie Antoinette-style wig.She was coached by Mlle. Antoine of the Comédie Française. Of her Vivien wrote later:

> She was a most inspiring teacher, and I owe a great deal to her care in correcting my diction and to her encouragement. "I believe you have a future in the theatre, *mon enfant*," she told me, "but you must go back to England and work… work…work. If you do that I shall see the name Vivien Hartley in big letters outside a London theatre one day. I promise you."[11]

Betty Harbord's mother took her and Vivien to see Ramon Novarro in *The Pagan Love Song*, after which Vivien declared she had fallen in love with him. In the interval both girls went to the lavatory and surreptitiously put on a little lipstick, an act dubbed somewhat fast in 1929.

Vivien had another friend, Jean Campbell, who had been with her at the Sacred Heart. They sometimes went to tea with Rosemary O'Malley Keyes, also from the Sacred Heart and now at a similar school run by Mlle. Boissier. Vivien, still naïve and young for her age, would come back and relate tantalizing tales of Rosemarie wearing make-up and escaping to nightclubs with men. But Vivien was closely protected by Mlle. Manilève, and not allowed out unescorted on the strict instruction of her parents.

Even so, the Hartleys decided that one term was enough. Vivien had written of midnight feasts, and Mrs. Hartley had no problem detecting the appearance of make-up – to say nothing of a rather dashing hat from the

Galeries Lafayette – when she visited her on her sixteenth birthday. On 18 December Vivien returned to Biarritz for Christmas and that was that.

Between January and April 1930, Vivien was at school near Biarritz, making expeditions to Loyola, Pamplona, and Lourdes with her parents and Tommy. At Easter Mrs. Hartley underwent another operation at Lugano, with Ernest, Tommy, and Vivien nearby, and then on 22 April she set off with her daughter on a four-day journey to Bad Reichenhall, in the Bavarian Alps, the next stage of Vivien's education.

It was a long and eventful journey. At the Hotel Bahnhof at Worgl, men continually peeped through the keyhold of the bedroom they shared. Finally, Vivien was left at a finishing school run by Baron and Baroness von Roeder. Here she stayed for four terms.

Vivien now benefited from enough French and German to enable her to dub her own films later on – a rare accomplishment in an actress. Her French, as can be judged from snippets in films such as *Lady Hamilton,* was excellent; likewise her Italian as heard much later in *The Roman Spring of Mrs. Stone*. During these years she also developed a passion for the visual arts and became a devotee of the Opera. Her mother spent ten days with her in Munich at the end of March 1931 and was amazed to find her totally gripped by the eight hours of *Parsifal*. She also skied a little at Kitzbuhl, though because of an inner ear problem, she found balance tricky.

John Merivale remembered Vivien telling him that when she was fourteen her mother slapped her "for kissing a German waiter."[12] Dido Merwin, an English friend from the Convent of the Sacred Heart, recalled that Vivien fell in love with at least one German boy during her stay there. With characteristic generosity she asked Dido to have a silver cigarette case engraved with his initials and smuggled out to her. Vivien got as far as demanding her parents' consent to marrying him, flying into her mother's arms and saying: "Please say yes – If you don't no one will ever ask to marry me again."[13] Later, Vivien said: "There was a pleasant absence of all chaperones in Foreign affairs."[14]

Chapter 4
Mrs. Leigh Holman

I was under nineteen when I married, and not quite twenty when my daughter was born. I felt too young to be the mother of a child, and very lacking in the qualities of restfulness and serenity which a mother should have. How many times since then Scarlett O'Hara's lines, speaking of her mother, have sprung to my mind: "I always wanted to be like her, calm and kind. I certainly have turned out disappointingly."

Vivien Leigh
What Success has Taught Me

Vivien arrived in London on 4 July 1931. Presently the Hartleys settled in Devon, which was a good deal cheaper than Biarritz. They remained there for the winter, as guests of the Martins. Ernest, Tommy, and Gertrude settled in a small bungalow at Polzeath called Troy, loaned by the Martins. This had little appeal for the essentially urban Gertrude and on 28 December she and Tommy headed back to Biarritz, leaving Ernest in London.

There was thus no question of Vivien enjoying any form of 'coming out' or debutante season. Instead she was stuck at home, under the watchful eyes of her father. It was Ernest who planted the idea of a stage career in Vivien's head by announcing at dinner one night: "You know, Vivling, you might make an actress yourself."[1] She was further influenced by reading a biography of Lillie Langtry, which suggested that the life of an actress could be fulfilling. Later she read D.H. Lawrence's *Lady Chatterley's Lover* in an early expurgated edition. Vivien went to see her school friend, Maureen O'Sullivan, in her first movie, *A Connecticut Yankee*, late in 1931. Soon after this she persuaded her father to enter her for R.A.D.A.

The New Year of 1932 found Mrs. Hartley taking injections of Homoverine Byla in Biarritz. Gertrude soon employed all her organizational abilities in creating a beauty business, which she continued to run well into old age.

Vivien began her own new year in Falmouth. "This place is dismal," she wrote to Jane Pauling, "and I am completely in the dumps."[2] However, all this changed when she went to Teignmouth to stay with her friend Mills Martin. It was she who introduced Vivien to her first husband, Leigh Holman, whom Mills had known since the age of two. The two girls set off in a two-seater Alvis to attend the Dartmouth Hunt Ball at the Two Bridges Hotel on Dartmoor, suffering a puncture on the way.

When Vivien met Leigh, he was still in love with Mills' sister, Dulcie. He had asked her to marry him but she had turned him down. He was "sore about it, but flattered at the obvious admiration of Viv: there she was looking up at him."[3] Leigh was beguiled by Vivien but not in love with her. But Vivien was soon determined to marry Leigh.

The Holmans lived at Holcombe Down, a house set high above Teignmouth. They had been friends of the Martins for two generations. Leigh's full name was Herbert Leigh Holman. Born on 3 November 1900, he was educated at Harrow and Jesus College, Cambridge. He rowed for his college and at Henley for the Thames Rowing Club, and was known as 'Holo' Holman. He passed his B.A. in 1921 and two years later became a Barrister-at-Law in the Middle Temple. In 1932 he had been practicing at the bar for nine years.

Leigh was the third son of Herbert Holman, again a barrister, also a Justice of the Peace, a shipowner and and insurance manager. The Holmans were a Devon family descending from a cordwainer called William Holman, who in 1718 married Judith Bleight, appropriately a cordwainer's daughter. For many generations they lived at Topsham, prospering, making money out of the joint business of building ships and marine insurance. In common with many British families, Leigh lost one brother at Ypres in 1915. He was destined to lose another, Alwyn, killed in an air raid with his daughter in September 1940. The early months of his marriage to Vivien would be overshadowed by the death of his mother in February 1933 and by an accident in which his youngest sister, Hester, a talented sculptress, was killed falling from her horse in January 1934.

Leigh had a friend called Oswald Frewen, a barrister at the Inner Temple, thirteen years his senior. A bachelor who only married late in life, he was a wise counselor and a keen observer of the lives of his friends. Leigh was devoted to him "from the first time I knew him in 1924 to the day of his death. It was his quality of gentleness that is most vivid in my memory and it mellowed his candor as a critic and his pervasive humor."[4]

Frewen was born in 1887, the son of Moreton Frewen, who veered between vast riches and bankruptcy and became known as 'Mortal Ruin.' His rich American wife was Clara Jerome, the sister of Lady Randolph Churchill. Thus Oswald was a first cousin of Winston. Oswald had seen the world, first in the Navy, and later during extensive and eventful travels with his dramatic sister, Clare (famous later as the sculptress Clare Sheridan). Oswald and Clare enjoyed a difficult relationship, based on the sincere conviction that they had been a married couple in some previous incarnation. They traveled across Europe in 1923, securing interviews with Maxim Gorky in Russia and General Primo de Rivera in Spain. Oswald cabled a long report to the *Daily Telegraph* headed *Coup d'État in Spain*. In 1924 he drove Clare into Russia from Poland, an unneeded dinner jacket and black tie tucked into his luggage.

Oswald Frewen was described by his cousin Shane Leslie as "the indefatigable diarist of his own life and times."[5] The many volumes of his leather-bound diaries, meticulously indexed and sometimes written in code, provided an important record of the lives of Leigh Holman and later of Vivien and of Laurence Olivier.

Oswald first spotted Leigh in the autumn of 1924, when he was called to the Admiralty Bar, hoping to make a good living. He was told some depressing tales by other barristers and noted: "When I realized that a nice child called Holman with long fair hair, in our chambers, who has just finished his year's apprenticeship with [Hugh] Dumas, is the brother of the senior member of the firm of Admiralty solicitors, and got a brief yesterday, I understood, and went down to Brede very greatly depressed."[6] Despite what could have been a growing jealousy of Leigh with his connections, a firm friendship was forged. "His four years at the Bar were lean indeed for him," wrote Leigh Holman, "but a glorious light relief to the rest of us in The Chambers who were trying to work but always willing to be entertained."[7] In May 1925, Frewen "fired Leigh Holman's enthusiasm for an Arctic mo'bike stunt"[8] and from 3 to 31 August they were traveling companions in Norway and Sweden. It was a daunting expedition, their cabin mates "seamen in process of repatriation and intoxication,"[9] and Frewen bemoaning "I have for a bedfellow a peculiarly active and voracious flea."[10] Leigh never shirked hard work, toiling manfully at an oar, pushing 'Satanella,' the motorbicycle, when its wheels spun, or helping lower it into a skiff. He was game for any kind of expedition, climbing happily for five hours to enjoy a particular view.

Subsequently, Leigh became a regular visitor to Brede Place, Frewen's home in Sussex, built as a great hall in 1350 and allowed to lie derelict until restored by Frewen's parents. Brede was a sad and beautiful house with its old hall and wings of pale red Elizabethan brick, in a sylvan setting. Foot-long rainbow trout swam in a pool in the woods, where Leigh proved himself "an old hand with the Big Saw, the Hand saw, the axe, wedge, or bill-hook."[11] In the winter of 1930 and 1931, Oswald had driven his eighty-year-old mother across the Sahara in his baby Austin, a vehicle described by his far from timid sister Clare as "the most disreputable car in England."[12] Since then old Clara Frewen had been running Brede, and Oswald was happily ensconced there. He was in the process of converting a tumbledown barn into an Elizabethan half-timbered cottage. Called The Sheephouse, it became Oswald's home, adjacent to the Brede estate. Leigh advised him on the construction and put his shoulder to any task. Frewen was delighted when he undertook "yeomen work in the dell"[13] or proposed himself for "a good hard-slogging job"[14] for the weekend. Leigh would drive down in his fourteen horse power Sunbeam 'Solicita' and sometimes used Brede as a base for sailing in his three-ton yacht *Katurah.* Frewen came to respect him as a barrister too:

> Then I looked at Leigh, spoon-fed by the family firm, a babe in years 'and/or wisdom,' with more work than he can cope with. For relaxation he rings up the Firm and they send him a brief! And he works hard. The Law 'eats him up.'[15]

Leigh had another friend in Hamish Hamilton, the publisher, who had rowed against him at Cambridge. Jamie Hamilton recalled him:

> He was not particularly scholarly, quite the reverse. If anything he was an an athlete and a very bad barrister. He had blond, curly hair and no particular ambition, but he was a good rider and we were great friends. We used to do trapeze dives at the Bath Club (alas no longer). He was always perfectly calm and I was in a great state because we had to dive at the interval of the Oxford and Cambridge sports, and he always said it would be all right on the night, and we would never rehearse. As a result when we did our double dive, I fell in.[16]

Through Leigh, Jamie Hamilton first set eyes on Vivien, "a vision of beauty far lovelier with her eyebrows unplucked before the theatre people got hold of her."[17] Vivien used to spend hour after hour watching the two men play squash. And they went dancing: "Leigh was no dancer," recalled Hamilton, "and would sit stolidly watching Vivien and me enjoying ourselves at the Old Berkeley opposite the Ritz. Both were my confidants and it was clear that little love was involved, Vivien wanting to get away from home, and Leigh hating to lose his independence."[18]

Leigh's mother, a somewhat fierce lady, was unlikely to approve of any bride that Leigh might choose, least of all a teenage girl with a dubious family background. Betty Harbord remembered being told that Vivien's mother was the one who was so anxious that she be "married off, as she had become rather jealous of her."[19] It was certainly a good marriage from the Hartleys' point of view and it is possible that in their straitened circumstances they welcomed a release from the financial burden of a daughter. Gertrude was not at this time a particularly motherly mother. Nor was she interested in Vivien until she became famous, whereupon she became almost transfixed with devotion. It is invariably said that Vivien was anxious to get away from home, but at this time she had no real home. She lived out of a suitcase, staying at clubs or with friends and being sent often to her grandmother and the maiden aunts at Bridlington. Marriage to Leigh therefore heralded the end of an unsettling nomadic life.

Monday, 1 February was an important date in the relationship between Leigh and Vivien. She wrote to him that she longed "…just to have those hours…back again only I should be very greedy and expect the hours never to slip away."[20]

In the middle of Feburary Vivien was condemned to nearly six weeks of 'vegetating' in Bridlington, "this deadly hole,"[21] with her grandmother and aunts. She had a great deal of time on her hands and spent it thinking, making plans, shocking her grandmother, knitting pullovers, reading Colette and shopping ("a faculty I have I believe in common with the rest of the female of the species").[22]

Altogether, it was a frustrating period for Vivien as she explained in a series of concise, well-written letters to Leigh.

> Do you know Leigh that if I had to stay here for more than two weeks I shouldn't care a scrap what anyone said – I should just come down (you would of course be in the conspiracy with me and help me, this would entail grave responsibilities – but maybe you wouldn't mind)… we would have to do some cute evading – either that or I should consider the easiest form of suicide. The sea is too cold, and I couldn't face a pen-knife. Perhaps it would just be the commonplace gas-oven![23]

Only letters from Jane Pauling and Leigh cheered her up. On receipt of one from Leigh she wrote:

> I think that you employed yesterday most satisfactorily, and you would think so too, if you could see the extasy *[sic]* radiating from me…[24]

Vivien was due to return to London on 17 March to attend the Pegasus Ball with Leigh. Her father forbade her to go to Leigh's flat, however, and as Ernest was still in the process of flat-hunting, she would stay with another friend, Jay Wilson. Smoking a cigarette as she wrote, Vivien declared:

> I think I shall present Papa with a large number of books all

> pointing out how absolutely useless it is for parents nowadays to try and restrict their offspring in any direction…[25]

After her visit to London Vivien went to spend a fortnight with Jane Pauling at the Prebendal, Thame, and Leigh went back to Holcombe Down in Devon. She recalled to him a particularly perfect day, Friday, 25 March, when they had driven down a hill together:

> We drove over that same road tonight, everything looked fairylike (I think everything does at night don't you?) I only had to shut my eyes and I saw the sunshine, and little gold things tumbling about in the breeze a little way above me – And so I had my Friday over again, only the most important factor was actually missing.[26]

Vivien's father led a peripatetic existence before moving to 29 Knightsbridge Court at the end of October. Vivien looked forward to seeing Leigh on 9 April. Then she was 'pushed off' to Bridlington once more for a fortnight. Leigh's letters arrived after lunch, a meal she rushed to the point of indigestion, "thinking that this will brace up the postman as well – the leisurely manner in which he deliver the letters is a continual source of agravation [sic].[27] She passed her time enjoying G.B. Stern's essay, *Man Without Prejudice*, and the letters of Madame du Deffand.

If plans did not go her way, Vivien conceived the fanciful idea of retreating to Kenya. She passed her exam on 24 April, and started at R.A.D.A. on 6 May, working there from 9:30 to 4:30 and often at home in the evenings too, encouraging Leigh: "maybe you can spirit me away some time."[28] In the evenings she liked to dance until very late "so that I can immediately go to sleep with a feeling of wonderful rest."[29] If she did not sleep at once she always pretended to and found "I can apparently take dear Papa in with success."[30] In the summer Leigh moved to 124 Eyre Court in Finchley Road. This would be their first married home.

Vivien's mother was still away in Biarritz when Vivien began classes at R.A.D.A. at their new modern building in Gower Street. She was auditioned by Sir Kenneth Barnes, the principal, and was taught Shakespeare by Ethel Carrington.

Leigh used to meet her after class, and as the summer progressed he took her to events such as the Henley Regatta. Leigh dined with Gertrude and Vivien on 13 June 1932. In 1949, Oswald Frewen recalled:

> One day I got a letter from [Leigh], could he come for the weekend, and he might be bringing his young friend VIVIAN [sic] Hartley. I said, of course, but what sex was "Vivian," so that I could arrange rooms (good for a girl, 2nd best for a boy). Leigh replied: "A girl; I might even marry her."[31]

Thus, on Sunday, 19 June 1932, Leigh motored Vivien down to Brede. Frewen continued:

> Leigh arrived with Vivling, indescribably lovely, gentle, sweet and friendly and I waited, agog, for NEWS. None forthcoming. I presently asked him, when he and I were alone in the Wendy Garden, "Well, have you proposed to her yet?" Leigh, in his vague, off-hand manner, said, "No, do you think I should?" and I, aghast, said, "Well, if you don't, *before* you leave *here,* you won't get her: *that* sort of thing isn't left lying about, *I* can assure you." I said no more, and Leigh looked enigmatic as a judge and they left. A week later he came down again, alone. After about 24 hours I could bear 'the weather and the garden work' no more, and said, "Well, *are* you engaged?" – "Oh, yes," said Leigh, still vague and matter of fact "I proposed on the way back to London, didn't I tell you?"[32]

Hamish Hamilton, who might have been a rival for Vivien's hand had he not already married Jean Forbes-Robertson, also encouraged Leigh, realizing that his friend was on to a very good prospect. "Jane, great thrilldom," wrote Vivien to Jane Pauling on 7 July. "Leigh and I are engaged. It was officially announced this morning."[33]

Gertrude went to see Vivien act at R.A.D.A. in two performances early in July. On 29 July, the Hartleys took Vivien to Scotland and Tommy motored them over to the Royal Hotel at Campbeltown.

Vivien was often sleepy, and always bored. She played bridge with the family and knitted Leigh a sailing sweater. She received a letter from Leigh that referred to her R.A.D.A. experiences and commented: "Nice to think one might have been a star."[34] At this point, Vivien thought he was being cynical and responded: "I can think of something much more adequate."[35] On 12 August Vivien went down to see her grandmother in Bridlington.

Vivien was to take Leigh to Leenane in Ireland for a week's holiday with the family, or 'the Victorians,'[36] as she called her parents, and their friends. Leigh was worried about the safety of driving in Ireland but was reassured that the presence of 'GB' on his car would be adequate protection from the ever troublesome Irish. Vivien wrote: "Mummy and Tommy are going over next week. They will let us know what it's like."[37] Vivien described to Leigh what Ireland meant to her:

> What a heavenly sight that light morning will be in Ireland enhanced by the knowledge that the day will be a beautiful one and that one will drive out to the 'silversands' where there's never a soul, a surf ride, at a tremendous rate right up Killarney Bay to a little scooped out beach. We always called our own particularly little bay the silversands. I know you'll love it there.[38]

November involved meetings between Gertrude and Mrs. Holman and preparations for the wedding. And there was another visit to Brede. While Leigh cut wood in the Dell Head in bitterly cold weather, Oswald Frewen set Vivien to work, polishing in The Sheephouse, to keep her warm. On 25 November, Frewen, Leigh, Vivien, and Patsy Quinn went to the German film *Rasputin*. At R.A.D.A. Vivien performed as Lydia in *The Rivals,* and Rosalind in *As You Like It*. The Shakespeare was made irksome by a spotlight that got out of control and which Vivien did her best to follow round. She also performed in *The Young Person in Pink*, but had "a sad disaster…said completely imaginary words which was most upsetting for everyone concerned."[39] Vivien abandoned R.A.D.A. at Leigh's request, a mere five days before her marriage. Sir Kenneth Barnes was disappointed that she was leaving, as she was clearly taking her work seriously. He told her: "We always say to our girls that if they choose marriage instead of a career they choose wisely. In your case I believe you would have succeeded on the stage."[40] It seemed final, but to friends Vivien announced: "Just wait and see. I'll be back."[41]

The wedding itself was a Catholic ceremony at St. James', Spanish Place on 20 December. Vivien looked "thin and shy"[42] according to one guest. Some time afterwards, Vivien's mother described the day as a "terribly sad" one, adding "went to see *Tell Her the Truth.** Couldn't enjoy anything."[43]

A small photograph of Vivien as a bride appeared by chance on the front page of the *Daily Sketch* below one of King George V and Queen Mary attending a Christmas matinée. In old age Gertrude wrote: "I thought her photo a good omen, on this page, for the future and it happened. She too became famous."[44]

Vivien and Leigh honeymooned in Austria and Germany, visiting Bad Reichenhall, Kitzbühl, Munich, Leipzig, and Dresden. From Sils-im-Engadin where they skied, Vivien wrote to her parents:

> We would have wired you Xmas Day but we were traveling. It is very lovely here with quantities of snow and hot sun. I am very stiff and hurting all over.[45]

The return to London was to herald a short-lived attempt by Vivien to enjoy the simple domesticity of married life at Eyre Court. Three days after her return, Vivien wrote to Jane Pauling:

> I am too d—busy for words, packing and unpacking and trying to be married. I feel about 50 years older and as if I had 3 times the amount to do than anyone ever has had. However if Leigh is well fed, it will be alright.[46]

A mere fortnight after returning home from their honeymoon she obtained Leigh's permission to go back to R.A.D.A. for French lessons. Oswald Frewen had a hand in this, as he recalled later:

> We were wandering up through my Dell, and out at its head when Viv laddered her silk stocking, and Leigh said "My

* A popular long-running musical at the Saville Theatre.

> dear, if you're going to wear *silk* stockings to go through Oswald's unkempt garden, I think you had better go back to your R.A.D.A. and ask them if they can get you a small part in a West End production to earn your own pin-money." Viv looked pleased...So I can claim that *my* brambles drove the lady onto stage and screen...[47]

Leigh's mother fell ill, but Vivien failed to appreciate just how ill when Leigh had to rush home to Devon on 2 February. She was bitterly disappointed at having to miss an evening party. She apologized by letter: "I am sorry. Of course I understand you had to go down at once..."[48] Leigh's mother died the next day, and Vivien wrote again:

> I find it difficult to tell you now, but I will show you with my life, all that you mean to me, and how much I want to keep all sadness away from you. I am longing to have you back with me. Everything is strange and empty without you.[49]

The letters that Vivien wrote Leigh when apart all expressed her feelings of dependence on him and loneliness without him.

To her considerable annoyance, Vivien became pregnant in the early months of her marriage and once again her acting career was curtailed. Yet she was able to perform in Shaw's *St. Joan*, dressed in ungainly chain-mail leggings and boots which were too large for her.

In August Leigh sailed to Amsterdam alone, Vivien being forbidden to go because of her pregnancy. Instead she went to stay with Oswald Frewen at Brede, making friends with his sister, Clare ("divine and huge fun")[50] who invited her to stay with her in Paris. Oswald was particularly pleased that Vivien accepted him as a contemporary, though she was twenty-seven years his junior and even her mother was younger than he. Besides missing Leigh, Vivien spent her time in the dell, and talking to a bearded old man sitting on a barge in Rye. She was determined to learn as much about nautical life as possible to impress Leigh on his return: "You can be quite technical now, as I understand quite a lot about ships and am really interested."[51] There was also some gentle teasing:

> This morning I have been lying practically naked while Oswald has been digging a hole for water for the cows, he has got a new tenant. He assured me I must take everything off I can, that he won't look but that I must write and tell you so as to make you jealous.[52]

Meanwhile Vivien's mother had finished her training as a beautician. It was quite a change from the earlier days of Calcutta and rich, easy traveling. Gertrude was already familiar with beauty parlors all over the world, but now threw herself wholeheartedly into the culture of beauty. Part of her training involved studying the structure of bones, muscles, and skin with a plastic surgeon in Paris, something that many beauticians did not bother to do. She began to lay plans for the Academy of Beauty Culture, which she opened nervously on 1 May 1934. Though Gertrude was in many ways quite feather-headed ("She would have been a flapper if she'd been the right age,"[53] recalled her cousin Xan Fielding), she was to make a great success of her work. It was to give her a life-long interest and prove the main means of financial support for herself and Ernest. Gertrude believed in the manipulation of the muscles to make them taut and strong, and in massage by pressure rather than pulling and stretching the skin. She approved of electrical stimulation. Her academy had two purposes, the first to treat, the second to train students to practice her methods. Some years later she defined her philosophy of beauty:

> Wanting to look young is no foolish desire; it is every woman's duty, to the world as well as to herself, to add to the beauty of it, and those that make the effort are the happier and more successful for it. This is a mission in life which all women can and should share: a bond of beauty, as it were. There is no virtue in being unattractive.[54]

While Vivien's mother opened her practice in Dover Street, her father became a bill-broker with the firm of Page and Gwyther, based in the Hong Kong and Shanghai Bank building at 8 Gracechurch Street, E.C.3.

Vivien entered the Rahere Nursing Home in Bulstrode Street on 10 October, and two days later her baby daughter, Suzanne, was born prematurely. Mrs. Hartley recorded: "I was in the room all the time."[55] She then spent several days and nights with mother and child at the nursing home. Vivien wrote to Jane Pauling with news of the birth:

> The spinster Holman is minute, and does not allow anyone to be very proud of her yet, as she only makes rude noises, rather sneering faces, and shows a tendency to greed and petulance, which, however, is all passed off as personality by the more kind hearted of my visitors! – her name is Suzanne, but we have decided to call her "Toosoon" until she starts asking 'Why?' – Leigh is frightfully funny, and most callous, won't even look at it, he shouts 'Shut up' even if it just sighs…I have produced such a small size infant that I shall have to feed it for months. The thought is too depressing. *Radiant* motherhood (if there really is such a thing) hasn't descended upon me yet. But I really like it quite a lot.[56]

Knowing from Gertrude that Vivien had suffered a tubercular patch on her lungs, Tommy was quick to write from his fishing holiday at the Leenane Hotel in Connemara:

> Dear Old Grandmama,
> I suppose you are very happy to have it safely over. Poor little Viv! It must have been a very anxious time for you knowing what you do about the possibilities…[57]

In conclusion, Mrs. Hartley judged 1933 "a lucky year for me."[58]

Vivien had given birth to her daughter a month before her twentieth birthday. She was soon restless:

> I was not cast in the mold of serenity and in any case, although you may succeed in being kind at twenty you cannot be calm, with all your life still before you, and your ambitions unfulfilled. I loved my baby as every mother does, but with the clear-cut sincerity of youth I realized that

> I could not abandon all thought of a career on the stage. Some force within myself would not be denied expression. I took the problem to my husband and asked his advice. He was many years older than I was, a deeply kind and wise man, with that rare quality of imagination that implies tolerance and unselfishness. We decided that I should continue my studies at the Royal Academy of Dramatic Art. We took a tiny house in Little Stanhope Street and got a good nannie for the baby.[59]

In other words, it was goodbye to domesticity.

Chapter 5
Things Look Up

Long before you have rung the bell of Miss Vivien Leigh's front door, you have realized with a thrill of excitement that you are about to see a house which is as unusual as it is individual in character.

Molly Kyle,
Return to Elegance

Eyre Court proved too small for a growing family, and so in the New Year Vivien searched for a new house. In February 1934 she and Leigh contemplated building a house in Hampstead Garden Suburb, but eventually they veered towards Mayfair. No. 6 Little Stanhope Street, the new home of the 'Holmen' (as Oswald Frewen called them), was a small Queen Anne house, sharing a courtyard with Shepherds Cottage, the house that gave Shepherd Market its name. It had a theatrical link since the British actress Lynn Fontanne had occupied a room there, paid for by serving as an artist's model in 1907.

The decoration of the house took several months and involved Leigh and Vivien and Mrs. Hartley in some enjoyable bargain-hunting.

Having completed her R.A.D.A. training, Vivien naturally hoped to be engaged instantly in the West End. However, nothing presented itself. She was luckier than some, she realized – if not at the time, then certainly later – for during the long periods of waiting, and on the many occasions when hopes were raised and swiftly dashed, she could fall back on the real-life role of wife and mother.

But Vivien was bored with domestic existence. Mills Martin once visited her and found her distinctly restless. "Sue was screaming her head off, purple in the face. It was Nanny's day off. Vivien had no feeling for the child. It is possible to give birth without the maternal glands working."[1] And Fabia Drake, already a successful actress, often lunched at Little Stanhope Street: "She was bored with her marriage to a barrister. She told me she'd married Leigh Holman because she thought he was intelligent and she'd found him a bore – but Leigh Holman remained her friend for life."[2]

Leigh did not always enjoy the parties Vivien gave. Sometimes he could be found sitting disconsolately on the stairs, wishing her guests would leave. Oswald continued to invite them to Brede, for working weekends at The Sheephouse, and often slept on their sofa in London. On 13 June 1934, Vivien was presented at court to King George V and Queen Mary, by her sister-in-law, Mrs. Alwyn Holman. Later in the summer Leigh arranged a sailing holiday with friends and as Vivien was not pregnant this year, she came too. However, she had heard of the chance of a small part as a schoolgirl in the a film called *Things are Looking Up,* starring Cicely Courtneidge, one of a bout of minor talking films that boomed in the 1930s. Ever hopeful, she left a forwarding address and set off for Goteborg and Sweden, and then sailed with Leigh to Copenhagen. There she found a telegram awaiting her saying that she might be needed. She knew that she must desert the party and return home without delay.

It was a testing time for both Leigh and Vivien, who were without news of each other for some days. Leigh wrote:

> Adorable little Vivling, you looked so angelic steaming away in a 3rd class carriage…I shall sleep in your bunk tonight and shall miss you more than ever.[3]

Still lacking news he made a rare attempt to lay down the law:

> There is one thing I want you to be very careful about – that is not to be away when I get back – none of this Rochester* business. Really if this film business is going to take you

*Where Vivien was filming at Cobham Hall.

> away too much I shall be wanting you to stop it. We must have a month together in September.[4]

Vivien thought this letter severe. She replied in five letters, which only reached Leigh considerably later:

> It was so awful leaving you on that platform – the two dirty little children in the carriage stared at me while tears dripped down my cheeks. Then I discovered I had two tickets instead of one!...I remember wondering vaguely why I had such a handful of tickets…When I got to Tujlev luggage was carried for me by two old men practically senile, no porters anywhere. On the other hand there were scores of railway officials who didn't deign to carry luggage. I asked one about getting the money back for the ticket and he thought it was a huge joke, and called up three other men and we all laughed and everybody thought it was so funny, having gotten two tickets instead of one, that I only just got into my next train in time. They held it back for 3 minutes, while they wrote unintelligible things on the back of the unused ticket. We waved goodbye pleasantly. In the next train a fat Dane talked to me in English, German and Danish, and also carried my luggage, and put me in the waiting room. The next train was very uneventful and we eventually got to Esbjerg where I was completely lost, until a very nice young Dane agitated about for me. The steward first of all said there wasn't a single cabin. Then he got pleasanter and told me to wait until the people had finished bothering him. I waited while I heard him tell a lot of plain women that there weren't any cabins. Then he turned around and said 'And now I will give you the best cabin of the ship', but unfortunately not for nothing! It was 20 Krone more as it was a single one, there were no double ones left, I was very glad to be alone tho I am afraid it was very extravagant of me. There were the *foulest* people on board…[5]

Eventually Vivien got home to find the film postponed, perhaps for a fortnight. "Oh my sweet," she wrote to Leigh, "it will be too miserable if I'm not here when you get back![6]

On Tuesday 21 August Vivien had to present herself at Lime Grove Studios: "and if by Saturday I can see that I won't have any lines, I shall really leave it alone. It simply isn't worth wrecking our month together for this rather little job."[7]

Work on the film involved a lot of waiting about, but Vivien justified her persistence by securing one line (subsequently cut from the final version): "If you are not made headmistress, I shan't come back next term."[8] Albert de Courville, the director, was pleased to have found an attractive, well-brought-up girl with some dramatic training to play 'just one of the schoolgirls'[9] in his light comedy.

Each day Vivien somehow dealt with her domestic responsibilities while spending the best part of her day at the studio, or on location. It meant a six o'clock start, and during the long delays of filming or in wet weather, Vivien vied with Anne Wilding, another 'schoolgirl,' over *The Times* crossword puzzle, for which she was a life-long enthusiast. It was at this time, too, that she perfected the art of raising one eyebrow on its own.

In the late summer of 1934, a friend of Vivien's, Beryl Norman (Mrs. Ivan Samson), also an actress, mentioned her to a young agent called John Gliddon. A failed actor, Gliddon had conceived the ambition to discover unknown British talent and convert them into big stars. He had been depressed that all the famous names in show business were foreigners. Thus he set himself up in his father's small office at 106 Regent Street, "without anything to sell and not a single client."[10]

Gliddon was to be the first agent to many stars, nearly all of whom subsequently deserted him when they became famous. Only Deborah Kerr had publicly acknowledged him as her discoverer.

Beryl Norman brought Vivien to Gliddon's office. He related:

> Our first interview went well. For my part I had made up my mind that here was a very beautiful girl who possessed that rare gift – star quality. I wanted her to be quite certain that I meant business. Firstly I needed to get her to sign a contract with me for a period of years so that I alone would

be responsible for her progress to stardom.[11]

Bunny Austin, the famous tennis player, was present at Gliddon's first meeting with Vivien. After she left, he gave his frank opinion: "Very beautiful – but no personality."[12] There was then the search for a new name There are many who take credit for thinking of Vivien Leigh, while Gordon Courtney, manager of the Prince of Wales Theatre, was generally blamed for thinking of 'April Morn,' which briefly found favor with Vivien in the form of 'Averill Maugham.' She also toyed with 'Susan Stanley.' Ivor Novello is said to have thought of 'Vivien Leigh,' but Oswald Frewen, by no means given to exaggerated claims, also took credit for this. He recalled:

> Vivling...came down to Brede with Leigh (in September 1934) and in the evening in the Old Library said she must find a stage name, and thought 'Averill Maugham' would be chic. I curled up inwardly like an earthworm on a kitchen range, but said ever so gently that that would be like the little house I passed whenever I went into Hastings' suburbs called 'ONTHEROX': what was the matter with her own name? Browning (I said) had written lyrically of 'beautiful Annabel Lee,' I had heard Wilfred [Sheridan, Clare's husband] recite it literally unforgettably and was not *hers* as beautiful? All she need do was to drop the 'Holman' and remain 'Beautiful Vivien Leigh' and at that 'Vivien Leigh' while *sounding* as melodious as Annabel Lee, *looks* more beautiful in print. Neither Leigh nor Vivling said a word. I had shot my bolt, I said no more and *they* never referred to it, but Korda's new star [in due course] appeared as 'Vivien Leigh.' And the man responsible was not I, nor Browning, nor even old Wilfred, but Edgar Allan Poe![13]

One of the first roles that Gliddon submitted for her was a one-line part in Ivor Novello's *Murder in Mayfair.* She fought for the chance to say a line such as 'Oh! What a lovely dress' with two other Gliddon protégées, Coral Browne and Sally Gray. Coral Browne recalled that the three of them were the first to be 'chucked out'.[14] The play opened at the Globe on 3 September.

In the autumn of 1934 Vivien went to see *Theatre Royal* in which Laurence Olivier was performing in his newly acquired status of matinée idol. She confided to a girl-friend: "That's the man I'm going to marry.' Not unnaturally her friend reminded her that they were both already married. "It doesn't matter," replied Vivien, "I'll still marry him one day."[15] She returned to see the play on many future occasions.

By December all sorts of curious plans were afoot, as Oswald wrote:

> The latest notion is that *if* Viv gets an offer of £500 a week to go to Hollywood, Leigh can't chuck his Bar, but *I* would go and chaperone her! [16]

Things are Looking Up was released on 25 February 1935 by Gaumount British, a Michael Balcon production. Meanwhile, Gliddon secured her a leading part in a 'quota quickie' film, called *The Village Squire,* an eminently forgettable comedy in which she played the sister of an actor (Leslie Perrins), who came to live in a village dominated by a squire (David Horne), who was fond of quoting Shakespeare. Vivien worked for one week at Elstree and was paid five guineas a day. She also performed in *Gentlemen's Agreement,* again with David Horne, this time playing an unemployed typist. Horne, a distinguished West End actor, was impressed by Vivien's beauty and suggested her to Matthew Forsyth, one of the directors. Gliddon continued:

> He knew they were having great difficulty in finding a really young actress with the right sexy beauty for the part. So they rang me up and asked me to bring Vivien down to the Q [theater] as soon as possible. We arrived at the Q but when it came to listing Vivien's stage experience the producer seemed rightly scared of engaging Vivien for the part, as it involved some big emotional scenes. I suggested that they let Vivien rehearse on approval for the day and then make a decision.[17]

The role of a young and flirtatious wife was not an easy one, however Vivien secured the role and was paid £5 for the week. *The Green Sash* opened at the Q on 25 February 1935. The advance publicity described her as 'making her first appearance on the London stage after two years at the Comédie Française.[18] Of her performance as Guista, a soldier's young wife in Florence who is widowed during a plague, Vivien wrote:

> I am sure I was not good in the part, which was a long one and far too difficult for anyone as inexperienced as I was. But Charles Morgan – the only critic who turned up on the first night (God bless him) – gave me two, not too scathing lines in *The Times*, with the result that Sydney Carroll was interested, and came to see me in the part.[19]

Charles Morgan wrote of Vivien:

> The dramatists have given so vague a sketch of her that Miss Vivien Leigh has little opportunity for portraiture, but her acting has a precision and lightness which should serve her well when her material is of more substance.[20]

Oswald Frewen liked the performance, after which he drove Leigh, Vivien, and John Gliddon home in 'Baby.' It was a bumpy ride, Oswald commenting: "At least, the agent got out at Hammersmith, dithering. It's a pity I drive so dashingly at my age![21] When the play ended after a fortnight, Oswald was disturbed by its effect on both Vivien and Leigh. While Leigh dug trenches for the new kitchen garden, Vivien regaled Oswald with excited tales of her achievements to date. Meanwhile Leigh "moped around, thoroughly dissatisfied with Viv's continuing glow over the accomplishments, which he thought were nil."[22]

Another character to be found at Brede was Clare's son, Richard Brinsley Sheridan, the dramatist's great-grandson, known as Dick, born just as his father Wilfred was killed in action in September 1915. His curious life included living in America and the Sahara as a child, becoming a sailor, losing the original manuscripts of *The School for Scandal* in a storm, being thrown overboard by a French skipper for falling in love with his wife, and dangling 100 feet above deck when a footrope broke on a voyage to Australia. He was the author of *Heavenly Hell.* Vivien was present during a weekend in December 1934 when Dick and his cousin, Jack Leslie, fell into a classic Jerome argument on the relative merits of an eighteenth-century frigate and a nineteenth-century clipper ship. Jack Leslie walked out in high dudgeon and his father, Shane, announced that Dick would no longer be welcome in their house. Dick used to bring his girlfriend, Diana Churchill, to Brede Place. Dick introduced her to Vivien, saying" "She thinks she can act."[23]

Oswald was one of those who had advised Leigh to let Vivien have her fling at acting: "Once she gets it out of her system, she'll be alright."[24] When Leigh asked the advice of Hamish Hamilton, he replied with more prescience: 'You can't stop her. But it will be the end of your marriage.[25]

All this time Gliddon was taking Vivien to restaurants that he could ill afford, such as the Ivy and the Savoy Grill. She began to be noticed due to what he called her "beauty, exquisite taste in dress, even the perfume she used [which] was fragrant in its subtle appeal to the senses. Laughingly she called it "rape."[26] When he took Vivien to studios he hired a chauffeur-driven limousine in order to impress the man on the gates. Gliddon succeeded in persuading Aubrey Blackburn, the casting director for Basil Dean, to take Vivien for a comedy film called *Look Up and Laugh*, starring Gracie Fields. J.B. Priestley wrote the screenplay. Filming took four weeks in the spring of 1935. Vivien would rise at 6:30, go down to Elstree and often wait about unused until 4:30. One afternoon she was so upset that she drew the Sub-Producer's attention to herself by washing off all her make-up with her own tears. Oswald Frewen, staying at Little Stanhope Street, heard her tell the story to John Gliddon on the telephone:

> "I nearly left then and there, I was so miserable, with*out* their damned permission," she said. I distinctly heard her agent nearly fainting with horror the other end at such a suggestion.[27]

Vivien played the nice daughter of a nasty tycoon (Alfred Drayton) and there were a lot of North Country songs from 'Our Gracie.' Basil Dean was more of a dictator than director, and he picked on Vivien for her lack of experience before the camera. He admitted later: "She was so uncontrollably nervous that for quite a while she seemed unable to take direction, a circumstance for which I made insufficient allowance. I became impatient…"[28] Gracie Fields noticed that Vivien was "so nervous of the director that several times I found her nearly in tears,"[29] but impressed to find Vivien studying Russian during breaks in filming, she wondered if Vivien was going there. Vivien said, "No, I just like to study different languages."[30] Gracie took Gliddon aside and said: "That young girl of yours will go places but she will need very careful handling."[31]

John Gliddon was far from pleased with the results: "When I saw the rushes of *Look Up and Laugh* I could not help but feel disappointed with the way she had been photographed.[32] What seemed like a setback followed. Basil Dean gave up his option to use Vivien for three films at £8 a day, offering a new one on reduced terms. This was rejected.

While filming was still underway, Sydney Carroll was searching for an actress for his costume play, *The Mask of Virtue,* to be staged at the Ambassadors Theatre. Hamish Hamilton recalled that Carroll first spotted Vivien lunching at the Ivy and asked her if she had ever acted. He said he had just the part for her. John Gliddon claimed that his wish to see her came from seeing rushes of *Look Up and Laugh*. He was quick to ensure that Carroll saw *The Times* notice about Vivien. Gliddon also said that the director, Maxwell Wray, spotted Vivien waiting in the queue outside the office and declared: "If that is the girl at the end of the row dressed in black, then as far as I am concerned the part is cast."[33]

Carroll himself maintained that he discovered Vivien independently.

> I gave her her chance without seeing any press notices, photos or pictures. I was influenced solely by my own judgment plus a knowledge of palmistry. Vivien allowed me to read her hands and her remarkable line of success or destiny struck me as being unique.[34]

Vivien was fortunate that none of Carroll's first choices – Peggy Ashcroft, Jane Baxter, or Anna Neagle – were available. And Diana Churchill did not feel she should leave her play. Vivien was given an audition. She recalled:

> I can still remember my excitement when I went along for it, and my absolute despair when the actual moment arrived. When Sydney Carroll handed me the script and

> asked me to read the part I literally shook from head to foot with fright. But Lilian Braithwaite, who had been invited to the audition, gave me a smile of friendly encouragement, and somehow I managed to find my voice. After I stopped reading there was a moment's silence. Then Lilian Braithwaite said briskly: "I think we have got the right girl, don't you, Sydney?[35]

Vivien was engaged at ten pounds a week to play Henriette Duquesnoy, a prostitute masquerading as a paragon of innocence. *The Mask of Virtue* was set in the days of Louis XV, adapted by Carl Sternheim from Diderot's story, *Jacques le Fataliste*, and translated into English by Ashley Dukes. Vivien was greatly encouraged by Frank Cellier, who played the womanizing old Marquis who was to be tricked into taking her on. Lilian Braithwaite, too, was a great help, urging her to do breathing exercises to increase her range and giving advice that Vivien always heeded – to take three deep breaths before going on stage.

Vivien feared dismissal throughout the rehearsal period. And it was tiring, as she was still filming. She knew she was lucky to have beautiful dresses to wear and Maxwell Wray made full use of her particular qualities – repose and graceful movement. In many ways Vivien was still quite naïve:

> Someone in the play had the line to say to me: "I shall make many demands on you" and I said "Not more than the gentlemen, I'm sure" and it brought the house down and I never knew why. I was that much of an ass. I suppose, though, I must have had some sort of timing to get the laugh.[36]

The first night, 15 May 1935, was a sensation. Vivien became an instant star. Opinions are still divided to this day about the quality of her acting, but when the curtain rose, the audience held its breath. It was one of those legendary nights in the theatre when an unknown beauty won all hearts. Vivien was reserved about her success:

> It was a romantic first night. I had a part that was both

good and decorative, and I was helped by the entire cast, with that wonderful loyalty and generosity of the theatre world towards a newcomer. The fact that I was young and unknown caught the imagination of the audience. The roar of applause when the final curtain fell told me that the miracle had happened. I had arrived.[37]

Chapter 6
Fame in a Night

Some commonsense streak in me kept me from having my head turned, made me understand how easy it would be to slip, unless I compensated for my lack of experience by hard work. I struggled far more to keep at the top than to get there.

Vivien Leigh
What Success has Taught Me

At the end of the first night Sydney Carroll made a speech describing his three leading ladies, Viola Tree, Jeanne de Casalis, and Vivien as 'The Past, the Present, and the Future.'[1] Lady Tree shook her fist at him in jest. Vivien went to the Florida nightclub, nervously asking her mother: "Was I r*eally* all right?"[2] The reviews soon confirmed the reactions of the audience under headlines such as 'Actress is a Discovery' and 'New Star to win all London.' The reviewers themselves praised her beauty while remaining guarded about her 'limited range.'[3] There were two important ones: Charles Morgan of *The Times* wrote:

> Ingenious in appearance, untouched in heart, but by temporary misfortune a girl of the pavement, the bait (or shall we say in tribute of her prettiness) – the fly? mingling very adroitly a demure repose with a lively understanding.[4]

And James Agate in the *Sunday Times*:

> Miss Leigh has inciveness, retenue, and obvious intelligence. She gives to this part all it asks except in the matter of speech. If this young lady wants to become an actress, as distinct from a film star, she should at once seek means to improve her overtone, which is displeasing to the fastidious ear.[5]

Sydney Carroll himself was quick to capitalize on Vivien's success, writing in his regular Thursday column in the *Daily Telegraph*:

> I congratulate myself upon having encountered on the threshold of her career a young girl whose mental balance of mind equals her physical poise, one who can bring a divine sense of humor to meet the many vicissitudes and setbacks that are certain to be her accompaniments to fortune so long as she pursues it… It is grand to think that Old England can turn out all this promising material out of which we hope see emerge the Bergners, the Bernhardts and the Duses of the future…[6]

Agate, disguised as Richard Prentis in *John O'London's Weekly,* responded and Carroll's theater remained full for many days.

Friends of the Hartleys were also pleased. One wrote from Sussex:

> I am *absolutely delighted* for your sakes that your little girl has done so well. And I know what a lot of it is due to you Gertie. I know how keen you were that she should study on the continent, it must give you great satisfaction to know that you gave her the right education and training.[7]

Early on the day following the first night, the press descended on Little Stanhope Street, numerous photographs were taken and Vivien became the victim of a great deal of sensational gush in newspapers. John Gliddon, who arrived to help keep order, was delighted with the interest and surprised that

Vivien appeared "rather annoyed at having been disturbed at such an early hour."[8] Much useful publicity emerged from the idea of photographing her with Suzanne, then aged nearly three. Later this inspired Walter Sickert to paint the scene from a cutting in a newspaper.

Hamish Hamilton was one who had not attended the famous first night, thinking it would be embarrassing. He got a slightly different reaction:

> Next morning I rang her and asked rather condescendingly how she got on. "Jamie," she screamed, "don't you ever read the papers? I'm a STAR!"[9]

The Hungarian film producer Alexander Korda had been in the first night audience. He summoned Gliddon to his office. Gliddon related:

> It seemed as if nearly every film company in England and the United States were wanting to make screen tests of the new discovery. Had I wanted to make quick money for Vivien then this was my chance, but I already knew her well enough to realize that she only wanted to sign up with one producer and that was Alexander Korda.[10]

Fortunately Gliddon had realized that Vivien was on the threshold of fame. Having turned down Basil Dean, he was free to negotiate with Korda:

> As far as Vivien was concerned she made it a condition with me that she wanted to continue her career as a stage actress. She would say to me sometimes "I would rather be a Marie Tempest than a Greta Garbo." It took nearly six months of legal work to get the Korda contract ready for signature. On that particular morning when I bargained over the film side with Korda we reached a verbal agreement. Korda asked me "What shall we say to the press?" I did some rough calculations and found that over the 5 year period (as Vivien's husband would not consent to a longer period) Vivien would receive about £50,000. So that sum

> was given out to the press and I had the thrill of seeing the evening papers with the words: "£50,000 film contract for Vivien Leigh."[11]

The details of the contract were that Vivien had to make time for two films a year. Her salary would rise from £1,300 in the first year to £18,000 in the fifth, hence the figure of £50,000. Oswald Frewen was amused that Korda had "had her Film Test in his office these two months past, and could at any time have made the same contract with her for 1/10th the sum."[12] John Gliddon anticipated problems with Leigh Holman and these duly arose. Leigh did not mind Vivien acting as a hobby, rather as a wife might undertake a spot of modeling. The next day he arrived with a solicitor "to see if they could break her contract."[13] Instead he proposed a different form of agreement, giving her the right to end their association under a variety of circumstances, all of which were on her side. But Gliddon remained resolute.

Oswald Frewen, a voice of reason amidst the jubilation, worried at first that success might overwhelm Vivien. The weekend after the opening night, Leigh, Vivien, and Diana Churchill were at Brede. Oswald inscribed a circle around Vivien and looked her up and down. He then announced: "Well, I don't *see* any change."[14] Vivien replied almost tearfully: "There isn't any change and there never *will* be, Oswald."[15] He added later: "And indeed there isn't, except perhaps that she is…just a wee bit more matured."[16] Frewen saw the play on 10 June and during the entr'acte Leigh went to sleep in Vivien's dressing-room, after complaining that he had seen the play three times and each time there were alterations aimed at diminishing Vivien's part. Oswald had no illusions about the play itself, or Vivien's part in it:

> Her natural sweetness cannot help getting across the footlights, as she is a lovely picture, she has to cry at two crises, and she can't cry. When she lays her head on the table it looks as though she were just tired out (or bored) or asleep.[17]

The Mask of Virtue brought Vivien to the attention of many other stars who were later to be important friends to her. They came in droves to see the play. "She made a fantastic first appearance," [18] recalled Fabia Drake half a century later, while Moura Budgerg wrote that she had "gasped at her beauty (especially…when she was kneeling)."[19] Douglas Fairbanks Jr., Noël Coward, and John Gielgud were amongst those who became aware of her at this time.

Vivien's beauty was her greatest asset. There are many that declare that she was the most beautiful creature they ever saw, with her melting eyes, Cheshire cat smile and beautifully shaped face – fine English looks with a hint of the Oriental. That arbiter of beauty, Cecil Beaton, described her as "in looks the acme of prettiness. Beautiful nose, lips, violet eyes, long neck, heartshaped face," though he added: "But did it add up to beauy?"[20] Gladys Cooper thought her "the most beautiful woman of her age, and to me her beauty was not of any period."[21]

Yet Vivien, like most famous beauties, had little confidence in her looks. Vivien was worried when James Agate wrote that her neck was like a tulip, and added that some tulips have 'too long stems.'[22] She continued to worry about this for some years, when, as she said: "I should been worrying about my acting."[23]

Vivien's hands were her major flaw. She thought them clumsy and ungainly. She used to wear gloves until she read in Ellen Terry's autobiography that it was wrong to hide the hands, because it only fueled the myth that one had something to be ashamed of. Vivien's other problem was her mouth, which she felt was too small. When making up she would accentuate and lengthen the lower lip to give it fuller effect.

Her fame had a welcome side-effect for Antony Beauchamp, whose photographs of her were much in after *The Mask of Virtue* triumph. As Beauchamp wrote: "Vivien Leigh was established – And so was I."[24] Presently Vivian was photographed by Norman Parkinson, and then for *Vogue* by Cecil Beaton. In the 1936 Summer Academy Exhibition a portrait of her in her nightgown by T.C. Dugdale caused quite a stir.

On 29 May Sydney Carroll transferred *The Mask of Virtue* to the much larger St. James Theatre. This proved over-ambitious and often the house was only half-full. Vivien plowed on in the play. She forged what proved to be a life-long friendship with Jeanne de Casalis, who though her "entirely adorable" and "as friendly and irresponsible as a kitten.'[25] This led to a certain amount of tomfoolery in the theatre. Jeanne de Casalis gave Lady Tree a farthing as a tip on stage and Lady Tree rose to the joke by saying

"Oh, Madame, it is *too* much." Having carried this off she got into a muddle over the line: "Who knows which of us the fish will snap up in the end?" This emerged variously as "Who knows which of us the ship will fish up... the fish will ship up...the shop will fish up," and on and on. Vivien wrote to Leigh, who was away:

> You can imagine how Jeanne and I *roared* – yes roared *unashamedly* and very loud and would you believe it we got a big hand on our exit again – most extraordinary.[26]

As ever Vivien relished simple things, included a disturbed night at Little Stanhope Street:

> I heard a scratchy noise in the ceiling and a little bird popped through a hole on to the pipe running along the side of the wall, turned its behind on one and went fast asleep. Then this morning I was woken up by the most terrific chirpings and had no peace until I'd managed to get it out of the room as it flew about pee-ing on everything. One landed just where your head would have been if you'd been there![27]

Meanwhile, Vivien left Suzanne in the care of Nanny in London.

After Vivien died, Gladys Cooper recalled that she "was allowed by her very kind, but rather strict first husband to go out once a week."[28] With Leigh away, Vivien, very energetic, was determined to enjoy her new fame and popularity. Daisy Goguel, her new lady's maid, remembered a number of young men who came to take Mrs. Holman out.[29] She dined frequently at the Savoy Grill, the Café Royal, and Quaglino's. She attended the Russian Ballet and danced at the 400. Amongst her new friends were two distinguished oarsmen, David Collet, who had rowed for Jesus College, Cambridge in 1921; and John Fremantle (later Lord Cottesloe), a formidable all-rounder with twinkling eyes, who had rowed for Trinity in the same year.

Another man who took Vivien out was Gladys Cooper's son, John Buckmaster. Vivien spent a weekend in Kent with him in August 1935. Nearly two years younger than Vivien, he was immensely good-looking, a male version of his mother. He was an expert batsman and tennis player. A lively character, dubbed 'Oh that man!'[30] for Leigh's benefit, he later became an actor and inspired nightclub entertainer in New York. His half-sister, Sally Hardy, recalled that he was very talented and versatile, if anything too diverse. She said:

> Vivien was the love of his life and the only person, according to my mother [Gladys Cooper], that Leigh didn't mind her going around with.[31]

Vivien told John Merivale that John Buckmaster was the first person with whom she had an affair after her marriage. They stayed with Sidney Herbert* who lived near Lympne in "a lovely house with an exquisite garden and some of the loveliest paneling I've ever seen, which S. Herbert said came from Philip Sassoon's house."[32] She enjoyed talking to Herbert, once a marvelous athlete but now incapacitated by the loss of a leg. Buckmaster took her and his father, Buck, to see the latter's 65-ton yacht at Folkestone and on the Sunday they sailed to the Sandwich and then back to Deal, returning to London in time for the play. Buckmaster drove her down to Brede, where they arrived at 2:20 in the morning. Oswald received them in his pajamas and they went to bed at 3. The next day they breakfasted at 11:30 and went over to Jeanne de Casalis's Bohemian party and variety show, returning again in the early hours of the morning. Vivien had wanted to perform a bit of *The School for Scandal* with Frank Cellier, but he had to film at 7:30 the next morning. Oswald judged John Buckmaster "a shy book, but is friendly and with a desir de plaire.[33]

After *The Mask of Virtue*, there was a lull in Vivien's career and she consequently became restless. There was talk of acting in *Hamlet* in America with Leslie Howard, and Korda hoped to film *Cyrano* with Charles Laughton as Cyrano de Bergerac and Vivien as Roxanne. Neither came to fruition – *Hamlet* because, by the time *The Mask* was over, he had made new plans; and *Cyrano* due to disagreement between Korda and Laughton, concerning the script, the props, and even the proposed use of Vivien herself. Matters were not helped by Vivien's refusal to dye her hair blonde for the part.

*Later Sir Sidney Herbert, Bt (1890-1939), MP and sometime Parliamentary Private Secretary to the Prime Minister.

Thus from a professional point of view the autumn months of 1935 were stagnant. John Gliddon, negotiating away, suffered too: "You have to be pretty cheerful to stand all that."[34]

On the other hand, Vivien nursed another ambition – to meet Laurence Olivier. She had seen numerous matinées of *Theatre Royal* in the autumn of 1934, since when he had become an obsession. She had conceived the idea that one day she and Olivier might emulate the Lunts as a celebrated stage couple. She now had a foot on the ladder. Indeed Olivier had seen *The Mask of Virtue.* Years later, with hindsight, he wrote of how she had attracted much attention, though not then as a promising actress:

> Apart from her looks, which were magical, she possessed beautiful poise; her neck looked almost too fragile to support her head and bore it with a sense of surprise, and something of the pride of the master juggler who can make a brilliant manoeuvre appear almost accidental. She also had something else: an attraction of the most perturbing nature I had ever encountered. It may have been the strangely touching spark of dignity in her that enslaved the ardent legion of her admirers.[35]

Vivien prevailed upon her ally, John Buckmaster, to take her to dine at the Savoy Grill, where Olivier and his wife invariably dined after his performance in *Romeo and Juliet.* This was another play that she saw frequently. Olivier's own marriage was unsteady. However, towards the end of 1935 Jill Esmond became pregnant. It has been suggested that it was the very night when the Oliviers were celebrating this event at the Savoy Grill that John Buckmaster finally introduced Vivien. Buckmaster remarked that Olivier looked a lesser man without his moustache and when Vivien leapt to his defense he realized how she felt about him.

Olivier and Jill had rented a small house at Burchett's Green, near Maidenhead, not far from Ivor Novello's Redroofs. Vivien recalled: "And so we went and we played football, and I remember Larry roaring around one minute and then unaccountably falling fast asleep under the piano the next."[36]

Some time after this Vivien paid one of her frequent solitary visits to

Romeo and Juliet. Olivier wrote:

> One afternoon I was making up for a matinée of *Romeo and Juliet* when she popped into my dressing-room at the New Theatre; it was ostensibly to invite us to something or other; she only stayed a couple of minutes, and then she gave me a soft little kiss on the shoulder and was gone.[37]

But Olivier knew that an irresistible temptation had crossed his path.

Vivien's career advanced thanks to Ivor Novello and John Gielgud. John Buckmaster had taken her over to Redroofs, where the actress Fabia Drake met her for the first time:

> I was there for the weekend and they arrived while we were having lunch and they went and sat on a hammock in the garden and when lunch was over we came out and there was John Buckmaster, and beside him was a little person in navy blue slacks, navy blue silk blouse and I stopped dead in my tracks and said to Ivor: "Who on *earth* is that?" And he said "That's someone called Vivian Holman"…But really, her beauty would stop the traffic.[38]

Terence Rattigan recalled his first meeting with her, also at Redroofs:

> Ivor had a crush on her, and vaguely, on me too – so she and I didn't like each other much at first. I thought she had the most beautiful face I'd ever seen – but that wasn't enough – Oh dear![39]

Novello offered her the part of Jenny Mere in Max Beerbohm's *The Happy Hypocrite.* Vivien's stagnant career was complicated by her film contract with Korda and Sydney Carroll's option on her next stage appearance. However, while staying with Leigh at the Lygon Arms in Broadway for New Year's Eve, she determined to accept the part. On New Year's Day, she wrote to John Gliddon, explaining that if necessary, she could film by day and act by night:

> After all, most people seem to do the two now, and working with Ivor can't fail to be a big and very good thing. Do, do try and arrange this. If you'd read *The Happy Hypocrite* you'd understand more how anxious I am to do it.[40]

Contractual differences were resolved and she was signed for the part. There was a delay of two months and meanwhile John Gielgud remembered Vivien's success in *The Mask of Virtue* and invited her to audition the part of the young Queen in *Richard II* at Oxford. His deputy, Glen Byam Shaw, recalled:

> She was very nervous at the reading and I must admit that I was not very impressed, but John said she would be very good, would look divine, and that all the young men at Oxford would fall madly in love with her. All of which proved true.[41]

Gielgud was impressed that Vivien wanted to make her career foremost 'in the living theatre' when with 'her natural beauty, skill, and grace of movement' she could easily have been tempted solely into films:

> She had a lifelong devotion to the theatre, and determined to work there diligently through the years in order to reach the heights which she afterwards achieved. Though in her first big success, *The Mask of Virtue*, she had taken the critics and public by storm, she knew that her youth and beauty were the chief factors of her immediate success, and she was modest and shrewd enough to face the challenge of developing herself so as to find the widest possible range of which she was capable.[42]

The lion's share of the work fell to Byam Shaw:

> She was wonderful to work with. She was tremendously serious, sensitive, eager for direction, punctual and professional and gave me great encouragement and help

> throughout the rehearsals. No leading lady could have been more generous in her attitude to an inexperienced producer and it was the start of a friendship that was always very precious to me.[43]

The set consisted of an ingenious Gothic triptych but *The Times* reviewer noted that 'in some lights the flying buttresses appear to need more support than they give'[44] At this time it was normal to have professional actresses for the women's parts, whereas earlier these would have been played by boys. Thus Florence Beerbohm Kahn, Max Beerbohm's wife, played the Duchess of Gloucester. But the male leads were taken by Oxford students, David King-Wood of St. Edmund Hall playing King Richard.

While Florence Kahn decorated her dressing-room with prints of fourteenth-century England and placed a Shakespeare Variorum on her table to help her get into the mood of the play, Vivien filled hers with undergraduates and music on the wireless. She soon became another Max Beerbohm heroine – Zuleika Dobson; as a member of the cast, Michael Denison, then at Magdalen recalled:

> She was certainly the most beautiful creature that I've ever seen and she was only in her 23rd year – at the absolute height of her beauty. And so the whole of Oxford was absolutely spinning. The great thing was if you got her to come to lunch in your rooms because in those days the College chef would provide you with a splendid meal, served by your scout in the rooms. So you had your chosen few to meet her – a pretty heady occasion. I was luckier than some insofar as one of my great friends at school was Hugh Martin.* Hugh told me at the time (he was as smitten as all of us) that He and Vivien shared a bath at the neutral age of about two…It gave me a Head start over some of the others who were queuing up to ask her to lunch.[45]

Whenever separated from Leigh, Vivien would write, almost automatically, of how much she missed him and how lonely she felt. From her room in the

*Son of Geoffrey Martin, Ernest Hartley's partner. Brother of Mills and Dulcie.

Randolph Hotel in the week of rehearsals, she wrote to her husband:

> I just refrained from exclaiming how lonely I should feel sleeping alone which I am sure would have shocked the undergraduates who are a very sober lot, but very sweet and kind...David King-Wood is very good and quite puts me to shame.[46]

Richard II duly opened on 17 February with Max Beerbohm prominent in the stalls. Vivien received a bad notice in *The Times*:

> Miss Vivien Leigh makes a pretty figure of the pathetic Queen, but she has yet to make herself at ease with Shakespearian verse.[47]

The second night went badly and then on 20 February Gielgud brought his friends from London to the matinée, a prospect that filled Vivien with dread. The week ended with an informal and witty speech from Max Beerbohm at the O.U.D.S. dinner and revelry which continued well into the night.

Soon Vivien was touring Manchester and Southport in *The Happy Hypocrite*, adapted in three acts by Clemence Dane from a story written in 1897 by Max Beerbohm. Like Vivien's first major play, the story concerned 'the function and significance of masks.'[48]

The play opened in the Manchester Opera House. Vivien's parents sat in a box and said they could hear Ivor Novello, Isabel Jeans, and Vivien clearly 'but couldn't hear the others, which is rather serious.'[49] Vivien hated Manchester but the play enjoyed a good reception. A 'wonderful' new prologue and other bits had been added which caused a lot of drying-up in the cast. She felt less depressed after a Pimms No. 1 at supper. The games-playing continued and Vivien was dubbed 'the games mistress' by her fellow players.[50] One woman in the audience described the play as 'sheer Shakespeare all the way through' but 'there were three tight bookies, one of which said the play was just a lot of pansies shooting arrows! They subsequently walked out.'[51]

The company then went to Southport and gallantly danced with 'all the Southport drearies'[52] at the Prince of Wales Hotel. After a disastrous dress rehearsal, the first night was a success but Vivien dreaded the London opening on 8 April. She had a song which she despaired of getting right and found that the more she did the play the less she liked herself in it. She became depressed until she read the 'marvelous' notices.

The Happy Hypocrite continued to play to packed houses to Vivien's surprise: "I can't think where the people come from as Southport is quite barren and one never sees anyone anywhere.'[53]. Vivien's only concern was that Isabel Jeans as La Gambogi got all the reviews: 'I have told Winifred [Clemence Dane] that if Gambogi is written up any more I shall insist on two more scenes, another dance and another song![54] The tour continued with 'glorious' notices in Manchester and Vivien writing to Leigh: 'I really hate to think of it not being a success as it is really so beautiful.'[55] Vivien found an occupational hazard in that Hugh Laing's brown make-up came off all over her bottom when he lifted her in the dance and her trousers proved impossible to clean.

Peter Graves's principal memories of the production concerned the endless game-playing. He said that Vivien would not give him time to get his make-up off in her urgency to get to the card table. Isabel Jeans struck up a great friendship with Vivien. She remembered that they gave a lot of parties called 'Our Routs,' mainly inspired by Vivien. At one of them Clemence Dane told Vivien's fortune and cried out with dismay: 'Oh, there is a devil in my Jenny's cards.'[56] Another member of the cast was Carl Harbord. In the late 1940s he asked John Merivale whether the Oliviers had split up yet. Merivale was surprised at this and Harbord explained: 'Even when she was sleeping with *me*, she was talking of Olivier.'[57]

The London opening took place at His Majesty's Theatre on 8 April in the presence of a glittering audience who received the play enthusiastically. Only Max Beerbohm had reservations, giving the impression of being 'in it but not of it,[58] and his fear that it would not be popular with the general public proved correct all too soon. Years later Max described Vivien's participation as 'of exquisite sensibility – a foreshadowing of how much to come in later years.'[59] Her performance inspired the diminutive red-faced Scot, Alan Dent,* from then on a devoted admirer, to describe her Jenny

*Ill-paid and exploited secretary to James Agate for fourteen years. Dramatic critic of the *Manchester Guardinan, Punch*, and *News Chronicle*. Film critic of the *Sunday Telegraph* and *Illustrated London News*.

Mere in the words of Wordsworth: 'a dancing shape, an image gay, to haunt, to startle and waylay.'[60]

Despite an excellent cast, the presence of Max Beerbohm, a good adaptation by Clemence Dane, music by Richard Addinsell, the light touch of director Maurice Colbourne, costumes by Motley, masks and photographs by Angus McBean, the play proved a failure. Novello's biographer, W. Macqueen-Pope, judged:

> Alas that thing of delicate beauty, that piece of gossamar idealism was not for the general taste. It was caviare. But it was a memory to treasure as long as one lived.[61]

In June Vivien took part in *Henry VIII* at the Open Air Theatre in Regent's Park, which had been the creation of Sydney Carroll some three years before. Vivien played Anne Boleyn to the Welsh actor Lyn Harding's Henry VIII in a cast that included Gyles Isham and Phyllis Neilson-Terry. The play was bedeviled by bad weather, Lyn Harding squelching his way nightly along the muddy path to his dressing-room. Vivien already suffered from inadequate voice projection, a problem that was exacerbated by the open air. The critics found her 'on the slight side for park acting'[62] and thought her portrayal of the ill-fated Anne lacked 'that inner hardness which might bring a cardinal down.'[63] The production left Vivien run-down and suffering from a bad cold.

Vivien then launched into three films for Korda in very quick succession. Her career was becoming well established. She was being noticed by critics and fellow actors and actresses. She had a kind husband and a healthy alert daughter. But this was not enough. And so she embarked on the dangerous and complicated course of having an affair with her idol, Laurence Olivier.

Chapter 7
The Quest for Olivier

We've a right to be happy. Everyone's a right to be happy.
Vivien Leigh
Fire Over England

Laurence Olivier was born in Dorking on 22 May 1907, the son of the Rev. Gerard Kerr Olivier, an Anglo-Catholic priest of whom he was afraid. Hs mother, whom he described as 'my entire world,' died when he was twelve, and Olivier, ever the puritan, felt this emotional experience might have helped make him a good actor. The Oliviers were a Huguenot family from Nay in France, dating back to 1520. They came to England in the seventeenth century to escape religious persecution, producing in due course a number of merchants, rectors, and colonels.

Olivier's early years were dominated by the Church and he became one of fourteen choristers at All Saints, Margaret Street. It made an indelible mark on him and he was consumed with religious fervor. He began acting at an early age, attracting the attention of Sybil Thorndike, Forbes-Robertson and Ellen Terry when he performed as Kate at Stratford. He was not popular at school, being thought somewhat sissy and florid of manner. He longed to follow his brother, Dickie, to India to grow rubber, but his father told him that the stage was to be his career. He obtained a scholarship to the Central School of Speech and Drama, where he studied under Elsie Fogerty.*

In those days he was, if anything, a little uncouth and no amount of

*Speech therapist, founder of the Central School of Speech Training and Dramatic Art.

physical exercise could succeed in building up his physique. Esmond Knight said:

> After this first term at the Central his teacher Harry Oscar wrote to his father and said: 'I really think you should withdraw your son. He's no good. He looks like a farm boy.' His hair grew down to his brown. He had buck teeth, and he looked like a sort of Breton peasant. Extraordinary. He used to shave his hair right back.[1]

Olivier made his way to the London stage by the age of twenty-one, and met his first wife, Jill Esmond Moore, when they acted together in John Drinkwater's *Bird in the Hand.* She was the daughter of H.V. Esmond, a well-known actor-manager, and the actress Eva Moore. Born in 1908, she first appeared on stage at the St. James Theatre, at age fourteen. Her career progressed swiftly and she starred in Noël Coward's *Hay Fever* in 1925. Jill had a strong face with heavy, dark yet soft eyes and a long down-turned mouth. Planted in a contemporary photograph with, say, Edwina Mountbatten, she would not look out of place. Yet she always appeared somewhat miscast in the role of romantic heroine in films such as *Secrets of FPI.* She was more convincing when cross than when gentle, probably because she was more intelligent than the average star. Had she been a bird she would have been a watchful owl or a predatory eagle.

Marriage to Jill was a good proposition of the young Olivier. They were married on 25 July 1930 (Princess Marie Louise sent a pearl knick-knack). According to his memoirs, Olivier was not exactly in love:

> With those antecedents, though not dazzlingly attractive she would most certainly do excellent well for a wife. I wasn't going to wait for anyone better to come along, I was desperate to get married...she did not respond automatically. In fact she took two years to agree to it and never did really respond at all.[2]

They proved ill-suited partners. Jill had been honest with him:

> She had admitted to me that she was in love elsewhere and could never love me as completely as I would wish.[3]

In those early days, Olivier still lacked self-confidence. Like many others, possibly even subconsciously, he molded himself in the likeness of a more famous actor, only breaking away when he was ready to be himself. It is said that he wore a moustache in imitation of Douglas Fairbanks. But it is fairer to attribute the pencil moustache to the style of the Hollywood actor, Ronald Colman, who had left England to become the archetypal Englishman abroad, more British than the British themselves. As such, Colman caused hearts to flutter for over thirty-five years, starring in *Beau Geste, Bulldog Drummond, The Prisoner of Zenda* and *Raffles*. David Niven and Douglas Fairbanks Jr. were likewise in the Colman mold.

In his Colman phase, Olivier played in Noël Coward's *Private Lives*, a part that Coward felt he did not enjoy, but which did him considerable good. A few weeks before his first wedding, when Olivier was still only twenty-three, George Bernard Shaw was describing him to Harold Nicolson as 'a born actor. Spoke of him with real admiration.'[4]

A year later, Olivier made his way to Hollywood where Douglas Fairbanks Jr. remembered him as a rather self-conscious Englishman, best known as Jill Esmond's husband – which, said Fairbanks, 'didn't appeal to his sense of pride.'[5] Olivier tested for the part of Garbo's lover in *Queen Christina* but the temperamental Swede rejected him. He made three films in two years and tried to write a play. In 1932 he gave up and returned to England, bringing with him considerable distaste for Hollywood. In so doing he persuaded Jill to pass up the chance of starring in *A Bill of Divorcement* for David O. Selznick, 'thereby losing her chance at Hollywood,'[6] as Irene Selznick put it. Soon Olivier acquired success as a matinée idol, before switching towards Shakespearian roles. He was much criticized for trying to play Romeo with realism rather than singing the part, a method favored by Gielgud and the cause of much swooning in an admiring audience.

By the mid-1930s, Laurence Olivier was at an early zenith of fame, strong, handsome, already the master of many diverse roles. His thick dark hair formed a widow's peak, which appealed to Vivien (when he cut it for a film in the late 1940s, it never grew properly again).

Just as Vivien was on the brink of her quest for Olivier, so too was

Olivier reaching a turning-point. Esmond Knight found himself a fellow dinner guest with Olivier and Jill:

> Jill Esmond was a terrific character. She was a great star. She was almost a bigger star than Laurence was, you know...Laurence was there with Jill, who was heavily in the family way and she sort of armed herself with the boldness of a creature married to a man who was obviously going to be a very great star...but he, at the moment he had just met Vivien – which was just at the wrong moment as far as Jill was concerned – and from that moment he just steered away.[7]

In his own memoirs, Olivier claimed that he had endured 'two years of furtive life, lying life'[8] before finally making his love affair with Vivien public in June 1937. However, the soft kiss on the shoulder occurred sometime between the opening of *Romeo* on 17 October 1935 and its closing in March 1936. It is more likely that the affair did not begin until the early summer of 1936. Olivier looked back ruefully on his adulterous phase which he found "a little nauseating to set down."[9] He felt "a really worm-like adulterer, slipping in between another man's sheets," making "darting sporadic little hops, covering some mileage"[10] to places like Stamford in Lincolnshire, where the lovers succeeded in remaining undetected. At first he found Leigh "a dull man, dry, cerebral, without sparkle."[11] Later he regretted the suffering endured by Leigh and realized that he was "highly intelligent, clever, but not exciting or outwardly romantic."[12]

These latter months of Jill's pregnancy were riddled with guilt, an emotion to which Olivier all too regularly enslaved himself. That notwithstanding, in August 1936, he was delighted to be invited to co-star with Vivien in Korda's *Fire Over England* to be produced by Erich Pommer and directed by William K. Howard. Jill was approaching the birth of her son and living quietly at Burchett's Green. Leigh was once more safely yachting with friends in Sweden.

As usual it was hard work, Vivien filming from 8 a.m. to 9 p.m., sometimes returning late to eat her supper on the floor at Little Stanhope Street. The apocryphal story revolved around a dashing sailor, Michael

Ingolby (Olivier), who narrowly escaped his father's fate of being burned at the stake. He then offered his services to good Queen Bess and returned to Spain to defeat the Armada. Vivien played Cynthia, the Queen's lady-in-waiting, the love interest in the film, and evidently in the studio too. The film's dramatic poster showed her clasped in Olivier's arms.

Fire Over England provided Olivier with ample opportunity to act dangerously.* In one scene, he had to leap onto a galleon, throw a firebrand on the deck (which, being soaked with petrol, immediately caught fire) and then dive head-first over the side into a safety-net. During one take the flames chased him and he slipped badly; the director actually wondered if he had broken his neck. Flora Robson as the Queen had the best part with lines almost entirely drawn from genuine speeches by Elizabeth I. She was dressed in an ornate costume with a false nose and a red wig and had to appear hostile to the youthful lovers.[13] The director, William Howard, did his best to keep order, urging the Tudor-clad extras: "Will you Ladies and Gentlemen be careful not to chew during a take?"[14]

While working with Olivier, Vivien kept in touch with Leigh and professed to miss him. "I was so depressed on Friday – last night – my darling. It was very dismal without you…"[15] Once she laughed in the middle of a shot and incurred the fury of the director, "a very quick sort of fury,'[16] which frightened her out of speaking to him until late the next day. Then she met Winston Churchill, whom Korda brought to the set: "He described Oswald as 'a very fine gentleman!'I liked him and we go on quite well."[17] Meanwhile she read the letters of Bernard Shaw and Ellen Terry.

Fire Over England afforded the two stars ample opportunity to spend time together and their affair was soon an open secret at the studio. They were known as 'the lovers.' Korda played an avuncular role. Vivien said later: "We went to him with every little problem we had. We usually left convinced that he had solved it – or that we'd got our way, even when we hadn't."[18] She found the Elizabethan costumes very heavy in the boiling August sun.

Vivien loved making this film, however, and was depressed at the prospect of beginning work on *Dark Journey* with only one day's break

*In America a scene in which Olivier weeps over his father's ashes was jeered at during previews and subsequently cut as intolerably sentimental and unacceptable behavior for such a hero.

between the two films in mid-August. She discouraged Leigh from returning on the grounds that she would be too busy.

> I am so unhappy when you are in London, when you could be in the country or sailing which is good for you. I think I'd almost rather you stayed on sailing my love. That isn't because I am not longing to see you and be with you but I feel so mean when you're waiting for me all that time, especially in this wonderful weather. We might work late on the other film or anything.[19]

She told Leigh that she did nothing but film and had only been out late twice, evidently a recurring temptation. There were occasional mentions of Olivier and Jill:

> I had dinner with Jill and Larry the other night. She is going to have hers (her baby) anytime now. They have the loveliest house overlooking the river with one immense room which was Whistler's studio…[20]

Two days later she wrote:

> Jill has started to have the baby and then it suddenly stopped just as the pains were going wonderfully well, so they are rather depressed, poor little things.[21]

Vivien heard this news from Olivier, with whom she continued to have an affair as he hovered on the brink of fatherhood. It was not an easy time for his wife, who was perfectly aware of the situation. The baby boy was born 21 August and named (Simon) Tarquin:

> Jill had her baby and I saw it last night. It is really very attractive and very big but not fat. Larry says it is like Edward G. Robinson which is a little cruel. He has already starting reciting Shakespeare to it. We drank its health at the studio yesterday.[22]

Korda was delighted with Vivien's performance in *Fire over England* but A.E.W. Mason was enraged to discover the film had little or nothing to do with his book. One actor thought Olivier was being worn down by his over-ambitious stunts, but Olivier confided: "I'm done in already. But it's not the stunts. It's Vivien. It's every day, two, three times. She's bloody wearing me out."[23] It was a complaint he would voice in the years that followed. Vivien herself retained a more idyllic remembrance of these days, as she told the journalist Godfrey Winn at Tickerage in the 1960s. She wondered if, when looking at the film, it was possible to detect that the two actors had reached a point of confrontation in their destinies. Winn quoted her:

> I don't think I have ever lived quite as intensely ever since. I don't remember sleeping, ever; only every precious moment that we spent together. We were so young. I mean all of us were so young. Like those who went to the war and did not come back. I trusted everyone and I imagined, like the very young always do, that everything lasts for ever.[24]

Vivien began work on *Dark Journey* without quite understanding what it was about. She was spotted out with Olivier within ten days of Tarquin's birth and felt it wise to inform Leigh:

> Larry took me to the ballet last night, which I adored. We missed the first one but saw *Choreatium* which is *superb* and *Boutique Fantastique* which you must remember with Danilova.[25]

Returning from Norfolk, Oswald Frewen stayed a night at Little Stanhope Street on his way back to Brede (which he had recently inherited from his mother but sold to his nephew, Dick, while he moved to The Sheephouse). He found Vivien with an influenzal throat chill and Olivier in attendance. Frewen took a tumbler round to the Pitt's Head and bought some rum:

> "Double?" asked the girl – "I don't know. How much *is* a double?" – "Oh, a single's hardly any use" – "Well, try a double." She did. I looked at it quizically, and said "Now

> add a single to it." We pumped it into Vivling, with hot water added, and sugar, and she hated it…[26]

Despite her throat, Vivien insisted on asking who had paid for it. Frewen was impressed:

> I had always regarded her as a very beautiful, spoiled girl, with charming manners but probably not a great lot behind the 5th rib or above the ears. After that I began wondering.[27]

Olivier made a less good impression by behaving in a possessive fashion. He did not want Frewen to sit on her bed or to stay on talking to her after he had left. Oswald said he had " a voice *calculated* to put anyone to sleep in 10 minutes; Vivling agreed (with a seraphic smile); Larry was not amused."[28] Olivier tried every ruse to get Frewen to leave with him, and when he failed, he rang the next day to enquire who the 'smasher' was. Frewen noted that this was a "trade term for stage-door pushful over-enthusiasts." He concluded that "Larry was just amusing."[29]

In her next letter to Leigh, Vivien mentioned Frewen's visit but not Olivier's. Victor Saville, *Dark Journey's* director, was pleased with her rushes and she began to enjoy her work more. Gertrude came down to the studio and in her enthusiasm called everyone by the wrong name. Jeanne de Casalis and her future husband invited Vivien for the weekend to attend the Lympne Air Show, and Vivien took the opportunity of a flight: "We…saw Steve's* house, Noël's and Victor [in fact Philip] Sassoon's houses. I loved it. It was a closed machine."[30]

During the show Godfrey Winn went "for a flip in a biplane with a German acrobatic ace, who proceeded to throw me about the sky until I almost prayed for death."[31] Not surprisingly Winn vomited violently upon landing. But he was hypnotized by Vivien:

> With her heart-shaped face, swan-like neck, and the smoky-blue eyes of a Siamese cat, she was without doubt

*C.D. Stephenson, who married Jeanne de Casalis in 1942. She was famous as 'Mrs. Feather' on the radio.

> the most beautiful woman who has ever come my way. To my astonishment, she seemed completely oblivious of the devastating effect she had on every male in sight.[32]

Dark Journey was made in five weeks, again at the London Film Studios, Denham. Vivien starred as a French spy masquerading as a shop-keeper, who traveled ostensibly to sell clothes, but in reality bore coded messages. Sometimes these were sewn into the hems or formed a pattern which was revealed over a map on a lampshade. She was demure and beautiful in mink, asking "What are my orders?" and "Who's the head of Section 8?" The film was set in 1918 and co-starred the bemonocled Conrad Veidt, famed for his 'liquid villainy.' There were some good lines: "It used to be all girls with no clothes, now it's all clothes with no girls," but the plot was confusing, and Vivien never really fathomed it. The *News Chronicle* summed it up:

> Conrad Veidt takes his monocle far out to sea with Q-ships and U-boats and Vivien Leigh.[33]

It is memorable as an early film in which action at least contains some credibility. George Perinal, the cameraman, produced effects in which the steel sides of the ship caved in and thousands of gallons of water swept through the hull. Vivien found the work of filming much harder technically:

> There's so much to remember– whether you are overstepping the chalk marks or leaning back too far or turning your face the wrong way – it is difficult to think of all these things and be sincere at the same time in what you are saying.[34]

One reviewer doubted the happy ending:

> I found it rather difficult to believe that two such scintillating double-crossers would ever end their lives in complete conjugal trust.[35]

Vivien was due to star in Victor Saville's next film, *Storm in a Teacup*, but she had ten days for a much-needed holiday and casually suggested to

Oswald Frewen that he might like to escort her. Leigh was conveniently unable to go since "the bar tethered him to the Temple."[36] Oswald asked his permission: "Leigh generally keeps a sort of smiling poker-face. He said he didn't mind my going but he thought Taormina was a long way to go to find the sun."[37] On 23 October Oswald and Vivien set off for Italy. From Rome they entrained and crossed to Sicily, arriving at the hotel Timeo at Taormina in thick fog.They found the beautifully carved Greek theatre, and a genuine Saracen keep tower. They explored Etna and Catania. In the evenings they took moonlight walks and Oswald put an arm around her to keep her warm. Vivien found him an admirable guide: "What he is not sure about he makes up and it still sounds good."[38] Vivien wrote to Leigh that they hoped to visit Pompeii and Capri, adding:

> We have wired Axel Munthe* to ask if we would go and see him and it would be fun to see Jill and Larry if they're still there.[39]

Munthe conveniently wired back with an invitation and they set off for Capri, where they found the Oliviers in the middle of a quietly bored holiday at the Hotel Quisisana. They welcomed Vivien with open arms and presently Oswald, the Oliviers, and she were installed in three adjoining rooms, the communal doors almost permanently open.

Vivien was so happy in Capri that she wired Leigh requesting permission to stay on longer, missing his birthday on 3 November, but returning in time for hers. Olivier and Frewen "agreed that Leigh *couldn't* say 'no,' but would, if he were wily, reply "Yes, please do, signed Leigh and Froufrou (or Mimi) and *that* would romp Vivien home forthwith. However, he was much too downright and replied "Yes darling of course do just as you wish all love Leigh."[40]

The weather was not good. "The sun so divine," "Vivien's line to Leigh, soon became a standing joke as they picnicked with chattering teeth. Nevertheless, Vivien wrote to Leigh:

> It really is so nice here and warm and sunny. Yesterday

*Axel Munthe (1857-1949), Swedish physician and writer, thought to be illegitimate member of the Swedish Royal Family. Author of *The Story of San Michele*, 1929.

> we spent the whole morning on the beach in little boats and had lunch down there. I upset mine trying to stand on the back like the natives of the island do, and my bag fell to the bottom so Larry dived and got it, which we thought was very good. In the afternoon we walked and went up to San Michele where there was a letter from Munthe saying he would like us to see the old Town he was living in (has been for 30 years) which he thought was even more interesting than S. Michele. He himself is in bed with severe influenza (the most enchanting letter he wrote). S. Michele was wonderful. I would love you to see it. As we came down we saw it by moonlight and it looked *lovely*. He has found some amazing things and has been collecting since he was 18 years old (and is now 80). Some of the mosaics and heads are stunning and the way he places his bits is so beautifully done. He has not lived there for 30 years but in a Tower Materita which we have been to see today. It is much more lovely and I completely fell in love with a lot of things. We must come back and see it all again. It was in the Tower Materita that Duse stayed with him and gave him the loveliest stained glass window which one can see now.. Darling Sweet, I do hope you are not miserable. It was so hard just to spend one night when it was so nice and we could bathe… What a nice letter you wrote to Larry. They were thrilled to see us, as they haven't spoken English to anyone for 2 weeks they said! and we got an avalanche.[41]

Oswald took a telling photograph of Olivier with Jill on his right and Vivien on his left. Though Olivier looked studiedly in Jill's direction, it was Vivien who was more closely held. Oswald concluded that Vivien was the perfect traveling companion:

> The same mentality which refused to change on achieving success kept her as simple and receptive and *joyeuse* as though she had been an unspoilt schoolgirl on her first journey with her elder brother. The same considerations

> that made her enquire about the price of the rum made my holiday feel as though she was looking after me, and because the girl has got a brain we were never bored from beginning to end.[42]

The question of sex did not arise. They were like brother and sister. "Of course," noted Frewen, "I *did* fall in love with her before we finished and if the holiday had been 3 weeks instead of 10 days she would, I'm afraid, have had to do something about it."[43] The only distressing part for Frewen was the discovery that he was part of Vivien's plot to see Larry. He was, after all, primarily Leigh's friend.

After their few days in Capri, the four traveled to Naples and Pompeii. Then Vivien and Oswald entrained for Rome on 3 November: "The Oliviers stayed sadly on the grim gloomy platform waving goodbye."[44] Frewen realized that Vivien was in love with Larry and noted later:

> She had a *crise de nerfs* in Rome when he phoned her from Naples after we left them. I begged her to give herself time, not to do anything impetuous.[45]

Many years later, Frewen further revealed that Olivier had rung to say he was finished with Jill and was prepared to send her home. He had wanted Vivien to return to Capri. Fortunately, this time, Vivien heeded Frewen's advice. She returned to London to *Storm in a Teacup*, the first of two films in which she starred opposite Rex Harrison. It was based on a play written by Bruno Frank who was outraged by the effects of the dog-tax in Germany. James Bridie set his version in Scotland, and the film concerned a pompous Provost (Cecil Parker) almost losing his seat over his treatment of an impoverished woman (Sara Allgood) and her mongrel Patsy (Scruffy – who won all hearts). Rex Harrison played the journalist who brought the issue to public attention and fell in love with the Provost's daughter (Vivien). The film gave Vivien the chance to demonstrate her excellent French, and some neat golfing strokes from her Machrihanish days.

Inevitably, Rex Harrison fell for his leading lady, but never declared himself:

> All she wanted to do was to talk about Larry, and so I went along with that, gazing on that beautiful face with unhopeful ardour. I loved Vivien. Although we never so much as held hands, I cannot say my love was platonic, it was more exciting than that.[46]

Harrison recalled that, when it seemed that she might not be able to play Ophelia to Olivier's *Hamlet* in Elsinore, "she broke down in the dressing room into wild hysteria, anger and anguish. She was very like a cat. She would purr and scratch, and she looked divinely pretty doing either."[47]

On 17 November Vivien took Leigh and Oswald Frewen to a theatrical party at which the Oliviers were present. Gradually Olivier and Frewen struck up a confiding friendship. Two nights later they dined together. When the film was over, Vivien was free to take a skiing holiday in Sils Maria with Leigh. The new year of 1937 found her with a twisted knee and sprained muscles. She returned to the stage to rehearse *Because We Must* at Wyndham's Theatre and was carried in by the producer, Norman Marshall, and the stage manager, Bernard Gordon.

Oswald Frewen suffered a considerable personal tragedy when his nephew, Dick Sheridan, died of peritonitis in Algeria on 17 January. Dick had tired of the stage as the stage tired of him, and returned to a seafaring life. In December he had persuaded Jess Dyall to elope with him, with marriage the eventual goal. Valentine Dyall rang to 'congratulate' him, adding, "I feel I ought to punch your head." Dick invited him round and the next morning turned up at his mother's house "with a black eye (a genuine one) and a certain difficulty in chewing from a bruise on his temple"[48] Vivien and Dick had fallen out, too, but, when after Dick's death Oswald announced that he intended to commune with him via a medium, she made a request: "Do give him a message of love from me, tell him all is well between us."[49] Frewen concluded that Dick was "pure gold, but mis-struck in the mint, and withdrawn from circulation."[50]

Olivier was then playing *Hamlet*, and Vivien was frequently in the audience. She took Leigh and Oswald to see the play. Frewen judged: "He acted it as though Hamlet were alive, and not a gramophone repeating quotations."[51] Olivier joined them for supper at little Stanhope Street. Two days later Leigh and Oswald attended a trade screening of *Dark Journey*.

Oswald admired her beauty, her acting, and her star-billing and was convinced it would 'make her' on the screen, adding: "Not that she desires it, the silly puss; she said 'Oh *never* call me a Film Star; I'm an *actress*, I *hate* the *films*.'"[52]

Fire Over England was released on 25 February. The glittering opening night at the Leicester Square Theatre was attended by the Duke and Duchess of Norfolk and no fewer than nine Admirals. In spite of the rain, a large crowd of cinema fans was undeterred and the traffic ground to a halt as far back as Hyde Park Corner. The film itself was criticized for its obviously fake models of ships, but Vivien was deemed to have acquired a stronger voice and was now "an actress, not merely a decoration."[53] One critic welcomed Vivien as "a refreshing change after the cheapness of so many heroines." He continued:

> Where else shall we look for such a combination of intelligence, beauty and emotional sympathy, lit up as they are by shafts of sprightliness and humour?[54]

One unexpected admirer of the film was Adolf Hitler, who evidently screened it almost as often as Churchill was later to view *Lady Hamilton. Dark Journey* opened a month later on 28 March. It was soon playing to record houses at the London Pavilion, taking £5,000 a week.

This was Vivien's most prominent film part to date and she was hailed as "the film actress we have been waiting for in this country as long as some of us can remember."[55] She was the finest discovery of British producers for some years: "This is her conquest of films, assured and complete."[56] She was praised for her composure and competence, and above all her wit, not then a notable attribute in leading ladies.

Storm in a Teacup followed on 6 June. Some critics felt she was worth better material given what she had coped with in *Dark Journey*; however, she performed well within the parameters of the script. The *Observer* went so far as to back "Miss Leigh and Mr. Harrison as England's 1937 double for screen fame."[57]

Meanwhile, Vivien returned to the stage. She starred as Pamela Golding-French in *Because We Must*, which opened on 5 February. Oswald Frewen thought she did "the best possible with a meandering part" but looked "quite lovely."[58] Vivien hated being called 'lovely' but was glad that someone told her she was acting as well as Gladys Cooper or Fay Compton at the same age. Dame Sybil Thorndike recalled Vivien's great kindness to her youngest daughter, Ann Casson, who had a small part in the play. But it was a waste of her talents and a disappointing return to the stage. Just over a month later, on 11 March, she opened in a tiny part in the new Sydney Carroll venture, *Bats in the Belfry*. Again it was a thin production, a conventional farce, but at least the opportunity for some jokes on stage, one of which was to put a heavy weight into the suitcase that Harry Kendall had to carry off: "We saw him literally staggering about and of course only succeeded in making ourselves laugh,"[59] Vivien wrote to Leigh.

Olivier, who saw both plays, became concerned at Vivien's lack of talent as an actress and particularly her voice. He helped her when he could and she also studied with the speech therapist, Elsie Fogerty. She was advised to give up high-heeled shoes as these diminished her lung power by causing her to stand in an unnatural way.

Meanwhile, there were several dinners at the Moulin d'Or with Olivier and Jill. Vivien began to rely on Oswald's advice. On 2 March she rang him, anxious that he should come to dinner the following night. They talked until 2:30 in the morning. Frewen noted later:

> I begged her not to run away with Larry 'anyway for a year,' and she was gentle and said it was 'good advice.' So it was, but she didn't take it.[60]

When not preoccupied with work or the Olivier problem, she read energetically and one of the books devoured was Margaret Mitchell's *Gone with the Wind.* Indeed she presented copies to every member of the cast of *Because We Must*. She urged John Gliddon to submit her name to David O. Selznick, who was already launched on his widely publicized search for an actress to play Scarlett O'Hara. Gliddon's application was acknowledged. On 3 February 1937 Selznick cabled his New York office:

> I have no enthusiasm for Vivien Leigh. Maybe I will have, but as yet have never even seen photograph of her. Will be seeing *Fire Over England* shortly, at which time will of

course see Leigh.[61]

In March 1937 Korda contracted Olivier and Vivien as co-stars in his next venture, *The First and The Last* (later known as *Twenty-One Days*), and they began to film at Denham in May. It was based on the short story by John Galsworthy with a script by Graham Greene. The plot was somewhat immoral: the brother of a distinguished barrister kills his mistress's husband. Fortunately for him an innocent man is arrested and held on remand for twenty-one days, during which time he lives with the mistress. Thereafter he is prepared to give himself up 'because innocent men don't hang in this country.' But, by chance, the innocent man dies in custody, letting the lovers off the hook.

Basil Dean oversaw the production but found Olivier and Vivien difficult: "Their joyous awareness of each other took the form of much laughter and giggling on the set; it was impossible for them to take the film seriously."[62]

On 11 April four names were written in Oswald Frewen's Visitors' Book at The Sheephouse – those of the Holmans and the Oliviers. The two couples had stayed at the Old Flushing Inn, Rye, and they came over the next day for a picnic. They also toured Brede Place. At the end of their visit, there occurred a telling incident. The butler rushed out and asked Oswald if the young lady (Vivien) was an actress. He wanted her autograph. Oswald asked if he would like the young gentleman's too. The three stars obliged, handed the book back and drove off. When Oswald inspected the result he found that Olivier had signed his name above the date in order to come before Vivien and Jill: "*I* think it's an amusing and typical star-story like the Conrad Veidt and Vivien Leigh one of the headline for *Dark Journey** but I had thought that Larry was different. However, I'm not on the stage!"[63]

Oswald was a keen fan of Olivier's. In March Vivien had given him a ticket for *Twelfth Night*. Arriving late he had not had time to check his program, and so heavily disguised was Olivier, with pads on his shoulders and sponges in his mouth, that Frewen failed to identify him until his voice betrayed him halfway through the second act.

The Wednesday after The Sheephouse visit, Leigh and Oswald attended Olivier's *Henry V* and then dined with Vivien, Jill, and John Fremantle at

*Korda had put Vivien's name first but Conrad Veidt insisted on having this changed. He never spoke to Korda again.

the Moulin d'Or. But time was running out for such friendly meetings as Frewen was all too aware. He had talked to Vivien on 1 March and he also had the chance to speak to Olivier:

> Later Larry discussed it with me (between the Old Vic and the Moulin d'Or) – he was deceiving himself, I felt, with arguments that it was for Viv's benefit that she should live with one who shared her artistry and her life, and not with Leigh, whose opinion on Drama is contemptible (in Larry's eyes; as must be mine!) and who does have to work by day when Vivling works by night. I made all the obvious demurrers, and Larry accepted them as true, but he also said he had been alarmingly loose before he married Jill, and with his terrific temperament he was afraid of fetching loose again, and that the only partner in the world who could keep him steady was Viv. I said "If she *should* fail (and statistics are against you) you will have wrecked *her*, and that is a very serious matter." He said if this *did* crash he would despair of himself and let himself go to the devil, and then, on the other side, said that Viv anyhow could never continue living with Leigh, so unsuited were their tastes and temperaments, and if it was not *him* it would be someone else: the one a selfish, the other a cynical, statement, but he did not realize it. As a last shot I told him frankly that I didn't expect the passions of 2 people of his age and Viv's to endure, and begged him to give themselves at least a year before doing anything irrevocable, and indeed he said he would…[64]

Chapter 8
The Break

> In a fit of temper Olivier kills Vivien's caddish husband and runs desperately to his brother for advice...Olivier and Vivien start life *anew.*
>
> *Sunday Express*, summary of plot of *Twenty-One Days...*
> January 1940

Murder was not in the offing, but the tension of a long, furtive affair was taking its toll on Olivier and Vivien, to say nothing of Jill and Leigh. Jill was aware of what was happening. Olivier had even arrived at Tarquin's christening with Vivien. Next, Olivier said he would only play *Hamlet* at Elsinore with Vivien as his Ophelia, and got his way.

For some time before Korda's films were about to be released, the wily producer had been urging caution. He knew that Americans were deeply sensitive to marital infidelity and that any slurs on the reputations of Olivier or Vivien could mean that the film might be banned in the United States. It was, after all, a delicate situation. Olivier's son, Tarquin, was scarcely weaned. Thus in the early months of 1937 both parties attempted to live reconciled lives with their partners. This was easier for Olivier than for Vivien as he was able to feel briefly at ease with his conscience.

In the light of this, his portrayal of *Hamlet* at the Old Vic takes on a new emphasis: When Tyrone Guthrie invited him to play the part he said: "I already know what it feels to be a Hamlet in real life."[1] Guthrie explained Olivier's unhappiness as "the conflict between his violent, immature love for Vivien…and his more mature, subdued attachment to Jill."[2] Guthrie encouraged him to use the production as a Freudian test-case, suggesting that the revenge for the death of his father was not so much based on fatherly love, but an Oedipal jealousy of Claudius, now the mother's husband, and the supposed murderer of his father. The critics were confused by the theme. Michael Redgrave, a young member of the cast, thought Olivier not sufficiently subtle, and Alec Guinness, his understudy, decried his show-off acrobatics. Kenneth Tynan later analyzed Olivier's popularity as a desire to be showman and entertainer first and actor second. He said that Olivier did not believe that audiences really appreciated the plays they saw, thus wanted them to "remember at least something of their night at the theatre."[3] Inevitably this led to over-acting. Of this Old Vic production Tynan said that Olivier admitted that his portrayal of Hamlet was entirely directed towards Vivien:

> With all its physical virility and acrobatic flash, it was his way of wooing her. And she confirmed it. She told me later on that she went to see at least half the performances, just so that she should be near Larry during a time when she was supposed to be staying away from him. Larry's performance was his long-distance Valentine to her.[4]

Thus there is the double irony of Hamlet rejecting one Ophelia on stage (Cherry Cottrell) while mesmerizing a future Ophelia (Vivien) in the audience. However, Vivien's determined quest for Olivier suffered a further setback when, soon after, Jill returned to the stage starring opposite him as Olivia in *Twelfth Night*. Then Korda intervened once more. He invited Olivier and Vivien to act together in *Twenty-One Days*. They gave up their struggle and resumed their affair.

The Coronation of King George VI and Queen Elizabeth took place on 12 May 1937 and Vivien participated in a staged procession of monarchs at the Coronation Costume Ball two days later. Olivier celebrated his thirtieth birthday on 22 May and at the end of the month the Old Vic company flew to Copenhagen to perform *Hamlet* at Elsinore. Vivien was still only twenty-three.

The Elsinore production, which ran for only six performances, was in celebration of the Silver Jubilee of King Christian X of Denmark. Olivier insisted that Vivien play Ophelia, which displeased Tyrone Guthrie, who had offered the role to Jill. Finally Guthrie had no choice and Lilian Baylis issued the formal invitation. Korda gave Olivier and Vivien a week's leave from filming. Until then they worked on the film by day, and rehearsed *Hamlet* in the evenings.

Apparently Olivier and Vivien had already planned their elopement. Yet there is no hint of trouble in Vivien's two surviving communications to Leigh from Denmark. On 30 May she cabled her safe arrival, and then, from the Hotel d'Angleterre she wrote:

> Darling,
> Had a very good journey, lovely sun all the way over. Played lots of delicious games and were very gay. Have just arrived back from a sort of nightclub! It looks the most lovely town, so clean and open. We leave for Elsinore tomorrow morning and I won't promise when next I write, as we certainly have our work cut out for us. What is more the Danes *hate* us ever going to bed. They say they only sleep 4 hours in summer time (Funny that a whole nation should feel like me!).
>
> Goodnight my darling. Longing to hear about the house. Don't be lonely and
> Take care of yourself.
>
> Vivling[5]

Kronborg Castle at Elsinore is a sixteenth-century building by the sea, along the coast from Copenhagen, The cast rehearsed in the evenings because by day tourists plied their way through the ancient fortress. Other hazards included hammering in a nearby shipyard, a chiming clock in the courtyard that Lilian Baylis ordered to be stopped. It was hard work, made harder by cold winds and driving rain. Vivien rehearsed under an umbrella and caught a bad cold. There was added poignancy to Claudius's line rendered by John Abbott, umbrella in hand: 'Is there not rain enough in the sweet heavens?'[6]

On the first night there could be no outdoor performance, yet cancellation was unthinkable. Elsinore abounded with royalty and socialites such as Lady Juliet Duff, some of them flown in by specially chartered plane. The British rose to the occasion, converting the Merienlyst Hotel's ballroom into an impromptu stage, 800 basket chairs surrounding the dance-floor on which the actors would perform. There were some splendid double doors with a flight of steps, perfect for entries, but these could not be used as blue-tits were nesting in the architrave.

Crown Prince Frederik and his wife, Princess Ingrid, were guests of honor. Prince Knud, his brother, stuck his long legs out before him, adding to an already fraught evening. Olivier enjoyed it, though, and when one of the audience persisted on chatting to his neighbor he steered the duel with Laertes (Anthony Quayle) right up to him.

Lady Diana Cooper was one of the celebrities. Later she wrote:

> Never was there such a performance. Disaster leads to finest hours, and Lilian Baylis in mortar-board and gown, told the audience in epilogue that they would never see a better rendering.[7]

But Conrad Russell reported:

> The crab is that Olivier can't act Hamlet as I knew from seeing him at the Old Vic.[8]

Everybody savored the gushings of tireless American hostess, Mrs. Corrigan, who approached the stars and explained that she had enjoyed *Hamlet* so much, "particularly as I am such a close friend of the present Danish royal family."[9]

Vivien coped better in the ballroom than outside where her voice was harder to hear. Anthony Quayle wrote: "I remember how beautiful Vivien looked; and I remember how far her talent fell short of her beauty."[10] The second night took place out of doors, and was almost a first night all over again. One newspaper correspondent thoroughly entered into the mood:

> Within the turreted courtyard of Kronborg more than 2,000 people sit rapt, not a mouse stirs. Light glows upon the high stage before the northern wall of the castle where Hamlet, his task accomplished, rests in Horatio's arms and hears the throbbing of the drums of Fortinbras.[11]

Jill Esmond had come to Denmark too. Olivier recalled the pressure of acting with his mistress in the presence of his wife:

> We could not keep from touching each other, making love almost within Jill's vision. This welding closeness tripped the obvious decision and two marriages were severed.[12]

Alec Guinness recalled that he was delegated to take Jill out on afternoon trips to give the lovers time to be together. He wondered whether perhaps if Jill had not been there, things would have turned out rather differently: "It might have just been an exciting new affair."[13]

Ophelia was the first of many tragic heroines that Vivien would portray in her lifetime (the most notable being Blanche Dubois in *A Streetcar Named Desire*). According to Thomas Kiernan's biography of Olivier, Vivien suffered some kind of manic depression while at Elsinore, veering from silence at one moment to hysterical yelling the next. The cast doubted she could perform, Olivier said "something about Viv having gone bonkers, having attacked him, having had a fit of some kind.' Then she appeared: "Not a word to anyone, just staring blankly into space."[14] However, she made herself up and the performance went ahead. Olivier remained concerned and, having fortified himself with aquavit, went to her dressing-room after the curtain. There was no explanation, but next day she was perfectly all right.

Soon after their return from Denmark, Jill went around to Little Stanhope Street to plead with Vivien. Daisy recalled that this was the first Mrs. Olivier's only visit. Vivien told her that they had important things to discuss and that on no account were they to be disturbed.

Jill arrived at the house fired with determination, but soon found herself disarmed, even nervous in Vivien's presence. Vivien served champagne, confessed she intended to marry Olivier and then proceeded to ask a lot of questions about domestic details – how he liked his eggs cooked, and so on. Jill probably only fell in love with Olivier after Tarquin's birth, harboring maternal feelings and a new respect for him as the father of their son. No doubt she felt additionally protective due to the threat of Vivien. She knew she would always have Tarquin, but she did not want Olivier's career threatened by Leigh Holman citing him as co-respondent in a divorce case. And yet in a disarming way, Vivien and Jill were friends. Olivier's wife could not help being fascinated by this beautiful and enthusiastic newcomer who had invaded their lives.

On 16 June, ten days after her return, Vivien moved out. Daisy recalled:

> Mr. Holman told me that she had gone. I couldn't believe it, I thought he meant she had gone early to the studio. Later she asked me to stay and look after him. Mr. Holman was very good about it. He never bore her any grudge. But it was a long time before I came to like Sir Laurence Olivier. We were such a happy house until he came along.[15]

Years later Leigh explained to Gertrude, Vivien's mother, what occurred next:

> When she left me for Larry she told me that after a month she would write me to say whether it was final. I got that letter and it was the only one from her that I ever destroyed. I felt utterly hopeless but I did not badger and beseech her to change her mind and had I done so I would only have got something equivalent to no flowers or cable on a first night. Since then of course we have got so much from each other's friendship, and friendship was the only possible basis on which we could get anything.[16]

Vivien's next letter, dated 19 July, does survive:

> Leigh, you will know how hard it is to write this letter, but you asked me to write after a month had passed. Although I am very very happy I do want to know, Leigh, if you are well and feeling happier, as I do wish and hope with all my heart you are. You know that I have seen Suzanne several times, and if that, in any way, is troubling you, for your own self or hers *do* tell me, as I would like to do anything that you think best. However painful it may seem at the moment, Leigh, I do feel that this is the right thing to have

> happened for you and me, and I hope that perhaps later we can still be friends, in spite of whatever has come between us. I do pray that it may turn out well, dearest Leigh,
>
> Vivien[17]

Oswald Frewen had been to Marseilles, so his advice had not been sought. He heard the news from Leigh and his first reaction was: "I think it is the unforgivable sin. To hurt someone for no cause but your own selfishness."[18] He soon became more sympathetic. He loved Leigh and Vivien equally, and had named them in his will to inherit The Sheephouse:

> It is *not* a case of a man hammering away at a girl in a long drawn-out, stoutly, resisted, effort of seduction, nor the converse. The warmth of Nature has been melting the snows of their self-controls, and the avalanche has fallen. It must be nearly a year, or even the full year, since they first fell in love, and they *have* fought against themselves, *each* of them, *hard.* Fought and lost, as we did against Italian rape of Abyssinia, as we are doing against German-Italian rape of Spain. But the disaster is none the less there, and I'm terribly afraid that *he* is inconstant and unballasted and that it won't last 10 years – perhaps not 5. Once cast loose from dear steady old Leigh's helmsmanship I have awful doubts for *her* too. She says in a letter: "It was a week of nightmares for us and torture for the others," – "I feel completely sapped" – "I wish you were here much more for Leigh's sake, as he needs people like you he can talk to." – Oh Peter I am sure this is the right thing and better in the long run for all four – it wasn't a hurried callous decision, and it is not as if I shall not have to go through suffering too" – not the words of a wanton. She has *brain* and a heart, but no ethical upbringing and instead an overdose of temperament. Can she remain unsubmerged? Will her intellect and her heart fade out?...[19]

Frewen concluded ruefully: "And *I* advised Leigh to marry Viv; and *I* advised Larry not to, I *am* a success." [20]

Olivier bought Durham Cottage, a concealed love-nest with a small high-walled garden just off Christchurch Street in Chelsea, paying for it with money advanced to him for *Twenty-One Days*. But the cottage was not ready so the lovers settled quietly in Iver.

There was more work to do on *The First and The Last*. One day the journalist C.A. Lejeune accompanied the crew when they filmed on the Thames. The conversation turned to the casting of the new epic film, *Gone with the Wind*:

> Somebody turned to Olivier and said "Larry you'd be marvelous as Rhett Butler," He laughed it off, but the suggestion was not too preposterous… discussion of the casting went on in a desultory fashion, until the new girl, Vivien Leigh, brought it to a sudden stop. She drew herself up on the rainswept deck, all five-feet nothing of her, pulled a coat around her shoulders and stunned us with the sibylline utterance: "Larry won't play Rhett Butler, but I shall play Scarlett O'Hara. Wait and see."[21]

Caroline Lejeune was writing in 1964, but the story is confirmed in a contemporary cutting. The special Film Correspondent of the *Evening News* visited stage 6 of the Studios at Denham:

> "I'm reading *Gone with the Wind*," said Vivien, "but if I brought it here I shouldn't be able to start working." Her voice grew ecstatic: "I've never been so gripped by anything in my life. It's the finest book I've ever read, what a grand film it would make! I've cast myself as Scarlett O'Hara. What do you think?"
>
> I muttered something inaudible. Quickly I decided to lie low. It was obvious now that I was the one person in Denham who hadn't read Margaret Mitchell's 600,000 words best-seller.
>
> "And Clark Gable as Rhett Butler…" suggested someone. But Vivien definitely wouldn't have that.[22]

Vivien's concentration on *Gone with the Wind* came but a month after the separations. For a journalist to write about it in a promotional piece about *The First and The Last* implies that Vivien was authorized to talk openly about her wish to play Scarlett with Korda's permission. He was anxious that Olivier and Vivien should become better known in America (which would obviously benefit him financially). Vivien spoke often about Scarlett in the hope that someone at Selznick International would register her interest.

The film was completed but Korda viewed it and decided to withhold it from release.* Olivier and Vivien then took a holiday in Venice.

The later months of 1937 remained riddled with complications. Vivien was happy to be with Olivier, but the future was far from resolved. She left Suzanne with Leigh at Little Stanhope Street and largely surrendered her role as mother to Gertrude who, in effect, brought Suzanne up. While at work, Vivien did her best to help Leigh with domestic problems concerning Suzanne and her nanny, whose occasional bouts of hysteria merely amused her six-year-old charge. Vivien offered to interview a new nanny for Leigh, wondering, also, whether it was not time for Suzanne to go to school with some children her own age. Presently a new governess arrived and Nanny departed, falling flat on her back as she left.

The question of divorce was to hang heavily over both Olivier and Vivien for the next three years. Partly in the hope of getting her back, and partly to be sure that in eloping with Olivier she had made the right decision, Leigh resolved inflexibly that she must wait three years for a divorce. During this period, Vivien re-established her relationship with Leigh on a firm basis of friendship, not wholly unlike the role that Tommy had played in her mother's life – loyal, supportive, loving, her best friend. As a first step, Vivien sent Leigh a *History of Furniture* for his birthday on 3 November, though she added: "I am sure that you know I would rather you did not write back."[23] At Christmas Leigh responded by sending her a ring.

Oswald Frewen noted that Vivien seemed considerably more concerned about Leigh than about her own plight. In November he called on Leigh and found him "aged, but so pleased to see me."[24] He was due to see Vivien too. Since Leigh was departing for Henley at 5:15, he told Frewen he could

* *Twenty-One Days* was finally released in 1940, and Olivier and Vivien went to see it in New York. They walked out long before the end.

invite her to Little Stanhope Street. Vivien duly arrived at 5:30, "sweet, gentle and affectionate, and as considerate of me as ever, but not without her own traces of the tragedy."[25]. Her main preoccupation was how to ask Leigh for a divorce without hurting him.

They went to see Olivier in Hertford Street. Frewen reported:

> They appear to be as much in love as ever, but are not having an easy time, even in *their* milieu. They are shifting out of a temporary site at Iver to Durham Cottage, Christchurch St., Chelsea, which isn't ready yet. We went to *his* ex-abode, 74 Cheyne Walk, where a secretary was busy, and I saw all the complications which the affair brings with it – many more than I had supposed it would cumber itself with in these days. But I'm not at all sure that the wave of promiscuity has not passed its peak, and that they aren't finding a back-wash. Only those who know them both intimately know that they *did* struggle against it for a long time, and were not, and are not, callous – and *they* aren't believed when they say so. My little line to Jill* fell on stoney ground. I said they *had* tried. She said flatly they hadn't, and didn't answer me! So there it all is, very sad; and I think probably Leigh and I are the only two people who look upon it without just cold disdain or cynicism.[26]

Frewen had the chance of a longer talk with Leigh about a fortnight later. After dinner they spoke for about an hour:

> It was news to him that Jill had refused to divorce Larry and told him to review his application in 3 months. Leigh's attitude is that Vic and Larry are iconoclasts, and he doesn't hold with the hypocrisy of remarriage. You only perform the marriage ceremony, he says, to steady you when temptation comes, and bring you through it. If it is unavailing then, it is useless to you, and a 2nd bond is just a

*Frewen had written 'just a line' to Jill Esmond in an attempt to pour oil on troubled waters at the end of June.

> hypocrisy, and he will do nothing to release Viv 'unless he is forced to' (I don't see how he can be). He still hopes to get her back, so powerfully that when you are with him you begin to believe that he may. Meanwhile he is more serene, and getting on patromaternally well with a Suzanne vastly improved by the change over from fool-nanny to efficient nursery-governess.[27]

Mills Martin confirmed this view of Leigh. Shortly after Vivien's departure, she called on Leigh at Little Stanhope Street and found that he kept her dressing-gown and night-gown in perpetual readiness for her. He told Mills: "She can come back whenever she wants."[28] Mrs. Martin, having observed the Holman marriage from the start, noted that if Leigh had not loved her in 1932, he certainly loved her now. But there was never any question in Vivien's mind either of returning or of leaving Larry. When Mills visited her on a film set she declared: "To do it once is forgivable, but never again."[29] Vivien was thus by no means secure in her new role. There was always the fear that Olivier might leave her on a whim or return to his wife and son.

There was also some hostility from theatre friends who had known Olivier and Jill as a pair. Lynn Fontanne describing her first meeting with Vivien as "icy."[30] Another friend commented on the unreality of their shared bliss: "For all their apparent happiness, he and Vivien struck me as two exquisite pieces of china teetering on the edge of a shelf."[31]

Korda loaned Vivien to MGM to make *A Yank at Oxford* in order that she should have American exposure. At first Louis B. Mayer was a little reluctant, but Michael Balcon persuaded him. Korda went so far as to contemplate Olivier as Rhett Butler and Vivien as Scarlett in *Gone with the Wind*. Her friend, the actress Eve Phillips, believed that, in her playing of Elsa Craddock in *A Yank at Oxford,* Vivien was in effect doing a screen test for Scarlett, playing her "as saucy and sexual, like an imperious modern-day Cleopatra," a kind of "English version of Scarlett O'Hara."[32]

Vivien worked on *A Yank at Oxford* in the autumn of 1937. Meanwhile Olivier starred in an unhappy collaboration with Merle Oberon in *The Divorce of Lady X* (delivering almost Shakespearian monologues in the court scenes). In November he and Vivien were able to move into Durham Cottage. It took her many enjoyable hours to convert it into the stylish and comfortable home she wanted. In due course she created a flower-filled sitting-room with a Sickert hanging over the fireplace, a small gold and cream dining-room with rich satin curtains, lit by sparkling glass chandeliers, and a blue and white striped kitchen. Olivier had a crowded study from which he oversaw his many enterprises and there was an open-plan staircase leading upstairs, providing ample opportunity for a dramatically theatrical descent. Vivien acquired many treasures over the years, including paintings by Degas and John Piper, and an Epstein flower-piece brilliant with peonies. One friend who dined there in later years described it as 'sweet and bijou,' noting that Vivien surrounded herself with "an almost claustrophobic prettiness."[33] Her taste was conventional and informed, and, as with Little Stanhope Street, her own ideas were coordinated by professional designers. Vivien fitted perfectly into these exquisite surroundings, but the same friend recalled: "I had an awful feeing of Larry being rather like an unfortunate bull in a china shop."[34]

Durham Cottage was not fully decorated but Olivier and Vivien invited Ralph Richardson and his wife, the actress Meriel Forbes (known as Mu), to dine with them on Vivien's birthday, Guy Fawkes Day. Olivier was then rehearsing *Othello* with Richardson. It had seemed to Richardson a good idea to bring some fireworks with him. Lady Richardson recalled:

> All he had was a box of rockets, very good ones and he set them off aiming to go through the French windows into the garden. Instead they missed the windows and went sideways and straight up and down those beautiful new curtains. Viv, of course, was absolutely livid and I was horrified. Larry didn't say a word. And Viv's anger was so great and everybody else's horror was so great that Ralph went to the window, rather surprised at the general reaction, and said, with immense dignity: "Mu, we will now leave. These people don't understand us," and disappeared into the garden.[35]

John Gliddon was still representing Vivien, but he gradually realized that she was depending more on Olivier than on him:

> I became of little real use over decisions which had to be made. I had been negotiating with Paramount for a possible deal for Vivien in Hollywood...One day I received a cable from Paramount which read: "Vivien Leigh. Please ascertain whether available play female lead C. de Mille picture *Union Pacific*. Leading man Joel McCrea. Stop. Other important leading women including Colbert being considered. Answer immediately.[36]

Paramount offered £3,500 for seven weeks' work with options for one picture a year rising to £14,000 for seven weeks with first-class return fare to Hollywood and £40 a week living expenses. Gliddon rushed to Durham Cottage and handed Vivien the cable:

> She glanced at the piece of paper showing only the mildest interest in this important offer from Paramount. Then she let the cables fall to the floor. I remained silent. There was little I could say. "This is a better offer than Greer Garson had," Olivier remarked casually. Vivien looked thoughtful for a moment. She picked up the cables and read them again. They began to discuss the offer.[37]

It was agreed that Gliddon should ask for £5,000 for six weeks with one option only for a further picture at £8,000 for six weeks – to be made within a year of the first film at a time that suited Vivien:

> I sent our reply to Hollywood which was like a certain rejection and a snub to a great company. No reply was received. I realized that I hardly mattered any more in Vivien's career. Weeks of work had just been a waste of time.[38]

A Yank at Oxford was a film which was in part a fantasy version of Oxford, romantically recreated like a Victorian public school. It also had undertones of Beerbohm's *Zuleika Dobson*, especially in lines such as: 'I love to help the undergraduates, especially the new ones,' and the concluding threat of future trouble: "We are moving to Aldershot" (a line devised by Sidney Gilliat). It was the first film that MGM ever made in England (it was released in New York on 25 February 1938 and in London on 1 April). Other stars were Robert Taylor, who acted much better than his detractors chose to admit, Maureen O'Sullivan (Vivien's convent friend), and Lionel Barrymore playing "the same old part…as competently as ever."[39]

Basil Wright wrote of Vivien's small part in the *Spectator*:

> Her quiet but almost vicious sense of humour makes one regret all the more that the producers did not rely more on Beerbohm and less on – whatever it was they used as a basis for the story.[40]

When the film was screened in New York one critic wrote: "Vivien Leigh is the sort of thing to make anyone want to go to Oxford."[41] Vivien was not always professional when filming. One night she particularly wanted to see Olivier so she developed 'foot trouble.' To be convincing she had to buy special shoes and then wanted reimbursement. She urged Gliddon to get the money back and cajoled him: "You're not tough enough. You're too weak, John."[42] Yet the actor, Robert Flemyng, who saw her for the first time on the set, was impressed by how very cool she was. She possessed a sense of authority which, though in no way dominating everyone around her, proved she was very much in control.

Ralph Richardson encouraged Olivier to concentrate on Shakespeare. He believed that, if a scandal broke, the public would be much less liable to condemn Larry if he bore the dignity of a distinguished Shakespearian. Olivier had joined the Old Vic earlier in the year and would remain a member of the Company until 1949. Besides his two *Hamlets*, he had also performed in *Twelfth Night* and *Henry V*. In December 1937 he was, in his own words, "not an unparalleled success"[43] as Macbeth. But he was delighted that the Queen attended a performance because this indicated "that the gossip concerning my private life had not reached far or high yet."[44] Richardson further urged that Vivien should join the Old Vic.

Shakespeare soon became a most profitable obsession with Olivier. He found tremendous satisfaction and a great challenge in attempting to present the Bard in a way previously untried by the famous Shakespearian actors of the past. Vivien entered *A Midsummer Night's Dream* at the Old Vic on 27 December 1937. It was a production made memorable by Tyrone Guthrie's direction, Robert Helpmann's performance as Oberon ("he glides into imagined invisibility")[45] and Ralph Richardson's as Bottom. The music of Mendelssohn embellished Shakespeare's poetry, Ninette de Valois undertook the choreography, and Oliver Messel produced lavish costumes and sets (covering much of the expense himself). The program went to pains to emphasize the links between Shakespeare, Mendelssohn, and the architecture of the Old Vic. Oswald Frewen noted: "The compromise resulting in early Victorian fairies."[46] Charles Morgan was also interested in this point:

> What matters is that the other contributory artists – Guthrie, Messel, de Valois – should exercise their own imaginations freely. They can call the result 'early Victorian' if they will. Perhaps it is, if you think in those terms, but it appears as one of the loveliest, most magical, and least affected productions of the play that the stage has seen for many years.[47]

This glamorous moonlit pantomime was also Lilian Baylis's last production. During rehearsals Ninette de Valois found her "tired and a little despondent."[48] When discussing a future *Sleeping Beauty*, on 25 November 1937, Miss Baylis died. Olivier was forced to open in *Macbeth* without this formidable figure in her traditional bow.

A Midsummer Night's Dream was Vivien's first introduction to the kind of light-hearted pastiche stage glamour over which Oliver Messel and Cecil Beaton vied to such good cause. Vivien, as Titania, wore a dress of organza, adorned with fairy's wings and a headdress like a coronet of large pearls and rhinestones with off-white velvet flowers and flat roses of bright pink ribbon. From this hung strings of oval silvered beads and sequins. Frewen observed: "Vivling lovely as ever, and I thought did it all gracefully, sweetly and *unecceptionably* [sic].[49]

On 12 January 1938 Queen Elizabeth fulfilled a promise to the late Miss Baylis that her daughters should see their first Shakespeare at the Old Vic. After the performance the stars were presented. Helpmann and Vivien bowed and curtsied simultaneously and their elaborate headdresses became inextricably entwined. They had to retreat backwards from the room like two stags locked in combat. Charles Morgan reviewed Vivien's performance in *The Times*:

> There are a few weak spots…Miss Viven Leigh, who looks extremely pretty, and at the opening of her performance, promises a genuine firmness in her verse, is as yet a trifle nervous of Titania's authority.[50]

Following which, Vivien commented in a letter to Leigh:

> Mr. Morgan was his infuriating self once more last Tuesday. It is so dreadful to consider for a moment that he really may be right![51]

Chapter 9
Hollywood Already

"What about Hollywood?" I asked.
"Are you likely to go there?
She shook her head.
"I don't think so. The trouble is that Hollywood seems to be interested in me only as a long-term contract actress. And I have no intention of tying myself for several years to any one company, particularly in Hollywood, where it would be difficult to take stage engagements between films. I am not going to neglect the stage, whatever happens."

Vivien, talking to John K. Newnham
Film Weekly, 10 December 1938

In the New Year of 1938 Vivien wrote to Leigh asking him to divorce her. Her decision had been neither a whim nor sudden. Time had proved it:

> But now it seems wisest for all of us, to make the position clear. I can never be sure of myself again or trust myself completely, having behaved and hurt you in a way I thought inconceivable after your great understanding, goodness and kindness to me always but as far as I can possibly tell, my feelings will not alter and I will truly try to justify the step I have taken. And perhaps, Leigh darling, it might be easier

> for you to forget if things were clear and definite, though I know it sounds easy for me to say so, the last few months have been full of pain and unhappiness, not only for you and Jill, and don't you think this might be remedied if there were no more indecision in our minds, and so I'm asking you, if you think you possibly can, to divorce me.[1]

Leigh did not budge, nor did Jill Esmond. While Vivien was both gentle and coaxing in her handling of Leigh, she was less discreet with visiting journalists. She began to feel it was best if her liaison with Olivier came into the open, thus provoking Leigh and Jill to sue for divorce. Her line was that Leigh and Jill were 'the villains,' forcing them to live in a state of adultery. One such journalist concluded that Vivien "seemed to suffer from enormous guilt."[2]

Vivien then took part in the film of *St. Martin's Lane*. She played a girl from the East End who steals from the cap of a street busker entertaining a queue of autograph hunters. Then she deftly walks off with Rex Harrison's silver cigarette case. Later the busker sees her dancing and they become partners. Eventually she rises to stardom in London. The prospect of America looms and the prophetic line is uttered: "Hollywood already. I say that's a bit quick." Vivien's part was considered complex, a mixture of hard selfishness with sentimental rushes of remorse. *Film Weekly* declared that Vivien "shows herself to be an actress of character with a fine sense of the complexity of human nature, and a real gift for creating a true pattern of its lights and shadows."[3] Her cockney accent, however, was inconsistent.

When filming was over in May, Vivien fell ill. She was due to open in *Serena Blandish* at the Gate on 26 May, an important part for her. Oswald Frewen found Norman Marshall patiently at her bedside, rehearsing her as best he could. Frewen noted:

> Saw Vivling, ill in bed, in pain, with an axilliary swelling in the nature of a choked follicle or subcutaneous cyst, but the doctors don't know really what, and I am a little anxious.[4]

Oswald was soon acting as an intermediary with Leigh, with whom he was staying. Leigh refused to see Vivien unless she left Olivier, saying that it "would only blur the outline."[5] Olivier himself was against such a meeting, fearing she might change her mind and go back. Leigh's message was that Oswald "had run [his] head into a brick wall and could see no damage on the wall."[6] However, later that day, Leigh relented.

On doctor's orders, the play was postponed and Vivien was told that she must not work again until after a holiday. Leigh agreed to see Vivien after dinner on Friday, 27 May. She postponed her holiday and asked herself to dinner. Leigh still would not give her a divorce.

She and Olivier set off for France. Charles Laughton put the holiday-makers on the right track by alerting them to the *route gastronomique* through France down to the Colombe d'Or at Saint-Paul de Vence and the Calanque d'Or at Le Dramond-Plage in Var. It was the first time that the pair could travel alone together, "the glowing fulfillment of every desire of the wayward lovers,"[7] as Olivier later put it. It was also their last period of relaxed bliss.

On their way down they lunched at Vonnas: "We haven't stopped eating and drinking since we arrived in France,"[8] wrote Vivien before they headed to Grenoble. At Saint-Paul de Vence they were able to visit John Gielgud and Binkie Beaumont to discuss ambitious Shakespearian plans. Olivier wanted to undertake the four great Shakespearian tragedies with Vivien as co-star – *Hamlet, Othello, Macbeth*, and *King Lear*. He wanted to create a theatrical couple to match the Lunts. Beaumont had encouraged him but on condition that Gielgud was involved and that the two great actors took the alternating leading parts. In the end this ambitious plan came to nothing.

Later Olivier and Vivien headed to the Calanque d'Or by the sea. To her parents Vivien wrote: "We are still here having a heavenly time. I am learning to drive and loving it…Haven't the vaguest idea when we're coming back."[9] The seaside hotel was also the home of eighteen Siamese cats, one of which Vivien took back to England. In mid-July the headed homeward, driving slowly through France, stopping at Sauveterre in the Basses-Pyrenees. They visited Nay, the small town from where the last of Olivier's Huguenot ancestors escaped to England in 1685, returning home on 29 July. Oswald Frewen saw them the next day: "Vivling sweet and gentle and affectionate as ever (and looking *very* well); Larry bronzed, friendly and inconsequent."[10]

While abroad Olivier received a cable suggesting that he, Vivien, and

Merle Oberon might like to play in Goldwyn's *Wuthering Heights* starting on 1 September. They delayed any positive reply until their return. Vivien was not keen to be cast in the role of Isabella. It was to be Cathy for her or nothing. Oliver was impressed by William Wyler and though Vivien had declined a part she insisted that Olivier should accept that of Heathcliff, even though it meant separation. It also meant that Vivien could assuage her guilt about Suzanne, whom she had neglected since her elopement. Her mother and some of her friends were making her feel a more than inadequate mother. Leigh, on the other hand, was coping well, though Gertrude undid a lot of his good work by spoiling her granddaughter.

The late summer was difficult. Olivier and Vivien had spent too much money and the Income Tax inspectors were in hot pursuit. No money was due for Vivien's new play for a while. Olivier had bought goldfish for the pond at Durham Cottage in July. Three had died. He did not like his catfish, his cupressus alumii had not grown in three months, his clematis, planted in a sun-baked flowerbed, had not flowered. In September war seemed imminent.

On 26 September Oswald Frewen lunched with Vivien and found her "agitating about gas-masks and gas-precautions."[11] After lunch they purchased felt, carpet-tacks, adhesive plaster, and other precautions for future black-outs. Hitler was due to broadcast at 8 o'clock, but they could find no wireless powerful enough to intercept him. Vivien went to the Gate Theatre, and Frewen followed after a brief talk with Olivier:

> Only had five minutes with him alone, during which he was pathetically saying "Is it worth going to prison for, would my little mite by going to prison secure Peace?" Also, he is under contract to go to Hollywood next month, and doesn't know whether to go, or whether he won't be allowed to go, or whether to enlist, and if so in what? Truly the 'To be or not to be' spirit has entered into him. Vivling, on the other hand, means to drive ambulances.[12]

Vivien had two remaining projects for 1938, the first of which was to play the eponymous role in S.N. Behrman's play *Serena Blandish,* based on Enid Bagnold's novel. Esme Percy directed the play, but Enid Collet, the manager of the Gate Theatre, was put out to find Olivier popping in during Percy's lunch break and surreptitiously running through Vivien's part with her. The Gate Theatre only staged about eight shows a year, most of which ran a maximum of three weeks. Stewart Granger (by virtue of being one of John Gliddon's clients) played Lord Ivor Cream. He found Vivien hard-working and ambitious. She had two passions, her love for Larry and her determination to play Scarlett O'Hara in *Gone with the Wind.*[13] Olivier and Vivien attended Granger's marriage to Elspeth March on 10 September. The bride recalled:

> They both came to our wedding and they were incandescent. They were so in love and it was wonderful to see them. I always say I spent my honeymoon in the Gate Theatre because directly after we were married – on the Monday they were rehearsing again. Vivien was ravishing in it. I don't think anybody has ever given Vivien enough credit for her performances. She was a thundering good actress.[14]

The Times judged that Vivien "decorates her part with the unreality it needs and makes genuinely witty nonsense of the luncheon party"[15] with Lord Ivor Cream.

Vivien wrote to Leigh, then staying the head of the family, Alexander Holman, at Shielbridge House in Argyll:

> I am afraid the notices for the play were appalling but not too bad for me, thank goodness. Bronnie Albery [the director] is very thrilled, anyway, which is encouraging. Tuesday itself was a chapter of accidents. I spent practically the whole day fitting and one hour before the curtain went up, my evening dress was still in pieces, so I went on in a great state (even worse than usual) all pinned up! We have had full houses and people seem to enjoy it tho' the last scene is very bad… Mummy sent me a wire on the 1st night saying she hoped I would have a 'happy' evening which made me laugh a lot.[16]

Frewen attended the play and noted: "Vivling looking *lovely* and saying her lines with a Larry intonation, rather attractive."[17] With Jeanne de Casalis, also in the cast, they scrutinized extracts from Hitler's speech in the evening paper. On their way home they passed the Duke of York's Headquarters in Chelsea. Frewen observed: "Red *buses* within: embussing A.A. units. 1914 again."[18] On 28 September Vivien and Ursula Jeans went in search of constructive wartime employment as ambulance drivers. They were too late. "Early applicants are said to be 'across the sea, already at the front.'"[19] Soon after this Frewen joined the Royal Navy and went out to Gibraltar. He was much cheered by seeing Vivien's film *St. Martin's Lane* and found her as polished as Laughton:

> I know she doesn't care for films at all, but only for flesh and blood theatre. But despite a degradation of her gentle well-modulated voice, to suit the part of the street-slut, there was my Vivling, with flashes of her own self (and one of Suzanne!) looking at me from the screen so that I felt all I had to do was go round to the stage door after, to see her in private! It was almost as good as meeting her, and like a cool drink in the desert. I hadn't realized till then that I was homesick![20]

Frewen did not see Vivien again until 1941.

Meanwhile, Vivien's mother, Gertrude was in Scotland. She had gone up there in August to nurse Tommy, who was gravely ill with cancer of the throat. Tommy died at the Royal Hotel, Campbeltown on 30 September 1938 at the age of fifty-one.* Olivier and Leigh Holman were amongst those who wrote to offer their sympathy. Olivier addressed his letter from Durham Cottage:

> These few flowers (which I've had to ask Vivien to get for me) bring you my dearest love, and sincerest sympathies

*Tommy left Gertrude the income of 100 shares of the Imperial Bank of Iran and 50 of the Hong Kong and Shanghai Banking Corporation to her for her lifetime. On 28 September 1938, two days before he died, he added a codicil which included a pecuniary legacy of £100 for Ernest Hartley. Gertrude was described in the will as "Mrs. Gertrude Hartley, wife of my friend, Ernest Hartley."[21]

> in your unhappiness and grief at the present time. I am so terribly sorry for you pet. I can never begin to tell you the joy and happiness that your Vivien brings to me, and I'm always wanting to thank you, at odd times, for bringing her into the world...[22]

Leigh wrote from his chambers, 4 Kings Bench Walk, Temple:

> If I had seen about Tommy I would have written. It must have been a very bitter time for you both. The world as we have known it is always crumbling, but fortunately the world which is growing up is quite oblivious of this. Suzanne said at breakfast today that when I am dead she will have to look after herself, and when she is dead she won't be able to look after herself. I am seeing Viv on Tuesday.[23]

Vivien had written to Leigh on 3 October, saying she wanted to see him: "There is a possibility of my having to go to Hollywood for 1 film sometime soon."[24] Again she wanted to discuss divorce, and again she was given a negative response. Vivien sent Leigh a Hawes and Curtis dressing-gown for his thirty-eighth birthday. She wrote that she had been offered a play in New York but that owing to casting problems it had to be postponed until January:

> I don't know whether that is true or if they are trying to get out of it but am ringing up tonight to see how the land really lies, so as you can guess everything is *very* dismal at the moment. It is a question of either waiting here, just to do the 'Dream' again at Xmas or for that play in January, anyway no immediate work which is what I really wanted, I suppose it's about time I had bad luck so I am trying very hard not to be furious or miserable.[25]

Vivien's plan to repeat *A Midsummer Night's Dream* for Tyrone Guthrie at the old Vic did not last long. Olivier had left for Hollywood on 5

November, her twenty-fifth birthday. During his voyage in the *Normandie*†, Olivier spoke to Vivien three times on the telephone, something he knew was fiendishly extravagant, but he explained to her mother that she sounded so poorly and that he was very concerned about her. He asked Gertrude to give Vivien his love whenever she thought of it.[26] Vivien also rang John Gliddon to say she intended to pay Olivier a quick visit in Hollywood but would be back in time for *Dream* rehearsals which began on 15 December. As Gliddon put it:

> That brief visit was to end in my having to see Tyrone Guthrie and ask him if he would release her from her contract. Yes, the impossible had happened.[27]

To Vivien's delight Leigh allowed Suzanne to stay with her for a few days in the middle of November, though she thought Suzanne was much happier when she had her father "to box and fight with:"

> In fact the first morning I didn't know how long it would last as she said in a very positive way "Oh this is dull."[28]

Vivien told Leigh that she was going to America on Saturday (27 November) for ten days:

> As there is nothing happening in the way of work just at the moment I thought I might as well go. I will read *Green Mansions* (Leigh's birthday present to her) on the way which I am longing to do…[29]

She sailed in the *Majestic* and found that a fellow passenger was Hamish Hamilton. He had been incensed, if not surprised, by her desertion of Leigh, and informed her that their friendship was over. Hamilton recalled:

> When I reached the dining-room that irresistible laughing

†Also on board were Leslie Howard, Anna Neagle and Herbert Wilcox, and Noël Coward. Cole Lesley wrote of Olivier: "He and Noël still great cronies since *Private Lives*, so they were happy as bird-dogs." [Lesley, *Remembered Laughter*, p. 199]

> face popped up and we danced the whole way over. Inter alia she said, "You will love Larry." I replied: "No I hate him for robbing my best friend of his wife." Vivien said: "You won't." And of course, she was right.[30]

He asked her why she was going. "Partly because Larry's there, and partly because I intend to get the part of Scarlett O'Hara." Hamilton laughed and bet her ten pounds that she would not succeed. "I fear it was left unpaid,"[31] he commented half a century later.

Chapter 10
Gone with the Wind

It handled the American Civil War with grandeur and with just the necessary touch of Whitmanesque poetry. It had Leslie Howard and Olivia de Havilland presenting as nice a pair of people as ever existed on the screen. It had Clark Gable as the most exciting bad man who ever smacked a woman for her good. It had the young, wild, ungovernable, devastating Vivien Leigh as Scarlett O'Hara- 'all a wonder and a wild desire,' in Browning's phrase.

Alan Dent, Vivien Leigh: *A Bouquet*, p. 119

Gone with the Wind is more than a love-story and more than a saga of the South. With its recurring theme of procrastination, it is a book which has continued to grip the imagination of readers over the course of several generations. Girls more accustomed to reading glossy magazines have studiously read and re-read its 795 pages, loving either Rhett Butler of Ashley Wilkes according to taste, and admiring Scarlett for her self-interested manipulation of all and sundry.

Gone with the Wind sold 326,000 copies within six weeks of publication. It won the Pulitzer Prize of 1937 and has sold millions of copies since. The novelist Muriel Spark pointed out that the book has always appealed to the eternal teenager:

It has an inspired (or at least unpremeditated) emotional

> immaturity, which is a requisite of every best-seller, and is sometimes a minor ingredient of great art.[1]

The story of America and the story of Scarlett are inextricably interwoven, yet, wrote Mrs. Spark in 1956: It is undoubtedly Scarlett, however, who has been selling the book these twenty-odd years."[2]

Gone with the Wind was written in the course of four years by Margaret Mitchell, a journalist on the *Atlanta Journal.* She took her title from *Cynara,** a poem by an alcoholic Roman Catholic convert, Ernest Dowson. Vivien was one of its earliest readers:

> From the moment I read [it], I was fascinated by the lovely wayward, tempestuous Scarlett. I felt that I loved and understood her, almost as though I had known her in the flesh. When I heard that the book was to be filmed in Hollywood early in 1939 I longed to play the part…[3]

Vivien knew well the importance of being single-minded:

> I have always believed that if you want something with all your heart and soul you get it.[4]

Inevitably Vivien will be remembered more for her part in the film of *Gone with the Wind* than for anything else she undertook. It was a form of type-casting she came to resent – just as Olivier bridled at being dubbed 'Mr. Scarlett O'Hara' for a time in the American press. Unquestionably she dominated the film from the moment she emerged in white crinoline from behind the pale blue coat of an unwanted beau on the steps of Tara until her parting decision to return to her homestead and contemplate the resolution of her future on the morrow.

The other principal characters, Rhett Butler and Ashley Wilkes, came and went spasmodically throughout the film (Ashley, for example, dropped out of the book from page 209 to page 392 while fighting in the Confederate cause),

*The relevant lines are:
I have been faithful to thee, Cynara! in my fashion.
I have forgot thee, Cynara! gone with the wind,
Flung roses, riotous with the throng.

but Vivien was there throughout. Thus she became associated with Scarlett in the minds of the general public, especially in the United States. She has been described as a survivor on her own terms, but still in the romantic tradition of the South, and one who used romance for her own purpose – survival – for as long as was possible. It has also been suggested that, in later films such as the two by Tennessee Williams, there are better clues to the eventual fate of Scarlett than those exploited in sequels to *Gone with the Wind.*

The film rights to *Gone with the Wind* were purchased by David O. Selznick, of Selznick International, sight unseen. He had founded his company in 1935 with financial backing from John Hay Whitney. Both men were in their early thirties. Jock Whitney was rich, roundly educated, interested in art and racing. According to Irene Selznick, David's wife: "He led a lusty, strenuous, swashbuckling life with seven-league boots on."[5] A considerate man, he shared Selznick's devotion to quality and was prepared to pay the cost. Irene Selznick explained: "Perfectionism brings delay, disorder and (naturally) expense."[6] There was considerable doubt as to whether a book on the Civil War, as yet unpublished, was the right material for a film. Selznick's bright and energetic story editor in New York, Kay Brown, was determined that it was. She obtained a synopsis and Selznick pondered. He consulted Whitney, who said that he would buy it himself if Selznick did not want it, and that proved the final spur.

Selznick only read the book itself (on a sea voyage to Honolulu) after he had paid his $50,000. By then it was already a bestseller and many of the passengers were likewise engrossed, but, recalled Irene Selznick, "he was reading it more slowly and he owned the picture rights."[7] Selznick made careful plans. He appointed Sidney Howard, the Pulitzer Prize winner and playwright, to produce a script (the first draft of which would have resulted in a film of five and a half hours). And he set about selecting actors and actresses. Clark Gable was an obvious, early, and expensive choice for Rhett Butler. He was loaned by MGM, the company of Irene's father, Louis B. Mayer. They put up $1,250,000 of the $4,250,000 and by securing the re-issue rights took half the film. Though Selznick threw away millions, he told journalist James Bacon:

> I have never regretted my decision. I wouldn't have made the movie without Clark.[8]

The others were less easy. And Selznick found himself launched on a widely publicized nationwide search for Scarlett O'Hara.

George Cukor was appointed director and as early as November 1936 he began his quest for locations and for a suitable Scarlett. Most of the famous names of the day were considered, as were a great number of unknowns. Tallulah Bankhead was a 'strong possibility'[9] in December 1936. Kay Brown, whose tentacles stretched far, suggested Vivien Leigh as early as January 1937 but Selznick cabled that he had 'no enthusiasm for Vivien Leigh'[10] but would reconsider her after seeing *Fire Over England.* Negotiations for Leslie Howard* to play Ashley opened in October 1937.

Vivien again came to Selnick's attention in February 1938 when he saw *A Yank at Oxford.* He was then searching for a star for *The Young in Heart* and wrote:

> I saw *Yank at Oxford* last night, which by the way is a swell picture. While I think Vivien Leigh gave an excellent performance and was very well cast, I don't like her for the part in our picture as well as Margaret Lindsay, Pat Paterson or Dorothy Hyson.[11]

The role went to Paulette Goddard, another Scarlett contestant. In April, Max Breen wrote that he had drawn Selznick's attention to Vivien as a possible Scarlett, but Selznick had said: "She is very beautiful, but she seemed to be a little static, not quite sufficiently temperamental for such a fiery role."[12]

By September Selznick was very clear about the kind of girl he was seeking, as he wrote to Ed Sullivan, the Hollywood columnist of the *New York Daily News.* He explained that after considerable research he was convinced that the public wanted "a new girl as Scarlett." He had spent $50,000 in the quest of such a girl, with talent scouts touring the country, George Cukor himself exploring the South, and both he and Cukor personally seeing hundreds of largely unsuitable candidates: "We've done everything conceivable," he wrote. The search was "on again with renewed vigor" because Selznick was contracted to start filming with Clark Gable the

*Howard had the same good looks as Leigh Holman. Had he lived to be an old man, he would have been the perfect figure to portray the spy and art expert, Anthony Blunt.

moment he finished *Idiot's Delight*: "and the best Scarlett that shows up by that time will play the role willy-nilly."[13]

Numerous young women were obsessed with the idea that they might be Scarlett. Even Jock Whitney's wife, Liz, underwent a screen test. No stunt was too ridiculous. One girl presented herself at the Selznick home inside a giant replica of the book. Bette Davis was the most publicly rejected Scarlett. Later she wrote of how perfect she would have been, and how, in the quest for a new face, she was used as the touchstone.[14] Paulette Goddard was another. She was in the running almost to the end, but thwarted by her irregular relationship with Charlie Chaplin, which puritan Hollywood could not condone.

By November 1938, Selznick was somewhat more than anxious: "I feel that our failure to find a new girl for Scarlett is the greatest failure of my entire career,"[15] he wrote. Meanwhile he made plans with excellence his aim. No detail was too small for his attention – even the best way to obtain the effect of candlelight on screen so that it did not resemble electric light. He also hoped that, with judicious cutting and editing, every word would somehow be Margaret Mitchell's.

More great names were raised and dropped – Ann Sheridan, Lana Turner, Julie Haydon, Janet Gaynor, Sara Haden. By 21 November his confidential short list of Scarletts was Katharine Hepburn (Cukor's favorite), Jean Arthur, Joan Bennett, and Loretta Young. Despite the indecision, George Cukor was impressed by Selznick's genius for publicity and the 'absolute fever pitch'[16] of interest in the as yet unmade film.

December 1938 found Selznick wondering if the fiery Tallulah Bankhead, another rejected Scarlett, might be tempted to play Belle Watling: "she would be a perfect illicit mate for Rhett Butler."[17] When asking Kay Brown to sound her out he warned her she might bite her head off. Filming was but four days off and the heroine had still proved elusive. Small wonder that Selznick lived on Benzedrine.

On 10 December Selznick reported to Jock Whitney that the film had started with the burning of Atlanta: "Shot key scenes at eight twenty tonight, and judging by how they looked to the eye they are going to be sensational."[18] It was an exciting start after more than two years of spade-work: $25,000 worth of old sets were given new fronts on the back lot of the Selznick Pathe Studio before being consigned to the fire. As many as seven

Technicolor cameras filmed doubles for Rhett and Scarlett in both medium and long shots. There was a practical reason for such a dramatic beginning. The burning cleared space for the construction of the exterior set of Tara and of certain sections of Atlanta.

This was, of course, the dramatic meeting point for Selznick and Vivien. It is as legendary in show business history as the encounter of Stanley and Livingstone. As if by chance, Vivien appeared, demure and beautiful, her long dark hair blowing in the wind, silhouetted against the roaring flames. Two days later Selznick wrote to Irene:

> Myron rolled in just exactly too late, arriving about a minute and a half after the last building had fallen and burned and after the shorts were completed. With him were Larry Olivier and Vivien Leigh. Shhhhh: she's the Scarlett dark horse, and looks damned good. (Not for anybody's ears but your own: it's narrowed down to Paulette [Goddard], Jean Arthur, Joan Bennett, and Vivien Leigh. We're making final tests this week…[19]

Later Selznick described the scene:

> When he (Myron) introduced me to her, the flames were lighting up her face and Myron said: "I want you to meet Scarlett O'Hara." I took one look and knew that she was right – at least as far as her appearance went – at least right as far as my conception of how Scarlett O'Hara looked. Later on, her test, made under George Cukor's brilliant direction, showed that she could act the part right down to the ground, but I'll never recover from that first look.[20]

The meeting was almost too fortuitous. Irene Selznick was certainly skeptical about Vivien's sudden well-timed arrival:

> At deadline, Vivien appeared. There had been magical interventions. David said, "See, I told you." It seemed so far-fetched that a dark horse could show up at the last

> moment that occasional tales still surface to challenge this fact. Vivien Leigh, a relatively minor actress under contract to Alexander Korda in England, came to town apparently to see her sweetheart, Laurence Olivier, who was making *Wuthering Heights.* Ten years later in London I learned* that her timing was not coincidental. Vivien was as determined as she was beautiful. What she desperately wanted was Larry and Scarlett, in that order; they were both in California, and each made the other more possible. Moreover, Larry's agent was Myron.[21]

There is evidence of Vivien's determination. Fabia Drake, who saw her often in the 1930s, was surprised when Vivien announced her intention to play Scarlett. She wrote:

> But Vivien, you could never play Scarlett O'Hara. She's too-too-ruthless' Vivien looked back, her eyes glinting and mischievous – and she smiled a secret smile – the smile of Scarlett.[22]

Olivier himself made an interesting comment on Vivien's determination. In his book, *On Acting*, he discussed Vivien's decision not to accept the secondary role of Isabella in William Wyler's *Wuthering Heights*: "Slowly we were learning that actors have to manipulate their careers with cool, determined heads.[23]

Later Irene Selznick said she did not believe that Myron Selznick was involved in Vivien's campaign. She maintained that his famous 'Meet Scarlett O'Hara' line was as much a way of sidestepping his late arrival as anything else. Fate assisted Vivien when a flash of light lit her just as he uttered the words.[24]

After the first meeting between Selznick and Vivien, events moved at a brisk pace. Selznick had one remaining anxiety: could Vivien act? George Cukor spent all of 14 December testing her. She wore a dress that she was sure had been worn but minutes before by a previous contestant. She spoke in an English accent, making no attempt at any Southern talk. As she was

*It was Binkie Beaumont who revealed this to her.

laced into her dress by 'Mammy,' she played the scene defiantly where others had been tearful and sentimental.

Marcella Rabwin, Selznick's executive assistant, described the outcome:

> And of course she was a brilliant actress. They tested her, silent tests, wardrobe bests, she was just the ideal. She was the most glowing, vibrant, dynamic woman I had ever met.[25]

Miss Rabwin thought that, like Scarlett, Vivien represented the idea of a strong, persuasive, determined woman. Olivia de Havilland found her exquisite and very feminine but "capricious, and a bit perverse, which made her interesting."[26]

From the Beverly Hills Hotel ("11 acres of sunshine for 12 months of playtime in the heart of residential Los Angeles[27]) Vivien gave her version to Leigh, who was looking after Suzanne in London:

> You will never guess what has happened and no one is more surprised than me. You know that I only came out here for a week. Well just two days before I was supposed to leave, the people who are making '*Gone with the Wind'* saw me and said would I make a test – so what could I *do* and so now I am working frantically hard and rehearsing, and studying a Southern accent which I don't find difficult anyway. These are the final tests they are making, and there are just four of us – they seem to be very pleased with me – and I don't know what I think or what I hope – I am so afraid it will mean me staying here (IF I get it) for a long time, and that I know I don't want to do. The part has now become the biggest responsibility I can imagine and yet it would be absurd not to do it if given the chance…I also forgot to tell you that I dislike it *very* much out here. Everything is so completely unreal and it will be wonderful to see England again. Even the climate is ridiculous…[28]

Meanwhile, of course, she still had a contract with Tyrone Guthrie for the *Dream*. Her career would probably not have ground to a halt had he refused to release her, but the situation would have been awkward. He did not stand in her way.

On Christmas Day Cukor invited Olivier and Vivien to a party. Steeled for the worst, and resolved to talk of anything but *Gone with the Wind*, she heard that the part was hers: "Well, I guess we're stuck with you,"[29] said her new friend.

Inevitably there was a rush to get the new contract signed. At this point, Korda (who was in Hollywood pursuing his romance with Merle Oberon) became involved as Vivien was still under contract to him. It seemed that Selznick would make one picture after *Gone with the Wind* and, subsequently, the two producers would use her alternately. Selznick explained to Jock Whitney:

> The lucky Hungarian has fallen into something, and we're going to make a fortune for him. However, if she's really as good as we hope, I suppose we're lucky too, and shouldn't be greedy that someone else gets something out of it.[30]

Vivien herself had problems. Her mother was very upset that she would have to make two pictures each half-year in Hollywood – even though she might take a holiday of six weeks between each and spend the other half-year working for Korda in England. Vivien explained that it was "really unavoidable– as if they get an unknown girl to play the most sought after part in the films for years they naturally want to make a star out of her and make their money back."[31] An additional reason for Vivien's appeal to Selznick was that she was not expensive to sign. Once a star, Vivien was sure 'they will be agreeable to any new terms I want to make, such as 1 picture a year.[32] Nor was Olivier pleased. According to Bob Thomas and confirmed by Irene Selznick, he burst into Selznick's office and declared that he would not allow Vivien to fulfill her contract. Selznick reminded him that he had already destroyed Jill Esmond's potential career in Hollywood by denying her a role in the film *A Bill of Divorcement* and dismissed him with this message: "Larry, don't be a shit twice."[33] News of the contract was relayed to Leigh, but Vivien cabled: "I cannot work here at all without your consent, so please find it possible to give it."[34]

The arrival of the cable caused Leigh considerable anguish. Maintaining his rights as a husband, he declined to give the required consent. This pleased Vivien as she hoped it would mean that she could modify her contract. She explained to her mother:

> I think it will make a difference to Selznick and they might just let me do 1 picture a year which is what I am going to try to get if this is a success. I know I could not stay here without Larry and I naturally cannot expect him to spend his whole time here…[35]

Vivien was sorry to have put Leigh in such an awkward predicament. She wrote to him:

> They told me at the Selznick office that I could not work here *at all*, without getting your permission, so I sent the wire which caused all the nuisance. Then, without waiting for a reply (because the studio was pressing to get the contract signed) they said I *could* work with a working permit instead of getting on the quota. This former involved no kind of fuss whatever…[36]

Vivien already hated Hollywood. "If Larry were not here I should go mad,"[37] she wrote to her mother. Hollywood, that curious phenomenon, had grown from a fig orchard in 1886 to attract the first motion picture makers in 1911. A curious invasion of wooden constructions had sprouted and the boarding houses were soon advertising 'no dogs or actors.' From the makeshift sets the vast studios had developed. The legend grew from the days when stars did their own stunts and the nudes looked innocent to a time when Anita Loos could write cynical sub-titles, and Cecil Beaton would observe 'a rather desperate glint' in the eyes of would-be-stars parading the streets in the quest of fame. It had turned sour too when Fatty Arbuckle was accused of raping and murdering Virginia Rappe, the 'Sunbonnet Girl,' at an orgy in San Francisco, and when the death of Rudolph Valentino heralded several suicides amongst his fans. Vivien continued to Leigh:

> ...As you well realize I loathe Hollywood, and for no other part would I have dreamt of signing a contract. My agent here assures me that if the picture is a success I can make demands and get my contract altered in such a way that is impossible at this moment. They cannot possibly say this is unfair of me, as all their standards are financial ones and I am doing *Gone with the Wind* for them for less money than I have been earning per picture for the past two years. I will never make a fuss about the financial side*but am determined to ask for more time for theatre, etc. I know perfectly well I could not stay here half the year (and I have intimated as much). The more I see of Hollywood the less possible it becomes...In fact I do not think there is anything nice about America except the football, and the politeness of men in garages...[38]

Vivien also took the opportunity to reiterate her reason for maintaining friendly relations with Leigh:

> I cannot help hoping also that it may mean you are beginning to feel a little more reconciled to the thought of a divorce later on.[39]

Margaret Mtichell, the book's author, had resolved to end her connection with *Gone with the Wind* the day she sold the film rights. Nevertheless she was kept closely informed of all developments. Susan Myrick (Selznick's technical advisor) wrote about Vivien conspiratorially, on 11 January:

> She is charming, beautiful, black hair and magnolia petal skin and in the movie tests I have seen, she moved me greatly. They did the paddock scene, for a test, and it is a marvelous business the way she makes you cry when she is 'making Ashley.' I understand that she is not signed but far

*Hamish Hamilton confirmed this: "Everyone thinks Vivien made a fortune, but she got no royalties whatever, and never held it against her agent-characteristically magnanimous." [Hamish Hamilton to the author, 19 October 1986.] Nor did Vivien mind having to pay tax: "I am coming home no matter what the Income tax does," she wrote to her mother in January 1939.

> as I can tell from George [Cukor] et al, she is the gal.[40]

Margaret Mitchell found the local press favorable to Vivien. She informed Selznick:

> Everyone thought it was fine thing to have a girl who was comparatively unknown in this country because her rendition of Scarlett would not be mixed up by past performances of roles of a different type.[41]

In America only curious groups such as the Dickensian Chapter, United Daughters of the Confederacy and the Scala Daughters protested in vain against the choice of an English girl. But the British press were very skeptical about her selection.

While Miss Mitchell was quietly pleased with the selection of Vivien, she was deeply reluctant to be involved in any publicity concerning the choice. Almost immediately there was controversy about how much Vivien should try to talk Southern. Margaret Mitchell pointed out that there were a great variety of Southern accents and hoped that Vivien would eliminate particularly British intonations but not attempt what could easily turn into bogus Southern talk. Vivien herself cabled the author:

> If I can but feel that you are with me on this, the most important and trying task of my life, I pledge with all my heart I shall try to make Scarlett O'Hara live as you described her in your brilliant book.[42]

It must have been considerable relief to Margaret Mitchell to find an actress who had read and understood the book. At first, however, her response was purely visual:

> While I have nothing to do with the production of the film of my book, I cannot help feeling a thoroughly normal pleasure that the role of Scarlett has fallen into the hands of a girl whose photographs show her to be so charming.[43]

As always whenever there was an announcement about the film, Margaret Mitchell was besieged by press and public and spent her time neither endorsing nor objecting to Selznick's choices. It was usually in vain. She was invariably confronted with headlines announcing 'AUTHOR OKAYS LEIGH.' She went so far as to complain to Selznick himself, saying that her only public statement concerning the choice of Vivien was that "she appeared to be a young woman of spirit and fire, with a very decided Irish look in her eyes."[44] She had had enough:

> Ever since the summer of 1936, your film has been the subject of public controversy and, for no good reason at all, I have been caught in the storm center of the controversy.[45]

Reassured in due course by Selznick, she complimented Vivien's approach to the part of Scarlett;

> I have the highest admiration for the way she has conducted herself. Her dignity and sweetness in her very difficult situation have won friends for her everywhere. For your private ear and not for repetition I am impressed by the remarkable number of different faces she has. In the stills you have been good enough to send me, she looks like a different person every time she is shown in a different mood.[46]

Vivien started work quite early each day, beginning by practicing a Southern accent (on which she had to work four hours a day, determined to master it in a fortnight), then rehearsing and undertaking photographic tests. Selznick took a close interest in her physical appearance, but urged that nothing drastic be done: "her hair should not be cut or the color changed, nor should her eyebrows be plucked in any way."[47] In due course Vivien was to resent the experiments made, especially when he began tampering with the shape of her bosom. Then he altered her origins, describing Vivien's parents as French and Irish. She and Olivier "laughed and laughed over her mother's concern as to whether they had found" a good man to play opposite her.[48]

To everyone's surprise shooting suddenly began on 26 January 1939, and a great number of problems normal and abnormal arose. Early on, after two weeks of filming, George Cukor was replaced as director. This upset Vivien considerably because she had enjoyed working with him. He was "a very intelligent and imaginative man [who] seems to understand the subject perfectly.[49] She explained to her mother how difficult everything was (especially since Olivier had not departed to New York for a play):

> …everyone is *hysterical* about this film, with the consequence that everything is disorganized – after two years they are still writing the script which means I don't know where I am. They have changed the director, which has upset me a lot, as I loved George Cukor (who was here before). I like this man alright [Victor Fleming], but the poor wretch is *exhausted* as he hasn't stopped working for ages, and he did not really want to do this film, as he was so tired, and has not even had time to read the book!! Then the photography is appalling, they all say. So *how* can I have any confidence. I am so homesick and long to be in London…[50]

The exact reasons for Cukor's dismissal have never been fully revealed, but it was thought that he failed to understand or encompass the wide canvas of the film. Clark Gable felt he was too interested in helping the female leads, Vivien and Olivia de Havilland, that he was not a man's director. Indeed, they both continued to consult him informally. Victor Fleming took over until he collapsed with ill health. Gavin Lambert felt that the loss of Cukor was to the detriment of the film. Referring to the screen test with Cukor he pointed out: "It had that kind of neurotic power, really desperate and frightening. Victor Fleming's version seems almost tame in comparison."[51] In later years Cukor joked that he was most famous for the film he did *not* direct.

In March Selznick was worried that his epic was not looking sufficiently impressive. He regretted the lack of location work: "Tara looks on the screen as though it were the back yard of a suburban home."[52] Sets did not look lived in and costumes looked as though they had come straight from the costume department. Nor were the costumes dramatic or sufficiently contrasting in colors. The Technicolor experts were meant to be giving technical advice and not "dominating the creative side of our picture as to sets, costumes or anything else."[53] Clark Gable refused to attempt a Southern accent. Selznick hoped at least for an occasionally accented word. Gable had a large neck but the costume department were making his collars too small. Selznick pointed out how well he dressed in private life compared to their efforts on his behalf. He decided that more money should be spent on bit actors than on the sets.

Vivien found life desperately lonely without Olivier. He had finished filming *Wuthering Heights* (another story of contrasting dark and fair heroes and a lone heroine), during which he had endured a running battle with William Wyler, the exasperation of Sam Goldwyn and 'real hate' with Merle Oberon. He explained later:

> I think I was being high-handed because my emotions were in a bit of a whirl. I was most deeply in love with Vivien, and I could think of little else.[54]

He then went to New York to act in S.N. Behrman's *No Time for Comedy*, "as there was nothing coming up here in the immediate future."[55] In *Confessions of an Actor*, he blames Vivien for the separation that ensued ("It was Vivien's turn to force a separation.")[56] At the time it did not seem so. Vivien was anxious to explain to her mother:

> Without Larry to go home to and talk to it is horrible but you must not blame him, as it was really the only thing to do and it will prevent another separation later on and it's not as if he were in Nyland. He only did this play in this country, because I was here and he could fly to me and phone. He will probably write to you anyway, and I wish you would to him, as he will be lonely too…[57]

Olivier did write describing the situation as "a very hard punishment to bear, this self-imposed separation."[58] He continued:

> But there is *sense* behind it, and a great deal of thought. It was an agonizingly difficult decision to make, but I

> believe we were wise to make it, and that it will bid more for our ultimate happiness together, to choose to work (even if we don't like it very much) at the expense of our temporary personal happiness rather than the other way about. In either case it was the choice between two evils, and we believe that in the end, in choosing this – by far the hardest way, we will have chosen the lesser of the two. We *are* so *determined* to be together in the end, and it would have been too easy to fall for the obvious comfort of being together as long as possible *now*, at the expense of our careers. We are both very ambitious and I think we both probably have futures. Therefore the important thing is to finish up together, for which we will gladly suffer now. But this now is *very* painful darling…[59]

Olivier consoled himself with the knowledge that they could write and talk every day and that, if anything was the matter, he could fly to California on a Saturday night, spend four hours with her, and be back in time for his play on Monday night. He used to go to concerts on Sunday nights and be the last man to clap so that Vivien could hear him on the wireless transmission. Meanwhile, he explained:

> She has a *very* nice girl living with her who looks after her. And she has a nice lot of friends here who are fond of her and will see that she is alright.[60]

The girl who came to work for Vivien was Sunny Alexander, a Texan, who had been trained at the Metropolitan Business School, Dallas, and had come to Hollywood in 1930. She had been given the not inconsiderable sum of $10,000 to establish Bobby Crawford's agency (representing stars such as Lana Turner) on Wilshire Boulevard, but he jumped off a tall building following a substantial horse-racing debt. Thereafter she worked for the Myron Selznick Agency. She was deputed to live with Vivien as secretary, companion, and guide and to negate any gossip about Larry living with her. Vivien was soon describing her as "such an angel of kindness and goodness."[61] Sunny explained:

> We liked each other right away. I hired a good cook, butler, gardener and personal maid. Larry was number one for her. Scarlett O'Hara was number two. I never saw two people so happily in love in my life and it was a delight to be around them.
>
> David Selznick gave us twenty-four hour guard service around the clock to keep the press away from the house so that in the event that Larry was seen going in or out, the press couldn't take pictures of him coming out of that particular house, which they knew was her home. But we had no trouble. We were well-protected.
>
> Scarlett O'Hara was a very challenging role for her. She knew that Selznick wanted perfection and he was a neurotic genius. The separation from Larry was very, very upsetting for her. She was motivated by how fast she could get the movie over and get back to Larry. It was a horse-race. She had a cute little way of going up to Vic Fleming and saying, "Darling, could we just do two more shots?" Being separated from Larry put so much fire and anger into her and it was projected out through Scarlett. She actually made her character stronger.
>
> Vivien hated resting. She would go to bed with the telephone on one side and the newspaper on the other. And she would write notes and make phone calls. Then she'd get out of bed, take a shower and say, "I had my rest." She gave excellent dinner parties on Saturday nights with wonderful china and crystal. She kept up her social life even without Larry.[62]

Before Olivier left, Sunny inspired them with a romantic idea. She said it was the tradition of young lovers in Hollywood to take a hamburger and ice-cream soda and cuddle in the back of the car. Substituting a meat-loaf for the hamburger, Olivier and Vivien went along with the plan. Sunny and her future husband, Harry Lash (a vaudeville actor who had worked with Bob Hope) drove them to a spot near the corner of Wilshire Boulevard and Rodeo Drive.

From New York Olivier explained to Gertrude:

> I never thought it was possible to love anybody so much or quite so completely, or that anybody should be so wonderfully abundant and prodigal to me in everything I wanted most.
>
> As we have settled down and become firmer in our minds, and more peaceful in our hearts, our life together has become so unbelievably beautiful. We have been through a terribly difficult two years as you know Darling Pet, but I really believe that our love will justify itself in the end.[63]

Once again, the letter bore residual undertones of guilt about the distress that their love affair had caused to all those around them, including Gertrude. But Olivier was determined to prove that their love for each other would prove it all worthwhile in the end.

Vivien and Olivier only met twice between March and June, once when Selznick called him and begged that he come from Indianapolis to calm her down. Olivier explained: "Exhaustion coupled with hysteria due to our harshly testing separation was producing dangerous symptoms…"[64] To keep busy, Vivien took piano and accordion lessons in the evenings and was able to master 'Banjo on my knee' and 'Suwannee River.' She worried about the inevitability of war and craved for reliable news other than the sensational reports in the American press. She also fretted about the dryness of her skin in the California climate, asking her mother if Helen Rubinstein's pasteurized cream for dry skins was a safe remedy. The film crept slowly on. Vivien found that long hours were spent and little achieved principally because "of the appalling dialogue."[65] She was pleased that Sidney Howard was being called in again, and assigned the rest of the problems to Technicolor "which I think looks horrid anyway."[66] Ever generous, she did not neglect friends in England. She wanted to help Jeanne de Casalis, who was suffering from lack of money, and hoped to pay for Suzanne's riding lessons. For relaxation she went to the beach house of the film director Anatole Litvak and his wife Miriam Hopkins ("they are both very charming and one does not feel one is in Hollywood in their company").[67] Otherwise she liked the English people in Hollywood, especially the Ronald Colmans and David Niven. Vivien's complaints about Hollywood must have appeared very ungenerous to those who held the colony in high esteem.

Leigh sent Vivien some snaps of Suzanne, who was growing fast. "She looks quite robust and much taller,"[68] noted Vivien. By the middle of May Vivien was feeling exhausted by the filming. Everyone was working harder and harder and the general reaction was good. However, progress was still "at snail's pace, and now they've taken to dawn shots – which is *v.* exhausting and miserable."[69]

Vivien experienced many problems during the filming itself. Ninety-seven tons of brick dust had been imported to California to give the effect of the red earth of Georgia. Her dress turned pink and her hair red, causing the Technicolor cameraman unusual problems. "That was not a thing to what the wind was doing to me," wrote Vivien. "It was an emotional scene and as I cried, the tears made great crimson rivers down my cheeks! My face was washed twelve times that day."[70] When they were nursing the wounded soldiers, thousands of bluebottles were imported. Vivien was amused when Olivia de Havilland commented, "Poor things, d'you think they'll get screen credit for all this work?"[71] And Vivien was in some danger when a horse reared up during the filming of the Siege of Atlanta. She believed she was saved by the billowing of her hoop skirt.

Vivien continued to be preoccupied by the hope of a divorce, while Leigh remained intransigent:

> Leigh, you said in your letter in April, that you felt that even if you divorce me I would not feel free, but you see darling, it's not that *I* don't feel free, it's you who wish that I shouldn't. If only, Leigh, you would divorce me from your *mind*. I am so sure that it would be easier for you instead of clinging to a hope. I know it's simple enough to give advice, but what else can I say, when to myself I *have* found the truth of this step, and am not still seeking. Jill has written to Larry and has said that she will either divorce him now, naming me as correspondent or next year, for desertion. She also said she was going to see you, so perhaps by the time you get this letter you will have discussed it with her. I remember you saying some time ago that you thought

> the desertion thing was the best, it is of course more to do with you and Jill which way you'd prefer, but I suppose the latter (desertion) is the lesser of the two evils. Will you tell me what you think?[72]

While on the set, Vivien was vociferous with complaints. Dedicated reader of the book as she was, she kept a copy close at hand and deeply resented any divergence from Margaret Mitchell's text. Selznick recalled that during her 122 days on the set "she groused plenty."[73] He continued.

> Before a scene, she would be muttering deprecations under her breath and making small moans. According to Vivien, the situation was stupid, the dialogue was silly, nobody could possibly believe the whole scene. And then, at a word from Victor Fleming, who was not merely a very fine director but a man who had the ability to conceal the iron hand in the velvet glove, she would walk into the scene and do such a magnificent job that everybody on the set would be cheering.[74]

Evidently Vivien disliked her few kisses with Clark Gable because of his false teeth and whisky-sodden breath. He later confessed that when obliged to kiss on screen he normally thought of a steak. Not everyone enjoyed working with Vivien. Evelyn Keyes, who played Scarlett's young sister, Suellen, remained bitter years later. "She still treated me like the bit player I had once been." [75] In the scene at Tara when everyone has to work with their hands, Scarlett slaps Suellen because she complains. Evelyn Keyes noted: "And she didn't pull her punches. My cheek wore the imprint of Vivien's fingers for the rest of the afternoon."[76]

Vivien always worked hard, at one time coping with a twenty-four hour day and then returning to a new scene after a mere four hours of sleep. Between shots she played canasta with Sunny. Later, as the long days of filming mounted, exhaustion took its toll and George Cukor found her asleep in her wet bathing costume beside his pool. He did not wake her, but covered her with a warm blanket. It has been suggested that this event led to her later tuberculosis. Cukor also felt that six days of filming a week was too much. And he recognized that, towards the end of filming, Vivien became "exhausted and impatient"[77] and was longing only for reunion with Olivier. Sunny remembered Melanie's death scene as especially moving:

> Vic Fleming was directing at that time and he had the shot redone several times but it was so real and everybody was so emotional and so tired out from working so hard that when he said 'cut' everybody on that set was crying – the crew, the electricians, the third and fourth assistant – everybody was weeping as though we had just been to a memorial service or something. That's how real it all seemed. Vic knew he had a good shot when he saw tears in everybody's eyes – including his own.[78]

When Vivien had completed her filming on 27 June, a fabulous epic was 'in the can.' The film remains as fresh today as ever it was in 1939 and there are still many who relish settling down to Margaret Mitchell's 'story of the old South,' as the titles roll over Max Steiner's majestic music. While slaves pick cotton in the fields the viewers are reminded of an earlier era in the titles written by Ben Hecht: "Look for it only in books for it is no more than a dream remembered, a Civilization gone with the wind." The much criticized direction was subtle in its silent screen approach to things hinted at but not seen – the servant chasing the chicken in predatory fashion fading to the cooked chicken being served for dinner, the surgeon's scalpel silhouetted on high in the hospital, Scarlett's face seen observing the grim amputation, her signature 'Scarlett Kennedy' on a check, revealing that she had married the hopeless Frank. There was considerable humor, too: Charles Hamilton's gallant death from 'measles and pneumonia,' Rhett's delight at giving his word 'as a gentleman,' the soporifically sweet Melanie emerging from her room after Scarlett has shot the Yankee, trailing Ashley's sword, as equal to action as Scarlett. And there was the eroticism of Rhett sweeping Scarlett into his arms and mounting the wide red stairs of their Atlanta home. Above all, it was a towering performance from Vivien, who sprang to life in this film as never before, the slight Southern accent adding a timbre to her voice, her self-confidence as an actress fully assured. She found her way to the part and in every way she vindicated Selznick's confidence in her.

When all the battles were over and the cutting and editing was done, David O. Selznick could boast with pride to Howard Dietz that his film was the longest motion picture ever made, that its only near equivalent was *The Birth of a Nation*, and that it would make *The Big Parade* and *Ben-Hur* look very small fry. Selznick concluded correctly: "This picture represents the greatest work of my life, in the past and very likely in the future."[79]

Chapter 11
First Days of Wartime

You know I have a feeling that from now on everything is going to take a turn for the better.

Vivien Leigh, Waterloo Bridge

As soon as filming of *Gone with the Wind* was over, Vivien did a test for Daphne du Maurier's *Rebecca.* David Selznick was not impressed, however: "It is my personal feeling that she could never be right for the girl…"[1] Vivien rushed to New York, arriving just before Olivier left the cast of *No Time for Comedy*. Such was her determination for the new role that she insisted on a second test, this time opposite Olivier. Irene Selznick judged:

> This was a woman obsessively in love. But the qualities which made her the perfect choice for Scarlett made her the worst possible one for this role.[2]

These tests survive and show Vivien more in the mold of her pre-*Gone with the Wind* screen heroines. The part was not right for her. It needed someone more demure and gentle. Vivien would have been better cast in a role such as Estella, Miss Havisham's ward in *Great Expectations*.

Following the release of *Wuthering Heights* in April 1939, Olivier became the object of an excess of unwelcome public hysteria. He soon discovered, though, that the obsession of a fan can veer swiftly from blind love to that breed of frenetic hatred that was later exaggerated into murder (for example, the 1980 shooting of John Lennon). Olivier was glad to have returned to the stage, for his involvement in films was almost entirely commercial. Vivien quoted him describing film acting as "just about as satisfying as looking at a Michelangelo fresco through a microscope."[3] He felt that on celluloid the actor was too much at the mercy of the director and the cutting editors. He concluded that the value of films was the chance to study technique: "It also teaches you the difficult trick of working up enough voltage to act for the camera – the stimulus you get on the stage from the audience."[4]

Vivien and Olivier were able to return to London in the *Ile de France* for a brief holiday. They arrived at Plymouth at the end of July. Britain was preparing for the eventuality of war with air-raid shelters a feature of London's parks. Meanwhile, in March, Olivier's father had died. He left £286 2s.11d in cash.

Vivien's mother had been depressed after Tommy's death, and was working hard with her beauty academy. Vivien decided to take her over to Hollywood for a short holiday. Thus Olivier, Vivien, and Gertrude sailed from Britain on the *Ile de France* on 17 August. Scarcely were they at sea when David Selznick cabled Vivien, explaining at considerable length that, much as he would have like to offer her the part in *Rebecca*, he and everyone else involved were convinced that it would only harm her reputation. To Olivier he was perhaps more truthful:

> Vivien's anxiety to play role, has, in my opinion, been largely if not entirely due to her desire to do a picture with you, which was best demonstrated by her complete disinterest in part when I first mentioned it to her as a possibility and until she knew you were playing Maxim…[5]

In Hollywood Vivien had some retakes to complete for *Gone with the Wind*. She continued to crave the part in *Rebecca*, but in vain, and became very angry with Selznick for denying it her. But her main worry was the possibility of being parted from Larry. Gertrude brought her cine-camera to Hollywood and filmed life at 606 North Camden Drive, Beverly Hills, which appeared relaxed as Olivier dived in the pool and Vivien picked flowers. At other times they attempted to teach Gertrude how to swim. Jerry Dale, a

United Artists press agent, felt that Olivier was secretly relieved that Vivien was not playing opposite him. His view as expressed to Thomas Kiernan was that "Vivien's constant affection toward him embarrassed him. The fact that her mother was there made it even harder for him. Her mother had a slightly disapproving air about the entire relationship, and Larry was uneasy with her around."[6] Joan Fontaine won the cherished part – though neither she nor Olivier enjoyed working together.

Filming of *Rebecca* had only just begun when fears of world war became reality. The news broke when Olivier, Vivien, her mother, David Niven and others were weekending on a chartered yacht off Catalina Island. Olivier "smashed as a hoot-owl,"[7] as Douglas Fairbanks related in one of many versions of the over-publicized incident, proceeded to row about informing the other weekenders that this was the end of the old world as they knew it. Vivien was upset. "It was," recalled David Niven, "one of the few times I ever saw her cry."[8]

On 11 September, Vivien wrote to Leigh:

> As you may imagine we have done nothing but sit glued to the wireless, tho' now it isn't worth while, as each country that comes on the wire seems to say what it pleases and all the accounts vary so widely that we don't know what to believe for the last few days there has been next to no news… Mummy is naturally frantically worried, about Daddy and Suzanne.[9]

Vivien had no plans other than that her mother should stay on. If Olivier was to be called up, then Vivien resolved to return home to make propaganda films.

Vivien's Texan secretary, Sunny Alexander, struck up a close friendship with Gertrude, who told her that she was always concerned about Vivien's health, because she had "once had a tubercular lung." Sunny explained: "Gertrude looked upon her as delicate."[10] Gertrude flew to New York to see the World Fair on her way home in October. Sunny wrote to her: "Little Vivien cried her eyes out after saying goodbye to you at the airport – in fact we both did all the way home."[11] More positively she reported:

> Larry is the same sweet wonderful boy and has been even more attentive to her since you went away. It is simply wonderful to be around such a beautiful love as theirs. Larry saw GWTW night before last – he thought she was absolutely magnificent – as everyone else does – and yesterday morning sent her the most beautiful bouquet of gardenias and red rose buds – looked just like a bride's bouquet. He asked me to waken her with this, which I did, and she was so thrilled.[12]

Vivien was planning to make *Waterloo Bridge* for MGM. She met the director, Mervyn LeRoy, and found him "terribly nice, and very intelligent and easy to work with."[13] Sunny felt she would be "happier when she is working."[14] She prepared her wardrobe for the grand opening of *Gone with the Wind* in Atlanta. Vivien was relieved that the showing had gone well: "Larry was terribly thrilled with me – thank goodness."[15] Olivier was certainly astonished by the power of her performance. Not a man who liked to be upstaged it would have been surprising, if, in secret, he was not also somewhat annoyed.

Olivier continued to work on *Rebecca*, and was sick one day after being obliged to smoke on the set. According to actress Ruth Gordon, who arrived one Sunday so punctually that the young couple were still in bed, Olivier hated the film. In the company of Miss Gordon, C. Aubrey Smith (shortly to play the avuncular Duke in *Waterloo Bridge*) and Dame May Whitty (destined to play the nurse in *Romeo and Juliet*, and a great support to the couple in the early days of their elopement), Olivier impersonated scenes from the film and made everyone laugh until they fell to discussing the war again.[16] Olivier's plans to make the film of *Henry V* were temporarily shelved and Vivien wrote to Leigh that she thought that in the war they could be "of use in a touring company."[17]

The British in Hollywood were in something of a quandary as to whether to go or to stay: "There is a very fine trade in white feathers going on here…" Vivien wrote. "The Americans are inconceivably patriotic."[18] Leigh responded by suggesting that Vivien adopt American citizenship, an idea which enraged her:

> I'd really rather die in England than be doomed to live here. Or perhaps that is very selfish when everyone is just praying for jobs. But then if my job is as inconsistent as it's started out to be I shan't be much better off, anyway, as they can apparently waste as much of my time as they see fit without paying for it. [19]

It was not an easy phase. One British M.P. spoke sneeringly of "English actors gallantly facing the footlights in America."[20] It was recalled that Ronald Colman had served in the "Old Contemptibles" in 1914, Basil Rathbone had served throughout the Great War, and Herbert Marshall had lost a leg in France. Of the actors of 1939, John Justin rejoined his squadron after filming *The Thief of Baghdad*, David Niven dashed home to re-enlist, Ralph Richardson joined the Fleet Air Arm and in due course flew a navy plane at Dunkirk, Bob Montgomery, an American actor, joined the Ambulance Corps. Richard Greene found himself harassed, and in October 1940, backed out of a big part in *Hudson's Bay Company* to join the Seaforth Highlanders in Canada.

In the long wait for filming to begin on *Waterloo Bridge*, Vivien took voice production lessons and played the piano. Later in November she and Olivier went to Santa Barbara for four days:

> We had such a terribly happy time, *very* quiet, not a soul anywhere, we just swam in the sea…[21]

Olivier was either to film *Pride and Prejudice* starting in January 1939, or to join Vivien in *Waterloo Bridge*. Greer Garson recalled that Vivien wanted the part of Elizabeth, tried to get Louis B. Mayer to replace her with Joan Crawford, or to have Olivier in her film. Afterwards they planned to do Ro*meo and Juliet* together in New York for four months:

> Larry would direct it himself. We can hardly think of anything else all day. I am having voice lessons 4 times a week and Larry has suddenly started *composing* music, and nothing will stir him from the piano. He is extremely proud of his achievements and writes them out and *signs* them.

> When I say *them* I mean *it* so far, but still, it's very good. It's his own entrance music for Romeo. Now he's going to compose mine for Juliet! unless I can do it myself.[22]

David Selznick resolved his final problems with his epic film, succeeding in convincing the Hays Office* to allow Rhett to say, "Frankly, my dear, I don't *give* a damn," and winning equally important battles for reserved seats and an interval to avoid bladder trouble. *Gone with the Wind* opened in Atlanta in true show business style and to excellent reviews. The Governor of Georgia declared a State holiday, the town overflowed with celebrities and there seemed to be a never-ending wail from the sirens of the motorcycle escorts. It was said that a town of 300,000 swelled to a million and a half for the day. Vivien was greatly relieved to have Olivier with her for moral support not only at the civic reception and screening, but also at the *Gone with the Wind* ball. Margaret Mitchell broke her silence and gave the film "a glowing tribute from the stage."[23] On 18 December the film opened in New York to similar acclaim, and on 27 December Hollywood (just overcoming the death of Douglas Fairbanks, Senior) went right over the top with so many arc-lights and incandescents that night became day. Vivien gave the briefest of summaries to her mother on New Year's Eve from Myron Selznick's mountain house:

> We left Hollywood on Dec. 12th for Atlanta and were there three days. The people were very mice and there were crowds everywhere we went. They all like the picture. I am send you lots of cuttings and will try and enclose them in this letter. After Atlanta we flew to New York where we spent five days, and then back just in time for Xmas, which was lovely... Did you see in the paper that I had received an award (from the *New York* film critics) for the best feminine performance of the year? And that *Wuthering Heights* won for the best picture? We were furious that Larry didn't get the man's award but Jimmy Stewart did.[24]

*A most censorious body run by Will H. Hays. It removed even the mildest innuendo from every film.

It took Vivien's secretary, Sunny Alexander, to give Mrs. Hartley the full picture:

> It would be impossible for me to tell you of her success in the picture – I simply don't know the words and won't attempt it. If you can just imagine the greatest things that every happened in all the world – that's 'your little Vivien.' The whole of our country is positively overwhelmed by her magnificent performance. She is all over the newspapers everywhere and the most wonderful reviews you have ever read…
>
> Every famous person in America writes her 'congratulations.' She is so unspoiled by it all and is still, and will always be I know, the same sweet girl. Larry is so proud of her, and maybe you think I'm not. I suppose *I'm* the one who'll get the big head for having the most famous boss in all our film world – and Larry too – believe me they are both 'tops' right now and all of Hollywood envys them.[25]

In December Olivier and Vivien moved into a larger house next to the Danny Kayes, 1107 San Ysidro Drive, full of fine antiques. Sunny thought Vivien looked particularly lovely in the Dubonnet and white bedroom. Vivien kept in close touch with her mother and Leigh in England. Mrs. Hartley was having problems over the rent of premises for her beauty academy. Durham Cottage had been loaned to Anthony Bushell and his friend Consuelo who was living there (while Tony was serving in the Welsh Guards). It suffered in a storm which blew some tiles off the roof. The house was swamped and fungus began to grow up the staircase. Leigh had rented Little Stanhope Street* and moved to the Bath Club. He then enlisted as a Sub-Lieutenant RNVR and was stationed in Ramsgate, sharing digs with Prince Dimitri of Russia. He was prevented by censorship from explaining the nature of his work to Vivien overseas, but was forthcoming to Gertrude, with whom he always remained on good terms:

*Little Stanhope Street was razed to the ground in 1941.

> They tell me that my work will consist in going off to ships anchored in the Dunes in order to cross-examine the passengers as to their origin, destination and the work they intend to take up. The idea is to prevent Germans getting out to submarine bases abroad or to other jobs of a hostile Description.[26]

Vivien informed Leigh:

> People are flocking to the film in spite of the stiff behinds they acquire on its account.[27]

In January she began filming the wartime weepie *Waterloo Bridge*. Her initial reaction to the plot had been far from positive:

> The story we do is so dreary, that I cannot look forward to it. It is a very sad affair which starts in this war and goes back to the Great War! And altho' I'm a good girl to start with I turn into a prostitute thereby ruining my chances with my fiancé (who is believed killed, but who of course isn't!) Eventually I either go mad or commit suicide, or am just plain blown up! – it's gay, isn't it? As I have no jurisdiction whatsoever as to what happens to me, or what I'm given to do, I'll just have to like it.[28]

When she was not knitting balaclava helmets for the troops (the neatest of which she sent to Leigh), Vivien undertook ballet lessons with the Hungarian-German choreographer, Ernest Matray, and his wife, Maria, for one brief dancing scene on stage early in the film. She asked to "be between two strong girls, who can prop me up."[29] Between filming Vivien either continued to knit, or played Chinese checkers with Mervyn LeRoy, inspected sketches for *Romeo and Juliet*, took voice lessons from Dame May Whitty, studied lines for her next scene, or gave an impromptu interview to some passing journalist. Vivien continued:

> Robert Taylor is the man in the picture and as it was written

> for Larry it's a typical piece of miscasting. I am afraid it will be a dreary job but I won't think about it, and just concentrate on *Romeo and Juliet.*[30]

In the wake of the success of *Gone with the Wind* and *Wuthering Heights*, *Twenty-One Days* was released in the United States in January (and in Great Britain in May) under the title *Twenty-One Days Together*. Foster Hirsch, in his book *Laurence Olivier on Screen*, noted:

> Olivier begins [one] scene by knocking over a vase of flowers, and his acting is so clumsy that it is impossible to tell if the spill is a deliberate part of his characterization or a mistake that hasn't been edited out.[31]

In January Leigh finally filed for divorce. "Scarlett's Mate sues for Divorce"[32] announced the *Los Angeles Examiner*. "I do so hope you will not have a very unpleasant time at the divorce thing, Leigh darling," wrote Vivien in February, "I understand it's tomorrow."[33] A conditional decree was granted in London, giving Leigh custody of Suzanne.* This meant that after six months Vivien and Olivier would be free to marry. Vivien's main dilemma was that, although she had suddenly become Hollywood's top star, she was by means in control of her destiny. She was obliged to film *Waterloo Bridge* without Olivier, while Greer Garson secured the part she wanted opposite him in *Pride and Prejudice*, a well-cast and well-acted film. Once the divorce issue was settled, Vivien trusted that the studios would lose their last hold – the irregularity of her relationship with Olivier. *Romeo and Juliet,* which she and Olivier rehearsed each evening, was the great hope for the new year.

Sunny recalled that Alfred Shenberg (who became her second husband after Harry Lash's death) was Mervyn LeRoy's assistant director and unit direction manager on *Waterloo Bridge*. He told her that he had never seen an actress "with the skill she had in her craft."[34] Vivien never lunched at the commissary but had lunch brought to her room by her butler, John. Her

*Olivier was divorced by Jill Esmond on 29 January 1940, the divorce becoming absolute on 5 August. She got custody of three-and-a-half-year-old Tarquin. Vivien's divorce became absolute on 26 August. Leigh and Jill named Olivier and Vivien respectively as co-respondents.

favorite was avocado salad. While at work on the film, Vivien received a visit from the Duff Coopers. Lady Diana wrote to her friend, Conrad Russell:

> We lunch with adorable Vivien Leigh in her caravan. There had been galaxies of kisses the night before, and now we had a birthday* bottle of champagne and more kisses, and back to pack, for we must leave these glowing flesh pots of Ming and jade, these beds of Chippendale and asphodel and moly, for the desert and the war.[35]

Filming of *Waterloo Bridge* was soon completed and so popular had Vivien been on the set that the crew gave her a party. Later she told her mother: "They had a sneak preview of *Waterloo Bridge* the other night and apparently it is quite good tho' I haven't seen it yet."[36]

A week later, on 29 February, the annual banquet of the Academy of Motion Picture Arts was held in the Cocoanut Grove of the Ambassador Hotel in Hollywood. Cinema fans lined the streets five deep and it was impossible to park for five blocks. Warner Brothers were alleged to have paid $30,000 for one camera spot for the evening. Vivien arrived with Olivier at 9:30. The press reported that she was "so thrilled her lips tremble. She isn't quite sure she's the winner. She doesn't know how these things are done."[37] She asked nervously "Wouldn't it be wonderful if I did get it?"[38] She toyed with her food until Hollywood ceded the microphones to figures who would dominate it in many ways for the next half a century. Bob Hope, with his rectangular grin, 'gagged' that the evening was more like "a benefit for David Selznick.'[39] A special award was given in memory of Douglas Fairbanks, Senior, and "the audience is silent while Young Doug, husky with emotion, thanks the industry."[40] Hattie McDaniel, Mammy in the film, specially invited to Selznick's table, was a sensational winner of best supporting actress, beating Olivia de Havilland and scoring a triumphant victory for her race. She returned to the table "still sobbing, her arms shielding her face."[41] Then it was Vivien's turn at 1:15 a.m.:

> She's not the confident Scarlett, but an excited, thrilled, sincerely grateful girl. Vivien goes back to her table to the

*Duff Cooper was fifty on 22 February 1940.

congratulations of Bette Davis and many, many others.[42]

Vivien's speech was eloquent. Speaking slowly, she said:

> If I were to mention all those who've shown me such wonderful generosity through *Gone with the Wind* I should have to entertain you with an oration as long as *Gone with the Wind* itself.[43]

When Vivien posed with Selznick, she held her Oscar to her breast. When she posed with Olivier, she let him perch higher than her, and tactfully kept the Oscar out of the photo. The Oscar was too heavy to transport to London in wartime so she left it with Sunny until 1950. Later she used it as a doorstop at home.

Gone with the Wind was released in London on 17 April, a windy afternoon in the middle of the Phoney War. It ran for four years, and Vivien was dubbed "the greatest star England ever gave Hollywood."[44] At the end of the year Winston Churchill, by then Britain's wartime Prime Minister, sat up until 2 a.m. watching it on Ronald Tree's private screen at Ditchley (where he would retreat for safety 'when the moon was high'). His private secretary, Jock Colville, recorded in his clandestine diary: "The P.M. said he was pulverized by the strength of their feelings and emotions."[45]

Waterloo Bridge was released in New York on 17 May (Vivien's third film to come out there since *Gone with the Wind*) and in London on 17 November. It owed much to the dialogue of Robert E. Sherwood's original play and to good, shrewd screen directing. Alan Dent, who first saw it in 1952, drew an analogy with "Marguerite Gautier's debatable dictum that the creature fallen by the wayside never can rise again."[46] Discounting the story as far from the inevitable tragedy, Dent concluded that the end was "as though *Anna Karenina* had fallen under the wheels of a *Streetcar named Desire*."[47] There would have been happier ending if the scriptwriters of Vivien's next film (*Lady Hamilton*) had been at work. In an early scene, Sir William Hamilton discusses the fate of a beautiful statue, which, though it had sunk 'lower and lower into the mud,' had been rescued until at last it found a home in the hands of one who understood "the glory of its beauty… despite its past."[48] In *Waterloo Bridge* everyone acted well – Vivien and

Robert Taylor as the stars, Virginia Field, the ever loyal fellow ballerina who takes to prostitution to help support her friend, Lucille Watson as the imposing yet basically amiable future mother-in-law, Maria Ouspenskaya as the harridan ballet mistress, and C. Aubrey Smith as the Duke. There was a memorably romantic scene in a nightclub which inspired Mervyn LeRoy to return to silence – music, dancing, flickering candles but no dialogue. As he explained: "A look, a gesture, a touch can convey much more meaning than spoken sentences."[49] Contemporary reviewers were unanimous over the most crucial point in Vivien's favor. The film proved that she was not a one-part girl, forever hidebound by Scarlett. She worked a different kind of magic in her poignant portrayal of the ballet dancer who became a gallant Captain's shy fiancé, but was reduced to walking the streets as a reluctant wartime prostitute. Howard Barnes was especially positive in the *New York Herald Tribune*: "The point is, that Miss Leigh is so brilliant and beautiful a leading lady that she gives a dated tragedy immense power and conviction."[50]

A few days later, Barnes wrote a further long and important article about Vivien herself, in which he declared:

> It is apparent, now, though, that her career is based on great talent and great beauty rather than on the supposed break she got when she was picked to play the most popular heroine of our day. Actually *Gone with the Wind* was extremely lucky to have her in it.
>
> Any film, or any stage work for that matter, is blessed by her participation. For here is an actress who combines all of the sorcery of a vivid personality with brilliant acting execution.[51]

Barnes was proud to have spotted her in *Dark Journey* and to have recorded: "Miss Leigh is a leading woman to be watched.[52] He extended his praise to her stage work: "She can do it on the stage, as she is currently serving notice at the Fifty-first Street Theater, where she is the most lovely and persuasive Juliet I have ever seen."[53] In common with most reviewers, Barnes did not think much of the production itself:

> The *Romeo and Juliet* in which she is appearing with

> Laurence Olivier is a highly disappointing Shakespearian revival, to my mind, but not because of her. As bad as Mr. Olivier is, both in his acting and in his directing of the production, as bad as several of the supporting roles are performed, the show is worth seeing for Miss Leigh's lovely Juliet. She not only looks the part that Shakespeare had in mind but she plays it with grace and eloquence.[54]

Romeo and Juliet began its ill-fated life with a disappointing opening at the Geary Theater in San Francisco. The idea was inspired by George Cukor, who thought it would be a good money-spinner. Olivier was keen for that and also to "a little extra impressive acclaim as Shakespearians, not just film actors."[55] One unfortunate incident involved Olivier's love for action. He made a solo entrance, spoke a few lines and then tried to vault over the wall into the Capulet orchard. Alas, he ended up suspended in the middle of the wall, an unfortunate reminder that the actor was no longer sixteen, but thirty-two. "It really does seem extraordinary, that the harder one works and the more effort one puts into a thing the less it is appreciated,"[56] complained Vivien, who, nevertheless, thought San Francisco a very beautiful city.

Though beset by problems, Vivien did not neglect her family, sending a cousin, Paul Fielding, five hundred dollars since he had been enduring "an awful time."[57] They then traveled in a series of private Pullman cars on the Sante Fe Railway to Chicago. The theatre there held 3,500 people and was normally used for concerts. Thus it proved almost impossible to act in. The reviews were consequently varied:

> I have come out better than I expected…as I find Juliet an extremely taxing and difficult part, not that I didn't know that before. However, by dint of strenuous rehearsals, it is getting better and by the time we open in N.Y. it should be alright. It is a perfectly delightful company, all very enthusiastic and young and eager.[58]

The only good things about Chicago were the fine van Gogh's in the Art Gallery and the lakeside walks. The people, Vivien found, "positively moronic."[59]

Romeo and Juliet opened in New York with the novelty of an elaborate revolving stage at the 51st Street Theatre on 9 May. "I know it can't possibly miss being a great success," Vivien's secretary, Sunny, had predicted in January. "What could be more perfect casting than those two darlings for R.and J."[60] And yet fail it did, most resoundingly, eating up $96,000 invested jointly by Olivier and Vivien, the bulk of their savings from recent film triumphs.

There were several possible reasons for this – public antipathy to a Romeo and Juliet who had recently passed through the British divorce courts in real life; the feeling that Hollywood stars were not capable of such major stage roles; the fact that Olivier had already given all he had to offer as Romeo some years earlier; the feeling this his performance was arrogant and lifeless; that he was publicly overshadowed by Vivien, whose recent successes outmatched his, and that he was overstretched by being director and having to deal with many administrative problems.

Brooks Atkinson, drama critic of the *New York Times*, known as 'the butcher of Broadway,' believed the production was too over-blown – twenty-one scenes on moving platforms, expensive doors that closed with a real bang, too many stars, an orchestra that played traditional airs, elaborate lighting designed by Robert Edmond Jones, religious scenes "overlaid with Palestrina chants."[61] Atkinson concluded that the production rushed the performance:

> They had to play so far upstage that it seemed as if they were in another Theater and that two strange actors were playing to some other audience. Shakespeare's casual 'two hours traffic on the stage' lengthened to more than three. A gifted actor had ingeniously designed his own destruction.[62]

Ruth Gordon had an even more bizarre theory. She asked Captain Joe Patterson, founder and proprietor of the *New York Daily News*, what he thought of the play. "I thought his costumes [by Motley] very coarse." Mrs. Gordon explained that the "the doublet was short-short and where Romeo's privates bulged under his tights swung two distracting golden tassels." She concluded: "If Shakespeare had seen the performance I bet *he'd* have been distracted."[63]

There was plenty of advance publicity, some of it somewhat questionable: "See real lovers make love in public."[64] And yet there was no saving it. After the grim notices Olivier offered to refund advance bookings. The play closed after a mere thirty-five performances. While Noël Coward chided them, the Lunts were kind. They were the only people who invited them to dine: "just the four of us, rather than a grand do with white tie," recalled Olivier, "it was kindly calculated to keep us looking *persona grata*.[65]

They left New York to stay in Katharine Cornell's country house in Sneden's Landing. One guest was the man acting the part of Balthasar, John Merivale, the step-brother of John Buckmaster, and the man destined to rescue Vivien towards the end of her life. But on this occasion he was merely accused unfairly of cheating at Chinese checkers and felt it better to leave before she got up the morning.

Meanwhile the Phoney War had turned into real war, and Olivier was anxious to go home and take part in it. He went so far as to announce that he would be leaving America as soon as *Romeo and Juliet* closed on 8 June. However, he was then told by the British Embassy in Washington that all British citizens over thirty-one were to stay in the States. Duff Cooper, the Minister of Information, cabled: "Don't hurry home. You may be more use where you are."[66] He also informed Olivier that Korda would presently arrive in Hollywood. Men were not needed, but planes, guns, and ammunition were. Thus they did their best from afar, with special fund-raising performances, working in the 'Bundles for Britain' office, Olivier completing 200 hours of nerve-wracking flying by November to qualify for a pilot's license. Vivien also went up once but felt she was "very uncourageous.[67] Sunny recalled that Olivier's only faults in life were that "he was a lousy automobile driver and a lousy pilot."[68] Vivien was a little afraid to go up with him, but Sunny politely declined on invitation to join her for moral support.

Leigh Holman decided that Suzanne should be sent to Ernest's sister, Florence Thompson, in Canada for the duration of the war. Vivien went to make some preliminary investigations and was impressed. After a hazardous voyage, Suzanne arrived in Vancouver with her grandmother* and soon afterwards Vivien went to see them in Toronto. She had not seen her daughter for almost a year. She brought her two costumes with velvet

*They traveled on the same boat as Jill Esmond, Tarquin, and his nanny, though the first Mrs. Olivier refused to speak to the mother of the (about to be) second.

jackets and plaid skirts and three Scarlett O'Hara dolls, a gift from David O. Selznick. "Suzanne was looking beautiful and was completely enchanting, she seems to have grown even sweeter."[69] But her mind was perhaps more on Korda's plan that she should make a film about Lady Hamilton, which would be good for propaganda. After a holiday in Martha's Vineyard, Vivien returned to Hollywood and eventually found a new temporary home, 95560 Cedarbrook Road, Goldwater Canyon, Beverly Hills. With it came an old English sheep dog, oddly called Jupiter in spite of being a bitch, and a stray cat. Vivien wrote to Leigh:

> Larry and I are to do a picture about Nelson and Lady Hamilton. I am extremely dubious about it. But now one does not plan a career much as it seems futile and we are certainly only doing this for financial purposes which are useful these days. Hollywood is more odious each time and I loathe it heartily and wish and wish I could come home.[70]

Vivien was preoccupied with a proposal to put money in Canada for the benefit of her mother and Suzanne, but feared it would not last more than seven years. Sunny married Harry Lash on 11 July, and even after that was happy to go on working for Vivien. Once, when Vivien telephoned with instructions late at night, her good-natured husband enquired: "Are you supposed to be working at 11 o'clock at night?"[71] On 15 August Vivien was voted the actress with "the most beautiful face" on the screen at that time, and described as "Britain's lynx-eyed beauty."[72] She was also able to do fund-raising for the Red Cross and paid for an ambulance. She was annoyed that she could not collect for armaments: "Do you think I could be of use if I learnt to fly? Or in fact in any way?"[73] she wrote to Leigh.

On 4 September she wrote again to Leigh:

> I really have no news. We were married as quietly as possible, and I wired you as soon as it was done and would have written beforehand if I had known myself it was going to take place as soon as that.[74]

Their state, described as 'the limelight of adultery,'[75] was at last over.

Chapter 12
The Oliviers

They will join the select company of great American lovers – the Duke and Duchess of Windsor, John Barrymore and Elaine Barrie, and John Smith and Pocohontas, who loved before their time.

Life Magazine, *20 May 1940*

The marriage took place as soon as possible after the two divorces became absolute, and in secret. Garson Kanin, then a youthful motion picture director, was sharing the Cedarbrook Road property with Olivier and Vivien to help with the rent. He went to see Katharine Hepburn, whom he was dating, but more importantly trying to persuade her to take part in a film about the wife of Ulysses Grant. Olivier asked him to best man at the wedding. Kanin enlisted Katharine Hepburn as a "snappy maid of honor,"[1]and the four set off to the Ranch San Ysidro, the exclusive country hotel run by Alvin C. Weingand and Ronald Colman at Montecito, Santa Barbara. The county clerk, Jack Lewis, had gone to some lengths to maintain the secrecy of the occasion, as State Senator Weingand explained:

> He took the filing and put it under a couple of papers and the press came in the next morning but he was out of his office. Afterwards we picked up the papers; they were on his desk and we took the chance of the reporter not seeing it.[2]

The journey was unusual, as Kanin recalled:

> It was absolutely hilarious. They started quarreling rather bitterly. She was sharp-tongued, Larry tough as hell. They were scrapping all the way to the banns.[3]

Unfortunately the wedding party got hopelessly lost and the Municipal Judge, Fred Harsh, succumbed to the alcohol offered to prevent him from retreating home in high dudgeon. When they arrived, the judge was "absolutely potted – out of it,"[4] as Kanin recalled. The union was solemnized (if such a term can be applied to such proceedings on the West Coast) in the presence of the county clerk, in the garden of the ranch, a romantic setting with mountains on the distant skyline. The judge rounded off the proceedings with the declaration: "All right. That's it. Bingo!"[5] Vivien became Mrs. Laurence Olivier shortly after midnight on 31 August. She at once rang her mother. On their honeymoon on Ronald Colman's yacht, the newlyweds were somewhat put out that their great event had not been discovered by the press, though Lee Van Atta was allowed to cover the story in the Santa Barbara *Morning Press*. They tuned in regularly to the radio, in vain. But Garson Kanin recalled that he heard something on the news as he was driving home. The news was already out before the Oliviers realized it.

While the bombs fell on Berkeley Square and Park Lane in London, the filming of *Lady Hamilton* began in Hollywood. Vivien continued to feel that it was ridiculous for her to be there:

> It seems so extraordinary to me to be here, in this country which I never had the slightest wish to come to, and cannot grow to like. My goodness what contracts are responsible for, and how idiotic ever to sign them.[6]

On 26 September, Wyn Holman, Leigh's brother, was killed in an air-raid with his eighteen-year-old daughter. Sympathizing, Vivien added:

> I don't suppose living on the verge of such things makes it any less shocking when they occur.[7]

As a result of this tragedy, Leigh came back from Stornoway to help run the family law practice at 1 Lloyds Avenue in the City.

It is said that Winston Churchill was directly behind Korda's idea of making a film about Nelson and Lady Hamilton. It has even been suggested that he contributed some of the script, Nelson's maiden speech in the House of Lords. Churchill had accepted work from Korda in the 1930s when he was lurking in the political wilderness. It was certainly the convenient presence of the Oliviers in the United States that brought the prospect of such a film to fruition. The plan was to produce a stirring love-drama set in time of war, with a far from subtle message of propaganda: "You cannot make peace with dictators! You have to destroy them – wipe them out."[8] It was exactly the sort of film that appealed to Korda – stirring battle scenes, love, and historical characters, a natural sequence to *The Private Life of Henry VIII* and *Fire Over England.*

The Oliviers were allowed to characterize Nelson and Emma as they pleased. They pored over books for inspiration. Vivien began work on 18 September, pleased to be making a film with Olivier at last:

> The costumes are enchanting, the sets very big, and the script pretty awful, which is about the usual Hollywood combination.[9]

The script changed daily, the scriptwriters working at the side of the set. At times they could have been writing the Olivier's own story, all the way from Emma declaring: "My life really began when I was eighteen. I was beautiful then."[10] Later, Emma's mother asks Emma if she is happy. Seated at the dressing-table, she replies: "Three years ago my only idea of happiness was to be married to Charles Greville…Then I wanted to be presented at court…I got everything, everything a woman of the world could possibly wish for, so why shouldn't I be happy?"[11] In a love scene on the terrace before he embarks for Malta, Nelson speaks of "all the wasted years I've been without you."[12] He continues:

> You are married and I am married and the magic and the music of the ballroom – these things become rather blurred – they stand out very clearly in the dawn. Your life is here.

> My life is there. We must obey the creeds and codes that we've sworn our lives to. I know that I must not come back. And I know that nothing in this world can keep me away…[13]

The encounter between Emma and Lady Nelson, played by Gladys Cooper with considerable *sang-froid* and the occasional raised eyebrow, had echoes of Vivien and Jill Esmond. And Kenneth Tynan would certainly have adhered to Lady Nelson's rebuke of her wayward husband: "Find a public hero and there you'll find as sure as fate a woman parasite. Don't you realize that all she wants is to flutter about in your glory, to use you for her own ambition and conceit…"[14]

The film was made in record time because Korda ran out of money after 7 November:

> Alex Korda is directing it himself and is very pleasant to work with – quite unlike anyone else to do with films, as one can talk to him of other subjects, and he will speak most eruditely and amusingly about them. The cameraman is Hungarian too, and they both speak the funniest English, but at the same time take it upon themselves to correct one another! Alex has been heard to say such things as 'Print both three!'[15]

Moura Budberg remembered Korda reproaching Vivien in his strong Hungarian accent: "My dear Vivien, Emma was vulgar." To which she replied: "My dear Alex, you wouldn't have given me a contract, if I had been vulgar!"[16] Korda also took full advantage of Vivien's type-casting as Scarlett in his directing of the film. Her sweeping run through the vista of rooms and along the terrace is very similar to her advance down the steps of Tara.

Olivier made himself up to look dashing and piratical, while delivering his lines with his customary English rhetoric. He was made to look somewhat wooden and stiff by historically inaccurate padded costumes. Thomas Kiernan believed that Vivien's portrayal was more complex than Olivier's:

> Indeed, she stole the picture from him, a fact that he immediately recognized and that left him not a little annoyed. He might have subdued his stage portrayal of Romeo in order not to dominate Vivien's Juliet, but in *Lady Hamilton*...he made no such concessions. The plain and simple truth was that as a screen actor, he still lacked the natural accomplishment of Vivien Leigh. Not only that, but as a screen team they failed to generate the electricity they had expected to, and it was his fault.[17]

Vivien's name was credited above Olivier's on the opening titles of *Lady Hamilton.* Significantly, they never appeared in a film together again.

Lady Hamilton ran into problems with Joseph Breen of the Hays Office, because the story showed a man living in remorseless sin with another man's wife. For a time it appeared that it might not receive a Production Code Seal of Approval. The matter was resolved by adding a moralistic scene with Nelson's gout-ridden clergyman father ticking him off for his wayward life and Nelson replying contritely:

> I know. You are right in all you say. I realize it is a wicked, inexcusable thing to do and I am ashamed at my weakness in surrendering to it.[18]

Once that matter was resolved, most of the scene was cut. Later Korda's motives in making the film were questioned before the Senate Foreign Relations Committee in Washington. Korda was due to answer charges that Alexander Korda Films was a propaganda and espionage center working for Britain in the United States. The hearing was set for 12 December 1941, but when the Japanese bombed Pearl Harbor and America entered the war on 7 December the matter became irrelevant.

Lady Hamilton was released in London on 4 April 1941, and as *That Hamilton Woman* in New York on 30 July. The film became a box office success and popular as far afield as South Africa and Russia. The reviews were by no means all flattering. James Agate declared that only Nell Gwyn or Mrs. Jordan could have done full justice to Emma:

> Miss Vivien Leigh gives us nothing of either side of the picture; she lacks equally Emma's charm and Emma's vulgarity. Her *Lady Hamilton* is an ultra-refined young woman, who, on Nelson's demise, must inevitably have declined to weeds, barouche and memories. Her performance throughout *Lady Hamilton* reeks of Muswell Hill at its most respectable; she is as much like a tom-boy as a tom-cat. Indeed, less. And if Vivien has any smack of Romney about her I ought to be cast to play Don Quixote. A thoroughly bad performance,* always presuming that Mr. Korda had any notion of presenting the real Emma...Mr. Laurence Olivier makes a brave, unaffected and successful Nelson...The picture is ultimately rescued by the Battle of Trafalgar, which is a grand job from start to finish, even if you have to forgive Mr. Korda's trained choir on board H.M.S. *Victory*.[19]

The film acquired a staunch and loyal admirer in Winston Churchill. When the Prime Minister took to staying at Ditchley, Sidney Bernstein and Jack Beddington, from the Ministry of Information, would send films down to entertain Ronnie Tree's distinguished guest. Tree wrote later:

> Whether it was the story of Lord Nelson or the beauty of Vivien Leigh, this film appealed enormously to the Prime Minister. He was delighted with it and on future occasions wanted it shown again and again, so I was told afterwards, much to the tedium of others who were forced to sit through it with him.[20]

Crossing the high seas for the Atlantic Charter Meeting with President Roosevelt in August 1941, Churchill had the film shown to those accompanying him in *The Prince of Wales*. Though seeing it for the fifth time, the Prime Minister was still moved to tears. He declared: "Gentlemen, I thought this film would interest you, showing great events similar to those

*Yet on 2 February 1942, Agate conceded to a friend: "You may be right in maintaining that Vivien Leigh can 'make rings' round Ellen Terry."(James Agate, *Ego 5*.)

in which you have been taking part."[21]

When old and in semi-dotage at Chartwell, Sir Winston had a screen and two projectors installed in the basement. He would sit there in a huge chintz-covered armchair, the smoke from his cigar curling up through the beam of the projector. And amongst the films shown – inevitably most of them Westerns – it was *Lady Hamilton* at which he stared "time and again."[22] While the film retains a strong period atmosphere of romance, some of the lines do not bear the passage of time. On television *Alias Smith and Jones* re-played a love scene between Olivier and Vivien to bursts of studio laughter in 1987. The pair were clinched on the terrace at a New Year's Eve party, 1799:

> Nelson: "Dawn of a new century."
> Emma: "1800. How strange it sounds."
> Nelson: "What a century it's been. Marlborough rode to war and Washington crossed the Delaware – Louis XVI and Marie Antoinette – the last of the Stuarts – Peter the Great – Voltaire – Clive of India – Bonaparte."
> Emma: "Nelson!"
> [They merge in a kiss.]
> Nelson: "Now I've kissed you through two centuries."[23]

When filming was over, Vivien toyed with the possibility of playing in Shaw's *Caesar and Cleopatra* opposite Cedric Hardwicke, but resolved to take the chance of returning home to London.

> Nelson: "We'll go back to London together."
> Emma: "I would have died if you'd left me here."[24]

First Vivien went to Vancouver to see her daughter.

Suzanne had begun school at a convent in Vancouver. Mrs. Hartley reported to Leigh: "She went off with Mother Bailey quite happily and thrilled with the idea of being with other children."[25] Vivien's visit in November resulted in some absurd publicity, the *News Herald* of Vancouver declaring that Vivien had arrived secretly because she was afraid that Suzanne might be kidnapped and held for ransom. Vivien was forced to issue a statement:

"There is absolutely nothing to the story. And it is certainly not a publicity stunt."[26] The visit had the unfortunate consequence that Mother Bailey forced Suzanne to leave the convent. In the New Year, Leigh was justly furious at "one of the most unpardonable things"[27] he had ever heard. Mother Bailey claimed that, now that it was publicly known that Suzanne's parents were divorced, they could no longer keep her. She had received a letter from the Symphony Society complaining that the daughter of a film star was at the school. Leigh wrote to Gertrude:

> I was often beaten myself by the lying artifices of the Press when I was married to Vivien, but that any professedly Christian woman should pay such attention to press reports as to risk injuring Suzanne by yet another change, would to my mind give Christ a nasty shock…I do implore you to bring up Suzanne in your own image and not that of the Mother Superior or the Sec. of the Symphony Society.[28]

Leigh managed to add £100 a quarter to the lump sum Vivien had put at the disposal of her mother and daughter. Suzanne was soon settled in a new school which she liked, and to judge from her grandmother's cine-films enjoyed a fairly carefree war with lots of skiing and riding and boat rides. From time to time Gertrude toyed with the idea of coming back to England, wanting to be reunited with Vivien. It was tiring and at times lonely having charge of a seven-year-old granddaughter, but she always stayed with Suzanne, more than fulfilling the role of mother which Vivien had relinquished.

Leigh kept in close touch with Gertrude, even confiding at one point that he thought he could marry again, "if I could think of anyone."[29] Charmingly he concluded: "What a pity you did not have some more daughters. I am sure I should have adored them all."[30] For once it was Leigh who was not entirely straight-forward. Towards the end of 1940 he had enjoyed a romance with a young ballerina, described by Oswald Frewen as "a sweet wild ingenuous creature, beautiful full-face with gazelle eyes."[31] Leigh was then living at 49 Arlington House, behind the Ritz. After dinner at Prunier's, the three made their way through bomb-ridden Mayfair to the flat, where there was some discussion as to whether the ballerina would stay. She was upset and felt she should return to her ballet-dancers' dormitory, so as not to excite gossip. She feared Leigh would be cross, but he said, "Why, of course," and offered to drive her back. Oswald loaned his car and, as they reached the garage, the attendant enquired, "Are your shoes all right? A man was killed in the alleyway you've come down, his head split open – but I think they've sanded it well."[32] When Leigh returned he was more forthcoming than usual, describing how he wanted to marry her. They had both agreed to write to her parents for permission. This Leigh had done, but the girl had not, probably from indecision. Oswald Frewen concluded:

> I think dear old Leigh will buy more trouble if he buys *her*. He was 40 yesterday and 40 can't marry 19 when 19 is on the stage.[33]

Nothing came of it, though Leigh was still in touch with the ballerina as late as February 1944. The other candidate was Prince Dimitri's sister-in-law, Countess Kutuzoff, but again, this fizzled out.

In December 1940 Vivien revisted Atlanta for a second premiere of *Gone with the Wind* in aid of British War Relief. It was not a success. Margaret Mitchell was incensed at the idea that Vivien and Hattie McDaniel might re-enact the corset scene on stage but the latter, in any case, declined to replay Mammie in segregated Atlanta. The Oliviers' plane was late and Miss Mitchell had to preside at the special luncheon, to her consternation and that of the Atlanta charity ladies and the MGM representatives. Olivier was about to return to Britain and Vivien determined to go with him. She ignored her seven-year film contract with Selznick on the grounds that it was wartime. Irene Selznick wrote:

> David's appeals went unheeded; she treated them as an imposition. The more time passed, the less she felt inclined to honor her obligations. In the early years I was frankly on her side; I felt she was being courageous and romantic, and that after the war she would make amends. I was wrong. It turned out that I was the romantic one.[34]

The Oliviers returned to Britain at the end of December. Asked why, they replied: "Because it is our home."[35] The *Excambion* reached Lisbon, where an air of hysteria prevailed. Vivien, listening to the German spoken on board, got the impression that they might be on the point of falling into Nazi hands. From Lisbon they could not fly direct to London. At length they made a seven-hour flight to Bristol (during which the cockpit appeared to be on fire) and landed in the middle of an air-raid. In due course they were back at Durham Cottage.

There was some publicity, none of it unfavorable. Having not slept for two nights, Vivien said that she thought a German airplane had been tailing them: "It didn't feel too good at the time."[36] She had heard of the air-raids naturally, but had not experienced them. She was surprised that people took so little notice of the warnings. Both Oliviers hinted at plans for plays and films and Olivier told a reporter at Paddington Station: "We feel we have stayed away long enough."[37] In their first days back they visited Roger Livesey and Ursula Jeans in King's Langley, attended John Mills's wedding to Mary Hayley Bell on 16 January and were reunited with the Ralph Richardsons. Lady Richardson remembered:

> They were enchanting, so much in love. It was one of their best times…They liked it to be seen. It was not a secret love affair.[38]

Leigh saw Vivien and thought her "a dream of beauty."[39] He saw her again in February, writing: "I have never seen her so lovely, but she looks a little tired, I think as the result of one of her usual winter colds."[40]

On 23 February they took part in the Services Variety Show on the radio, broadcasting from 'a theatre in the South.' Olivier played the cameo role of a trapper in Emeric Pressburger's propaganda film, *The 49th Parallel*, as a public demonstration of his patriotism. His accent left much to be desired. Olivier failed to get into the RAF but was seconded to the Royal Navy Air Station at Worthydown, just north of Winchester, a school for trainee air-gunners. He lived in a bungalow at Headbourne Worthy, three miles from the aerodrome. According to the racing driver, Rob Walker, who was undertaking advanced pilot training, Olivier was "a terrible pilot."[41] Having learnt to fly in the clear skies of California, Britain's thick fog presented him with more than a few problems.

Vivien's first idea was to try to join the Old Vic, but Tyrone Guthrie decided that she was too much the film star and "not a good enough actress."[42] She therefore settled with Olivier in the country, making occasional, hurried visits to London, meeting old friends such as Leigh and Oswald Frewen, the latter briefly on leave from Scapa Flow. She also sat for her portrait to David Jagger.

In July the Oliviers lunched with Noël Coward, his secretary Lorn Loraine, and Joyce Carey. Coward noted: "Larry not very happy. Think it a great mistake for him not to live in Mess."[43] *Lady Hamilton* opened at the end of the month, assuring the British of the patriotism of both Oliviers. Olivier and Vivien went to see the film in London in August and Vivien then began rehearsals for Shaw's *The Doctor's Dilemma*. The play was to tour in the provinces for six months before opening in London on 4 March 1942. This meant more periods of separation but in the 1950s Vivien looked back on their meetings as happy memories:

> I realize that the memories I cherish most are not of first night successes, but of simple, everyday things: walking through our garden in the country after rain; sitting outside a café in Provence, drinking the vin de pays; staying at a little country hotel in an English market town with Larry, in the early days after our marriage, when he was serving in the Fleet Air Arm and I was touring Scotland so that we had to make long treks to spend our weekends together.[44]

When Vivien came down to Winchester, Olivier would get out his prized Invicta car "with it chromium entrails bursting through the bonnet,"[45] to collect her. Sometimes she drove herself in a small box car, and Lady Richardson recalled a journey to the station and an accident which turned the car right over. Vivien emerged "completely unruffled."[46] But many of Vivien's journeys were made by train where she was a small figure in raincoat and headscarf, invariably deep in a novel by Dickens (she read the entire canon in the war years.)

Vivien rehearsed in London and then opened at the Opera House in Manchester on 8 September. In Liverpool she was joined by Leigh and Oswald Frewen, and all three stayed with Maurice Stern, whom she described as "Mamma's cotton beau," though Oswald mis-read it as "Mamma's rotten beau."[47] The play was performed at the Royal Court Theatre, and Oswald found it "a *most* entertaining and damned well acted play…she's as adorable as ever, and greatly improved in her acting. I *think* her stage speaking voice is even more beautiful than her face."[48]. Maurice Stern's two daughters drove them to his house, Upton Place. Oswald wrote: "When Maurice Stern heard that she and Leigh were staying the night he asked if they wanted a double room. I'm hardly surprised. Answer *was* no (alas).[49]

Leigh thought Vivien spoke a bit slowly in the first act, but in a letter she explained that that was "because I think it gives the weight and maturity Jennifer requires."[50] The play moved to Leeds in October, and then went on to Blackpool (breaking records). Vivien, living in the country, was able to ride for the first time in four years. She went through the formality of registering for national service, though as a member of a reserved profession she would never be called up. The company proceeded on to Leicester. Before going to the King's Theatre in Glasgow, Vivien saw Orson Welles's masterpiece, *Citizen Kane*, and thought it "most original and interesting, though not such an advance on French or Russian pictures, as one was led to believe."[51]

Later in November Vivien was playing in Edinburgh at a time when Cecil Beaton was there taking photographs to illustrate a *Vogue* article being written by Lady Stanley of Alderley, which concluded that the city was relatively unscathed by war and a popular place for leave. Beaton was delighted to have the chance to see *The Doctor's Dilemma*, a play he knew well. As stage-struck as ever, the mere ringing of the bell for 'Curtain Up' was "like gunfire"[52] to him. He noted:

> Play dated and poorly produced – seemed very out of date. Vivien monotonous – though lovely…We went behind – Vivien in dark purple velvet costume and black hat, with sables of last act looked so beautiful and beguiled us by being so completely unspoilt. She is a remarkable little person to have the character not to be spoilt by her tremendous success…[53]

Beaton took a memorable photograph of Vivien at her dressing-table. Four days later he went to collect her, arriving to see her dry in the third act. He inspected her costumes, which, close to, were like circus clothes. He questioned her dresser and later wrote a characteristically perceptive account of all he saw and heard:

> The dresser said how much both she and Miss Leigh preferred stage to cinema but of course Miss Leigh's life is her work. Vivien was as sweet as ever and as lovely – though older and more tired. She said that she liked to arrive early at the theatre so as to be in her dressing room as much as possible. She loved talking to people in her dressing room and dressing - receiving messages and letters. She loved the life of the theatre so much that she could never stop realizing how happy and lucky she was to be in the theatre. She is the trooper *par excellence.* Her dressing room has it flowers – its mascots – the electric heater – the tin kettle that go with her – in a basin her dresser is washing her 'smalls.'
>
> We went to the Deguise for supper – not once did Vivien's face show that she knew she was being stared at – and she dealt firmly but nicely with the irritating requests for autographs. We gossiped about the theatre until after 3 o'clock in the morning. One by one the other tables emptied and the lights were turned down until we had to move. We went back to the lounge of the hotel and here we sat for further hours while the night porter hoovered the carpets and dusted the armchairs – more lights out until we sat in the light of one overhead lamp – Vivien looked tired and drawn – and said how exhausting the theatre is – everyone prematurely old and each time they assemble at the station for the next journey they look smaller and tireder than before.
>
> Vivien is almost incredibly lovely. Hollywood is at her feet. She knows if all else fails she has merely to go out there to make a fortune.* Meanwhile she can experiment and indulge her fancies in the theatre. She wants to do Shaw's

*On 14 October Vivien had written Leigh: "I seem to be getting a great deal of money one way and another." (VL to LH 14 October 1941)

> *Caesar & Cleopatra* next. She is madly in love with her husband – who adores her – and is convinced he is a much greater person than herself. Her former husband dotes upon and adores her still – she is unspoiled – has many loyal friends and only ambition to improve as an actress. The adulation of her beauty leaves her cold – she loves talking late into the night and here she found someone intrigued and stimulated to continue even until she was tired.[54]

Soon afterwards Vivien was able to join Olivier at Headbourne Worthy for Christmas. She wrote to Leigh that their Christmas had been "hilarious and not very restful. This little bungalow looks very strange with two beautiful Sickerts. We are thrilled with them both."[55] Early in 1942 *The Doctor's Dilemma* came to London. In February Leigh reported to Gertrude in Canada: "There is the most charming poster of Viv in the tubes for the play. It makes traveling on the escalator a great pleasure."[56]

The Doctor's Dilemma was the first of many plays that Vivien undertook for Hugh (Binkie) Beaumont, whose company H.M. Tennent dominated the London stage in the 1940s and 1950s. It was also her first Bernard Shaw. Alan Dent believed that this version surpassed all other revivals of the play and, indeed, of any revivals of any Shaw play. In a particularly lavish production Vivien's hair was styled afater a 1901 picture postcard of Dame Irene Vanbrugh. She fitted Shaw's stage description of Mrs. Dubedat to perfection: "beyond all demur an arrestingly good-looking young woman. She has something of the grace and romance of a wild creature, with a good deal of the elegance and dignity of a fine lady."[57]

Dent pointed out a problem that would dog Vivien's stage portrayals for the rest of her life:

> There was an axiom in the craft that a good actress had better be a plain Jane with no beautiful nonsense about her, that pretty features were both a distraction and a handicap, and that the business of a player's face was to register and communicate emotion – and not to reduce the beholder to a state of driveling adoration whatsoever she might be trying to say, register, or communicate with those too lovely features.[58]

Thus many reviewers were critical or wholly mute, but Ivor Brown wrote in *Punch*:

> She sails exquisitely into the play as it were from a Sargent canvas (the costumes being 1906, the year of the play's publication), and brings to it all the quick loveliness which she has lately bestowed in the film-studios on two less reputable beauties – Miss Scarlett O'Hara and Emma, Lady Hamilton.[59]

In 1943 Cecil Beaton wrote a well-considered article about the theatre in wartime. He detected a renaissance and urged:

> If ever the theatre were given an opportunity to show its independence and superiority over the cinema, it is at this time, when Hollywood is producing a particularly inept assortment of lifeless re-hashes and phony heroics. Now is the moment for the theatre to strike a body-blow against its mechanized rival.[60]

He gave *The Doctor's Dilemma* a favorable mention:

> It is heartening that there has grown a considerable public for revivals of such a high order that Shaw and Turgeniev can be put as successful commercial propositions and can run until the cast no longer knows what it is intending to portray. *The Doctor's Dilemma* did not fill the Haymarket for over a year solely on account of the flower-like beauty of the Scarlett O'Hara of the films…[61]

Beverley Baxter, the M.P. and one-time editor of the *Daily Express*, whose wife Edie was Gertrude's best friend from Canada, took the same line in the *Evening Standard*:

> Vivien Leigh has accomplished what Katharine Cornell did in New York. Their feminine charms have beaten the critics

> who for 50 years tried to drive Shaw's plays into the discard or Sloane-square. Except for *The Doctor's Dilemma* and 2 or 3 admirable British documentary war plays there is not one English play of ideas in the West End today.[62]

Kitty Black, who worked for Beaumont, hailed Vivien as "the brightest star Binkie added to the Tennent stable."[63] Vivien played opposite the Irish actor, Cyril Cusack. On the second night (5 March) all funds were devoted to the Royal Naval War Libraries. St. Patrick's Day, a fortnight later, was memorable for another reason. Cusack celebrated his national saint's day with such enthusiasm that he was utterly incapable of appearing at the evening performance. This earned him the sack, and there was a monumental row because the understudy had not learned the part and was obliged to read his lines from the book. The next contender was Peter Glenville,* a young actor later famous as a director. Getting to know Vivien at this time he thought her "almost too much in command of herself, of her beauty, and of her success."[65] He judged that "her ability to entrance, entertain, and even to manage and organize every group of people she encountered would have done credit to an ambassadress."[66] Another new and lasting friend was Sir Kenneth Clark, Director of the National Gallery, whose office was near the Haymarket's stage door. A worshiper of beauty, and often a lover of the beauties themselves (though never Vivien's lover), he recalled:

> On matinée days I used to call in between performances. I noticed then that when she put a turban round her head and grease all over her face she looked more beautiful than ever: which shows how much her beauty was based on structure and proportion, independent of artifice. From then on we met frequently.[67]

In his memoirs Clark expanded on his reasons for liking her:

> I used to make for her rather better tea than her dresser would have done. At first I went because I enjoyed looking at her…

*In 1943 John Gielgud stepped into the breech when Glenville fell ill, having learned the part over the weekend. This marked the beginning of a long and close friendship with Vivien.

> But very soon I went because I enjoyed her company and was fascinated by her character. She was not only intelligent, she had style... Vivien's conversation had much in common with that of Gwendolen in *The Importance of Being Earnest*; which examples imply an ear for the rhythm of words, a personal voice, and an occasional sacrifice of the whole truth in the interest of economy. These seem to me the chief characteristics of style, and Vivien had them all.[68]

One day Clark was lunching with Vivien at Wheeler's when the tireless hostess Lady Colefax emerged from the back room. Clark wrote:

> I greeted her, but some naughty instinct prevented me from introducing my exquisitely beautiful companion. As soon as I got home the telephone rang – it had been ringing all afternoon – and Sibyl's voice, hysterical with fury, asked: "Who was that? Who was that?" "Vivien Leigh." "Oh, of course, how stupid of me." In ten days time we were asked to luncheon to meet the Oliviers. "Have you met my young people?" said Sibyl as we entered.[69]

Alan Dent also met her while she was rehearsing *The Doctor's Dilemma*. He became a friend by declaring that he believed she had brains as well as beauty. Mindful of her role as Lady Hamilton, Dent was given the task of persuading Vivien to review a new biography of Emma, *Milady* by Bradela Field, published by Constable. The piece appeared in *John O'London's Weekly* and was a rare literary venture. Vivien went to some pains to justify why she should agree to review the book, and outlined her duty as a critic. She felt the author's task was completed "with great verve, assurance, vividness, accuracy, raciness and ease – and at the expense of words which some may find *overwhelming*."[70] She criticized the author for telling only half the story – the years 1765-1800 – and felt she should have told "the *whole* story in about *half* the number of words."[71] She concluded that: "A novel or biography of this one's inordinate length needs to be done with the gusto, the wit, the fun and the drive of one of my own favourite authors, Charles Dickens."[72] Vivien's brief career as a reviewer proved that she was conscientious and well-read, thoughtful and not afraid to say what she believed.

Vivien continued to act in *The Doctor's Dilemma* for over a year. The play ran for an unprecedented 474 performances, largely because cinemagoers, delighted with *Gone with the Wind* at the Empire, invariably went straight round to the Haymarket to see Scarlett in person.

As for Olivier, he was still in the Fleet Air Arm, pleased to have a chance to display his patriotism, but frustrated as an actor because he longed to play the great classical roles. Peter Glenville recalled:

> He also wanted to appear with Vivien Leigh because he was very much in love with her. But his love second – a close second, but still second to his obsession with acting the great parts. [73]

Most of the time Olivier was in Hampshire, running an ATC Cadets Camp at the aerodrome, on call all day and part of the night. Looking back on this phase of the war, Olivier wrote: "In these limpid conditions life pursued its uncertain way with quite a lot of happiness in its uncertainty."[74]

In the summer of 1942 Olivier was given leave and Binkie Beaumont let Vivien take the same week. Olivier wrote to Gertrude:

> Vivling's play is *still* a wonderful success. She is most beautiful in it & I think the venture has done her a lot of good – tho' the poor pet is getting so sick of it now that she doesn't know what to do & I'm rather afraid her performance must suffer in consequence on occasions, but she is wonderful.[75]

Leave was therefore nothing short of paradise:

> We went to the furthermost corner of Wales, just to get as far away from every kind of association as we could (most unpatriotic I fear, as we had all been asked for some time to stay put & not move about) but I really do think we needed

> it as both our nerves were in quite a bad way, & we really felt a change was essential. We stayed at a hotel in a place called Aberdaron, 17 miles from any railway & just forgot everything for 8 whole days (at least tried to, & very nearly succeeded). We slept practically all the time for the first 2 days, & then went for walks taking lunch with us & bathed (we had three glorious days in what must be the dreariest summer for years) picked blackberries, talked & read – the sort of life one had forgotten existed. Nobody has ever been made so happy as Vivien makes me – She's my whole life.
>
> If it hadn't been for the continuous drone of a few aircraft always on some horizon we would really have been able to forget the bloody war. We came back much refreshed & proceeded to undo all the good we had done by 3 riotous nights in London in which I'm sorry to say we simply sat up all night? Then both of us back to school again. Oh dear & Oh dear…[76]

Whenever Oswald Frewen was in town, Leigh would arrange a dinner after the theatre with Vivien. At the beginning of September, Vivien was expected but announced that Olivier had gotten an unexpected leave and that it was a case of either both or neither. Oswald wrote:

> "So it's both," said Leigh-oh quizzically. I said "Is this the first time he's darkened your threshold since…? "It is." We dined *à quatre* & after, Leigh & Larry sat on the sofa looking at pictures of Leigh's new house, Woodlands, at Mere & Vivling & I conversed apart, & it was a complete success.[77]

Olivier confirmed this view in his letter to Gertrude:

> A lovely thing happened the other day. Leigh had me to supper with Vivien & Peter Frewen and was perfectly enchanting to me. I found him quite changed – greatly grown in stature & personality. We had a grand evening &

> so after five years that's alright, which is marvelous, isn't it?[78]

Gertrude was still in Canada, but moved Suzanne to Banff. Vivien's daughter, now nearly nine, sometimes skied to school and often rode along the paths of the Rocky Mountains. Suzanne all but became a child star. David Selznick was about to make *Jane Eyre* with Orson Welles as Rochester. At the end of the year he wrote to his brother-in-law, Bill Goetz, very excited at the potential publicity value of casting Suzanne as the young Jane:

> From what I hear of Vivien's child, she is perfect for it. Further, as she has been living in British Columbia through most of her childhood, her accent probably will be greatly in her favor...[79]

The part eventually went to Peggy Ann Garner, because Leigh had no intention of allowing Sue to follow her mother's perilous path.

Chapter 13
Desert Antics

Vivien: "I am a real queen at last – a real, real Queen! Cleopatra the Queen! Oh, I love you making me a Queen."
Claude Rains: "But Queens love only Kings."
Vivien: I will make all the men I love Kings."

Caesar and Cleopatra

In the New Year of 1943 Olivier was granted time away from the Fleet Air Arm to film *The Demi-Paradise* for Anthony Asquith, a propaganda film to encourage the British to like the Russians. He was frequently used to make recruiting speeches, and was finally won round to the idea that actors could do more good within their own profession than masquerading in uniform. Jack Beddington also wanted Olivier to make a film of Shakespeare's *Henry V*. Apparently he thought of Vivien for the small role of Princess Katharine, but on 6 March it was announced that David Selznick object to this under the terms of her American contract. The film was to prove a turning point in Olivier's life and a considerable challenge to his skill as actor and director. After *Henry V* he would never be the same again.

While filming *The Demi-Paradise*, Olivier leased a house previously lived in by Noël Coward at Fulmer in Buckinghamshire. There were a number of fellow actors and actresses in the vicinity, John Mills and his wife, Rex Harrison and Lilli Palmer, David and Primmie Niven. David Niven told John Cottrell that he arrived at the Oliviers' house with Brendan Bracken, then Minister of Information:

> There was Larry in some sort of rug singing the Messiah – that was something appalling; Vivien was draped in some extraordinary garment like a sheet and Bobby Helpmann wore a leopard-skin jock strap with a kitten in it.[1]

Roger Livesey and his wife, Ursula Jeans, took Vivien to meet Rachel Kempson, Michael Redgrave's wife, who was in the London Clinic in March following the birth of her daughter, Lynn. Lady Redgrave began a long friendship with Vivien, always preferring to see her alone rather than at large gatherings:

> I'll never forget my first sight of her in reality. So exquisitely beautiful with the happy, mischievous, gay yet almost fragile joyous look. She lit up the room.[2]

The Doctor's Dilemma celebrated a year on the London stage on 5 March* with a party attended by Olivier, Diana Wynyard, Carol Reed, Ivor Novello, a bearded Ronald Squire, and Kay Hammond. Vivien's image was much on display. A new portrait drawing by Serge Rodzianko of her in stage costume was shown at the Knoedler Gallery in April in aid of the Yugoslav Relief Society, and in May three new drawings by Augustus John were exhibited at the Leicester Galleries in a private view dubbed "surely the most colourful private view of this war."[3]

In the early summer Vivien joined a group of stars, including Dorothy Dickson, Nicholas Phipps, Leslie Henson, and Beatrice Lillie (who had lost her son in action the year before), to tour North Africa in a revue called *Spring Party* produced by John Gielgud. They set off with Binkie Beaumont in June after several false alarms and stopped for an excellent breakfast in Lisbon. This was a poignant moment for Vivien, for on 1 June Leslie Howard had been shot down flying from Lisbon, following a visit to Spain and Portugal for the British Council. They flew on to Gibraltar and, after four days of rehearsal, began to play to packed and receptive audiences. Vivien described it to her mother:

> We always had two performances a day and frequently

*It finally closed 25 April.

> 3. A ship or hospital in the morning. It was particularly exciting playing on board the aircraft carriers where the men not only sat in the body of the hangar but up in the struts (or whatever they're called) so we just saw their feet dangling.[4]

Vivien recited Lewis Carroll's 'You are old, Father William,' or Clemence Dane's 'Plymouth Hoe.' Sometimes she took part in 'The Decoy' with Leslie Henson. She wore a crinoline Scarlett O'Hara-style dress. From Gibraltar they went to Algiers and gave eight performances in three days, spending one evening with General Eisenhower and another with Sir Arthur Tedder, Air C-in-C Mediterranean Air Command, both of whom Vivien found "absolutely charming." Harold Macmillan was a spectator on 9 June:

> The rumblings of a storm are beginning to reach me, and the Americans are beginning to get all het up again. But nothing will prevent me going tonight to see Beatrice Lillie, Leslie Henson, Vivien Leigh, etc…[5]

The troupe then went to a small town called Bougie to play to the Eighth Army for the first time:

> We arrived a very short while before the curtain was due to rise and the costumes which were coming by road had not arrived so the show started with us going on in the clothes we could muster from our own baggage. It was *boiling* hot and I think it was there we first came into contact with all the various insects that make things unpleasant. Another difficulty was water for baths of which there was none, so none of us felt particularly refreshed after our traveling and after the two shows. However the following evening after the theatre we went swimming on a most exquisite part of the coast.[6]

Alec Guinness was serving in the Navy in Djidjelli and was surprised to receive a summons from Vivien and Bea Lillie to attend the show. He and a friend thumbed a lift to Bougie but were not allowed into the theatre. However, they were able to see their friends in the dressing room for twenty minutes or so. There was some anxiety about their return journey but Vivien came to the rescue. Guinness wrote:

> Vivien said she would fix it for us and went straight into bold action. She buttonholed, with all her wheedling charm, a starry-eyed Admiral. Caressing the lapels of his uniform, admiring his campaign ribbons, she suddenly asked what he was doing for the next few hours. His eyes danced with excitement as he blushingly replied "Nothing!" "Then," Vivien went on, "you won't be needing your car."[7]

To his chagrin she then commandeered the car to transport Guinness and his friend to their ship. The bemused Admiral was rewarded with a kiss.

The party then traveled by car to Constantine, "a breathtakingly lovely drive with scenery which is a cross between California and Bavaria,"[8] where they performed in a small opera house set in woodland. Nor were there any curtains. "None of these sort of things matter one bit though, because the boys are thrilled to be entertained and are so touchingly grateful for it, and when they all join in "The King" at the end it is unbearably moving."[9]

In Tunis, Bea Lillie, Dorothy Dickson, and Vivien stayed in a villa lately occupied by General von Arnim, before the spectacular defeat of the Afrika Korps at Cap Bon. "I slept in his room, which felt very odd when one considered what a short time before he had actually been there, also of all the unpleasant last hours he must have spent in that room."[10] Peter Daubeny, the theatrical impresario, then serving with the Coldstream Guards, sat up one night at the villa while Beatrice Lillie, "stricken with dysentery, still managed to look poised and gracious under the strain of nature, and to entertain me at the same time."[11] Daubeny (who lost an arm in the Salerno landing soon afterwards) was among those who watched the troupe perform before King George VI at Air Marshal Sir Arthur Coningham's villa at Hamamet. Vivien wrote:

> We played in the open air on a white marble terrace with three great white arches behind us – the centre one leading

> into the house and from where we made our entrances and exits. The audience, about 60 people, sat on a further shallow terrace. It was a night of perfect beauty with a huge moon which shone on the sea only about 30 yards behind where the little audience was sitting. We were all presented to him afterwards, and he told me how much he'd liked my 'Ode to Plymouth' written by Clemence Dane (which was one of the pieces I did in the show). We talked for quite some time. He was looking extremely well and never stuttered once the whole time and stayed at the party until about 1:30, and we all drove back after what we felt had been a most memorable and wonderful evening.[12]

The next port of call was Tripoli, where their show in the Roman Amphitheatre at Leptis Magna was attended by General Montgomery. He described their work as "a battle winning factor."[13] Marshal of the RAF Sir John Grandy, then serving with Fighter Command in the Middle East, recalled being surprised that Vivien was to 'give recitations" from the classics to the troops, as he felt this an odd choice for "an open air audience of tough, rough, hardened men on temporary rest from battle."[14] However, he continued:

> I was completely wrong. The sight of this small, beautiful woman, by herself, in that vast Arena, speaking the most perfect English was breathtaking; there was dead silence for each piece, followed by a great roar of applause and acclaim. The soldiers, sailors, airmen, all of us there, and there were many nationalities, were spellbound; it was a resounding success.[15]

On 28 June they flew to Cairo, an extraordinary oasis in wartime, filled variously with those winning the war and those actively avoiding it. There was more news for her mother in Canada:

> The Flambeau trees were all in blossom and looked absolutely wonderful. They are rather like Acacias only a

> brilliant scarlet. We stayed at Shepheards and I remembered you'd sent me postcards from there when I was at school. The heat was appalling all during our stay, just like living in a Turkish bath all day and night. We gave two performances at Suez, one in a ship and the other on a little stage put up in the sand while the men, 6000 of them, sat in the Open Air. We played two days in Alexandria which I thought very lovely and then back to Cairo. It could all have been perfect but for the heat which was terribly exhausting. The war is non-existent in Egypt and to see huge tables spread with every sort of deliciousness, and bowls of cream was extraordinary. There were parties every night and altogether it was the sort of life one has quite forgotten about.[16]

The party arrived shortly after Basil Dean had faced criticism that ENSA's activities in the Middle East had been "a story of missed opportunities."[17] Transport difficulties had prevented performers getting to remote outposts, nor had they performed enough in Cairo or Alexandria where boredom had led to excessive drinking by the British troops. Patrick Kinross judged the show "much too sophisticated" for the troops and Vivien's renderings "pathetic" and "sentimental," though the troops seemed pleased and liked looking at her. Maie Casey, wife of the UK Minister of State in the Middle East, gave a luncheon at which the military stuck to one end of the room and the less serious to the other. Kinross attempted a few words with Vivien but was "ejected by Sholto Douglas* who monopolized her for the rest of her visit."[18]

Sir Miles Lampson, the British Ambassador, attended the show at the Ezbekiah Theatre on the day his wife produced a daughter. He though Vivien most attractive to look at, and talking to her judged her "a nice little thing."[19] The stars dined with the Ambassador on 2 July, having requested a quiet evening followed by sitting out in the garden. They arrived very late and sat down to dinner at 1 a.m. Prince and Princess Aly Khan were amongst the few guests. By the time they reached the garden Bea Lillie was "completely

*Later Marshal of the RAF Lord Douglas of Kirtleside (1893-1969), then A.O.C.-in-C. Middle East Command. His *Times* obituary described him as a "companion who could play as hard as he worked and could bring to his play the same measure of concentration with the result that it sometimes proceeded to most unusual lengths."

blotto,"[20] causing concern to the others, while becoming more amusing with every glass she drank. Dorothy Dickson kept an attentive eye on her. The stars departed at 3:45 in the morning, leaving the Ambassador to bemoan the punishing inroads on the Embassy's whisky supply.

The next night Vivien was taken to see the Pyramids and the Sphinx and then Cairo "more dead than alive, hardly having been to bed at all."[21] After a show in the desert for the most neglected of all the military stations, the party returned to Tripoli at the express request of General Montgomery. News arrived of the invasion of Sicily on 10 July.

They returned to Gibraltar for three weeks. Vivien arrived there soon after the airplane crash in which General Sikorski had died on 4 July. It was a time of general reunion, for Anthony Quayle was ADC to the military Governor and John Perry* was also stationed at Government House.

HMS *Charybdis* had arrived in Gibraltar from Plymouth. Its captain, Lachlan Mackintosh ("a quite wonderful person")[22]+ had met Olivier and Vivien while at the naval air station at Gosport. While she was playing in *The Doctor's Dilemma* in Liverpool, Captain Mackintosh had invited her on board and she had attended a party for the crew at the Adelphi Hotel.[23] She gave *Charybdis* a signed photograph of herself which hung in the wardroom, near those of the King and Queen. Aboard *Charybdis*++ was Noël Coward who have given two solo concerts on successive nights, one for the crew and one for the officers. When they entered the harbor at Gibraltar, the Captain ordered that some of Coward's music should be played by the Royal Marines Band. There was some hasty rehearsal of "I'll see you again," the waltz from *Bitter Sweet*. Noël Coward was delighted and the Commander was informed that he had been seen "embracing the bandleader."[24]

Coward stayed at Government House. The next morning he and John Perry went to meet the concert party at the Rock Hotel. He found them "all deeply sunburned and bubbling with their experiences in North Africa. Binkie [Beaumont] was in charge of them, if such it can called, and seemed, although a trifle weary, to be rising above it with commendable fortitude."[25]

*(1906-1995), director of H.M. Tennent, friend of Binkie Beaumont.

+ Later Vice Admiral Mackintosh, C.B., D.S.O., D.S.C., The Mackintosh of Mackintosh, 29th Chief of the Clan.

++*Charybdis* was sunk off the Channel Islands in October 1943. Noël Coward noted: "This is the end of the happiest ship I have ever known." (*The Noel Coward Diaries*, 23 October 1942, p. 22)

In the evening Coward and Anthony Quayle went to the show:

> In the middle of it Leslie Henson made an impromptu speech recounting some of the Company's experiences in the Near East and eulogizing the gallant little ladies of the company for the magnificent way they had faced the unendurable hardships of traveling in service aircraft through the heat of the desert. This was, I fear, inaccurate, as the gallant little ladies had told me that morning, with the utmost sincerity that they had never enjoyed themselves so much in their lives. The men received this heartrending account of their Odyssey with remarkable composure.[26]

In the first week of August, Coward took Vivien, Beatrice Lillie, and Dorothy Dickson to lunch on board *Charybdis*: "When finally we went away in the Captain's boat most of the ship's company had collected to wave goodbye.[27] They swam in the chilly water of Rose Bay. The same afternoon Coward and Vivien were having tea together at the Rock Hotel when "an elderly Colonel came up and told us that he had just heard on the news that the matinée idol, Owen Nares, had died suddenly of heart failure. [28]. That night there was a ball at Government House. Coward noted:

> The gallant little ladies came and the gallant little gentlemen too and we all sang songs and danced. Leslie, with tireless vivacity, organized some of us into a performance. H.E. made a speech and thanked us, Curfew time came, everyone said goodnight and went home to bed, and that was that.[29]

Vivien left Gibraltar later in August, feeling that they had made many new friends, wondering when and if they would see them again and praying "so hard for their safety."[30] She returned home, landing at Plymouth, where, like everybody else, she had to be inspected for lice, a process deemed most humiliating by Air Vice Marshal John Elton, who flew with them.[31] Vivien concluded:

> Although I was miserable being away from Larry it's an experience I shall always look back upon with gratitude and great pleasure – in fact I think it is what all actors should be doing during the war as it's a really worthwhile job.[32]

When she returned she found Olivier "working day and night on *Henry V*"[33] and the cherished role of Katharine given to the more or less unknown actress Renée Asherson (who believed she got the part because she fitted the costumes made for Vivien). But Vivien was relieved that Olivier was doing a film rather than risking his life in a war zone.

Work on *Henry V* occupied Olivier from the summer of 1943 until June 1944, during which Vivien kept house for him not far from Denham at Old Prestwick, Gerrards Cross. Oswald Frewen went down to stay and found Vivien forever on the telephone. Her most frequent caller was Alan Dent (who was advising Olivier on *Henry V* from the point of view of critic). They were soon in heated discussion of the crossword puzzle and Oswald slightly resented the intrusion.* Oswald and Vivien walked over to Denham (which took an hour) and found Larry in No. 5 shed. Oswald recorded:

> I found His Majesty the King among the bell-tents of the fields of Agincourt, wearing his royal arms, to whom I bowed low and said with dignified deference "Your Majesty's humble liege." He replied "How do you do, Sir" gravely and unsmiling. I realized that *Lieut.* Laurence Olivier, RNVR, was greeting *Commander* Oswald Frewen, RN, but not till later did I know that Henry V's nose was false and might crack off if he smiled! (He was obviously dog tired.)[34]

Filming was not helped by bombers roaring overhead, so that the sound had later to be redone indoors. Oswald was impressed by Olivier's unprecedented step of producing, directing, and starring in a film and his wish to return to the Navy:

*Oswald had by now promoted Vivien to a high spot in his affections, so much so that from May 1944 until his marriage in June 1945 he intended to bequeath The Sheephouse to her. Years before Leigh had also been in the will.

> It will be an anxious time for Vivling if he does, but I agree with his desire. Meanwhile he's overworking and like to have a nervous breakdown. [35]

In the same month Vivien was reunited with her traveling companions and other stars including Michael Wilding, John Gielgud, Jeanne de Casalis, Richard Haydn, and Cyril Ritchard to perform before an audience of a thousand at a bomber station in England. Another wartime venture was a revue devised by Benn Levy and Constance Cummings and taken over by John Clements. On Sundays a group of straight actors would go to isolated places, normally connected with the RAF, accompanied only by a pianist and his compere. Clements told Alan Dent:

> I remember Vivien very vividly as the awful child in Herbert Farjeon's sketch 'How to Get There,' with Larry as the bewildered guest – and she and Larry often doing the 'wooing' scene from *Henry V*, and another Farjeon sketch called 'Bridge.' Vivien had no compunctions whatever in contriving to make herself look hideous when the occasion called for it. She had no need to have! Five minutes later she would come on something or other looking ravishing and the troops adored it. It was then, in those odd scratch rushed-up affairs, that I first became conscious that Vivien was a real professional. Everything she did was done meticulously to the best of her ability and with the minimum of fuss.[36]

The actress Judy Campbell recalled her first two meetings with Vivien during this phase. She noticed that Vivien could be a changeable character. She had taken over at the Haymarket after *The Doctor's Dilemma,* playing two Noël Coward plays alternately, *This Happy Breed* and *Blithe Spirit*. Vivien came round after the show, very moved by *This Happy Breed*. She asked if she could do something about her face as she had been crying. Judy Campbell found her very friendly:

> She sat at my dressing table, dabbing away, blowing her

> nose, borrowing my face powder, while I was getting out of my clothes. There she was with her face naked…After she had repaired her face she embraced me and said how wonderful it was.[37]

Ten minutes later, they met in the taxi to go to dinner and Vivien's mood had changed again. She was formal and reserved, addressing her as Miss Campbell. Vivien said:

> "Goodbye, so nice to have met you. I have *so* enjoyed it." (little pussycat smile). And I thought you are not the same lady who was in my dressing room. Quite different.[38]

Later, at one of the Sunday troop concerts at Aldershot, the Oliviers performed the courting scenes from *Henry V*, and Vivien sang a song, 'I'm Scarlett O'Hara, the terror of Tara.' This was followed by a formal reception "and she was behaving beautifully. She wasn't Lady Olivier then. Yet she was behaving like Lady Olivier."[30] After the reception those that were staying returned to the hotel and came to Judy Campbell's room:

> By this time it was after midnight. You know: 'We've got a bottle of gin and a bottle of whisky and bring your toothmug.' So we all did and it was the first time I had ever heard four letter words. I'd read them. But I'd never heard anybody say 'Fuck' until she said it. She was rapidly getting stoned out of her mind. She was flinging it back and I won't say that I felt my idols had feet of clay but I thought 'this is the other side of the coin.' Afterwards when one heard about drunken parties and that sort of thing, I thought, 'Yes I know. I've been to one.' But what fascinated me was that it was the same things that happened when she came to see the plays. In my dressing room she was in tears and therefore somehow had a nakedness, and then later on became very exquisite and formal and here it was the other way around.[39]

Early in 1944 Vivien became godmother to David Niven's son, also called David, giving him a Jacobean drinking mug, engraved D.W.G.W. When Niven complained she said: "I'm not going to change it so from now you'll just have to be called 'Wiven,' that's all."[40] Thereafter she always called him 'Wiven' or 'Wiv.' The ill-fated Primmie Niven (who died falling downstairs at a party in Montery in May 1946) also became Vivien's friend. In March 1944 the *Hollywood Reporter* revealed that Vivien would not be returning to Hollywood as had "decided it was her duty to remain in England for the duration."[41]

Early in 1944 the Oliviers were still at Old Prestwick, but looking for a more permanent country house. Leigh Holman, following a similar quest, had walked miles and miles of Wiltshire and found Woodlands at Mere, on the Somerset border. This he bought from the Meyrick-Joneses in 1942, taking it over in September 1943. The recently re-nourished friendship between Leigh and Larry had borne fruit when the Oliviers went to stay with him in March 1944. Vivien was very impressed with Woodlands:

> It is so thrilling, Leigh, that you have been clever enough to find something so incredibly lovely – which suits you better than it would anyone else in the world.[42]

It is possible that, in searching for country houses, both Leigh and Vivien were influenced by their early stays at Brede Place. As a child Vivien had stayed often at the Prebendal, Thame, another medieval house. They certainly veered towards the Middle Ages. Vivien had her eye on Stavordale Priory, a beautiful twelfth-century monastic church converted into a house, not far from Woodlands. The drawing room was built in the upper part of the choir, and there was a good garden. It was for sale with 84 acres for £8000. Unfortunately the rewards of *Henry V* were not yet forthcoming and somebody else snapped it up.

The completion and eventual enormous success of *Henry V* was a turning point in Olivier's career and had a considerable effect on his character. An Olivier production in every sense, it was the first successful attempt to bring Shakespeare to the screen. Olivier often related tales of making the film, how he offered to demonstrate any stunt and how this led him to jump from a tree onto a moving horse, suffering a painful sprained ankle, and how he acquired a scarred lip when a horse hit a camera.

Olivier's inspiration of beginning on the confined stage of the Globe Theatre and then transferring to France with 'a flourish' of Walton's music and the words "Now sits the wind fair, and will aboard" made full use of the new possibilities of film. He spent weeks in Ireland filming at Powerscourt, a beautiful Palladian house built in the silvery granite of Co. Wicklow. The completed film gave him critical and popular success and his first Oscar. Kenneth Tynan believed that, in *Henry V*, Olivier had "turned Shakespeare into a vibrant cinematic force all on his own."[43]

Contemporary actors speak of the relaxed and friendly Olivier of the pre-*Henry V* days and the feudal figure that emerged from it. At last he had won in the medium of film. He had suffered in the past. In Hollywood, he had played second fiddle to Jill Esmond's early popularity and whisked her away, denying her the chance to star in *A Bill of Divorcement.* Then he had watched Vivien eclipse him all over again with *Gone with the Wind.* He had been forced into the much disliked role of second billing. But now he was triumphant and unassailable. When he won his Oscar, Vivien made a fuss over him, conveniently ignoring the Oscar she had already won five years before. It was at this point that Olivier began to entertain the idea of living in an historic abbey, soon to be embodified in Notley. And Harold Nicolson spotted him as a new member of Beefsteak Club in July 1944.

Olivier had been given leave from the Navy to make the film. His first thought on completing his work was to return to active service. However, all they offered him was a posting as a 2-1/2 stripe officer in an aircraft carrier. Oswald Frewen pointed out that that was a job which any second-line pilot could do, and urged him to make his contributions to the war effort on stage. Olivier certainly longed to return to the theatre. Even before *Henry V* was finished, he was given his chance. He was invited to join Ralph Richardson, John Burrell, and Tyrone Guthrie in reviving the Old Vic company. In 1944 he performed in Ibsen's *Peer Gynt*, Shaw's *Arms and the Man*, both outstanding successes, capped only by his triumph as the hunchback Gloucester in *Richard III*.

Vivien was not invited to join the Old Vic company, partly because she was as good as committed to filming Shaw's *Caesar and Cleopatra* and partly because her success as a film star would give her an undue prominence on stage in what was meant to be a repertory company. Further legal wrangling occurred over her performance in *Caesar and Cleopatra,* a film she longed to do, Selznick earning about £50,000 as part of the arrangement of leasing her to Gabriel Pascal.

There have been many films of the Cleopatra story, most of them immensely costly and accident-prone. Pascal's film was no exception. George Bernard Shaw believed that Pascal was nothing short of a godsend: "Pascal is doing for the films what Diaghileff did for the Russian Ballet,"[44] he proclaimed. Yet he was to be disappointed. Pascal had already filmed *Pygmalion*, but this profited considerably from the inspired direction of Anthony Asquith, who added touches like 'The Rain in Spain,' later set to music in *My Fair Lady*. He had also filmed the very expensive *Major Barbara*. Shaw warmed to the medium of film, enjoying its considerable scope and possibilities. Comparing films to the theatre he pronounced one day at Denham: "We were like children playing with wretched makeshift toys. Here you have the whole world to play with."[45]

Originally Shaw wanted Gielgud for the part of Caesar, feeling that he was the perfect follower to Forbes-Robertson who had starred in the original film, but Gielgud took an aversion to Pascal and turned it down. The role went to the excellent Claud Rains instead. Vivien craved the part which she had been allowed to read in an Olivier 'Food for Britain' broadcast. Shaw had written: "For charity and Vivien Leigh once: for commerce never."[46] Vivien was taken to see Shaw. He referred to her disobligingly as "that Leigh woman" but secretly enjoyed being photographed with her for publicity purposes. Shaw was surprised that Vivien wanted the part because most aspirant Cleopatras turned out to be "giantesses over fifty."[47] Later she warned Lilli Palmer not to step out onto the balcony with Shaw. He was evidently a bottom-pincher.

In the film Pascal presented a direct challenge to Hollywood. He did not mind extravagance; he was prepared to work for twenty-one months, and he wanted everything meticulously accurate from an historical point of view. Shaw kept a close eye on the production, showering Pascal with memos about every detail of costume and pronunciation. Cecil Parker's eyebrows in the role of Britannus were scrutinized to such an extent that he resorted to penning an ode about them. Shaw urged that Vivien should pronounce Ftatateeta to perfection and helpfully suggested she begin by saying "Aftatateeta," eventually dropping the A: "It will then be as easy as saying "left a message" or "laughed to scorn" or "lift a suitcase" or any other phrase with an ft in it."[48]

Vivien was signed for the film in November 1943 but shooting at Denham did not begin until 12 June 1944, six days after D-Day. The problems were not long in arising. Pascal was nearly blown up on the Pharos set when a flying bomb exploded in a field 150 yards away, and then the French windows in his own sitting room were blown in. The weather was consistently terrible so that the actresses in Oliver Messel's elegant but lightweight finery often trembled with cold. It was difficult for the actors and staff to get to and from the studio and lack of sleep at night left many exhausted. When the flying-bomb raids increased, most of London's dressmakers, girls under the age of call-up, were evacuated to the country so that costumes had to be run up by the proprietors themselves, helped by elderly members of staff, causing tiresome delays. Plaster and paints were difficult to obtain and dyes almost impossible. Some soldiers were dressed in toweling. Claude Rains, never an easy man to work with, grew impatient. He was scheduled to return to America in the middle of October and when they delayed him, the backers, the Rank Organization, were forced to pay thousands of pounds of his income tax. Every time a handful of beautiful girls was found to languish by the pool, and their costumes were fitted, a percentage of them were packed off to work in factories in the North of England.

Later, after Vivien's part in the film was over, the mighty Sphinx and various other properties were shipped to the desert at Beni Ussef, near Cairo, in the hope of better weather, but instead devastating rail fell. The production team had to wait for a genuine sandstorm to subside before staging a more manageable fake one. Twelve hundred local extras and 250 horses were placed at Pascal's disposal, at which point a bizarre new hazard presented itself. The troops discovered the papier-mache shields were edible and that the fish glue made them appetizing. Marjorie Deans recalled: "Three hundred new shields had to be made in Egypt to supply the deficiencies caused by this outbreak of shield consumption."[49]

The technical problems set aside, the major flaw of the film was the lack of any constructive action. Max Beerbohm had condemned the original play in 1901, writing: "Most of the scenes are mere whimsical embroidery, a riotous sequence of broadly humorous incidents,"[51] and James Agate pointed out that what Shaw had really done was to write a story of what was going on in Caesar's mind: "Caesar is Mr. Shaw's hero because he is Shavian. His ideas are unclouded by idealism or any kind of romantic nonsense."[51] Agate believed that neither Cleopatra nor any of the action really gripped Shaw. Therefore he saw "no point in making Alexandria a red-rose city half as old as Denham unless that city is going to serve some purpose."[52]

Stewart Granger played Apollodorus in jaunty style with many a flashing smile of perfected formed teeth. At first he had been confused to be chosen "as I think Shaw meant him to be queer, which was not exactly my scene."[53] Granger gave an account of the film in his memoirs and seemed to think that Pascal did not mind bankrupting the Rank Organization. His wife, Elspeth March, was heavily pregnant during part of the filming. A man by his own admission "not unattractive to the ladies,"[54] he began to resent the inevitable embargo on sex. In due course he could resist no longer and embarked on an affair with Deborah Kerr. Making a muddle of his lines one day he was taken aback when Vivien told him "in the waspish voice she sometimes used"[55] to concentrate on his work rather than on Deborah. Until this point he had not realized that his affair was known to everyone except his wife.

The cast was rich in other ways too – Francis L. Sullivan was a spendidly magisterial Pothinus, his mighty stomach prominent under his toga, Ernest Thesiger a predictably effete Theodotus, and Stanley Holloway was easily spotted in a pre-Doolittle role as Belzanor. Holloway remembered filming summer scenes in the winter: "We had to clear away great slushes of snow, and even our breath was coming out in clouds so clearly that the cameraman practically committed suicide."[56] Flora Robson had her own problems as Ftatateeta. Because of coal rationing, she could rarely have an adequate bath. Thus she became browner and browner as the film progressed. Also in the cast was fifteen-year-old Jean Simmons as the harpist, and Kay Kendall, un-credited, as one of the serving girls, while the future Saint and 007, Roger Moore, wore a red toga and held a spear.

On Shaw's only visit to the set on 29 June 1944, he had been annoyed that Vivien said "cummineecho" and "oaljentlemin" in "The Romans will come and eat you" and "Old gentleman."[57] When the film was completed, he attended a private showing with Pascal and Kenneth Clark. He did not like Vivien's screen performance. Throughout the film he muttered: "Oh, she's ruining it. That was a delightful piece of comedy. It goes for nothing now."[58] At the end he turned to Pascal and said: "Gaby, you've ruined it."[59] Vivien naturally rang Clark to ask what Shaw thought. Clark claimed Shaw felt she had caught the spirit of the heroine. He wrote: "There was nothing for it but to lie; but I didn't make it sound very convincing and I am surprised that she forgave me."[60] This opinion was matched by C.A. Lejeune in the *Observer*: "there was more of Cleopatra in her Scarlett O'Hara than in this pale elf."[61] But Stephen Watts, though critical of the film's lack of entertainment, thought Vivien invested her role with a touch of ridicule where others would have been content to be glamorous: "this shrewd actress gives the shallow, vixenish Cleopatra the occasional flick of Beatrice Lillie-ish comment which enlivens the whole scene."[62]

Godfrey Winn was another visitor to the set, describing the scene when Caesar tells Cleopatra about Mark Antony:

> Because of his intensity of the feeling that she was displaying both in her body and in her voice, I half expected at any moment a Freudian slip of the tongue. Mark Antony… Larry Olivier. For I was to hear exactly the same intonation so often when she was speaking, off the set, no longer of Cleopatra's great love, but of her own.[63]

Marjorie Deans was impressed by Vivien's professional approach to her acting:

> Everything she did seemed effortless, but perfectly timed and final…Laying aside a blue satin dressing gown and a crossword puzzle, she would take her place before the camera, and be, instantly, not Vivien Leigh at all, but Cleopatra, matching gestures and dialogue with grace and accuracy, and repeating them, when called upon, again and again and again with the same tireless certainty and thythm.[64]

Vivien had her own problems during filming. On 16 August she wrote to Leigh:

> *What* do you suppose has happened. I'm to have a baby.

> Everyone is very, *very* cross and keeps asking me how I suppose they are going to make me look like the 16 year Cleopatra and I keep saying I can't help it, that it's an act of God and that they're not to be mean to me in my condition! I think it is a very good thing really because they'll just have to hurry up with the film…[65]

The schedule was reorganized to film Vivien's scenes first. She wrote to Alan Dent: "I've had a fine time this morning running up and down the Memphis Palace beating the slave."[66] This ended badly, Stewart Granger blaming Pascal for not employing a double:

> She slipped and fell heavily. Two days later she miscarried. She never forgave Pascal for this and from then on was constantly trying to have him replaced by another director, but without success.[67]

Granger did not tell his wife about this during her own difficult pregnancy. Elspeth March remembered that later she and Vivien had long talks on the subject:

> I used to say to her "Just give it a chance. Go to bed," but she couldn't. She was so hyper-active, and I am sure that was the T.B. which made her so strung up all the time.[68]

Vivien's miscarriage occurred in the first week of September 1944. Oswald Frewen called on her with chocolates in the London Clinic, finding her room "*bowered* with flowers, but (rationed) chocolates rather scarcer! Of course she was gentle and sweet as ever."[69] It is discreetly noted by Marjorie Deans that Vivien "was taken ill and we were held up for a matter of from five to six weeks all told."[70] This illness proved to be not merely the result of the miscarriage but another manifestation of the manic depression which was to dog her for the rest of her life. So little was understood of the disease that its cause was often misinterpreted. In those days the doctors did not know how to control it with lithium. The illness came in cycles, spasmodically and moderately to begin with, later more fiercely and more often. And from it there was no escape. As Robert Lowell, another sufferer wrote: "When you finally see a light at the end of the tunnel it's the light of an oncoming train."[71]

Richard III opened at the New Theatre on 13 September. Olivier was up until 4 a.m. at Claridge's the night before while Vivien and Garson Kanin helped him with his lines. Though he shrank apologetically before the magnitude of the role, he had a suspicion that he had embarked on something spectacular: "I stood up and looked again in the mirror. The monster stared back at me and smiled."[72] Vivien relished every moment of his triumph. James Agate judged the performance "a masterpiece of *gouaillerie,* and the death scene is as tremendous as, judging from Hazlitt, I take Kean's to have been."[73] For years Agate had been reviewing Vivien's performances in the *Sunday Times*. Now he met her. The three dined on roast partridges and champagne at the Café Royal. Agate noted:

> V.L. turns out to be as intelligent as she is pretty. Over and over again she said how much she preferred theatre to screen, and was backed up by Larry saying that film-acting is no job for an actor.[74]

He was interested that off-stage they were anxious to be ordinary people. No head turned as they entered the restaurant "because she doesn't *sail*, and he won't *stalk*."[75] Vivien tried to persuade Agate to accompany her to *Arms and the Man*, but he declined, pleading an antipathy to anything by Shaw after *St. Joan*. As for *Caesar and Cleopatra*: "I shall look at you in the film because not to do so would be impossible. But I shall not listen to you."[76] Vivien was thirty-one on 5 November, Oliver giving her a black Alsatian puppy which mixed uneasily with her cats. And, before the end of the year, Gertrude returned from Canada with Suzanne, who had acquired American clothes and a Canadian accent.

This was not an altogether easy homecoming for Gertrude. In her absence abroad her beauty academy had been ably run by Delia Collins, one of her assistants. Ernest had been serving in the Home Guard as a grenade expert. Unfortunately these duties had not prevented him too from being taken over by Miss Collins. When it was discovered that Ernest had been far from lonely, he was put 'in the dog-house' and not spoken to for some time. Delia Collins was sacked and set up her own successful business which still flourishes in Beauchamp Place in London. She also became Gertrude's arch-rival.

When the filming of *Caesar and Cleopatra** was over, the doctors wanted Vivien to have a complete rest at Old Prestwick, but she resolved to return to the stage in Thornton Wilder's *The Skin of Our Teeth.* She wrote to Dent on 13 January 1945:

> I don't think I have ever been more excited on the eve of any venture – or more nervous.[77]

*The film was released in London on 11 December 1945 and in New York on 6 September 1946. Vivien was recuperating at Notley when it opened. She first saw it six years later.

Gone with the Wind, 1939: Scarlett watches Ashley and Melanie on their way to bed

Vivien aged nine

Vivien aged sixteen

Vivien on her pony in India

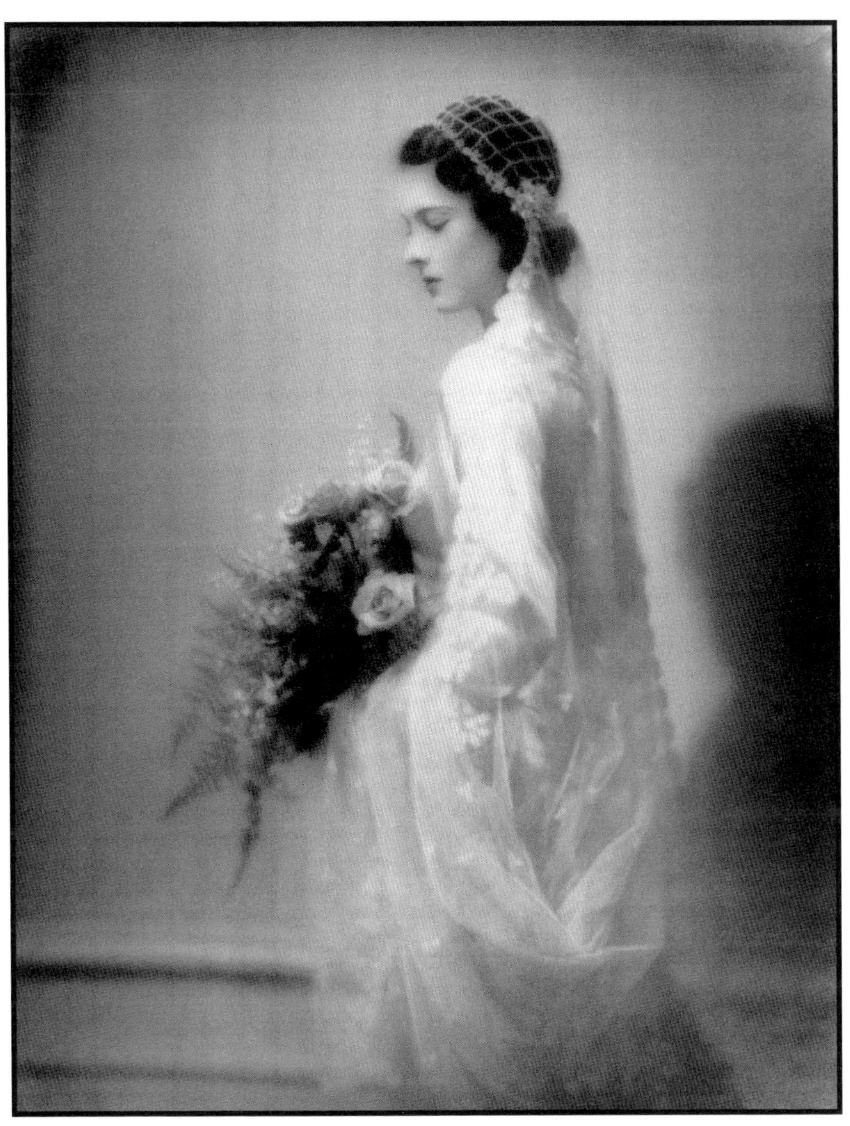

Vivien on her wedding day, 20 December 1932

Vivien; a photograph she gave to John Buckmaster in 1935

Vivien with Rex Harrison, 1937

Jill Esmond, Laurence Olivier, and Vivien in Capri, 1936

Fire Over England, 1936

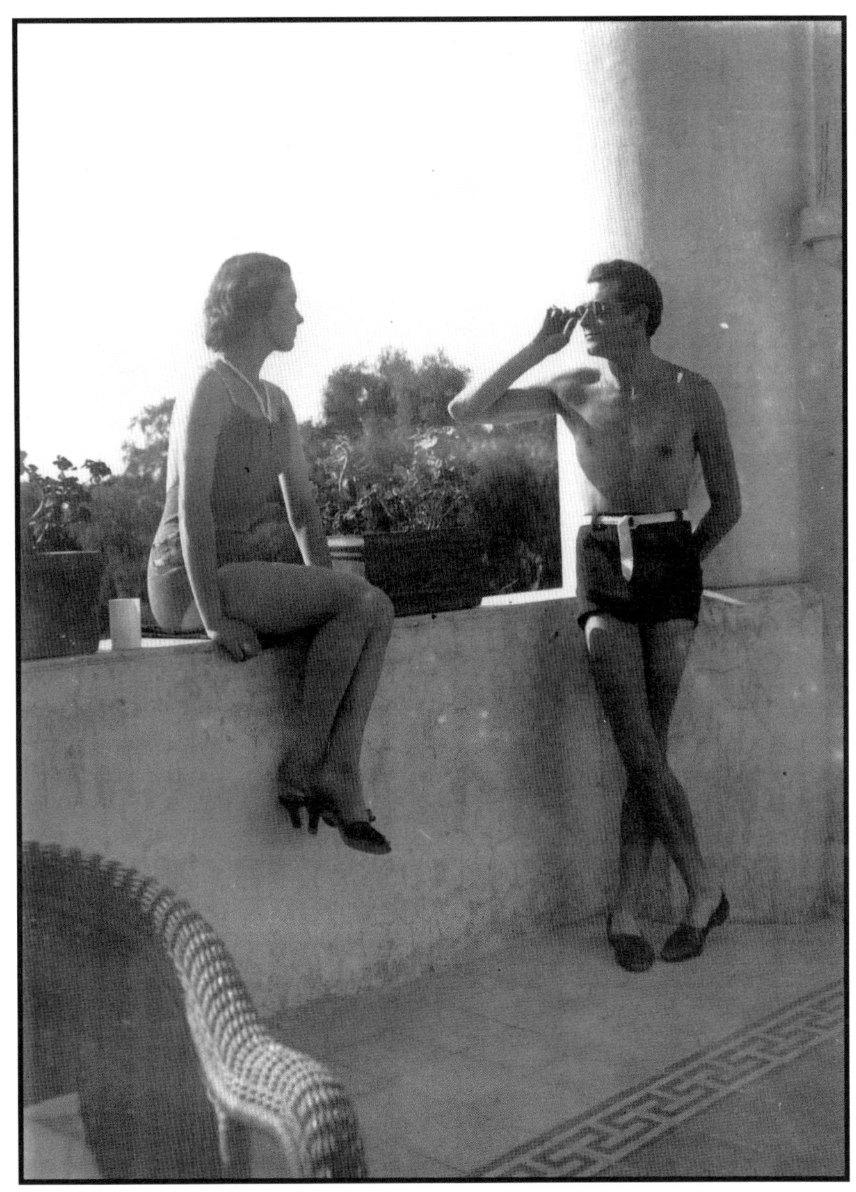

Vivien with Olivier in Capri, 1936

Hamlet at Elsinore, 1937

Oswald Frewen

Scarlett at Tara

Scarlett with Mammie

Scarlett with Rhett Butler

Scarlett with Ashley Wilkes

Oscar ceremony, 1940: Vivien with David O. Selznick and the Oscar

Vivien and Olivier without the Oscar

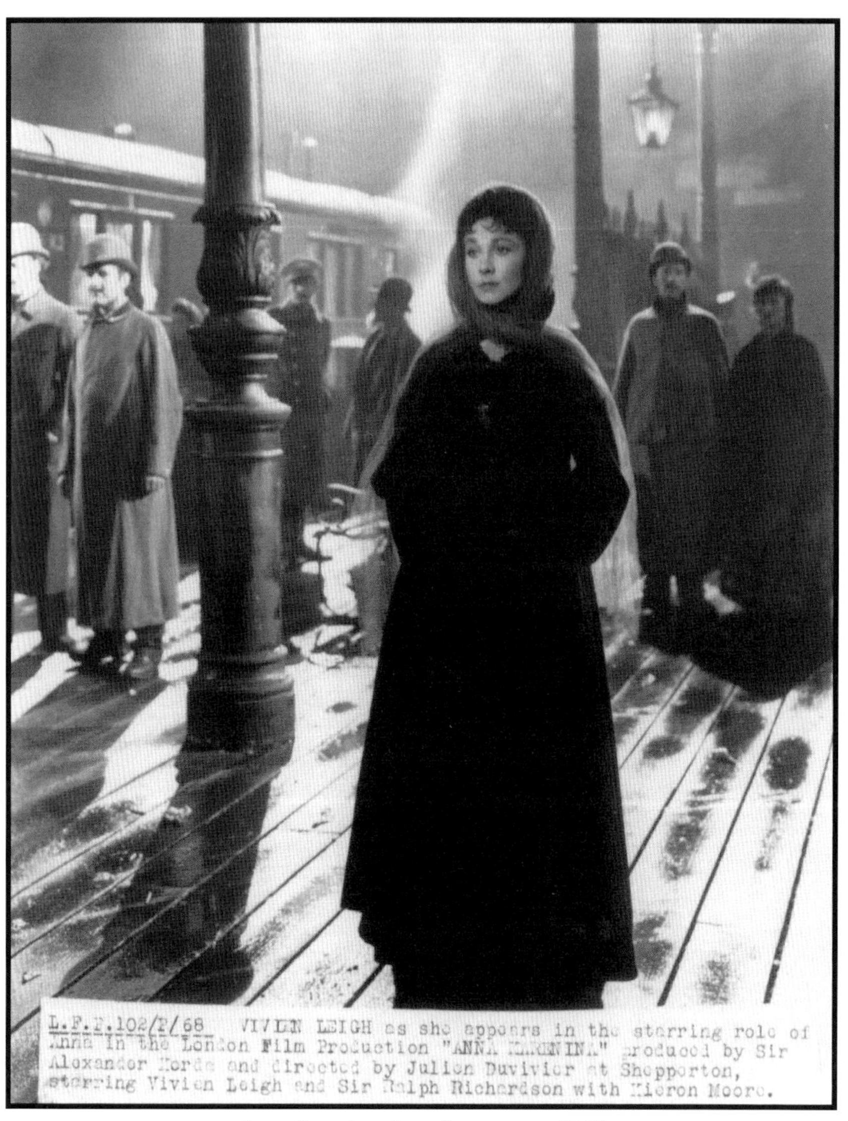

Anna Karenina: the railway scene, 1947

The School for Scandal, 1948: Cecil Beaton's design

Vivien with Marlon Brando in *A Streetcar Named Desire*, 1950

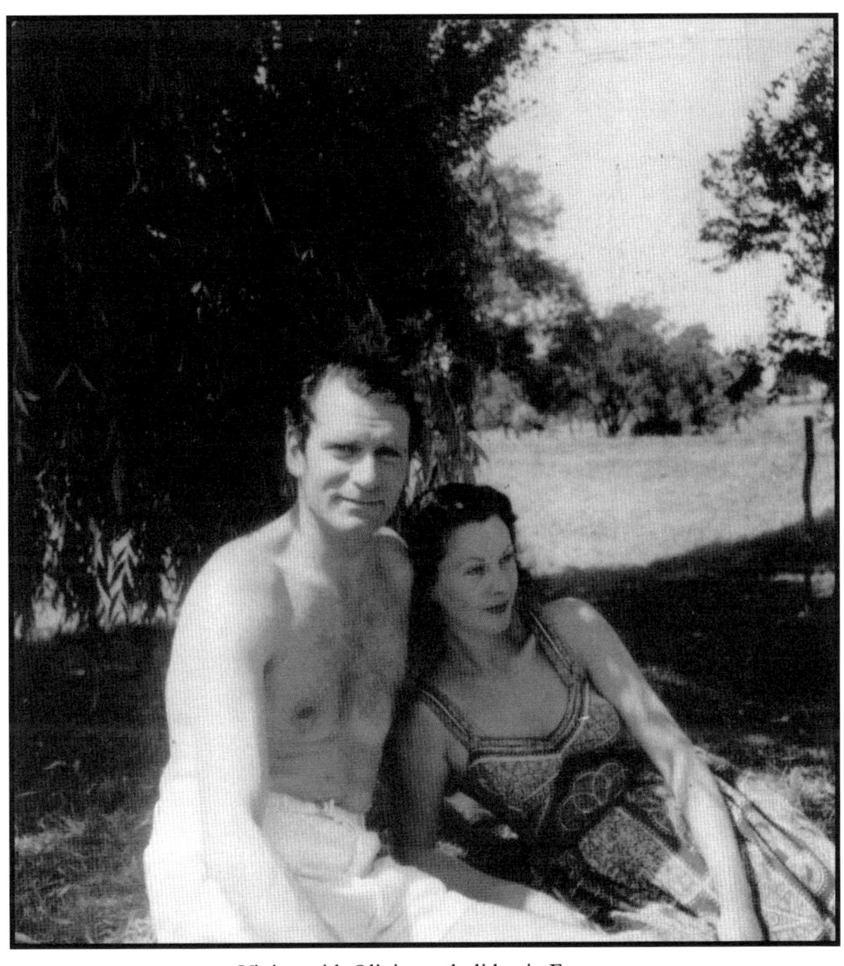

Vivien with Olivier on holiday in France

Vivien and Peter Finch in Ceylon at the time of *Elephant Walk*

The Oliviers at a gala

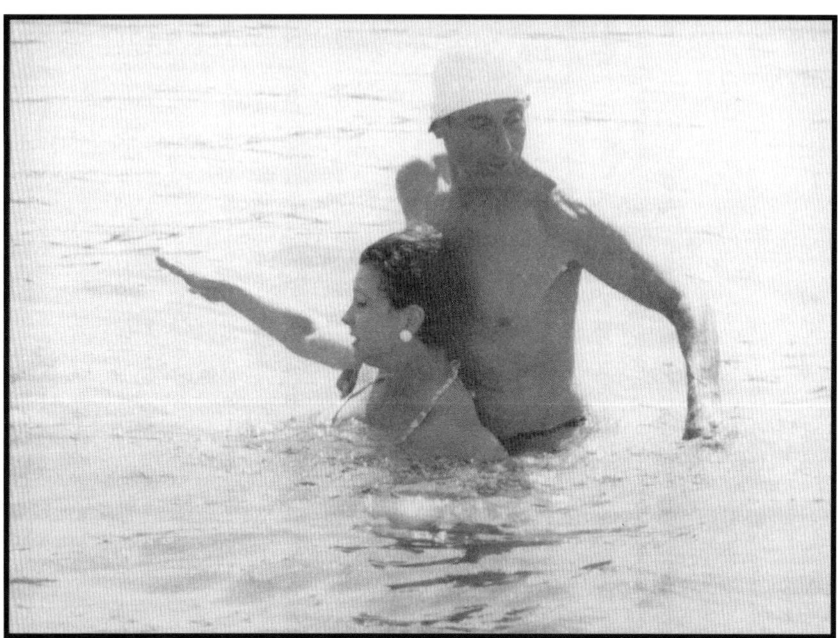

Vivien learning to ski with the help of Paul-Louis Weiller, La Reine Jeanne, 1957

Vivien at La Reine Jeanne with Princess Maria Pia of Italy

Vivien and Olivier at Suzanne's wedding, 1957

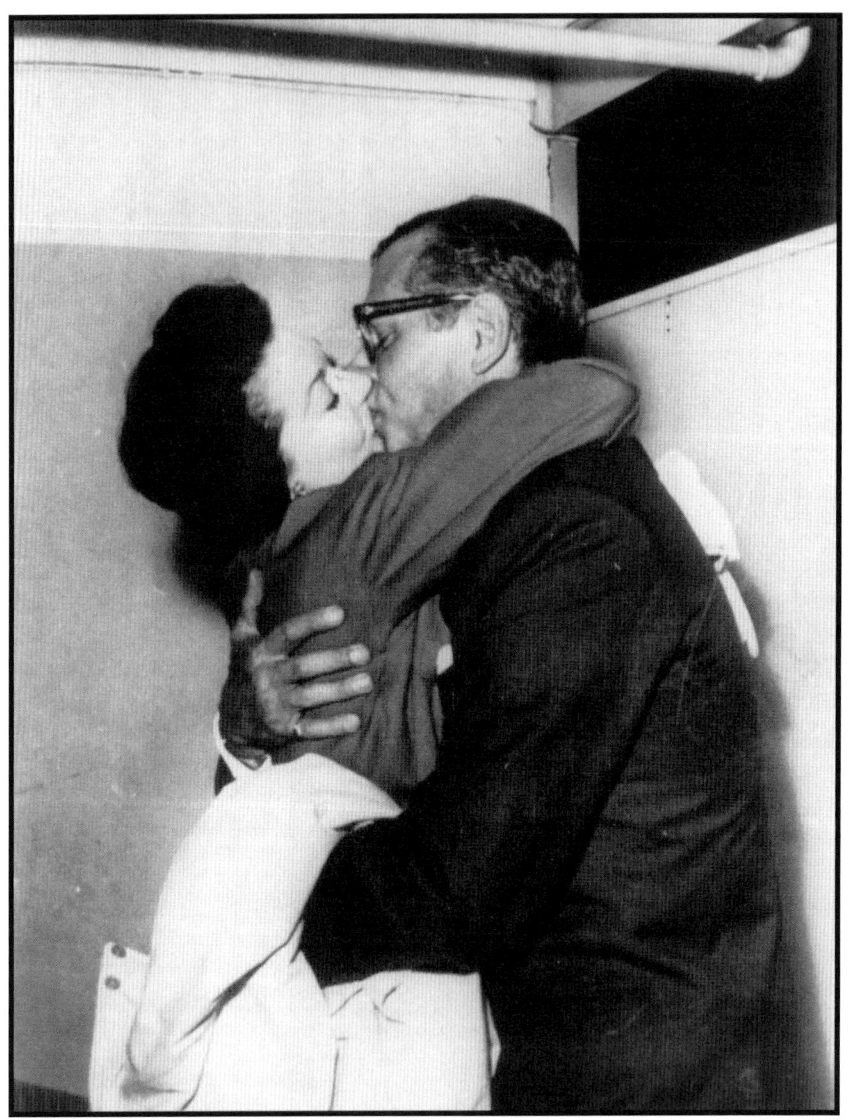

A kiss for the benefit of the Press, Heathrow, 1958

Vivien and Peter Wyngarde

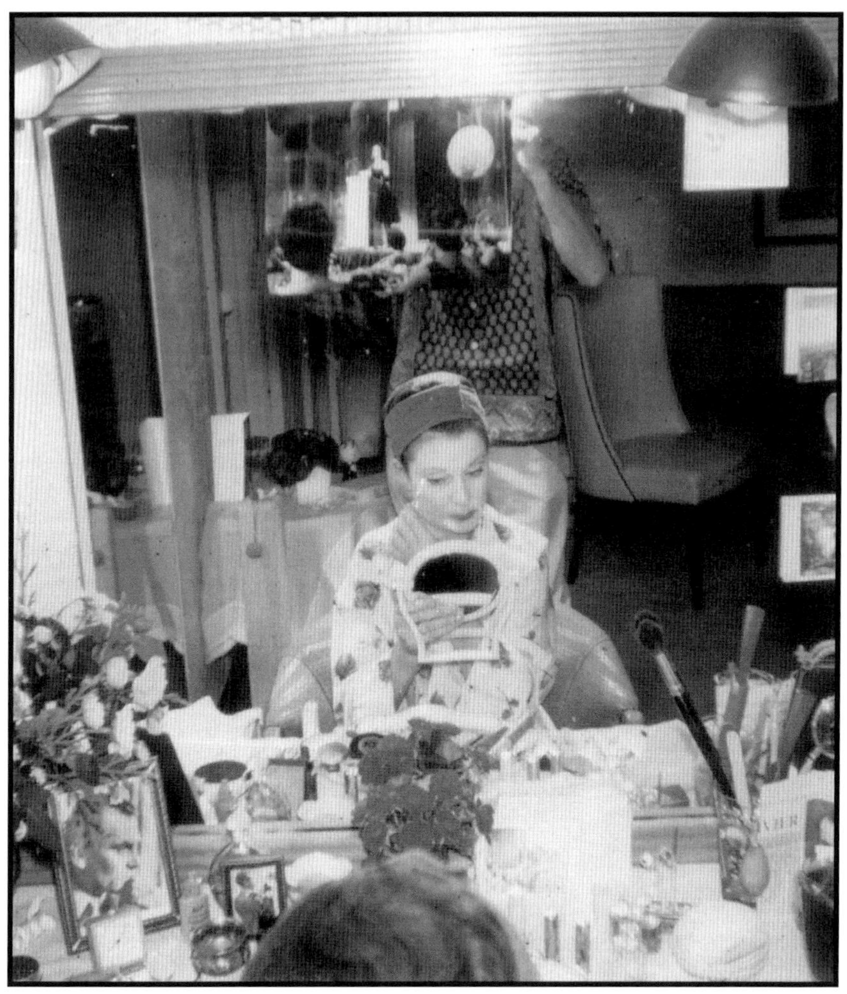

Vivien making-up in Hollywood

Vivien with Robert Helpmann at George Cukois swimming pool in California.

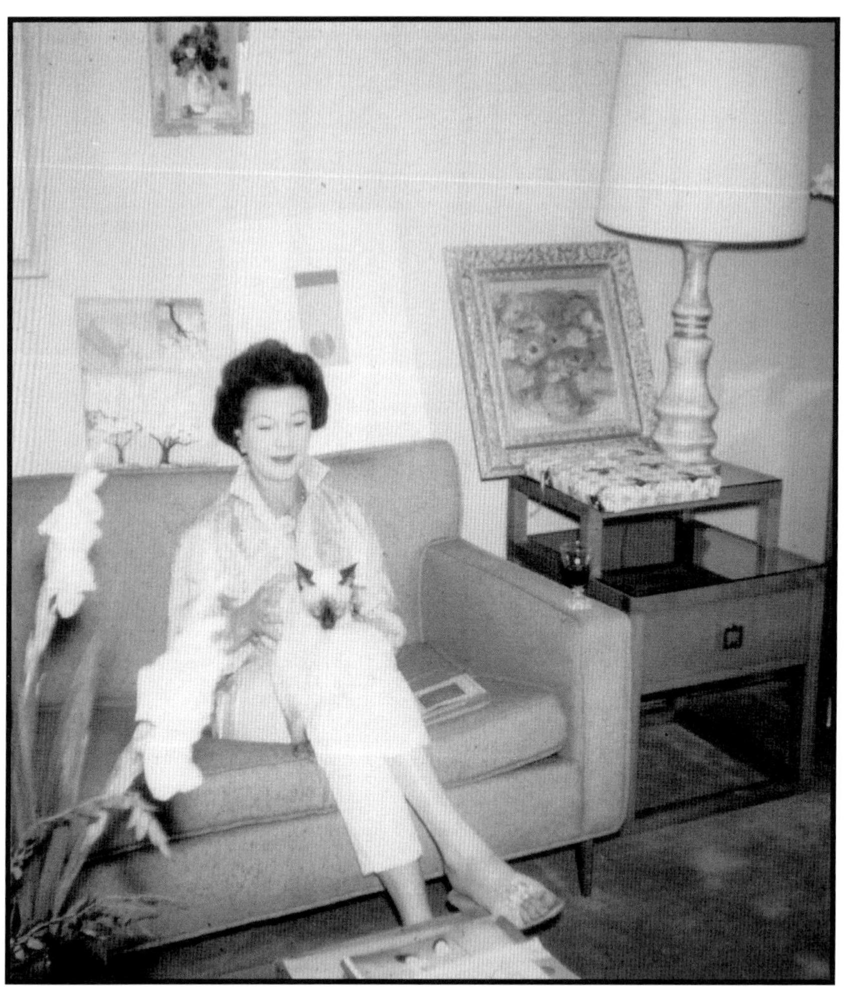

Vivien with 'Poo Jones' at Chateau Marmont

New Year's Eve 1960 at Eaton Square
From left to right: Gertrude Hartley, Mrs. Mac, Vivien, Michael Benthall, Robert Helpmann, Alan Webb, Lotte Lenya, Jose Quintero, Warren Beatty, Joan Collins, Bumble Dawson.

Warren Beatty, Vivien, and Joan Collins on the set
of *The Roman Spring of Mrs. Stone*

Bumble Dawson, Vivien, Bobby Helpmann, and Consuelo Langton-Lockton
at Tickerage Mill

Vivien arranging the sweet peas at Tickerage

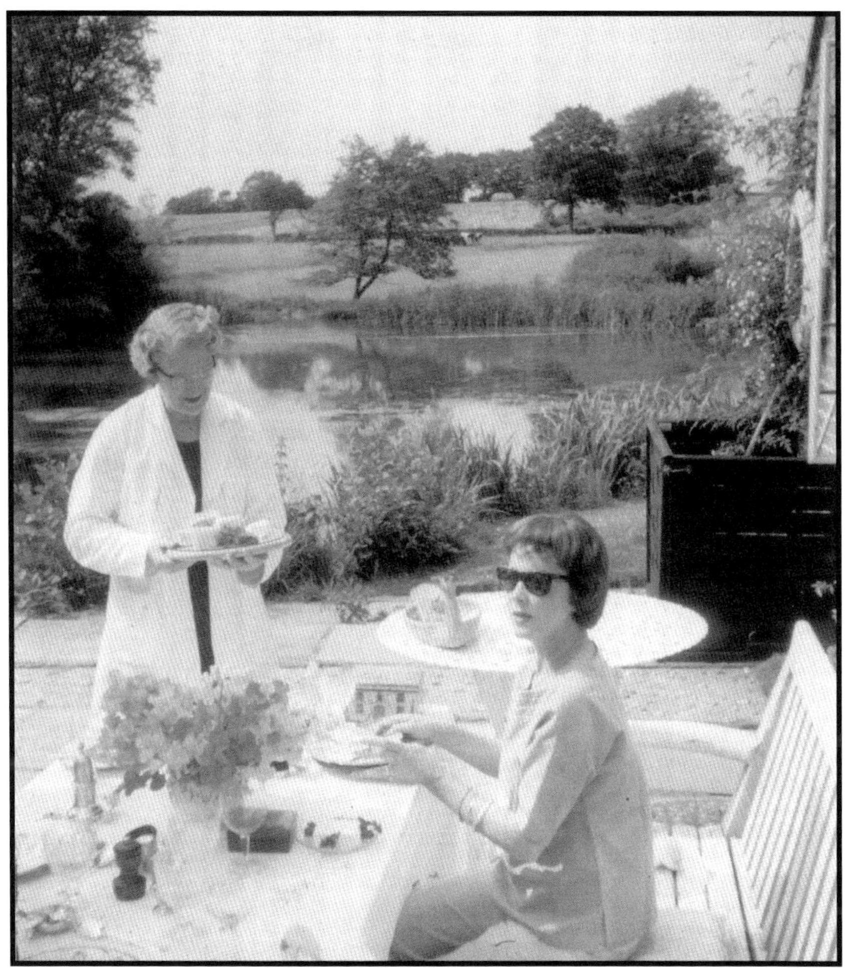

Mrs. Mac with Vivien at Tickerage

Vivien on a boat

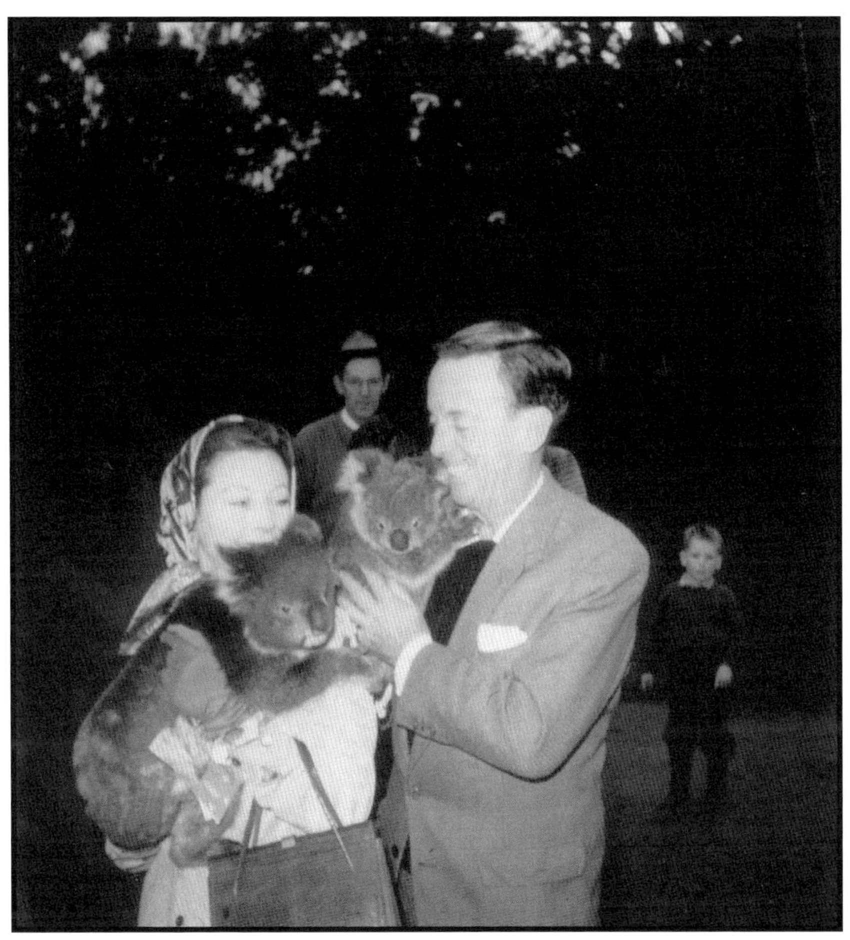

Vivien, Bobby Helpmann, and koalas

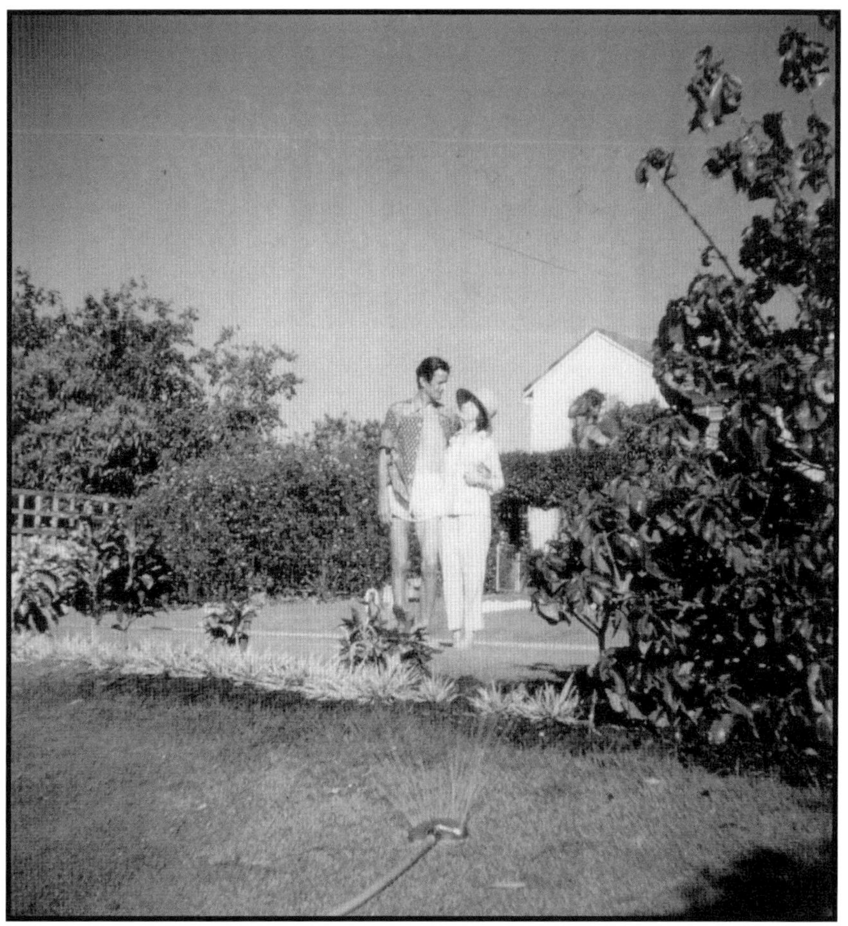

Vivien and Jack in Brisbane

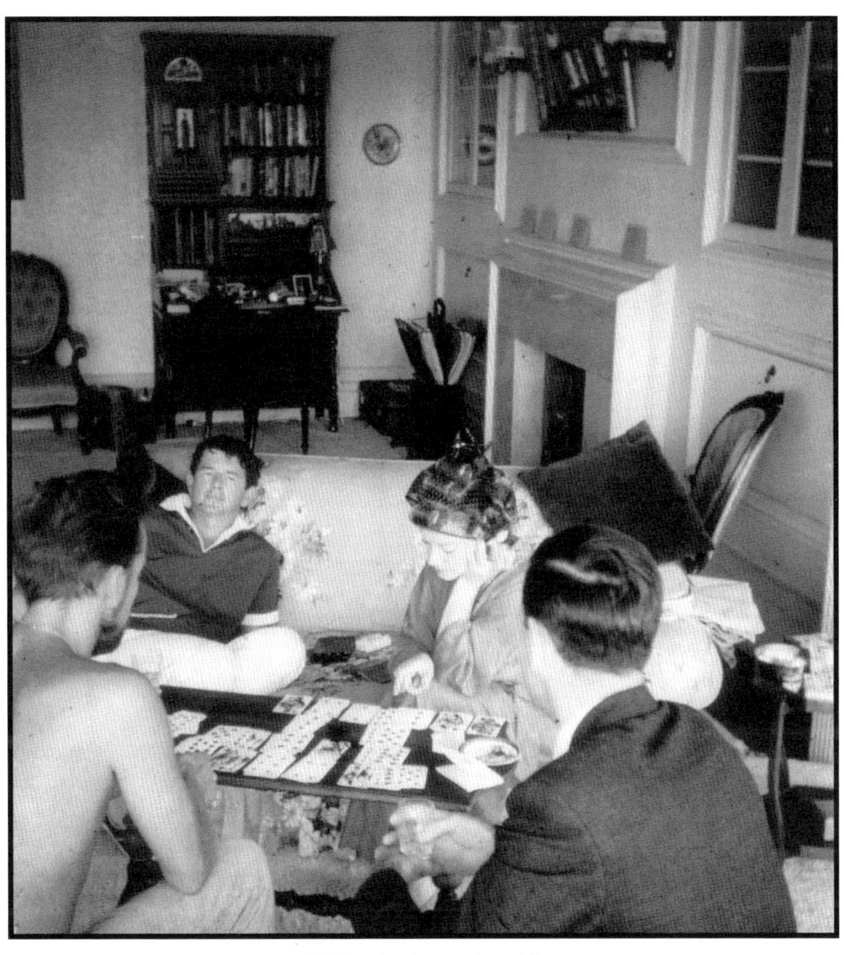

Vivien playing cards with
David Dodimead and friends

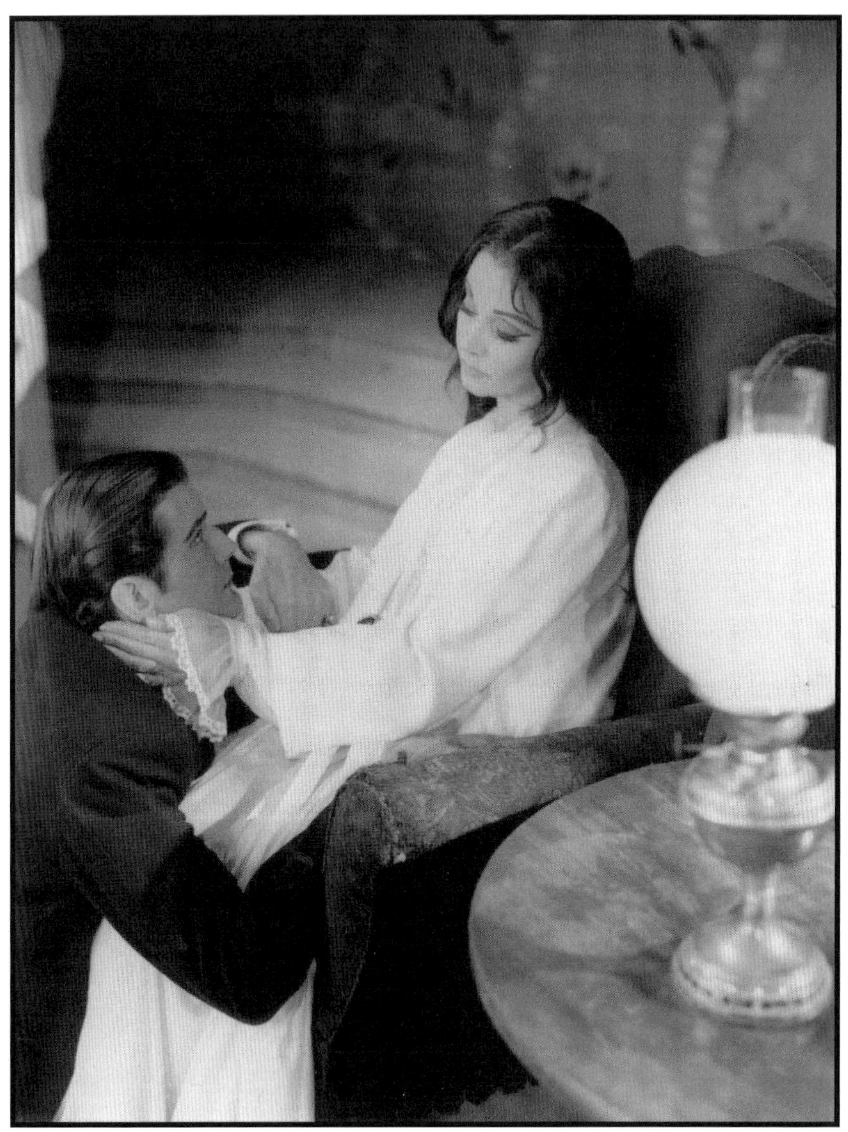

Vivien and Jack in *Camille*

Vivien in her *Tovarich* costume with Noël Coward

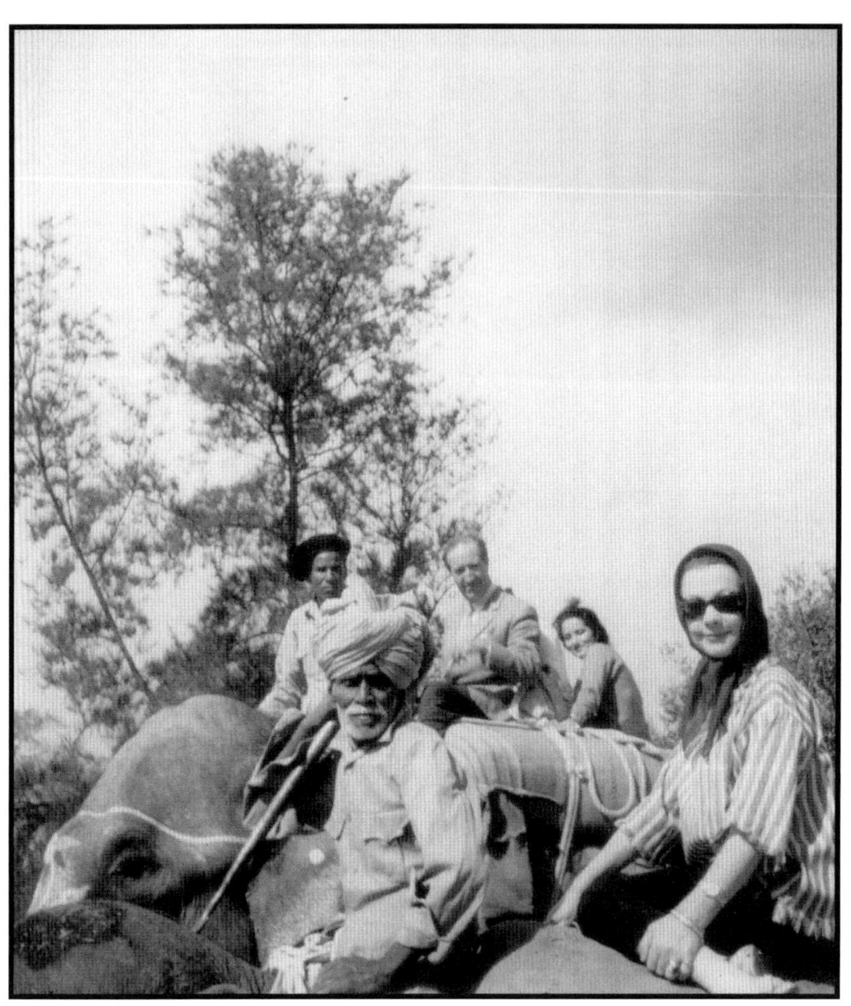

Vivien and Hamish Hamilton on elephants in India

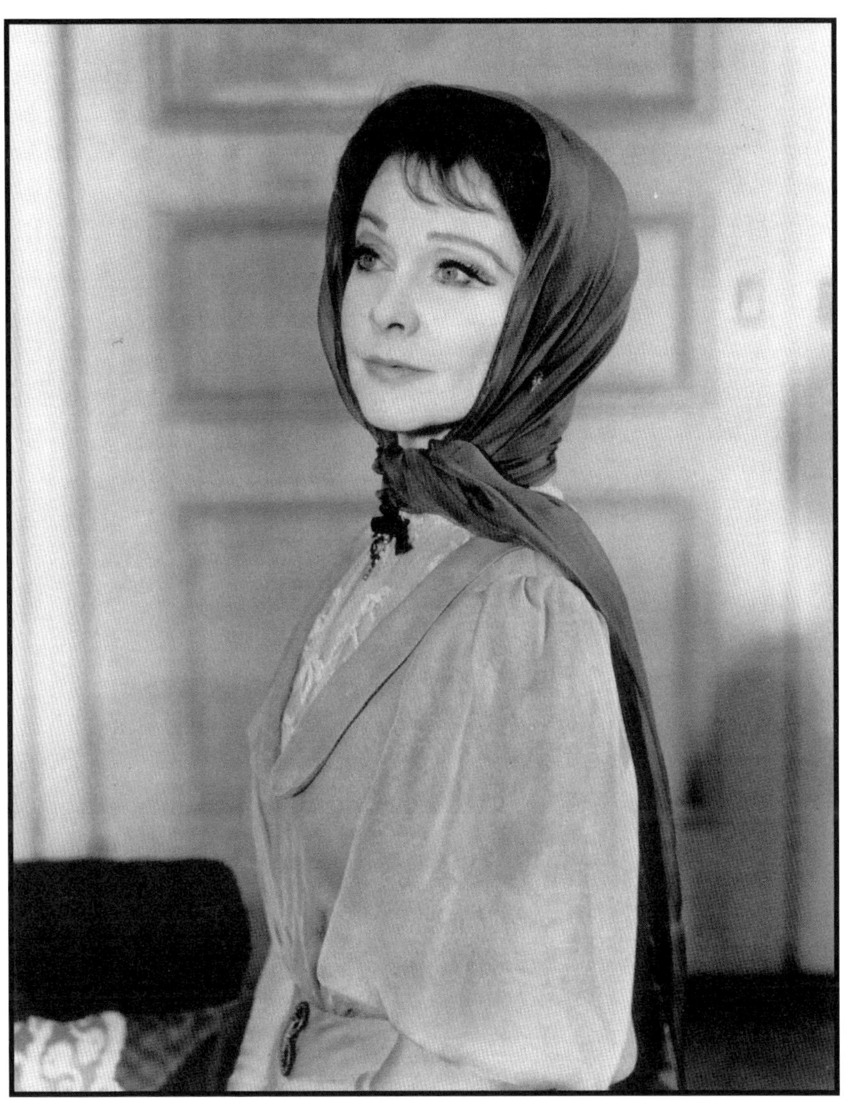

Vivien's last stage appearance *Ivanov*, New York, 1966

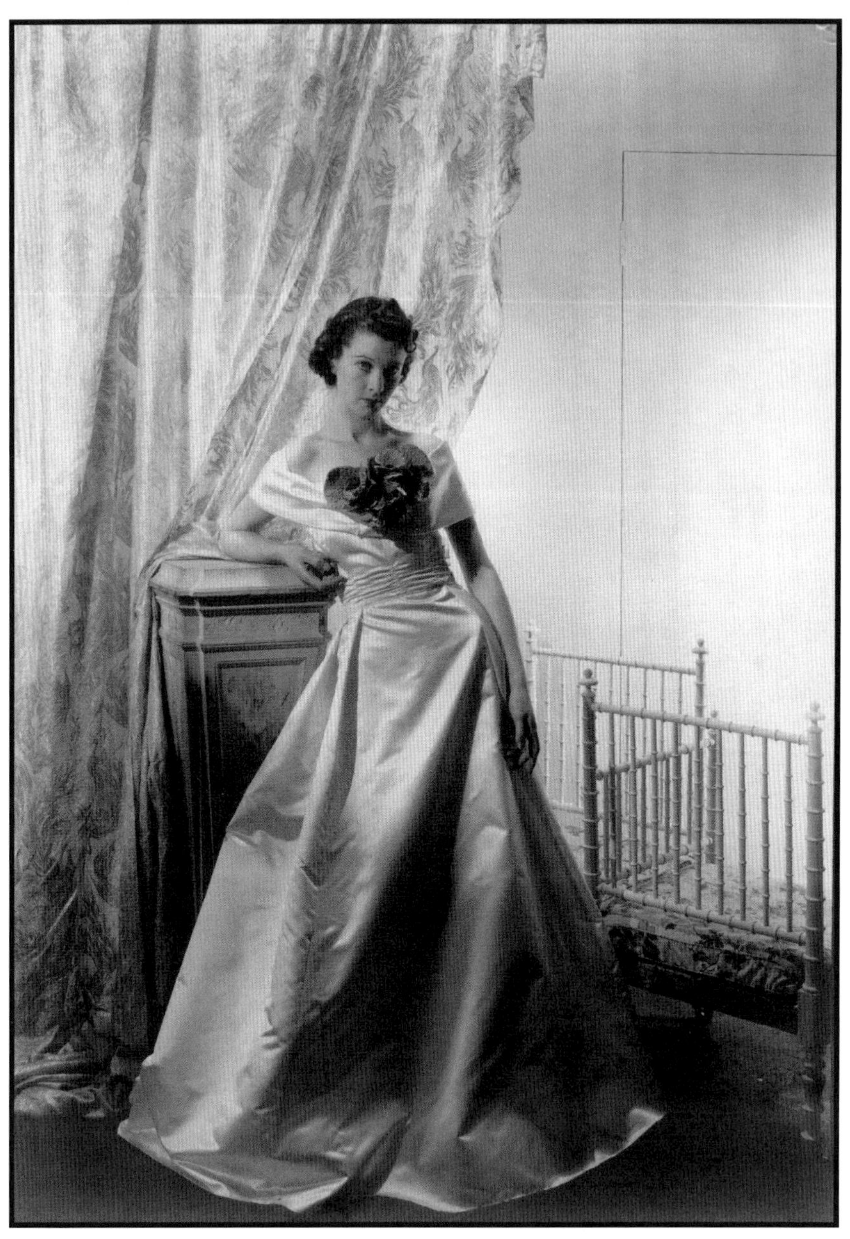

Vivien - an early photo by Cecil Beaton

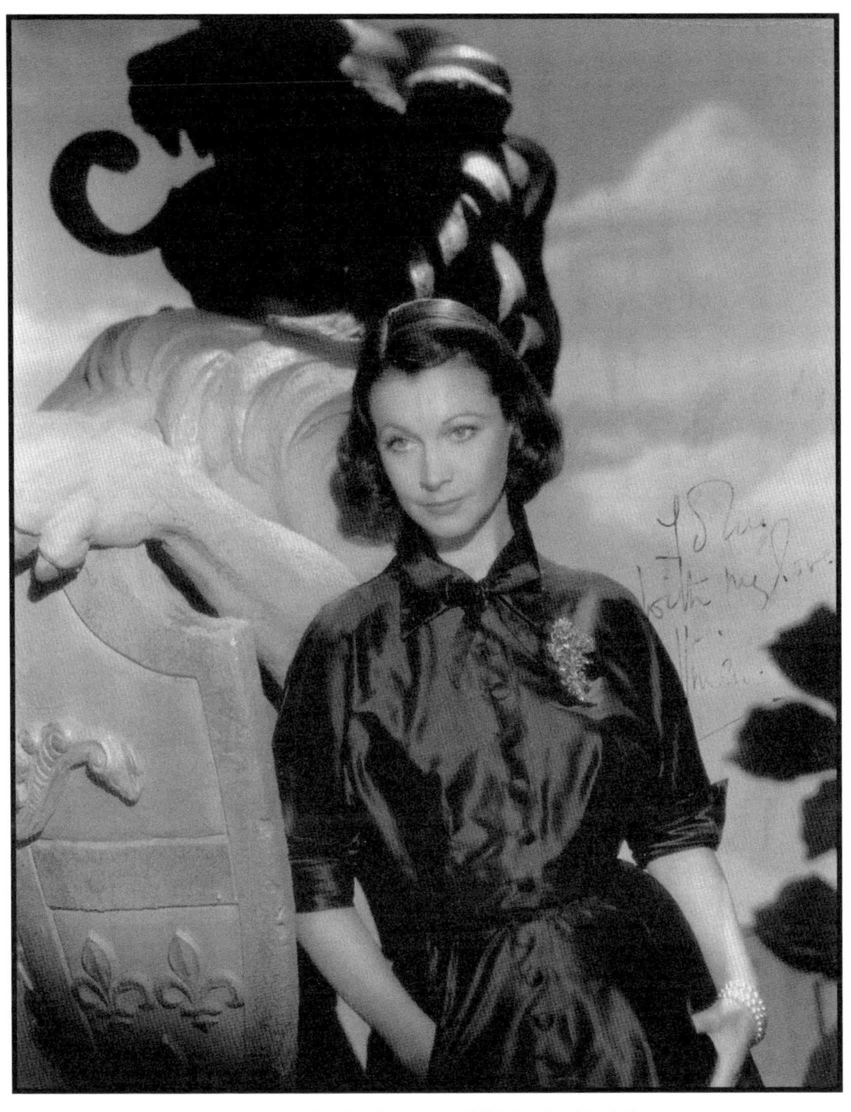

A photo given to John Buckmaster of Vivien by Paul Tanqueray

Another early photograph of Vivien by Cecil Beaton

The Oliviers

"WATERLOO BRIDGE," A Metro-Goldwyn-Mayer Picture
Made in U.S.A.

Vivien with Robert Taylor in *Waterloo Bridge*

Vivien and Olivier in *That Hamilton Woman*

Olivier and Vivien in *That Hamilton Woman*

THEATRE ROYAL HAYMARKET

6^{D.}

VIVIEN LEIGH

in

"THE DOCTOR'S DILEMMA"

by

BERNARD SHAW

Photo by Angus McBean.

In Accordance with The Requirements Of The Lord Chamberlain—(i) The public may leave at the end of the Performance by all exit doors and such doors must at that time be open. (ii) All gangways, passages and staircases must be kept entirely free from chairs or any other obstruction. (iii) Persons shall not in any circumstances be permitted to stand or sit in any of the gangways intersecting the seating, or to sit in any of the other gangways. If standing be permitted in the gangways at the sides and rear of the seating, it shall be strictly limited to the numbers indicated in the notices exhibited in those positions. (iv) The safety curtain must be lowered and raised in the presence of each audience. (v) Smoking is not permitted in the Auditorium.

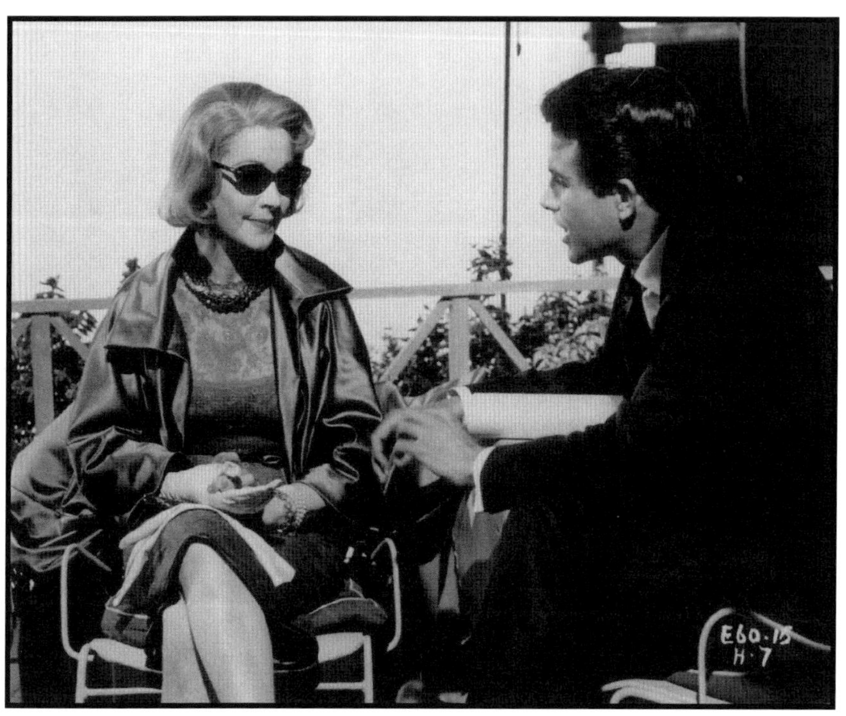

Vivien with Warren Beatty on the set of
The Roman Spring of Mrs. Stone

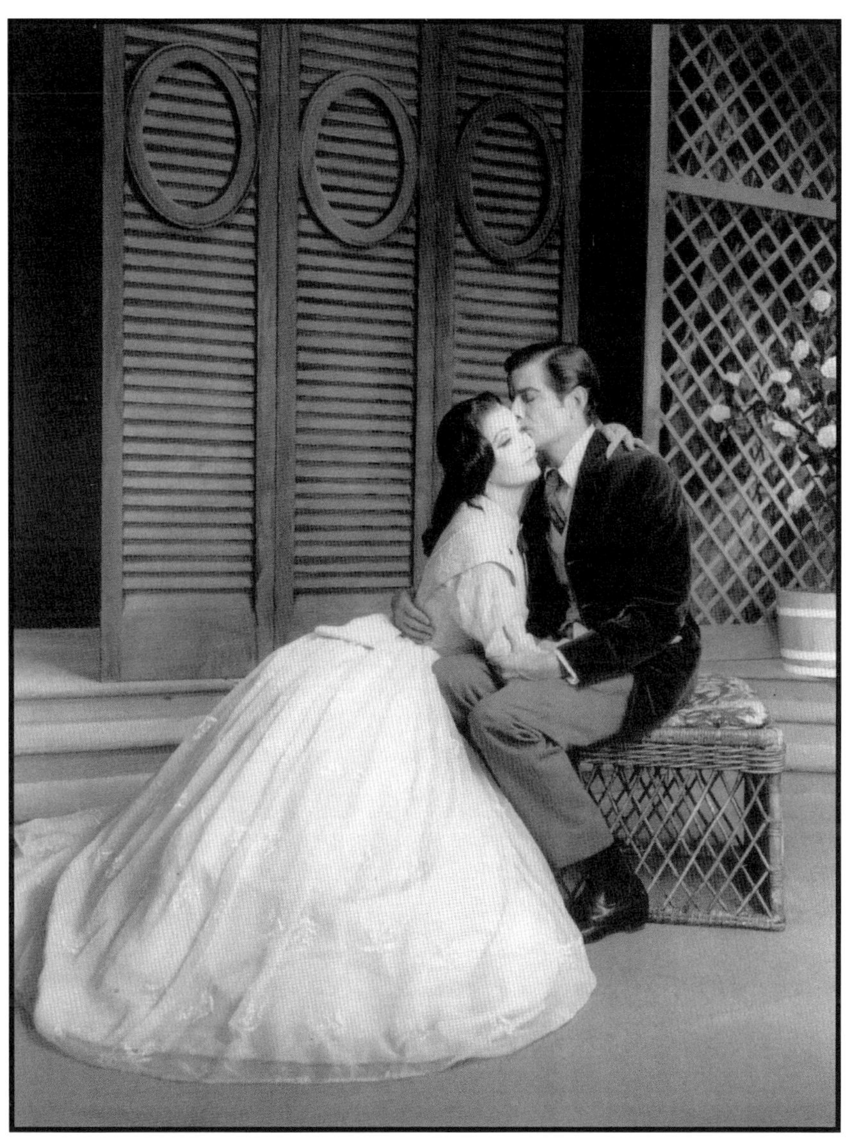

Vivien with Jack Werirale in Camille

A photo for the fans

Vivien in *The Roman Spring of Mrs. Stone*

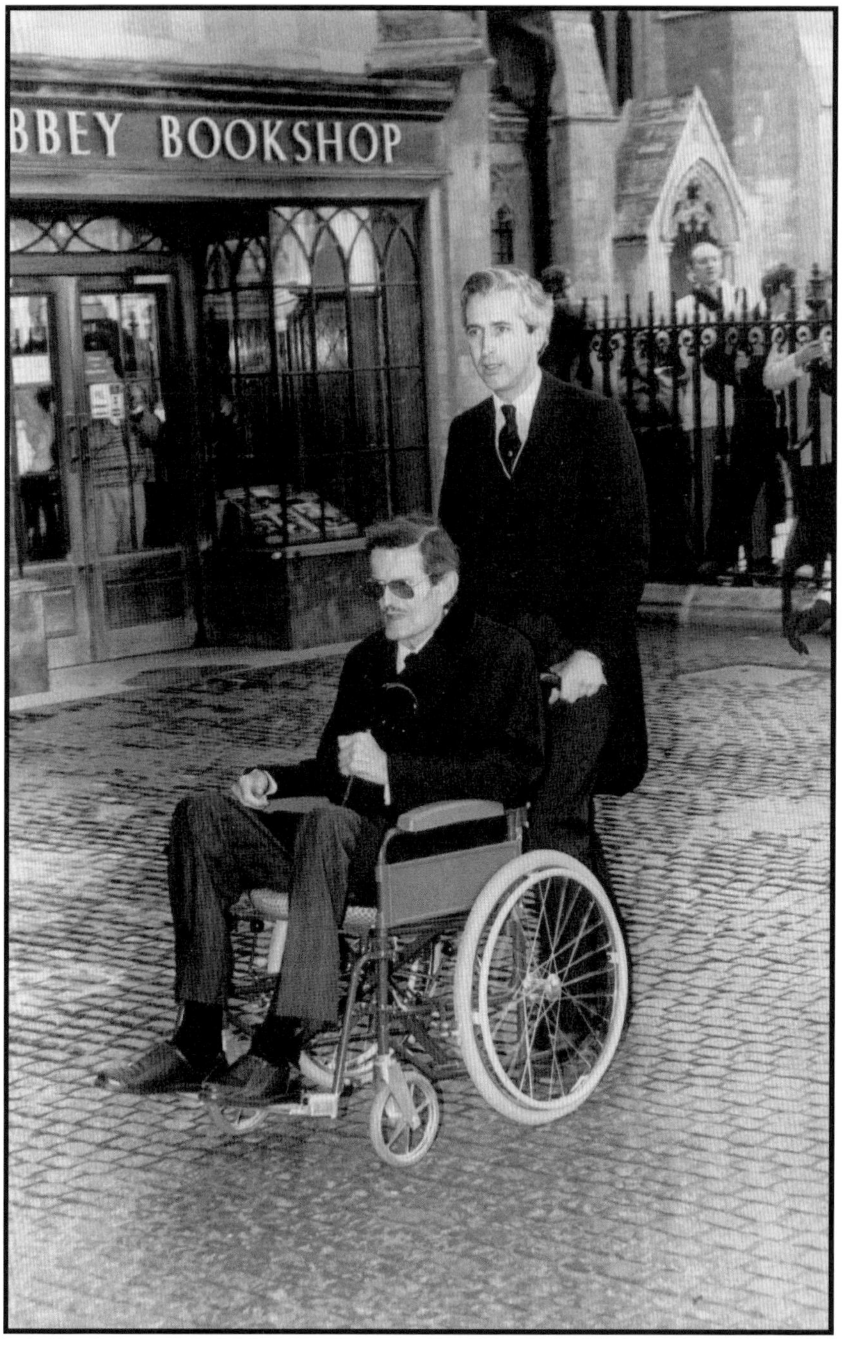

The author with Jack Werirale at Lord Olivier's memorial service, Westminister Abbey, 1989

Chapter 14
Lady Olivier

I don't know why we go on living at all. It's easier to be dead.
Sabina, Act One, The Skin of Our Teeth, Thornton Wilder

The Skin of our Teeth was to give Vivien the chance to prove herself on stage as a comedienne. A complicated allegory on the history of mankind written by Thornton Wilder, both Olivier and Vivien were enormously excited about it, and having purchased the British rights, longed for the moment when Vivien could play the role of Sabina. It was one of Olivier's rare excursions into directing for Binkie Beaumont.

Thornton Wilder wrote the play, with considerable difficulty, between 1940 and 1941. He judged the question of the struggles of the human race and its survival "the most ambitious subject I have ever approached."[1] He was confused by whether he believed what he was saying, and how to present his theme with simplicity without boring the audience. His characters begin as a man 20,000 years old, and a heroine of the same age, 8,000 years his wife. He offers some explanations of man's will to continue living, "the existence of his children," "the inventive activity of his mind," pressing him to "continued and better-adjusted survival."[2] He solves his problems by a number of technical tricks. The players soliloquize, speak either as individuals or as symbolic figures and wander on and off the stage seemingly at will.

The author had wallowed in considerable confusion. Small wonder that audiences were bemused. In New York the part of Sabina had proved a resounding success for Tallulah Bankhead, who enjoyed extracting fun from the confusion on stage, under the inspired direction of Elia Kazan. Even so, a number of theatergoers left at the interval. In London, so odd was the play that, when a mentally distracted theatergoer succeeded in climbing onto the stage, she was steered into the wings without the audience realizing that she was not part of Wilder's scheme.

Vivien faced problems even before opening. David Selznick decided to invoke his contract and press her to return to Hollywood. Reviewing the matter in February 1945, he noted that Vivien had only been granted "a twelve-week leave of absence"[3] to go to England in 1941 because of the war. Subsequent concessions had been granted but now she should make a gesture to return:

> …it might be stressed that she has consistently refused to even consider any such attempt, although we have stood ready and still stand ready to make pictures with her that could have enormously beneficial effect on British-American relations, with a potential audience of between fifty and one hundred million people throughout the world by comparison with the small number any play could reach…[4]

She prevaricated until Selznick resorted to applying for a legal injunction. The Selznick organization briefed Sir Walter Monckton, the man who had advised Edward VIII during the Abdication crisis. Before the Chancery Division he contested that Vivien was still Selznick's property and she should not be exposed in such a production. Vivien was represented by Sir Valentine Holmes, KC, who maintained that she was a married woman and subject to national service regulations. The judge ruled that Vivien was better employed on stage than in a munitions factory and there the case rested. In due course Selznick's contract was settled and Vivien had won her averred wish to be free of Hollywood.

During the court action, rehearsals continued. Vivien went on tour to Edinburgh and Liverpool and finally opened at the Phoenix Theatre on 16 May 1945. Cecil Parker, her erstwhile Britannus, played Mr. Antrobus, Joan Young was his wife, Terence Morgan the son, and Ena

Burrill (who stayed with Vivien at Durham Cottage, servantless), the daughter. Vivien was widely praised, and again the influence of Beatrice Lillie was noticed. Looking back, Olivier declared: "In the face of all critical prejudice, she had now established herself as a stage actress and star of the brightest metal."[5]

Almost all Vivien's stage contemporaries and friends cite this role as her best, proving her accomplishment as a comic actress on the stage – Moura Budberg, John Gielgud, Fabia Drake, Lady Richardson, Oswald Frewen (who had recently married). Binkie Beaumont admired her willpower in overcoming tuberculosis by tackling this part rather than retreating to a Swiss sanatorium. Kenneth Tynan, that most acerbic of critics, turned his attention to Vivien for the first time:

> At last a pale featherweight beauty has found her own pretty level: Sabina is the flirtatious self-sufficient housemaid who accompanies the Antrobus family on its desperate emergence from the cave to the centrally heated apartment, and Miss Leigh's particular brand of frail, unfelt coquetterie fits the part like an elbow-length glove…She executes all the accepted repertoire of femininity – vapid, eyelash fluttering, mock-unconcern, plain silliness – with convulsive effect and yet always with her brows slightly arched in affected boredom. She treats her lines as if she were going through a very fluent first reading, with little variation of pitch or tone; and puts important phrases in prodigiously inverted commas…[6]

James Agate also gave her a favorable review, despite being ten vital minutes late for the second act and receiving a blow on the shoulder from Olivier, who was vexed that he would miss the play's message (such as it was). Agate ended by judging Vivien's as "the best performance in this kind since Yvonne Printemps."[7] Vivien herself loved Sabina – "I always found her a real joy"[8] – and Thornton Wilder praised her for her "great beauty, an enchanting nature, lively imagination and observation and the skill with which to project them."[9] But he felt she was let down by her voice:

> In private life her voice was a constant delight, exactly conveying her kindness, her caressing pleasure in the friends about her, her searching honesty, her strength of character. It lost nothing in the moving pictures.
>
> On the stage however, it limited her performance to a narrow range of parts. She was enchanting, malicious, joyous, hard and pathetic, in turn, as Sabina…[10]

Perhaps the most important point was that Vivien was once again developing, proving that she was capable of putting famous Hollywood roles behind her, moving on from playing Shaw on stage and screen to tackling a complicated Wilder. The Vivien seen as maid or beauty queen was very different from Scarlett, Emma Hamilton, or Cleopatra.

Unfortunately, after seventy-eight performances the play had to close. Vivien had become "strangely overtired and quite alarmingly thin."[11] A cough, developed in Liverpool, had worsened in London, and she became worried. She found that "noisy and smoky restaurants" made her feel "frightful."[12] Vivien saw two doctors who diagnosed a tubercular patch on her lung. One wanted her to go to Switzerland or Scotland, the other just to stop work at once. The situation was made no easier by Olivier's absence in Germany on an Old Vic tour. So *The Skin of Our Teeth* closed in July, and Vivien spent six weeks in University College Hospital. Ralph Richardson's wife, Mu, was also suffering from T.B., but at home. She and Vivien used to do *The Times* crossword puzzle over the telephone to the annoyance of their husbands who found the line consistently occupied.

When Olivier was free he took Vivien to Scotland. The peace of their holiday coincided with the Japanese surrender on 15 August 1945. "This holiday had been a good idea," wrote Olivier, "but on account of it I had missed half my rehearsal time for the new season…"[13] Late in September Vivien retreated to the country for nine months of total recuperation. Olivier thought she would be better there than in Switzerland, with the windows open and a good log fire burning.

After two long years the Olivier's house-hunting had borne fruit in the discovery of Notley Abbey, between Long Crendon and Winchendon in Buckinghamshire at the end of 1944. Notley Abbey was in a state of considerable disrepair, but the knowledge that it had been endowed by

Henry V appealed inordinately to Olivier. "For me it has mesmeric power; I could easily drown in its atmosphere. I could not leave it alone, I was a child lost in its history. Perhaps I loved it too much, if that is possible."[14]

The Abbey was founded by Augustinian friars in the twelfth century. The house the Oliviers lived in was the fifteenth century Abbot's Lodging, consisting of Abbot's Hall, Parlor and Solar. The Hall and the Upper Chamber above it had straight-headed two-light windows and panel tracery. The south range of the Abbey contained some beautiful thirteenth century arcading with stiff-lead capitals, pointed trefoil arches and richly decorated spandrels. In 1954 the architect Philip Tilden wrote that within living memory there had been a great Gothic staircase of stone, but that the stiars had been destroyed in the 'unenlightened' nineteenth century and the stone used to repair the drive.

During their tenure, the Oliviers often found old bones amongst the ruins, not perhaps as exciting as the discovery in the late nineteenth century of "the skeleton of one of the monks of Notley, sewn up in folds of stout leather, together with a rosary."[15] in the brick vaulted grave of a nearby church. Notley comprised a hall and study, three large reception rooms, five principal bedrooms and a nursery, and land of 68½ acres. There was also a cottage where first Tony Bushell and, later, Olivier's brother, Dickie, lived as estate manager.

Notley was in no sense a natural home for Vivien. Grey, with mullioned windows, there were too few doors leading to the garden. Nor did it lend itself to Vivien's bright, chintz style. Whereas Leigh decorated Woodlands in a sparse, understated way, Vivien slightly over-decorated Notley, not perhaps remaining sufficiently in the period. Notley Abbey became their country home in February 1945. Vivien came to know and love Notley during her months of recuperation. She enjoyed discussing plans with Lady Colefax and John Fowler, though it was the latter who did all the work, gradually converting a monument into a home.

Of Vivien's close friends, two became notable visitors at this time, Robert Helpmann and Bumble Dawson. Helpmann, an Australian born in 1909, enjoyed a distinguished career as dancer, actor, director, and choreographer. A controversial figure with friends and enemies apace, he achieved posthumous notoriety in his obituary in *The Times* which broke the normal bounds of convention by describing him as "a homosexual of the proselytizing kind…capable of cutting a person down in public without mercy…an amusing companion, with an abundance of wit and fantasy."[16] He described himself as "a narcissus, who loves where he is loved; who responds to admiration from either sex."[17]

Helpmann first met Vivien in 1934, when she informed him that she had seen him dance: "You have very beautiful legs."[18] He called on her in her dressing room during the run of *The Mask of Virtue* and their friendship grew. He told Elizabeth Salter, his biographer:

> Like so many other men I fell in love with her. She had a superb sense of humor, and a great deal of character – not at all the frail little thing she appeared to be.[19]

They played together in 1937 in *A Midsummer Night's Dream* and might have done so again had Vivien not made her determined voyage to America in the quest of Scarlett.

Helpmann was one of those who advised the Oliviers not to pursue the idea of Notley. But during Vivien's illness he was a frequent visitor. His biographer wrote:

> With him she could be sure to laugh and so forget the boredom of enforced idleness. Olivier, Helpmann said, could be moody and often withdrawn… With petrol rationing at its height, he was usually met at the station by Olivier himself in a trap.[20]

The trap was pulled by Olivier's grey gelding, Blaunche Kynge. Evidently at a rendering of "Once more into the breach" he broke into a spontaneous gallop. Hamish Hamilton recalled that when Vivien felt times were rough she would say "I want my Bobby."[21] Other friends felt that he was not altogether a good influence on her. He was inclined to urge her to do as she pleased, rather than to do what was best for her.

Beatrice (Bumble) Dawson, on the other hand, was a consistently staunch friend. Born in 1908, she had produced the jewelry for *Caesar and Cleopatra* in 1944 and five years later designed the costumes for the London stage version of *A Streetcar Named Desire*. Bumble's early life had not been easy.

The photographer, Barbara Ker-Seymer, who met her at the Slade, recalled:

> Bumble spent her youth barricaded in a mansion flat by Westminster Cathedral. They didn't answer bells for fear of debt collectors…She got herself where she was by sheer hard work and a great deal of stamina…I was amazed at how well she got into the costume designing world as she couldn't draw for nuts when we were at the Slade, though she painted very well…I don't think she ever felt well and as a result couldn't be alone for even a short time, which is probably why she had such a passion for entertaining. It was a form of distraction.[22]

In her early days Bumble had been secretary to the society photographer Olivia Wyndham, one of the "Bright Young Things," and a friend of the painter Edward Burra. She married Gerald Corcoran and converted him into an art dealer by persuading him to buy some of Burra's work for cash. She inspired two Burra exhibitions at the Redfern Ballery. Bumble then began her career as a designer of costume jewelry, belts, and handbags in Shepherds Market. Her designs were startling – a glass earring with water and a model fish inside, with the habit of breaking and splashing everyone in its vicinity.

Her brother, 'Boy' Dawson, had been a friend of Terrence Rattigan at Oxford. Later she made a good living as a costume designer, a career that gave her plenty of opportunities for lionizing stars, John Merivale recalled:

> She was accomplished, extremely well-read, had a lot of affairs when she was young, and she was an extremely good cook and an amusing conversationalist. And she used these assets, as Noël Coward said, "like a shrimping net."[23]

As the years went by, Bumble played a close supportive role in Vivien's life.

When there were no visitors, Vivien lay in bed reading Dickens, Confucius and Montaigne; James Agate sent her his *Ego 7* (which included references to their dinner at Café Royal). She replied on 30 October:

> I am absolutely delighted to have your *Ego 7.* Whether you thought of me in my enforced purdah or whether you had quite forgotten that – for me – unhappy circumstance, it was extremely kind of you to think of it…[24]

Agate replied: "Hurry up and get well or people will think Larry thrives in your absence. *He is becoming a great actor…*[25]

Olivier continued to rise to great heights on the stage, more than eclipsing Vivien. An actress told Thomas Kiernan that if Vivien had gone back to Hollywood things might have been different:

> She might have become so preoccupied with her own career that she wouldn't have had time to dwell on her fears and anxieties. But after the war Larry so overwhelmed her with his talents and achievements that she lost her sense of her own worth…[26]

Others believed that as Vivien's melancholia grew, she was unable to fulfill Olivier's dreams of pure, romantic love. In his frustration he veered away, releasing his anger on stage, throwing all his energy into creativity. Many maintain that he fell in love with the characters he portrayed, a prime example being Richard III. Olivier acted in *Uncle Vanya*, both parts of *Henry IV, Oedipus Rex*, and *The Critic* in the 1945-6 season at the New Theatre. Not only was Olivier battling for a resolution of his private life, but he was fighting to be the theatre's king. Ralph Richardson saw the rivalry as friendly, but noted that between Gielgud and Olivier it was more guarded:

> Johnny still thought Larry tended to overact and found it hard to understand his popularity. Larry looked on Johnny as being much on the cool, remote side.[27]

Sadly, though Vivien made progress at Notley, she did not become completely well. She gave up drinking and smoking for a time, though she never drank inordinately unless held in the grip of a manic cycle. The tuberculosis also appeared to be under control, although sufferers are always in danger of its return. It seemed that Vivien's mood changes were due to some other cause. However, they set into a pattern which could be recognized. She was impossible while in a cycle but completely normal when not. Esmond Knight recalled her illness as "like a worm in the blood, as Viola says. It probably began to eat away something in her and this extraordinary deterioration began."[28] Olivier's performance as Oedipus was another example of how he coped with his plight, particularly the grim end when he put out his eyes, blood spurting forth onto the stage. Audiences found the scene hard to take and suffered, as they would suffer again when they saw *Titus Andronicus* in the 1950s. Kenneth Tynan found this moment of self-blinding and the cries of Olivier memorably powerful:

> In those agonized, agonizing utterances were contained three thousand years of mankind's confrontation with the fates, with the gods, with himself. They were the cries of a woman you might imagine discovering the bodies of her children in the rubble of a building in London during the blitz…[29]

Thomas Kiernan maintains that, with two houses, two wives and Tarquin (the son he barely knew) to support, Olivier was feeling the need to earn more money and that he contemplated a return to Hollywood. Kiernan pointed out that, due to Vivien's contractural difficulties with Selznick, he was a marked man. Selznick would do no business with anyone who employed Olivier. Therefore he was boycotted by the American film industry for two years.

In the spring of 1946 Olivier took *Oedipus Rex,* the two *Henry IVs* and *Uncle Vanya* to New York, where the *Henry V* film was also on the point of release. He also took Vivien.

Olivier stormed the New York stage in the same manner that he had conquered London. He was voted the best actor on Broadway in the 1945-6 season by the *New York Times* drama critic and played to packed houses. It was his turn to be exhausted. Vivien's two month stay was generally more relaxed. She was in great demand for films and plays but had resolved just to keep her husband company. Inevitably this led to a certain amount of "tension caused by inactivity."[30] One night Vivien began to bicker with Garson Kanin over the pronunciation of Machiavelli's 'LaMandragola,' which developed into a row about who was better educated. Eventually everyone apologized but some harm had been done. Kanin wrote: "I wonder if such flare-ups are ever completely forgotten. They are like little fuses blowing, reminding you that they may blow again."[31] He apologized to Vivien, "but I wonder if she really believed me and I wonder if I really meant it."[32] More constructive was dinner at the Colony with Somerset Maugham, whom Vivien had never met. Author and star were soon mutually bewitched, and as Kanin wrote:

> Vivien falls in love. As for WSM, I have never seen this side of him – the gallant, the courtly gentleman, the man on the make. Every warm instinctive exchange passes between them. Vivien is enormously impressive with her tremendous erudition, her wide reading, her beautiful French, her glorious speech. It is a pleasure to sit there and shut up and listen.[33]

The evening was going so well that Kanin unwisely brought up the word 'Mandragola' and asked Maugham for his verdict. Suddenly he fell victim to his stuttering and after a seemingly endless struggle, produced: "MMMAGENAMERINGOLAMEDRANLOLO." As the Kanins flushed red with shame, Vivien saved the day by announcing in triumph: "There, what did I tell you? Mandragola!"[34]

It was during the New York visit that the Oliviers suffered two incidents connected with airplanes. They had always resolved never to fly separately, but on returning from a ceremony at Tufts University near Boston where Olivier was made an honorary LL.D., Vivien and Jerry Dale, now publicizing *Henry V*, caught the plane, but Olivier missed it. Contrary to stories that have Olivier collapsing in tears on the runway, he could be seen laughing as the plane took off. Dale told Thomas Kiernan:

> Vivien got in a terrible fret about it, and she clutched my hand all the way down to LaGuardia. She kept chattering away about the fact that Larry had been laughing – "I'll kill him," she said, "he knows how much I hate to fly without him." [35]

A few days later, on 18 June, the Oliviers set off on their flight to London.

This time there was real danger. The airplane caught fire and lost an engine, and there was a very frightening forced landing at Willimantic, Connecticut. "It was very awkward flying around with a motor missing," said Olivier.[36] Two days later they arrived safely in London. Thomas Kiernan maintains that Olivier was once again seriously strapped for cash and that the "solution to their economic problems was for Vivien to go back to work."[37]

It was decided that Vivien would revive *The Skin of Our Teeth* and Olivier would stage *King Lear.* Before that, they enjoyed a healthy summer at Notley. Olivier did his best to become a gentleman farmer though not everyone was impressed. Lord Cottesloe was amused at Olivier's fear of what he thought was a field of bulls. These were in fact steers.[38]

Opinions differ about the pleasure of Notley life. Vivien went to immense trouble to create a good atmosphere. Unlike Olivier, who was always an actor and thus playing the role of country squire, a tweed-jacketed figure in a cravat at the head of the table, Vivien was a more natural country dweller. Significantly, she ceased to be an actress at Long Crendon. She was the headscarfed Lady Olivier, rather than Vivien Leigh, even if she did go shopping in a chauffeur-driven Rolls-Royce. Lady Walton recalled the room she stayed in later in the 1940s "with curtains chosen to match the sheets, as well as the breakfast set, and the color scheme continued down to the loo paper. It was sybaritic."[39] Breakfast was served in the bedroom, which not every guest appreciated, and the house was perpetually a hive of activity, the formality relieved perhaps by Robert Helpmann impersonating Dame Edith Evans, playing bowls, or the kind of games that Vivien loved to organize. David Niven wrote of great arguments as causes were attacked or defended and professional reputations assessed, adding "there were few tears and gales of laughter," particularly when, accompanied on the piano by a hysterical Vivien, Larry, dead seriously would sing *Messiah.*[40]

Then there was the uncertainty of the unexpected. It was once said: "There was nothing Vivien wouldn't do on a wet afternoon." Evenings stretched on until dawn and, while Larry and other guests wilted noticeably, Vivien would end the evening as fresh as she had started it."

Godfrey Winn thought that to be at Notley was like "being part of an exquisite charade, performed by an all-star cast."[41] It was certainly no surprise to find Marlene Dietrich or Katharine Hepburn weeding the garden. Winn recalled driving in convoy to Notley with Orson Welles, Rex

Harrison, and Lilli Palmer in the 1950s. They arrived at 1 a.m. and, just as he was wondering if he dared ask for a biscuit, a lavish candlelit dinner was served. The evening ended in broad daylight, at which point Vivien took him on a tour of the garden. Then he went up to bed. Scarcely asleep, he was awakened by a maid who announced, "Her Ladyship would like you to join her for a game of bowls, as soon as it is convenient."[42] Winn stole some more sleep between lunch and tea and then another evening ended with bacon and eggs in the kitchen at 2 a.m. He was roused once more, after too little sleep, this time for gardening.

On the Monday, back in London, Vivien was acting and going on to Beatrice Lillie's show at the Café de Paris, while Winn retired to bed with instructions not to be called until Wednesday morning.

There was a market garden at Notley, run by Olivier's brother, Dickie, from the summer of 1954 until his death four years later. It owed its success to the energy of his wife, Hester. There was a wild garden and formal one, and Olivier planted an avenue of limes, which only reached their full glory some years after he had left. Olivier loved to garden, and Michael Redgrave would come across him early on a Sunday morning "pruning what he called a 'where'er you walk' of pleached hornbeams or beech."[43] There was also a variety of pedigree cows named after Vivien's stage roles, Sabina, Blanche, and Cleopatra. The farming side was perhaps more amateurish and diverting than professionally viable.

Caesar and Cleopatra was released in New York on 6 September, and "doing tremendous business," according to David Niven, eleven days later.

Vivien revived *Skin of Our Teeth* at the Piccadilly on 11 September, with George Devine as Antrobus and Esther Somers as his wife. Vivien told Cecil Beaton that Miss Somers could not act at all:

> When at the end of the run Larry laid into her and said he's never had so much trouble with anybody, she threw her arms in the air and laughed: "Oh isn't he just darling!"[44]

Noël Coward was soon describing Olivier's *King Lear* as "unequivocally great" and dubbing him "a superb actor and I suspect the greatest I shall ever see."[45] All seemed to be going well, but, within days of opening, Vivien was writing to Leigh: "I am not allowed to play tonight or tomorrow matinée which is horrid."[46] The play only ran for 109 performances, closing around the end of the year. On Vivien's thirty-fourth birthday she danced for the first time in many years and wrote: "It felt quite strange."[47]

The Oliviers were hoping to film *Cyrano de Bergerac* together in Hollywood, largely for the money. It was a serious blow when this fell through. Soon afterwards Vivien's manic depression entered a new cycle and she had to drop out of her play. Olivier was soon diverted into planning to film *Hamlet,* while Vivien was set to play Anna in *Anna Karenina*. In February 1947, before work began, Olivier took Vivien to Paris where they stayed with the Duff Coopers, now installed at the British Embassy. They were soon included in the group that Lady Diana called 'La Bande,' faithful and unusual talented friends who more than relieved the tedium of diplomatic life. Cecil Beaton was staying there, confined to bed with a cold. Vivien spent the afternoon cheering him up: "She has no pretentions about being anything but a very loving wife and devoted stage trooper."[48] Olivier was less at ease in the Embassy, confessing to Beaton: "I find it difficult when Duff comes into the room not to straighten up too much at attention, or alternatively to be so casual as to ignore him almost entirely and finally greet him in an off-hand way."[49] In discussing plans for *Hamlet* with Beaton, Olivier acted out his plans with much schoolboy joke spluttering. Vivien watched with rapt amusement, while Roger Furse and Tony Bushell looked on in pain. As Beaton noted: "They knew this of old and their slight looks of anxiety were inspired by the dread that this performance might continue late in the night."[50] Just before they left, Vivien came in to Beaton's room and told him:

> She had decided to play *Ophelia* in Larry's film as well as *Anna Karenina*. It is an exciting life – they have their future planned two years ahead and there is no gainsaying their success.[51]

The Oliviers then left Paris for a holiday in Santa Margherita Ligure. This trip included a visit to Bernard Berenson at Villa I Tatti, which proved such a success that the old art critic invited Vivien and Olivier back the following day. He was known to love beautiful ladies just as he loved beautiful pictures. On her return to London Vivien wrote:

> Of course you have exercised the worst possible influence for I have no wish to work again, my only desire being to rush back to Florence for another visit. The stern reality is that *Anna Karenina* starts next month and so does *Hamlet* for which Larry's hair is now an alarming ginger en route to being a ravishing blonde. It is also of an unusual cut which frightens the children in the village.[52]

Vivien had assumed the role of Ophelia would be hers, but the Rank Organization had other ideas. As the film's backers, they refused to put up the money unless a younger actress was chosen. Olivier agreed. The part went to Jean Simmons. Vivien could not dissociate Olivier from the decision, and he now became the victim of her outbursts when she was overwrought. This was not helped by Jean Simmons looking very like Vivien. In some scenes of *Hamlet* she could almost be Vivien. If Vivien was afraid of losing Olivier or in any way suspicious of infidelity, then this beautiful young actress more than fitted the mold.*As Olivier became increasingly engrossed in every detail of Hamlet he had less time for Vivien and her moods. When filming began he used to stay at the studio and she would ring him late at night accusing him of abandoning her.

During the filming of *Hamlet*, Esmond Knight became an occasional visitor to Notley. Having partially overcome his wartime blindness, he had taken part in the film of *Henry V* and was now playing Barnardo. One of his tasks was to restrain Olivier when his father's ghost appeared on the battlements, no easy task as Olivier played the scene with considerable strength ("it was like holding a Bengal tiger")[53]. At Notley Olivier put him to further work cutting nettles and he was much stung. He returned to the house:

> I went into this lovely hall with its beautiful winding wooden staircase going up and at the top was Vivien, standing there in the brilliant sun. I think she probably realized she was cutting a rather good picture—an absolutely stunning one—and she was talking to some guest about half way down on the first landing. I just stood absolutely transfixed by this incredible creature standing there. She was in a loose gown

*They did not have an affair.

> of some sort, practically stark naked underneath, which one was very aware of I may say, because she was absolutely unselfconscious about all that. But one was thinking "If only I could nip up the stairs and seize this gorgeous creature and carry her away."[54]

Esmond Knight's wife, Nora Swinburne, had a different memory of Notley:

> The thing that really fascinated me was when we went into the abbey, there was the most gorgeous smell of jasmine. She had some sort of spray which she used when guests were coming. When I came back to my rather meager little house I used to rush to my perfume bottle to copy her.[55]

Vivien then embarked on *Anna Karenina* at Shepperton Studios in May. It was a Korda production and Vivien played opposite Ralph Richardson as Karenin. At this time Korda was still in the phase of recreating great historical dramas such as *Bonnie Prince Charlie* with David Niven. He also made Wilde's drama, *An Ideal Husband*, with Paulette Goddard and Michael Wilding. They were lavish productions, the last two benefiting from Cecil Beaton's contributions as designer.

Vivien was to prove a very different Anna from Garbo's 1936 performance. Curiously they shared one trait – neither was the least bit maternal. Vivien relished Tolstoy as an author and in a conversation with Thornton Wilder in 1951 caused him to rethink the book, a convoluted process for him at the best of times. In his journal he wrote:

> I now see that I have all my life been an idiot about Anna Karenina – which came to such a bouquet of ineptitude in my conversation with Vivien Leigh about it: I have never had the faintest glimmer about that novel and now it is all to be reread.[56]

Cecil Beaton's involvement with the Oliviers over *Anna Karenina* and, later in the year, *The School for Scandal,* led him to stay at Notley Abbey at the end of March. He described his visit to Greta Garbo:

> It is very romantic in a medieval way and it is lovely to see something that has been neglected for so long taking on new life. They have planed avenues of trees, 500 rose trees and are making great improvements both in and outside the house. This morning a tapestry was hung with everyone giving advice in their pajamas. Larry looks very strange as he goes about the place and is disguised as a sort of village wight. He has dyed his hair yellow in order to be a blond Hamlet on the screen, and it is worn in the tradition of the middle ages with fringe and shaved high at the temples... The life they lead in the country is most suitable for Shakespearian actors. The whole atmosphere of the place is suitable for giving performances of *Twelfth Night, Midsummer Night's Dream* and *Hamlet.*[57]

Korda experienced considerable problems with the script of *Anna Karenina*, discovering just in time that the director Julien Duvivier and the screenplay writer Joan Anouilh planned to make it 'an existentialist glorification of suicide.'[58] Cecil Beaton and Vivien went over to Paris for two nights on 14 May, staying with the Duff Coopers, at what the Unit Production Manager called the 'British Embassy Hotel.'[59] The next day Beaton supervised the fitting of Vivien's clothes, which were being made in Paris to avoid rationing problems. He described the scene to Garbo.

> Vivien complained that her corsets were torture...At the fitting in Paris they still hurt. The clothes were carefully fitted, in spite of Anna's bosoms being wedged into a very unflattering shape – so unflattering indeed that when the storm of photographers invaded the small fitting room, Anna had to keep an arm discreetly hiding the corset. At last she could bear the pain no longer...[the expensive new corsets were then re-cut in several ways]... When we got back to the Embassy a call came through from Karinska to Anna to say they had discovered that the corsets had

> been put on upside down…the corsets worn upside down pushed in everything that should be pushed out, and vice versa…[60]

While Vivien was in Paris, Olivier received news that he was to be made a Knight. He rang Vivien, as Felix Barker has related:

> "You won't take it, of course?" she asked with mock innocence. "Of course not!" he answered, and promptly sat down and wrote to say that he would be honored to accept.[61]

Later, when the news was made official in the King's Birthday Honors List, Beaton went to congratulate Vivien in her dressing room. "Oh, I'm so happy about the great honor," he declared. "A face of furious scorn greets me: 'Really it's too stupid,' says the reflected face in the mirror." Beaton concluded: "The leading lady, so carefree and intelligent in her private life, becomes entirely different as soon as the strain of picture making begins to tell."[62]

Beaton observed Vivien closely on the set, impressed like everyone at the speed with which she adopted and relinquished her role. At the race meeting scene, the horses were smeared with soap suds to represent sweat. Vivien did not need time to work up to the atmosphere. Between the shots she read Thurber's *Is Sex Necessary?,* and roared with laughter. Beaton thought her convincing in the role of Anna, though not physically as Tolstoy had intended. He also detected a duality in her nature:

> The Star has developed a technique whereby she preserves herself from showing her feelings. She has bottled up her emotions so successfully that for weeks on end she is working only on media value. All the time she is in reserve and feels that she is successfully hiding her real self from the world. Therein lies her fault. She is carefully scrutinized by all her assistants. The girl who holds her powder box, the electrician and the continuity girl are all conscious of the various most subtle steps of artifice on

> which she is acting. One wonders: does the outlet come at home? She cannot keep herself in reserve indefinitely howsoever great her resources.[63]

Beaton also noted that Vivien was beginning to develop a phobia about her appearance:

> It is not at all what she would like. It has deteriorated and appalls her. Each photograph shown to her is further confirmation of her fears. She is always seeking to be in a dark light – muffled up in veils and furs.[64]

Beaton's eccentric friend, Stephen Tennant, famous posthumously as the recluse of Wilsford Manor, visited the set in June. Later he wrote:

> I loved your dresses and hats. They are very beautiful and unusual. Vivien Leigh's toilette – the tart's ensemble – is exquisite, and the hairdressing accents her individuality perfectly, extreme though it is.[65]

Mary Kerridge played Dolly Oblonsky, and recalled Vivien as a "totally unaffected" actress. She remembered the scene when Anna returns, very distraught, to see her little boy. On this occasion, the cameraman spent ages on the lighting and Vivien complained: "Oh, do get a move on! I'm thinking of all the things that make me cry. It's all being wasted."[66] Miss Kerridge attributed the faults of the film to a badly miscast Vronsky in Kieron Moore and to Duvivier's determination that Vivien should play the part differently from Garbo. While Vivien could not fail to respond badly to Kieron Moore, she was more alive when playing opposite her old friend, Ralph Richardson.

As filming progressed into June, Beaton found both Duvivier and Vivien most exacting. He did not help matters by replying to Vivien's complaint that he had made her gloves too small: "No, it isn't that the gloves are too small but that your hands are too big."[67]

The temperature soared, which did not help as Vivien wrote to Bernard Berenson:

> There has been a heat-wave during which I have had to pretend I was living in Moscow in *deepest* winter! – covered in velvets and sables and corseted down to 19 inches. I thought this last would gain me some sympathy when I told Larry. But not a bit of it. *He* too is corseted and pretending it's winter in Elsinore! It really does seem a strange way of earning a living sometimes.[68]

In July they filmed the last scene on the station platform: Beaton again wrote to Garbo:

> By the end of the day's shooting Anna's sable cape looks like an old drowned rat, and the ostrich feathers in her hat look like the flu brush. Time and again Anna has to get out of the train while the wind machines blow a mixture of Perspex and salt and cement onto her. Personally I think it is a lot of fun – and that is the part of films I like the best – the imitation icicles and snow – the imitation train – but by now Vivien doesn't share my views and she is thoroughly disgusted by the smell of the steam. Even so I think her a very lucky girl to be getting so much expert attention (from Tolstoy downwards) and to be paid such a fabulous sum for doing it. However she is not really of a contented frame of mind and does not see things in a rosy light. Her triumph is of such comparatively short duration and I think she should get more fun out of her spell dressed in a little brief authority.[69]

Both Garbo's and Vivien's versions of Anna had their good points, if neither Frederic March's nor Kieron Moore's Vronsky was at all satisfactory. Both had memorable moments – Garbo standing indecisive in the arcade of her garden, wondering whether to turn left to Vronsky or right to her son, and Vivien's romantic first appearance through the misty-snow-circle window of the train. Her last, of course, echoed her sad walk along *Waterloo Bridge*. John Barber of *Leader Magazine* judged Vivien "as better casting than the noble Swede,"[70] while Paul Dehn wrote that the film was "the screen's most brilliantly *continuous* piece of character development" since James Mason's Johnny McQueen in *Odd Man Out:*

> Mason has shown us a physically wounded man dying a slow death in the flesh: Miss Leigh, a mentally wounded woman deteriorating, as slowly, in the spirit.[71]

The general line was that *Anna Karenina* was a beautiful failure. This caused Vivien considerable distress. Lunching at an oyster bar with Mu Richardson, she said: "I know about Anna. I *was* inside her. I know everything about her, and yet they say I can't do it."[72] Lady Richardson said, "She had steeped herself in it. Yet what she was not able to do was to show the love for her son. And so those scenes were not really moving at all.'[73] The film compared badly with Olivier's *Hamlet,* which received considerable praise from the critics, if not entirely from the ever-critical Cecil Beaton:

> Well, after all the blaring fanfare of trumpets it is fairly damn good. Not the work of a first rate artist or man of taste and erudition, but a very boisterous and dramatic entertainment. There are some excellent rows, and the final fight is the best thing in the film...The albino dyed hair made [Olivier] look very froggish and thick set and the years are nimbly advancing on his countenance.[74]

On 8 July Vivien accompanied Olivier to Buckingham Palace for the investiture and witnessed him dubbed a Knight Bachelor by King George VI. Her early disdain for the whole affair had not dissolved, but the ever-patriotic Korda closed the *Anna Karenina* set down specially for the day. At forty, Olivier was the theatre's youngest ever Knight.

Chapter 15
Australia

Martita Hunt (Princess Betty): "Do you know, my dear, I believe you're rather inclined to the tragic side."
Vivien (Anna): "Yes, yes, perhaps I am."

Anna Karenina

On 6 March 1948 it was announced that King George and Queen Elizabeth, accompanied by Princess Margaret, would visit Australia in the spring of 1949. It was a visit that would never take place. In November 1948 it was announced that the King was not well enough to go. By November 1949 his doctors were satisfied that he could go. But it was too late to arrange it for 1950 and the Festival of Britain was occupying much of 1951. By 1952 he was dead.

The Old Vic tour made by the Oliviers between February and November 1948 was therefore never eclipsed by a royal visit. It is remembered by older generations as an important landmark in their lives.

Olivier chose *The School for Scandal* because he agreed wholeheartedly with Sir Herbert Beerbohm Tree: "Few will dispute that *The School for Scandal* is the most brilliant comedy that has been given to the world."[1] Vivien had already been seen in the quarrel and reconciliation scenes in her charity matinée opposite Cyril Maude. This was Olivier's first portrayal of crusty old Sir Peter, thus a new challenge for him. Olivier chose *Richard III* as an already proven star part for himself with Vivien in the light role of Lady Anne, and the third play was *The Skin of Our Teeth* for her benefit, with himself as Mr. Antrobus. Cecil Beaton did the décor and costumes for *School for Scandal*, the sets like Hogarth engravings, the clothes, "very sophisticated…mustard color, grape, toad, newt, mushroom, cinnamon."[2] Beaton undertook the preliminary work before a long-planned visit to New York. He left his young assistant, Martin Battersby, in charge. Conflicts soon arose, not helped by the mutual antipathy of Battersby and the wardrobe mistress, Emma Selby-Walker. On 9 December 1947 Battersby reported to Beaton on his visit to rehearsals at the Haymarket:

> Peeking through Miss Calthrop's delicious set I could see the company grouped in admiring attitudes round L.O. who was giving out cuts for the text with all the zest of a frenzied Chinese executioner. The company appears to consist of two or three thousand quite presentable young men, several older ditto, various mouselike women and of course Miss Leigh – no cuts for Miss Leigh at all. Feeling sure that if I were to poke my nose round a doorway L.O. would shriek "Cut that," I went about my business, returning home to find a message from L.O. – most urgent – I must be there at 2:00. When I got there nobody took any notice of me at all but I briskly put an end to that by inquiring in a loud voice "What about the pearl buttons?" This shook them somewhat but Miss Leigh and I climbed into the ring and really got down to the question. She said that when you said mother-of-pearl buttons you didn't mean mother-of-pearl buttons but 'those dear little mother-of-pearl things that drop off so easily!!!" And anyway they'd weigh a ton and she hated a dress which she couldn't work in. I said there was a fashion for buttons at the period of the play and that smart people sewed them on like mad on everything (not strictly true, of course, but the time is long past to bother about that) and that Mr. Beaton had put them in as a sort of leitmotif to express the period nuances and so on and so on. A hard glint came into Miss Leigh's eye, a hard tone in her voice and a very hard line in her jaw. "We won't bother about that and I *don't* want buttons."

> Round one to Miss Leigh with Battling Battersby retiring to his corner snarling hideously, and feeling that it is better to win the last battle than the first.[3]

Vivien discussed the color of her ball dress at some length and it was resolved that lime green would be the best. Olivier conceived a plan whereby the sky, as seen through windows, was replaced by linen. The effect of night could thus be achieved by "placing a Teazle blue flood behind the drop."[4] Battersby was sure it would not work:

> However, it is the easiest thing in the world just to stick a bit of canvas back again and L.O. will have had his bit of fun. When I was talking to him this morning, he suddenly looked up, twinkled at me and said "I don't know a thing about period clothes or furniture" without the slightest trace of shame. Perhaps he was joking.[5]

Vivien rejected Battersby's design for the embroidery on her ball dress, leaving him bemoaning:

> It really is difficult to know exactly what to do with someone whose criticisms are entirely destructive and who has not the knowledge or taste to put forward a constructive suggestion…[6]

She also proved difficult over her wigs.

Battersby was able to pass on a vignette about a *Richard III* rehearsal, uncertain as to its veracity, but true to character, he thought:

> Apparently L.O. and V.L. returned from lunch looking daggers at each other and having obviously argued like mad all the way through the meal. They plunged into a rehearsal of Richard in which V.L. is playing the Lady Anne. L.O. said "I think that Lady Anne should fall off her chair here," V.L., who never lets a chance slip by of contradicting him piped up "Larry, she wouldn't do anything of the sort – it's

> right out of character…" and so on for some time. L.O. bore it all for a while and then said through clenched teeth "The Lady Anne will fall off her chair if I have to bloody well push her off myself!" Probably I shall feel like that after the first dress fitting.[7]

Battersby's conclusion on Vivien was:

> I get the impression of V.L. that she has fought to get to the top of the tree and can't stop now even if she wanted to – which I don't think she does – and that on the whole she was ideally cast as Scarlett O'Hara.[8]

Not long after this Emma Selby-Walker succeeded in ousting Battersby. He claimed that his main fault was a determination to see Beaton's designs executed as faithfully as possible. Olivier confirmed to Beaton that the resignation had been accepted "owing to certain friction with wardrobe staff."[9] Battersby was allowed to inspect the finished costumes, which he deemed as bad as they could be – especially Vivien's ball dress: "It says a lot for V.L. that she managed to look very lovely in this abortion."[10] Emma Selby-Walker commented later:

> He really was making life impossible and there was very little time, and he was upsetting Vivien and everybody else. Poor man, he was obviously a designer manqué and didn't really want to be Cecil's assistant. It was a way in – he hadn't arrived.[11]

Maud Nelson, Beaton's difficult lesbian secretary, wrote to him:

> Sorry to tell you that, after all, I do not think the Oliviers are great friends of yours especially V.. and I am beginning to hate her in consequence and to feel quite definitely that she may be at the bottom of the A.K.* difficulties – a Siamese cat and very hard and grasping at that.[12]

This view did not prevent Maud Nelson working as Vivien's secretary a decade later, and bringing her customary chaos to the role.

Olivier was excited at the prospect of visiting Australia because he had been "assured of a tumultuous welcome and an acceptable little package of dough."[13] It was a challenge because Australia had been almost totally neglected by the theatre – Perth, for example, had not seen a professional theatre company for twelve years. Vivien had longed to see Australia since learning Banjo Paterson's verse by heart at the age of ten. Olivier chose each actor and actress entirely on merit and suitability in order to get exactly the team he wanted. Peter Cushing's only reluctance was separation from his wife, but Olivier was adamant: "I'll have none of that. There was too much of it forced upon most of us during the war. You bring Helen with you."[14] Inevitably those left behind were disappointed, and it was not long before they were conspiring for revenge.

The company formed, and the problems of costumes and sets resolved, the Oliviers and their team set off from Euston Station on St. Valentine's Day, 1948. George Relph and his wife, Mercia Swinburne, were of the company. As staunchly loyal friends of long standing, it was natural that they should make a foursome with the Oliviers, sharing a sitting room and dining at the same table. Mercia Swinburne was a great admirer of Vivien's "zest for living," her appreciation of her friends, and taste in furniture, gardens, food, and pictures. She realized that Vivien was enduring "a great struggle theatrically against the overpowering thing of Larry. Criticism was inevitable. Yet she was always trying to build up her own abilities.[15] She recalled: "The cast were devoted to her. At first they were a little nervous as we rehearsed on board, but both the Oliviers were delightful with the company."[16]

The tour was a success before it even began. It was nothing for Australians to travel a hundred miles to the theatre and one young girl in Darwin went two thousand miles to Adelaide for a single performance. The Oliviers were legends, particularly Vivien, who was still the living embodiment of Scarlett to so many.

From the moment that the Oliviers arrived in Fremantle, they were treated like royalty. The contemporary press-cuttings show the smiling

*Korda had complained at an Olivier dinner party of his exasperation with decorators and designers behaving in *prima donna* fashion…seeing themselves as the principal stars of the show. (Maud Nelson to Beaton, 2 January 1948)

couple disembarking, Vivien holding an enormous bouquet. Besides bringing culture to the Antipodes, Vivien brought the "new look" from Paris. She wore a suit in soft brown woolen material with a white fleck, the short jacket made with nipped-in waist and padded hipline, the skirt with sunray pleats of fashionable length (estimated by an Australian fashion editor to be "12 inches from the ground").[17] The trip included a great number of civic receptions, visits to hospitals, and eloquent appeals from Olivier for "Food for Britain" (still enduring food rationing after the war). Vivien was photographed in Canberra seated next to Ben Chifley, the Prime Minister, at an Anzac service. They visited the State Parliament House in Melbourne where Olivier assumed the local vernacular and declared: "You have all been absolute beauts and we've had a bonzer time here."[18] At Garnet Carroll's party, they met two future Prime Ministers, Robert Menzies and Harold Holt. Unlike royalty, they were not spared a grueling series of press conferences causing even some journalists to take pity on them. In Sydney, towards the end of the tour, Olivier was made to sit on the lowest couch imaginable. He was then asked every possible question. "They did everything but play football with him," wrote one commentator.[19] And, as he attempted to explain his plans for the theatre, a journalist at the back yelled: "Break it up; let's have a go at him."[20]

On the voyage out Vivien had gathered a list of birthdays. Michael Redington had the luck to be twenty-one in Melbourne and a star-studded birthday party was arranged with Chico Marx of the Marx Brothers present. The Oliviers also made a point of giving dinners for each member of the company in turn in small groups.

Another member of the cast was John Barnard, known as "Pip." He wrote from Australia:

> There was a special warmth woven in that 1948 tour which I doubt has ever quite been equaled for any member of the company since...We enjoyed the times we were together as a company, and especially those moments when we were close to Larry and Vivien. We called them "Larry and Vivien;" they let it be known they wished to be so called, though I admit I found it embarrassingly hard to do so at times, preferring to think of him as "sir," and normally trying

to avoid having to use any particular form of address.[21]

Pip Barnard also recalled a telling scene of Vivien backstage:

> One night while watching the stage I heard a dress rustle, and looking around beheld this bewitching Dresden figure of 18th century Lady Teazle next to me. She saw my look of obvious admiration and smiled at me in her almost shy way as she smoothed the creases of her voluminous skirt. I gasped at the exquisite picture. Suddenly the magic was shattered. Realizing she had forgotten something important, she muttered angrily "SHIT!" and rushed away to fix whatever it was. I grinned at the irony.[22]

In Perth they opened with *The School for Scandal* after only two dress rehearsals, the third having been cancelled for the sake of the costumes in the hot weather. Michael Redington wrote home to Jack and Winifred Keates, the managers of the Brighton Theatre:

> Well, the first night was a very good success, though it could not be heard all over the house. The laughs were very slow in coming, there are some people you cannot hear at all, it depends on the tone of the voice. Everyone came in evening dress, including the Governor of the State [Sir James Mitchell], who arrived a quarter of an hour late, incidentally he hasn't a H to his name.The house was packed and must have looked lovely as they stood for the King, but I am afraid not half as lovely as Cecil Beaton's sets and costumes, and the whole production and music…I think Vivien Leigh is giving a brilliant performance as Lady Teazle, especially after the discovery.[23]

In Perth they played to capacity audiences at night, while rehearsing *Richard III* by day. Olivier hurt his foot, because of having to dance, and for a time played Teazle with a stick. After one matinée the schoolchildren "cheered like mad things, all was well until Sir Laurence tried to leave in his car and practically knocked them all down in trying to get away."[24] As the Oliviers' popularity grew in the company, they became known as "God and the Angel."[25] An example of the way the Oliviers endeared themselves to the company occurred in Perth. The Capitol Theatre only had two real dressing rooms, which were assigned to the Oliviers. But they put the company first, insisting on changing in the wings, Vivien behind a simple screen.

The next stop was Adelaide, an uncomfortable ten-hour fight after two performances. Vivien, who did not even attempt to sleep, woke all the weary company with the enthusiastic cry, "Here's the sunrise!" [26] Georgina Jumel (Mrs. Terence Morgan) recalled: "I didn't want to look at the sunrise, and I suddenly saw this vision coming down the aisle in a pale blue negligée…We were all creased up – everything was creased. And she was immaculate."[27] The company spent a fortnight in Adelaide, launching *Richard III* to a first-night audience of 3,000. Once again, Olivier was in his element as he played the hunchback King, described by Terence Rattigan as "one of the most sexually attractive characters ever to disgrace the stage."[28] Much has been made of the swordfight between Olivier's Richard and Dan Cunningham's Richmond. According to an Adelaide reviewer, Olivier's sword snapped off a foot from the point and flew across the stage, narrowly missing a group of men-at-arms. Another sword appeared from the wings and the vigorous fight went on. But Michael Redington wrote that the dying King 'suddenly threw his sword at Richmond, which Dan just managed to shield off him. Sir Laurence remembered Kean had done that; he had never rehearsed it or anything!"[29] The ruse inspired tremendous applause.

In the second week the company staged *The Skin of Our Teeth*, Vivien's chance to shine. As ever the play was deemed confusing but even if most audiences were bemused they appeared to enjoy the evening. Mr. W. Stewart of Millswood, Adelaide, was an exception:

> Quite frankly, what the play was all about or what idea it was intended to convey, I have not the faintest conception, and to say I was bored almost to tears would be to put it very mildly. Judging by the remarks of many around me, I was not alone in this opinion.
>
> The charm and beauty of Vivien Leigh exceeded my expectations, but apart from these attributes, coupled with

> her vivacity, I found nothing in the whole show to keep my attention fixed.[30]

Vivien's stamina caused her to be nicknamed in the press: "Miss Vitamin B."[31]

They reached Melbourne in April, by which time some of the younger members of the cast were getting a bit homesick, while Vivien ran a temperature and developed bronchitis, missing five performances. To raise morale, Olivier hammed up his part of Antrobus, playing him drunk or in imitation of John Gielgud. Olivier was understanding when an actor inadvertently stood on his wig at the end of *Richard III,* bringing it off. Then he too became ill. The inevitable fatigue caused ructions, and Vivien and Elsie Beyer, the General Manager, fell out badly. Soon afterwards the company went on to Hobart, Tasmania, which was so cold that Vivien sat in the wings in her mink coat with a hole cut in the scenery and an electric fire behind it. In Hobart they performed only *Skin.* They also had something of a holiday in Brisbane and Cecil Tennant, the Oliviers' manager in London and an intimate friend, was with them for some days. Surfers' Paradise, south of Brisbane, proved crowded but beneficial. Olivier, at least, emerged from it all wholly refreshed.

Garry O'Connor, in his book on the tour, maintained that the Oliviers were not getting on well. He wrote "Only Mum and Dad 'in loco' fell out, not knowing if they loved each other any more, but like proud, old-fashioned parents, kept it from the children, and presented to them a devoted and united front."[32] Olivier has lent some credence to this in his memoirs: "Somehow, somewhere on this tour I knew that Vivien was lost to me."[33] But other members of the company noticed little untoward. Terence Morgan recalled:

> She used to play it up a bit and flirt with other men in the company just to make him jealous because he used to sit there watching her rehearse and he would embarrass everyone by getting erections.[34]

The Morgans found her restless, however, sitting on a balcony adjoining their room talking and drinking champagne until three in the morning. "We couldn't keep up. We wanted to go to sleep."[35] Floy Bell added: "She would be up herself pretty early – as bright as a button."[36]

Floy Bell was an Australian running a small secretarial agency, who was taken on by Vivien to help with other engagements on the tour. One of her duties was to take Vivien to various doctors to have check-ups to see that her T.B. was not returning. She recalled:

> I know Larry says thing started to go wrong then, but in retrospect it is forty years ago. I was not aware of anything wrong with them and I was in the same hotel or house as them.[37]

Vivien liked to be part of everything the company did. Emma Selby-Walker remembered:

> We had all those terrible company picnics on days off and frightful supper parties on the beach and she always looked splendid. She didn't dress up… Of course they missed out on a lot of it in a way because in Sydney there was a wonderful block of bedsit flats we were all put into known as 'The Block of Shame' because the younger members used to behave terribly badly. Vivien would have loved to be in on that but of course she and Larry were always slightly grander.[38]

After the holiday, they had traveled to Sydney, where *Skin of Our Teeth* opened on the coldest night of the Australian year. They were due to give sixty performances of each play, playing to an estimated 120,000 people. There were problems. Olivier injured his right knee at the second performance of *Richard III* and thereafter performed with a crutch. As Michael Redington noted a few days later:

> The fight at the end is still out, but he gives a terrific scream off stage and then staggers on and dies, which is just as effective.[39]

This was not only immensely brave, but certainly led to a bizarre new craze. Certain fashion-conscious Australians took to sporting a stick even though there was nothing wrong with them.

When not playing, Vivien bought gumtrees, tree ferns, and furnishings for Notley, as well as paintings by Australian artists such as Hans Heysen, Daryl Lindsay, and Dahl Collings. She also bought a jerboa rat as a pet for Ralph Richardson. She wanted an agile wallaby, but not a platypus because they cost £40 a week in worms. From Sydney she wrote to Leigh:

> The papers here are hair-raising though they are an irresponsible lot. Some would like to know just how one feels at home. I'm heartily homesick now but Sydney is certainly a stimulating city. The little beaches and bays all round the harbour are quite exquisite. We took the whole company to this one [Whale Beach, N.S.W.] for a picnic one Sunday. The sun shines but it is fairly cold and dreadful in the buildings.[40]

It was during the Sydney visit that Olivier received news that his team at the Old Vic was to be disbanded by the Board of Governors. As he wrote to Lord Esher:

> The Memorandum made me feel a little woeful and one was apt to picture oneself as a pioneer disowned by his country in the middle of a very distant campaign.[41]

The Memorandum wanted the Old Vic to expand into a National Theatre under an administrator who was not primarily an actor. Inevitably Olivier was depressed about this, while Vivien was described as "ill and trembling with over-strain."[42] For once unsmiling, she left the theatre to rest between performances while Olivier announced: "Miss Leigh is quite exhausted. She will need all the rest she can get before we leave tomorrow."[43] Brisbane, their last stop before New Zealand, was easier because they performed only *School for Scandal*. But Vivien was greatly distressed by the death of New Boy, her Siamese cat. The company then made an uneasy flight to Auckland, during which Vivien seemed dangerously out of breath and needed oxygen.

It was now September and there remained five weeks of traveling and performing. When writing from New Zealand, Vivien crossed out 'Australia' on her letterheading 'The Old Vic Tour of Australia and New Zealand' noting: "over – God be praised."[44] The New Zealand tour was crowded and rushed on purpose so that the company could get home as quickly as possible. In Auckland they achieved world-record takings. Vivien reported to Leigh:

> This must be the most subdued place in the world. The quiet is unearthly. They're thrilled to death with their 40 hour week, which makes for all sorts of complications. But nevertheless much more couth and better mannered all round than the Australians and a much better audience. We hear about the beauty of it, but I fear we will have little chance to see anything at all owing to the extra performances we have to give because of our earlier sailing date for which we are most grateful.[45]

Emma Selby-Walker recalled that Vivien did not like the special photographs of her in her *School for Scandal* costumes for the front of the house, and replaced them with more youthful versions taken at the Cyril Maude readings in 1942.

In New Zealand there was a recurrence of the stabbing pain in Olivier's knee. Presently he was telling the press: "You may not know it, but you are talking to two walking corpses."[46] The pain in his knee was enough, but then lumbago also struck. One night he had to have an injection to enable him to go on stage. After the last performance of *Skin* on 9 October, Olivier went to hospital in Wellington for the removal of the ruptured cartilage in his right knee. The surgeon, Kennedy Elliott, believed it was just in time to avoid the danger of lasting disablement. It was left to Vivien to make the final moving farewell speech to the tour.

Olivier was not idle in hospital. He found time to dictate a three-page letter to Cecil Beaton about costume changes, describing Lady Sneerwell's ball dress as resembling a dark brown tea cozy, and concluding: "You, Sheridan, Handel and me – *quelle* combination – particularly with Little Puss to crown our cake."[47] On 16 October the company boarded the *Corinthic,* Olivier hoisted on board on a stretcher in a scene reminiscent of Cleopatra's delivery to the feet of Caesar wrapped in a carpet.

The tour was a success both financially and critically. A united company sailed back via the Panama Canal, busily rehearsing *Antigone.* Garry O'Connor's alleged suggestion (albeit understated in his book) that Vivien may have had an affair with Dan Cunningham on board annoyed members of the company when they read it. Once again, it was Olivier who fueled the story in his memoirs. The general opinion was that Vivien, easily bored, needed attention while Olivier languished in his cabin and she found the ebullient Dan good company. Floy Bell said: "When Larry was in hospital getting his cartilage done, Dan did squire Vivien about a bit.:[48] On board *Corinthic* the company was sent on its way with a great many bottles of champagne. Vivien asked Floy Bell, "Who do you think is the least drunk that we can get to come and open this case of champagne?"[49] Dan Cunningham proved the obvious choice. They docked at Tilbury on 16 November, and as the press surrounded the Oliviers, Michael Redington realized that the tour was over: "It would never be the same again."[50]

Australia had further important affects on the lives of the Oliviers. They engaged Peter Hiley, destined to be a staunch friend to both of them, and one who quietly maintained good relations with all the protagonists in the story, even those who were to some extent at loggerheads with each other. He was an Old Etonian, working with the British Council, and had been involved with the social (rather than the theatrical) side of the tour. The Oliviers needed someone to help them with their expanding interests in England. Notley needed overseeing and so did Laurence Olivier Productions, the theatrical management company set up with Cecil Tennant in 1947. Hiley became company secretary to Laurence Olivier Productions and personal assistant to the Oliviers in all aspects of their lives, except in the theatre itself. He arrived in London early in April 1949 and remained in a paid capacity until 1962. However, he continued to help them both in many ways thereafter. When he first met Vivien he was impressed by her "dazzling beauty, infinite charm, and a sort of stimulating magnetism."[51] He wrote:

> I was in a position to see the extent of her genuine interest in other people and her delight in giving pleasure…I always felt that in whatever age or class she had been born, she would have found prominence in one role of another – that bright star would have come to the fore.[52]

Another of Olivier's new friends in Australia was Peter Finch, who was playing Argan in Moliere's *The Imaginary Invalid*. Olivier went specially to see him perform at a factory during a lunchbreak. Olivier was then veering from actor to manager, or at any rate to actor-manager, and he encouraged Finch to join him in London. It is not fair to say that Olivier discovered him, as he had been acting for fourteen years and had already taken part in several films. Finch was very soon absorbed into the Oliviers' social scene in Sydney. Yolande, one of his wives, wrote of the importance of that meeting between Finch and the Oliviers:

> He had met the greatest actor in the world, and he had met the woman who was to be his greatest passion, his mistress and very nearly the death of him.[53]

Floy Bell recalled:

> I remember the meeting with Finch but I'm quite certain nothing had started between Vivien and Peter Finch out there. Nothing at all. He used to come and see them a lot [only in Sydney] because they were both so mad about his acting.[54]

Finch arrived in London with his then wife Tamara on 17 November 1948 and in March 1949 he appeared as Ernest Piaste in a Laurence Olivier Productions version of James Bridie's *Daphne Laureola*. He was the first actor that Olivier put under contract.

The Oliviers were delighted to be back in London. The company they had formed was not disbanded. They prepared at once for *The School for Scandal*, opening at the New on 20 January, and the new play, *Antigone*, destined for 10 February. There was the Old Vic crisis to face. The changes in the administration were announced discreetly, though Olivier was prepared to say privately that he had been fired. Fortunately he was too busy to be unduly concerned. And despite their lengthy travels they spent Christmas in Paris, attending Noël Coward's play *Joyeux Chagrins* and the company party with Orson Welles (who had been filming *The Third Man* in Vienna).

The London production of *The School for Scandal* was Britain's first chance to see the Oliviers on stage together. It opened with a tremendous burst of publicity. Students queued from 4 a.m., some said to have waited thirty-six hours for the chance of a standing ticket. In the dressing room Vivien and Olivier exchanged first night gifts in the period of the play – a set of antique ruby and garnet cuff links for him, an eighteenth century painting and French scent for her. The star-studded audience arrived – the Richardsons, Margaret Leighton, Lady Hardwicke, David Niven and his new wife, Hjordis, Sir Michael Balcon, Terence Rattigan, Robert Helpmann, and Margot Fonteyn. And there was a shy spectator, Tarquin Olivier, aged thirteen. After the show the crowds cried "Good Old Larry" and Olivier was heard to comment: "It's like being back in Sydney."[55] The production with Cecil Beaton's costumes and Sir Thomas Beecham's arrangement of the incidental music was a great success. The fans did not mind Olivier's departure from traditionally dashing swashbuckler to "drawn cheek, grey hair and the frog of age in his throat."[56]

Oswald Frewen and his wife, Lena, came to see a performance on 3 February, and Frewen was amazed at the avenue of fans through which the Oliviers passed on the way to their car, and how the fans were content to send autograph books into the dressing room for signature without even meeting the stars.

Leonard Mosley thought Vivien "sometimes a little too like Scarlett O'Hara."[57]. Other reviewers wrote of her radiance, her quality as a good comedy actress, and described her as "a ravishing minx" and "the fetching cream-fed kitten that Vivien Leigh made of Lady Teazle."[58] W. A. Darlington thought the production exquisite to look at and the acting often like a ballet. Cecil Wilson wrote:

> Vivien Leigh's Lady Teazle is a baggage of all the sweetest impishness – a mincingly mannered performance combining all the prettiness of a doll with the fascinations of a demon.[59]

Princess Elizabeth was taken to the play by the King's Private Secretary Sir Eric Miéville on her twenty-third birthday in 1949. The party included Prince Philip, Princess Margaret, and Lord Porchester. Afterwards the Oliviers joined them at a floorside table at the Café de Paris before going on to the 400.

The School for Scandal also caused the celebrated rift between the Oliviers and Cecil Beaton. All seemed well on the first night when they cabled him at the Plaza Hotel in New York:

> Dear Boy just to gladden your heart by telling you that at the very mention of your name you received the most wonderful of any acclamation last night.[60]

Beaton's contribution was confirmed by Simon Fleet, Lady Juliet Duff's young companion, who wrote:

> *School for Scandal* is a real hit. You have come out of it with greater acclaim than anything you have so far done for the stage. You are considered to have moved from the state of being a 'fashionable designer' into a 'man of the theatre.'[61]

But Beaton's absence clearly annoyed the Oliviers and the production team at the New. Emma Selby-Walker recalled: "Cecil did his usual thing of whisking off. He was never there except when the photographers were there."[62] And Beaton himself complained to Garbo of the way Olivier had bombarded him with requests for new costumes and alterations, a year after he felt his contributions had been made:

> No sooner the first night of Gielgud over than the Oliviers were stampeding at my door and once more the thousand details of wigs and corsets and wings and floats must be lengthily discussed...The play should be a jewel of a production.[63]

Later he wrote more warily: "Too much Olivier trouble. I just don't like theatre-folk. They're too self-centered and spoilt."[64] Back in London in March, Cecil went to see the show and reported again to Garbo:

> I was very thrilled by this – and thought it looked better than

> anything I have ever done. The Oliviers rather grudgingly in their generosity and I fear they are not good friends behind my back.[65]

Later, this incident, so lightly set aside at the time, was magnified into an exaggerated version in his diaries, *The Strenuous Years,* which ends with a curt dismissal of the Oliviers: "They were both out of my life forever."*[66]

In fact, their paths crossed several times, and in May that year Cecil went to see *Richard III* and sat in the front row. With some glee he wrote again to Garbo:

> I heard the Oliviers were absolutely furious with me for going to *Richard III*… and not going round to congratulate them afterwards. I guess they just found an excuse to put me in the pan or the double-boiler.[67]

Richard III was already a proven triumph for Olivier. Stephen Williams wrote:

> His death struggle was like the convulsions of some giant scorpion one kills in a nightmare. And when at last the twitching limbs were still, one felt that this had never been a man: just so much refuse.[68]

For the first time London audiences saw Vivien as Lady Anne, a small part which she played in complete contrast to her more Dresden china Lady Teazle. Her friend Alan Dent wrote:

> Here is Vivien Leigh giving this feckless and be-wimpled bobby-soxer far more strength and compulsion than I suspected were in either (a) the Lady Anne or (b) Miss Leigh…[69]

*John Merivale recalled that the true origin of the antipathy between Vivien and Cecil occurred in New York when Vivien saw a photograph of Garbo in his bedroom and looked to see what she had written. "She had it in her hand when Cecil came into the room and he exploded with wrath." (John Merivale to the author, December 1986)

There was some fun to be had. In the scene near the end when the ghosts walked round Richard's tent, Vivien and Danny Kaye disguised themselves as specters and came on the stage.

Jean Anouilh's *Antigone*, the third of the plays, marked another turning point in Vivien's career. Michael Redington was very excited to have a small part but more so to witness Olivier produce a play right from the beginning. Rehearsals began on board the *Corinthic*. Then and later Vivien worked hard to lower the register of her voice. James Pope-Hennessy, the biographer, was favorably impressed:

> The biggest surprise of the performance is the acting of Miss Vivien Leigh, who brings to *Antigone* a taut strength, and a restraint which may surprise even the most loyal fans of this beautiful actress. Her voice, which it is permissible to suggest has not always been her strongest point, is deeper, more intense and controlled, less genteel than we remember. She gives Antigone the loneliness and desperate courage of a lost and determined child, while at the end, when the condemned girl is dictating a letter to her lover, she is properly tragic. This is a splendid performance.[70]

Felix Barker described the scene as the curtain rose with Vivien seated at the back of the stage, her arms folded on her knees:

> The eye traveled at once to this pale, dark-eyed creature, whose whole appearance of sullen misery marked her as the tragic target of the gods. It was a performance far beyond any that Vivien Leigh had hitherto given in a serious part; it had strength and a taut, emotional power. Her voice had lost nearly all trace of its usual silly undulations and had somehow become deeper; it had about it from the first a ring of authority and passion. A previously unsuspected tragic actress had appeared.[71]

Not all the critics were won over. T. C. Worsley judged:

> The part of Antigone is not a great emotional part...but it does require an emotional intensity, a fanaticism which Miss Leigh does not command.[72]

Of her performance *The Times* wrote:

> Mute and helpless she commands the pathos of the part, but when vehemence of argument is called for she has not all the power that splendid defiance requires.[73]

Beverley Baxter was surprised when Olivier addressed the first night audience and proceeded to assume the role of dramatic critic, leaving any criticisms voiced by the professionals seemingly "frivolous or untutored or blasphemous."[74] Olivier declared that he had never seen two finer performances than those of Vivien and her counterpart, George Relph. Alan Dent was convinced of one thing – that the Oliviers had reached such a point of fame that they could do no wrong in the eyes of their public. There were still two sides of the story, though. The first was the remark he overheard from an American in a theatrical restaurant: "Take that guy, Olivier – he was not great shakes as an actor till he married that lovely dish, Vivien Leigh" – and the second an impersonation in a satirical revue called *Oranges and Lemons*, which had a spoof of Vivien saying: "It's very difficult to teach a kitten tricks – but Larry has taught me one or two!"[75]

Olivier wrote in his memoirs that soon after their return to London, Vivien announced, "I don't love you anymore."[76] This occurred at Durham Cottage one spring day. He quoted her as saying: "There's no one else or anything like that, I mean I still love you but in a different way, sort of, well, like a brother."[77] This proved something of a thunderbolt, unexpected and wholly numbing. And as so often in his life, the moment of Olivier's greatest triumph was also that of his greatest despair. The crowds that formed to greet "the Oliviers" could not be disappointed. Thus he resigned himself to a double life – preserving an exterior myth to cover a private unhappiness. It is too simplistic to suggest that from now Olivier's life was one of permanent unhappiness; however, he was set for a difficult ten years in the 1950s. He wrote later: "I had not the faintest inkling of how life would have taken me and shaken me like a rat before the decade closed."[78]

The summer of 1949 included a three-day holiday in a rented house at Opio, one of the hillside villages near Grasse in the South of France. Both Olivier and Vivien were guided by Winston Churchill's book, *Painting as a Pastime*, and, inspired by the need to use a different part of the brain, they took to the brush. There was the usual to-ing and fro-ing between Notley, Mere, and London by Vivien, Olivier, Leigh, Suzanne, and Gertrude Hartley. Leigh having taken Suzanne on holiday to Cannes with Gertrude in 1948, it was Vivien's turn to have her for the summer. It is a surprising truth that Suzanne rarely ever had the chance to get to know her mother. An unwanted baby, she was deserted in the nursery, only seeing Vivien in scenes reminiscent of the mother's return in *Anna Karenina* between the ages of four and six. Thereafter Vivien was in Hollywood while she spent nearly four years in Canada. An actor who knew how diligent Vivien was in recalling the birthday of every member of the cast in Australia was horrified to hear Vivien apologize to her daughter for forgetting her birthday. To this day Suzanne can only recall a few occasions when she was alone with her mother. She had been at school at Sherborne. In 1949, at the age of sixteen, she was sent to Vaud in Switzerland, from where she wrote sadly to Vivien:

> I felt depressed and homesick…and also there aren't any horses here to speak of, at least not like Kilbuck but that all comes secondary to you my darling who I am simply aching to see again, also for a chat. That one in the Green room seems to be the only one we have had and we were only just getting to know each other cause we haven't seen a lot of each other until last summer hols…[79]

Vivien's response was to send the letter to Leigh, with a note: "I thought you'd like to see these letters. They're so terribly sweet and funny."[80]

Then in October, Vivien embarked on *A Streetcar Named Desire*, her most frightening role to date.

Chapter 16
Streetcar

Deliberate cruelty is not forgivable. It is the one unforgivable thing in my opinion and it is the one thing of which I have never, never been guilty.

Vivien as Blanche DuBois, *A Streetcar Named Desire,* Scene Ten

Tennessee Williams invariably wrote of the turmoil of his own life in his plays, and it is said that he was prone to the "ungentle animal instincts"[1] of both Stanley Kowalski and Blanche DuBois. Vivien's portrayal of Blanche DuBois was equally too real for comfortable viewing. Obviously she was no more an identical Blanche than she had been an identical Scarlett, indeed some speculate that Blanche is more what Scarlett, transmuted into another century, might have become. To watch *A Streetcar Named Desire* on film today is to fuel all the worst and most exaggerated stories put about by Vivien's various biographers of the past.

It is a story of the disintegration of a woman reflecting the disintegration of an entire class, the decaying aristocracy. Blanche DuBois drifts about in tattered chiffons, flirty and coquettish. Kowalski forces her to face reality briefly and then she sinks into the safe unreality of madness. It is a powerful play, which became in due course a powerful film. Benjamin Nelson wrote that, technically, it was almost flawless as a work:

> The construction is tight, with each ensuing scene gaining

> momentum from its predecessor. The language is for the most part lively and melodious with the passion and rhythm of real speech. Although Williams is not, in any strict sense of the word, a poet, he nevertheless possesses the genius of transforming ordinary speech into poetry.[2]

Nelson was right to point out that the audience is left at the end knowing "that something terrible has happened, but nothing has been gained, no one has quite realized what the catastrophe was for or about."[3]

Tennessee Williams was hugely amused that Thornton Wilder, the confused playwright of *The Skin of Our Teeth*, condemned *Streetcar* as being based on a false premise, the love of Blanche's sister Stella for the brute Kowalski.

> No female who had ever been a lady (he was referring to Stella) could possibly marry a vulgarian such as Stanley. We sat there and listened to him politely. I thought, privately, this character has never had a good lay.[4]

Streetcar had been produced on Broadway by Irene Selznick, now divorced from David O. Selznick. She had been daunted by the prospect, alarmed by Tennessee Williams, finally stimulated by the challenge. She chose Elia Kazan as director. With her customary attention to every minute detail of the script, she proposed a subtle change to the end of the play, maintaining that Blanche's destruction would be more complete if, during the rape scene, she began to respond and Kowalski rejected her. "It would be her fatal humiliation," wrote Irene Selznick. "I would have him fling her across the stage and just stand there, laughing savagely."[5] But Kazan did not want his audiences deprived of a rape. Signing Marlon Brando was the most imaginative coup that Irene Selznick secured for her New York production.

Streetcar had such a successful run in New York that many English managements clamored for it, including Binkie Beaumont and Laurence Olivier Productions. When Irene Selznick arrived in London in 1948, Beaumont was there to greet her in person. She suggested Vivien for the part and he responded that she was a great friend. Vivien had heard about the play from Cecil Beaton (often the first man with the cultural news from across the Atlantic) before their row. Later Vivien wrote:

> So many people have condemned the play for its sordid theme. To me it is an infinitely moving plea for tolerance for all weak, frail creatures, blown about like leaves before the wind of circumstance.[6]

Irene Selznick returned to London in May 1949, insisting that Tennessee Williams himself come from Rome to watch Vivien in the three Old Vic productions. Mrs. Selznick wrote:

> Vivien in essence did an audition for three nights running, and she was all too aware of it. By the third evening the matter was settled, so we all had a quiet supper at Binkie's. By this time I had learned that he and Vivien were thick as thieves and it had been Binkie who had helped plot Vivien's path to Scarlett O'Hara. Here he was again getting her her heart's desire.[7]

There was a great deal of discussion about Olivier's wish to cut the play, and a somewhat eerie party at Durham Cottage, at which Irene and Williams arrived late to find that Olivier had disappeared. "We heard his footsteps back and forth, back and forth, throughout the evening. Tennessee was not the only one disconcerted."[8] There was a weekend at Notley at which Vivien was especially kind to Williams's boyfriend, Frank Merlo, evidently a warm and lovable man and a good influence on the volatile playwright. Williams felt that Vivien understood him and wondered if "she realized that I lived with the same nervous torment."[9]

As the production got underway, Irene reminded Olivier that he could not effect cuts without the author's permission. Williams himself urged Irene: "See that everything possible is done to protect *us* and the *play* as distinct from Sir Laurence and his Lady."[10] Thus there was the kind of clash that occurs in the theatre when two determined figures stand up for their rights. Irene Selznick was horrified by the brutality of Olivier's direction of Vivien, observing him pushing her left hand back against her shoulder to stress his point. She did not believe that he understood this modern American play.[11] The inevitable showdown followed at Binkie's house with Vivien in attendance. "It was," wrote Mrs. Selznick, "a bruising experience for one and all."[12] Eventually Irene got most of the cuts restored but she left the Oliviers arguing the night away, and collapsing into bed at 6 a.m. The play opened in Manchester and then came to London in October.

"I feel as if I'd been bulldozed, and can't believe I have to 'go through it' every night,"[13] wrote Vivien to Leigh a few days after the opening. It was a grueling performance in every respect. John Gielgud commented:

> It must have been a most dreadful strain to do it night after night. She would be shaking and white and quite distraught at the end of it. Perhaps it was unwise to let her do it.[14]

Alan Dent tried in vain to prevent her as he did not feel Vivien should play one of Williams's "walking and wandering casebooks, nympholepts, inconstant nymphs, the victims of men who could be sadistic and even cannibalistic."[15] Having seen the play, he thought Vivien's Blanche "certainly one of the most harrowing things I have ever seen in any theatre anywhere. In trying to tear at my heartstrings she certainly tore at her own. It was like looking on at some beautiful little town being destroyed by an earthquake."[16] Years later Olivier said:

> Vivien was too much affected by the parts she played…it had a great deal to do with playing Blanche DuBois being ill in the same way.[17]

Visiting her in the dressing-room after the performance, Dent found her "shaking like an autumn leaf, and her lips were trembling."[18] Both player and critic were shattered by the performance. Noël Coward's view, seeing it in October 1949, was: "Vivien magnificent; audience sordid and theatre beastly."[19] Olivier chose to direct Vivien's scenes keeping a bright light fixed on her: "Her fading features are exposed to the merciless light of an unshaded bulb,"[20] wrote *The Times*. Their reviewer went on to praise her performance "considered merely as a feat of memory."[21] He continued:

> But the impressiveness of the performance grows as the

> violence of the action deepens. She is hard put to it during the first half of the play, for rarely in the history of the drama can a heroine have been given so many words in which to say so very little.[22]

Kenneth Tynan was critical of Olivier's direction:

> Olivier is a darkly brilliant atmospheric actor of enormous range: but his work in production has at no time been outstanding. His *Streetcar Named Desire*, at the Aldwych, is a good illustration of the way in which a good play can be scarred by unsympathetic and clumsy direction.[23]

He then launched into an onslaught on Vivien, who was now firmly fixed in his sights as an actress to be gunned down. Tynan was perhaps the best example of a failed actor turned brilliant, if vicious, critic. He was also an anarchist. When attempting a revolution, certain heads must roll. The victim must be identified publicly. Tynan railed against the happily married couples on stage, Michael Denison and Dulcie Gray,* and actors such as Robert Flemyng, indeed anyone who took part in a drawing-room comedy or entered the stage via French windows swinging a tennis racket. Vivien he attacked mercilessly in the belief that she was holding Olivier back:

> Olivier's first error was to cast Vivien Leigh for Blanche: through no fault of Miss Leigh's (she struggles gamely), it became clear that the play should have been retitled "A Vehicle Named Vivien." His second error was to direct her to play the part in a condition of crazed, hysterical languor from the moment she walks on to the stage: a posturing butterfly, with no depth, no sorrow, no room for development, and above all, no trace of Blanche's crushed ideals. Miss Leigh's Blanche is a bored nymphomaniac with a frenziedly affected tremolo, a Hedda Gabler of the gin-

*Michael Denison wrote of the conviction (shared by Vivien) "that 'the scintillating quality of his writing' would be used primarily to express his scorn for us as people; as for our work we were guilty before the curtain rose." (*Double Act*, p. 40.)

> palaces; and in the love-scene with Mitch, which should be inexpressibly moving, she becomes almost comic. This cardinal error in casting did what I should never, having read the play, have thought possible: it made the whole action shallow and salacious.[24]

Streetcar ran in London for 326 performances. "We did good business for the eight months Vivien lasted,"[25] wrote Irene Selznick. She saw one of the later performances, in the spring of 1950, at Vivien's request and thought her "wonderful."[26] She was delighted to support the choice of Vivien for the film. Kenneth Clark recorded that Vivien suffered a bad manic depression at the end of her run. He attributed this to the inability of actresses (with the exception of Peggy Ashcroft) to shake off the part: "Their parts get into them and influence them."[27]

While Vivien was busy with *Streetcar,* Olivier had set his Theatre Company in motion. He began at the King's Theatre, Hammersmith with Donald Wolfit in *Julius Caesar* for a fortnight. Then it was announced that he had taken over the famous and much-loved St. James Theatre in King Street, build opposite Christie's in 1835. Olivier launched Laurence Olivier productions there with Christopher Fry's poetical and much acclaimed *Venus Observed*, in which he himself starred. It ran for 229 performances from January 1950.

Vivien closed at the Aldwych in the spring. She had free time in the summer and went often to see Rex Harrison in *The Cocktail Party*. She was impressed by the way Harrison cracked his knuckles on stage, and asked him to explain its significance. Harrison replied that it meant nothing but that he had cramp in his left hand. In August Vivien flew to America to make the film of *Streetcar.* Originally neither Tennessee Williams nor Elia Kazan favored Vivien, though the Producer Charles K. Feldman wanted her from the start. Lucinda Ballard was chosen to create the costumes and was sent to England to discuss them with Vivien: "She was very anxious to do what was right for her character."[28] This had a second advantage in that Lucinda Ballard came from Louisiana and had a perfect, slight Southern accent which the director Elia Kazan hoped Vivien would imitate.

Vivien began her stay in America in Connecticut at the home of Elia Kazan. Once in Hollywood she settled at 2745 Outpost Drive, a comfortable house near the Studio. And she was allocated Bette Davis's dressing-room. She was immediately swept up into the business of makeup and costume tests. Sunny Lash (a widow since the previous year) came to work for her again. Not having seen Vivien for ten years, she noticed a slight change in her personality: "She wasn't always as cheerful as she'd previously been."[29]

Suzanne arrived with Olivier on Sunday, 13 August. In a ghosted account of her first ever flight, she wrote that Olivier reassured her: "No need to worry, I'll hold your hand." The moment for take-off approached and she became nervous: "I stood up in my bunk and looked up to Larry, but by then my stepfather was fast asleep."[30] Olivier (once again a moustached figure) came to Hollywood to be near Vivien and made the film *Carrie* for William Wyler. While in New York Olivier saw Garson Kanin who thought him tired and drained both professionally and emotionally. Olivier confided that he had problems with Vivien: "We never converse – we only confer."[31]

Filming on *Streetcar* began on 14 August. Vivien starred opposite Marlon Brando, who had made a noted success of the New York stage production. Brando never forgave Truman Capote for an interview he published in 1956. Amongst the revelations was a suggestion that Brando owed his screen success to a broken nose, acquired in a brawl in the theater's boiler room. Irene Selznick had urged him to have the nose re-broken and set. Later she concluded that the broken nose made him look tougher and gave him sex appeal. And he made his fortune.

Warners paid Vivien $100,000 for *Streetcar*. To secure Brando's services they were forced to agree to $75,000 for a one-picture deal. At this point Brando was squandering any money he earned, though his father was beginning to make wise investments on his behalf. He lived in an apartment in New York and his room-mate was a pet raccoon called Russell, which perched on his shoulder and accompanied him everywhere. Brando was well-behaved on the set, living down a reputation for being difficult, but Russell the raccoon scurried about biting cables, knocking things over and scratching members of the crew. Karl Malden and Kim Hunter recreated Mitch and Stella from the stage, so Vivien was the only newcomer on the team. The Hollywood press liked to play up the 'meeting of the lady and the tiger,' but Vivien announced: "Mr. Brando is only a tiger when the role demands it."[32] Nevertheless, their first encounter did not bode well. After shaking hands he said: "Go ahead and eat your food."[33] Her three co-stars were determined to make her welcome, and she fitted in very easily from the outset. Marlon Brando had to take second billing to Vivien and he found it difficult acting with her, since once again it was suspected that Olivier was counteracting Kazan's direction on the quiet. Brando was bemused by her very English politeness on the set. She, in turn, was impressed by his ability to do near perfect imitations of Olivier's performance in *Henry V.* Brando shared her general distaste for Hollywood and came to respect her fortitude and the way that she fought fatigue and illness, never missing a day's filming. In the end he became quite tender towards her.

The script of *Streetcar* was modified considerably to satisfy the over-sensitive prudery of the Movie Production Code. Very little was permissible on screen in 1951. The rape was merely hinted at, the homosexuality of Blanche's first love was veiled, and the strong sexual base of the Kowalski marriage was considerably reduced, amongst other changes major and minor. Memos passed instructing: "Dupe down Leigh's animal cries when she goes mad."[34] Despite all this it remained a harrowing film and in due course secured Oscars for Vivien as best actress,* Karl Malden (best supporting actor), Kim Hunter (best supporting actress),and another for best art and set decoration. Elia Kazan gave this verdict on Vivien:

> She had a small talent, but the greatest determination to excel of any actress I've ever known. She'd have crawled over broken glass if she thought it would help her performance. In the scenes that counted, she excelled.[35]

The Hollywood visit was a chance for Vivien to get to know Suzanne better. Jeffrey Selznick, son of David and Irene, recalled: "It seemed to me that she was making it up to her daughter at this time."[36] On her way over, Suzanne had enjoyed her first hamburger in New York and seen Gian-Carlo Menotti's opera, *The Consul*, which Olivier later brought to London (losing money for his pains). In Hollywood she found everyone very different. She thought Jeffrey Selznick "very pleasant and easy to talk to and rather more grown up than other boys there that I've met."[37] And she liked his cousin Judy Goetz and went riding with Judy Kazan, the director's daughter. She

*Vivien won best actress awards from the New York film critics, from BAFTA and at the Venice Film Festival.

remained on the sidelines, however, and Vivien forbade her to come to the four thousand dollar Danny Kaye party, which was deemed such an event that those not invited were leaving town fast. Lucinda Ballard Dietz recalled: "It was not a large party. It was a dinner-dance. But people were almost threatening to commit suicide at Vivien's feet if they were not invited."[38] Sue wrote her grandmother:

> Mummy and Larry have just gone off to the Danny Kaye party after great excitement. Mummy in beautiful olive green dress looking perfectly stunning. They have done a sweet joint speech of thanks together in verse form but as is intended it doesn't rhyme.[39]

The Danny Kaye party was to welcome the Oliviers to Hollywood, a lavish affair in the Crystal Room of the Beverly Hills Hotel. Guests included Groucho Marx, Eddie Cantor, Errol Flynn, Ginger Rogers, Cyd Charisse, the Ronald Colmans, Lana Turner, Louis B. Mayer, and Johnny Hyde, a rich William Morris agent, in the last year of his life, whose date was the youthful Marilyn Monroe, then a dumb blonde who knew nobody. Montgomery Clift gate-crashed. Olivier and Vivien saw many old friends and forged an instant friendship with Humphrey Bogart and Lauren Bacall.

It was the Oliviers' first visit to Hollywood for nearly a decade and in the meantime their status had magnified considerably. They soon found they were overwhelmed by invitations and had to restrict parties to the weekend. Vivien needed rest and she explained to the press that Thornton Wilder had told her: "If you really want to learn how to relax, watch a cat, how it sleeps and stretches."[40] Bobby Helpmann came to stay and John Buckmaster lunched on the set. Olivier strayed across a black tarantula in their garden. Katharine Hepburn asked if he had killed it, but he had put it in a bottle and released it elsewhere. Vivien said she found the role of Blanche more exacting than Scarlett: "I had nine months in the theatre of Blanche DuBois. Now she's in command of me in Hollywood."[41]

Vivien's already declining health and the fact that she was now nearly thirty-seven came as a surprise to those she met after such a long absence. Certainly any fans expecting to see the bright and smiling Scarlett were in for a sharp awakening when her faded Blanche appeared on the big screen.

The film of *Streetcar* opened in New York in September 1951 and in London the following March.

While Olivier was finishing *Carrie*, Suzanne returned to London via New York. At the end of October Vivien went to New Orleans for three intense days of location shooting, sometimes filming from 8:30 p.m. to 3:45 a.m. Eventually the Oliviers were free to sail home together by freighter.

In 1951 Olivier's plans for his company and the St. James Theatre took on new life when the daring experiment was made to perform Shaw's *Caesar and Cleopatra* alternately with Shakespeare's *Antony and Cleopatra*. Vivien starred opposite Olivier, her age as Cleopatra changing twenty years or so night by night. It was an ambitious project and during rehearsals Vivien and Olivier appeared "amost as if they loathed each other."[42] Jill Bennett played Iris and Maxine Audley Charmian in both productions. Maxine Audley recalled:

> For the first six weeks rehearsal we just gazed at Vivien. She was so unbelievably beautiful. When she came to rehearsals all eyes immediately went to her. She was at great pains to make sure we liked her. She took endless trouble with Jill and me particularly, because we went everywhere with her on stage. We followed her about, kneeling down or standing up behind her. It was very tiring, but she made it all great fun.[43]

The idea of alternating Cleopatras had been the inspiration of Roger Furse,* a staunch ally of Olivier's. He designed an ingenious set which revolved, with Rome and Roman monuments on one side and Egypt and the Sphinx on the other. Similarly Vivien wore the same Coronation robes in both, though she was so often bathed in perspiration that Audrey Cruddas had to design a special costume. This time Michael Benthall directed. Vivien studied for the part by reading Plutarch's chapter on Mark Antony in *Lives of the Noble Grecians and Romans*, Emil Ludwig's *Cleopatra*, Olivier Coligny de Chaufleur Ellis's *Cleopatra in the Tide of Time*, and Thornton

*He designed the costumes and armor for *Henry V* and the entire production of *Hamlet*. Later he was closely involved in the St. James's Theatre Productions, *Macbeth* at Stratford 1955 and the film of Richard III.

Wilder's *The Ides of March.* She took singing lessons with Maestro George Canelli. Vivien found it a strain to do eight performances a week, sometimes each version on the same day. She explained that *Antony and Cleopatra* was a particular strain because Shakespeare took "many liberties with the iambic pentameter pattern. Aside from the complexity of it as dramatic dialogue, it is hard to do it to sheer verse."[44] Maxine Audley judged Vivien's performance:

> I think she was perfect. She could do the kitten bit standing on her head but she worked like a beaver on getting her voice down. I'ver never seen anybody better. I saw Peggy Ashcroft, Edith Evans (admittedly not beautiful ladies – in fact I've never seen another beautiful Cleopatra) but I haven't seen anybody touch her, not only because of her looks but because of her fantastic mercurial changes of mood, which is absolutely essential for that part. You've got to be able to swing up and down, being violently bad tempered one moment and happy as a grig the next. She was sensational. There were definite undercurrents that she and Larry weren't getting on well too. Now and again there were little flare-ups, but we took that in our stride."[45]

There was one amusing drama in *Caesar and Cleopatra* which involved Elspeth March as Ftatateeta. Vivien had told her that she could only play the part properly if she looked ugly. Elspeth March said:

> She made me have this rubber nose made, a rubber negroid nose. On this particular day I sneezed and it blew off, and Vivien fielded it and I then quickly stuck it on again. It all happened terribly quickly but Vivien, Jill Bennett and Maxine laughed so horrendously that I thought I'd stuck it upside down with nostrils pointing to the ceiling. So I kidded myself it was some wonderful Egyptian gesture and played the scene peering through my fingers. Oh dear, that nose![46]

Elspeth March found Vivien "thoughtful and generous as usual,"[47] while she thought Olivier "such a concentrated man that sometimes you would come in and see him and say 'Good Evening' and he would walk past you as if you weren't there. People used to think that he was cold or rude, but it was because he was absolutely concentrated on what he was thinking about."[48]

Esmond Knight was in *Antony and Cleopatra*, playing Menas. He always enjoyed being in Shakespeare with Olivier because, as John Laurie said to him: "The great thing about Larry is he has no respect for the Bard."[49] He recalled that Olivier was very strict about actors not drinking before the performance. "He used to say, 'Darling Boy, don't drink during the play. You can get as pissed as a newt afterwards.'"[50] Helpmann was another member of the cast, playing Apollodorus and Octavius Caesar. Esmond Knight described him as:

> The naughty chap. Of course at that time he and Larry and Vivien were very much *comme ça*...He was great fun Bobby Helpmann, naughty, naughty boy. But he used to make us laugh. He became the kind of jester at Notley. He armed himself with the boldness of a lover, but Bobby Helpmann, you know, he used to move around with those two as if he was part of the ménage.[51]

Norman Wooland told Knight: "I'm never going to act with animals, children or the Oliviers, because no one looks at anyone bloody else when they're on stage."[52]

The two Cleopatras ran for over four months until September 1951 and proved in the best traditions of the St. James's Theatre. The two dramas were separated in writing by over three centuries but audiences were inspired by the contrasts in Shakespeare and Shaw. Vivien herself told Harold Nicolson that she preferred Shakespeare; "Shaw is like a train. One just speaks the words and sits in one's place. But Shakespeare is like bathing in the sea – one swims where one wants."[53] Nevertheless, Nicolson, seeing *Antony and Cleopatra* with Vita Sackville-West, thought "the production is excellent; Larry and Vivien good – she beautiful to look at, but not grand enough for so superb a part."[54]

Olivier wrote later that despite his reservations about Vivien as

Shakespeare's Cleopatra:

> She was brilliant, and in my opinion the best Cleopatra ever. She was radiant and beautiful and shone through the lines as if they had been specially written with her in mind… Vivien and I were sailing, we were set in the galaxy, and fortunately everyone wanted to see us.[55]

Hardly had they announced the plays – their particular celebration of the Festival of Britain – than the production was sold out for twenty-six weeks and plans were afoot to take both to America.

Kenneth Tynan saw his victim reaching to new heights, casting her net "wider than her special talents would permit."[56] He wrote his most scathing attack yet, what he called "a sober consideration of Vivien Leigh."[57] The piece was unkind to say the least. He employed the ruse of quoting others describing her as being as "calculating as a slot-machine."[58] He deeply resented the verdict of fellow critics that in the two Cleopatras she was now considered "great."[59] Of the Shaw production he wrote:

> Taking a deep breath and resolutely focusing her periwinkle charm, she launches another of her careful readings; ably and passionlessly she picks her way among its great challenges, presenting a glibly mown lawn where her author had imagined a jungle…[60]

And of the Shakespeare he continued:

> She picks at the part with the daintiness of a debutante called upon to dismember a stag, and her manners are first-rate. "She plays it," as someone said "with her little finger crooked…"[61]

It was in this piece that he first attempted to justify his onslaught – the belief that Olivier's greatness was being held in check by his wife's lesser acting: "He subdues his blow-lamp ebullience to match her. Blunting his iron precision, leveling away his towering authority he meets her halfway."[62] Emlyn Williams was one who discounted this view:

> Nonsense. That was snide press misinterpretation… Certainly he had more experience in the classics than she had. But she was a considerable actress in her own right. Sensitive and highly intelligent.[63]

Besides, the play would not have profited from Olivier upstaging Vivien. The performance had to be balanced. Sometimes Olivier's acting had the effect of outshining those around him, but he never tried that with Vivien. At her Memorial Service in 1967 John Gielgud judged her Shakespeare Cleopatra as "her finest classical performance."[64] According to Maxine Audley, Olivier's reaction to Tynan was stronger: "He threatened to knock his block off."[65]

In the course of the summer Olivier celebrated his birthday at a midnight supper given by Winston Churchill, who had become an ardent fan of both Oliviers and presented Vivien with one of his flower paintings. Not long after this, Clementine Churchill was writing to her husband: "Christopher [Soames] says that you both are in love with Vivien Leigh but that he hasn't a look in."[66] Vivien, Olivier, and Danny Kaye played as 'terrible triplets' at a glittering 'Night of a 100 Stars' in memory of the comedian Sid Field, on 25 June, with lyrics by Howard Dietz, "rehearsed as assiduously as if Shakespeare or Shaw had written it."[67] On 13 July the Oliviers were present when Queen Elizabeth laid the foundation stone of the National Theatre, which (when realized several decades later in another location) was to be so important in Olivier's career.

Then the Oliviers launched a season at the St. James's Theatre with Jean-Louis Barrault and his wife, Madeleine Renaud, starring in Marivaux's classic play, *Les Fausses Confidences*. It opened on 25 September (the only reason that the two Cleopatras ended) and there was a glamorous first night with a party at Claridge's, photographed for the *Tatler and Bystander* by a young society photographer, Antony Armstrong-Jones. The Barraults had been presenting plays at the Marigny Theatre in the same way that the Oliviers were producing plays at the St. James's. The Oliviers persuaded them to come with the words: "They will eat you."[68] The spectacular opening was dubbed by the *Tatler*: "The off-stage event of the century."[69]

The guests comprised a glittering array of society and theatre figures – the French Ambassador, René Massigli and his wife Odette, Jeanne de Casalis, Alexander Korda, 'Puffin' Asquith, Terence Rattigan, Oliver Messel, Kitty Miller, Peter Ustinov, Katharine Cornell, Mary Martin, Chips Channon, Peter Brook, Felix Aylmer, Jack Buchanan, Dame Edith Evans, Hamish Hamilton, and many more. Unfortunately Vivien was suffering from a bad cold, so Noël Coward took her home early. Later Jean-Louis Barrault wrote: "Vivien and Larry formed a princely couple. Presented by them to the Londoners, we made acquaintance with one of the best theatre publics in the world."[70]

After the two Cleopatras, the Oliviers relaxed in the Mediterranean on Korda's yacht, *Elsewhere*. Embarking at Piraeus, they found Graham Greene and Margot Fonteyn aboard. The Oliviers told the press their plan was to do "absolutely nothing"[71] since they were both exhausted. The *Elsewhere*, a luxury yacht of 140 tons, toured the Greek Islands, and headed for Istanbul. Arriving at Calvi in flowing kaftan and straw hat, Vivien drew an eager crowd of star-spotters. She was amused when an elderly English lady turned to her friend and said: "Pay no attention Agnes, they're just theatricals!"[72]

They were not therefore at the St. James's Theatre when Orson Welles opened in *Othello* on 18 October. Welles was fulsome about Vivien. He said that English women had a reputation for being ugly, but that in every generation there was one who tripped the imagination of the Continent:

> Today it is Vivien Leigh, because of her greatness as an actress, because of her personality and charm and *in spite of* her good looks.[73]

Vivien greatly admired Maxine Audley's performance in *Othello*, writing "You made her [Emilia] a really whole and exciting character."[74]

In November the Oliviers took Welles and Margot Fonteyn to Noël Coward's evening at the Café de Paris. Soon afterwards they sailed from Liverpool in *Mauretania* with a full company and many tons of scenery to dazzle Broadway with the two Cleopatras. Maxine Audley (who had not gone to New York) sent Vivien a wire, and she replied: "It cheered me and Goodness knows I needed it."[75]

Olivier had begun to notice a change in Vivien's character. She had become frightened, displaying "a funny little, childlike, clinging need for protection."[76] In a curious way this new reliance on him made him feel happy and wanted. Alas, the mood was soon to change.

The opening of the Cleopatras at the Ziegfeld in December was once again a resounding Broadway hit. Everything looked good on the surface, but underneath trouble was brewing. The production which opened as a sell-out competed well with the great musicals of the day such as *South Pacific*, but because of the expense of the sets and their transport to New York, the Oliviers were not making money. Before the opening Vivien suffered from psychosomatic laryngitis, a complaint not uncommon to her before a new venture. She gave an interview to Maurice Zolotow of the *New York Times*, discussing the difference between the Shaw and the Shakespeare and outlining the character of Cleopatra:

> Shaw got the shrewdness, quickness, ambition of her character, but he wasn't taken by her passion, her emotion – and not only in love affairs – she was intense about everything – she had a fabulous collection of jewels, gold, silver, clothes. She was even intense about her dying. All her life she studied poisons. She would have prisoners brought before her and she would try out various poisons on them. She found out the quick poisons hurt too much and the tastier poisons took too long. Finally she decided that the bite of an asp was the least painful and you died without being in agony.[77]

Maurice Zolotow thought this showed a streak of cruelty. "No, no," said Vivien, "the prisoners were condemned to death anyway."[78]

Olivier found Vivien "abnormally nervous about our social reputation."[79] Sometimes he found her sobbing on the corner of the bed "in a state of grave distress,"[80] which his soothing words could not relieve. The urbane old actor Wilfrid Hyde White (Britannus and Lepidus) saw that she was ill, "so ill that she would be shivering with weakness while waiting for her cue."[81] Her performance never suffered, but the real Vivien did. Olivier sought psychiatric help, but found this course hard to pursue, because Vivien dreaded each visit and was terrified of being spotted by the press. He noted that though manic depression took hold of her, she could still hide the condition from the outside world. Her case was always hard to treat because of her powers of deception.

New Year's Eve 1951 was celebrated at a party given by Mrs. Gilbert Miller, wife of the theatrical impresario. Diana Vreeland, arbiter of such matters, still found Vivien exceptionally beautiful:

> Only England could have produced her. She was the perfect English rose. When the door opened and she was there, she was so terribly good-looking. She had such an exquisite unreality about her.[82]

Nor is there any sign of trouble in the light-hearted letter that Vivien wrote her daughter a few days later. Both Vivien and Olivier had bad colds:

> …so my days are spent in bed wondering just what kind of noises are going to emerge on the stage each night! There have been various excitements pleasant and unpleasant. First with the revolve which just *wouldn't,* and then there were all kinds of plans for dressing up stage hands as Roman soldiers to push and heave us in and out of sight. However, at the first night all went well. It is worked manually here by two tough gentlemen but I never dare look in case I see them fainting dead away in the middle of a manoeuvre.[83]

Cecil Beaton, still smarting in the wilderness, gave his opinion of *Antony and Cleopatra* to Lady Juliet Duff:

> Although I expected very little, I was most disappointed. I cannot but think that she must have deteriorated for her voice was quite phony. I was never once moved and could not understand what she was saying as Larry has taught her to put on a fake voice to disguise her own little birdlike pipe. It is not a success.[84]

Brooks Atkinson, reviewing the production for the *New York Times,* called the two plays: 'the finest theatre work of this wretched season."[85] In an earlier review he wrote:

> There has not been an *Antony and Cleopatra* to compare with this in New York, in the past quarter of a century. Miss Leigh's Cleopatra is superb. We all knew that she would look glorious in the Egyptian costumes and that she would be every inch a queen. But it is a pleasure to report that she has also captured the infinite variety of the ruler of the Nile. She is smouldering and sensual, wily and treacherous, but she is also intelligent, audacious and courageous...It is as though *Antony and Cleopatra* never had been played before. Everything about the Olivier production is glowing or crumbling with vitality.[86]

In New York Vivien suffered a severe depression. "She was in a pitiful state,"[87] recalled Irene Selznick. Vivien tried to avoid getting involved with doctors and a vist to a psychiatrist proved fruitless.

After the Cleopatras, Olivier invited himself and Vivien to stay with Noël Coward in Jamaica. They arrived at Montego Bay on 13 April. Olivier told Coward that he feared Vivien was undergoing a suppressed nervous breakdown. Coward talked to her and tried to explain that nervous exhaustion resulted from physical exhaustion and that she needed a prolonged rest. Though he told Olivier, "If anybody's having a nervous breakdown, you are,[88] he remained worried about Vivien "who is terribly overtired and obviously suffering from nervous exhaustion."[89]

Olivier then embarked on the film of *The Beggar's Opera,* while Vivien spent long quiet months at Notley. Olivier believed that Vivien had recovered from her illness. Later he wrote ruefully: "I was quite unprepared for what was in store."[90]

Athene Seyler recalled the occasional tension of life at Durham Cottage:

> There were some wonderful parties in that little cottage. I remember I went to one and we were all crowded on the spiral stairs and Larry, who had been filming all day and

> was very tired and rather dirty, suddenly came in and saw his cottage filled with people all drinking and shouting and talking and she really paid no attention to him at all. And he went up these stairs to a bath and bed I expect.[91]

Suzanne was now at RADA, taking part in a play every now and again. Her faithful grandmother attended a production of *Twelfth Night* on 2 April, and then on 11 July the students performed *The Women Have Their Way*. Suzanne played two parts and the production is noteworthy for the sinister presence of one John Orton, as a sacristan, and Kenneth Halliwell as Adolfo Adalio. Orton made little impression on Suzanne. Also at RADA were Sylvia Sims and Joan Collins.

Much of the time Vivien was unwell. However, later in the year Noël Coward's diaries reveal that she attended a charity preview of *Quadrille* and Douglas Fairbanks' dinner for Charlie Chaplin in September, that she was at the opening of Chaplin's film *Limelight* in October, and that Coward drove her home from a party at the Millses (because Olivier had left early).

Gertrude's dairies record a weekend with Vivien on 1 August and that they spent a 'very happy' evening at home on 30 October. On her thirty-ninth birthday Vivien joined Rachel Redgrave and Noël Coward to see the Queen Mother (recently widowed) lay the foundation stone of the Vanbrugh Theatre. Coward weekended at Notley and the party went to Blenheim Palace where they found a young house-party headed by Princess Margaret. Then from 29 November to 5 December Coward's group, Larry and Vivien and John and Mary Mills, flew to Paris. They were met by staunch friends, Paul-Emile Seidmann and his wife, Ginette Spanier (the directrice of Balmain), a couple who held more or less open house to visiting stars at 70 avenue Marceau. They stayed at the Hotel France et Choiseul, attending theaters and nightclubs, a dinner party given by Korda, and enjoyed themselves so much at another dinner that they skipped one act of the play, inadvertently disappointing a reception committee and a bunch of photographers. The Oliviers returned to London as they had invited Gertrude for the weekend, but found themselves fog-bound in London, while Gertrude (who had been driven down the day before in the Bentley) enjoyed herself at Notley in the snow. New Year's Day 1953 found the Oliviers, Gertrude, Ernest, Leigh Holman, and Suzanne having spent a happy, if predictably late, evening together.

Chapter 17
Elephant Walk

> *"It's that damn bull come back again," George muttered. "Haven't seen him for a year or two now and I hoped we'd seen the last of him."*
>
> Robert Standish, *Elephant Walk*, p.59

In January 1953 Vivien set off to Sussex to see a new play at the White Rock Pavilion in the afternoon and to attend a party in Brighton given by the Ralph Richardsons. The roads were icy and she was accompanied by the chauffeur, Trudgett. Having some time to kill between engagements, she asked Trudgett to see if she could call on the Frewens at The Sheephouse.

Oswald Frewen's health had deteriorated considerably in recent years. He became prone to blackouts and often slumbered in the afternoons. He had felt particularly ill since Christmas due to having eaten oysters. Trudgett's phone-call woke Frewen up and, despite his devotion to Vivien, he had to say that he was too ill and could see nobody, not even her. Trudgett rang again at five o'clock and caught Lena Frewen just back from the village. Vivien was still determined to come, so Lena "hurled herself into preparations and soufflé, mutton loin and plum pudding into the cooker."[1] Vivien arrived at 6:30. They drank gin and vermouth, a bottle of red wine (given by Leigh) at dinner and then brandies afterwards. Vivien amused Oswald with her story of engaging Trudgett:

> "And what is your name?"

> "Trudgett, my lady."
> "Well I hope we shall never have to trudge it home together."[2]

At 10:30 Vivien left for the Richardson party intending to return to London that night. Oswald commented:

> And that is the way she lives: sweet and plumb crazy. No *wonder* she had a breakdown. Told us she was off to Ceylon directly to be filmed with elephants, and then to Hollywood to complete the film…Trudgett looked a little anxious when she said *she* would drive, but they off a'taunto and and completed their programme.[3]

Olivier has written of the feelings of shock he experienced when Vivien announced that Peter Finch was to be her lead in *Elephant Walk*. He had rejected the role himself, believing the film too slight. Korda alarmed him by appearing to know exactly why she had chosen Finch. He had not been deceived by Vivien's off-hand announcement of her choice.

"If ever there was a flawed masterpiece it was Vivien,"[4] Peter Finch told Trader Faulkner. Finch had played an important role in the lives of the Oliviers since he came over to England in 1949. It has been suggested that he was so much around that, when Vivien was ill, she could not determine the difference between him and Olivier. He took this as enormous encouragement, believing that she loved him for himself alone. In many ways they were well matched. They both had an Eastern background, Finch was easy-going and tolerant. He liked to stay up late, talking and drinking. He was fascinated by Vivien. There are many testimonials to Finch's stud-like qualities. And Vivien, who often berated Olivier for poor performance in the bedroom, found with Finch an extraordinary sexual rapport. Maxine Audley knew Finch:

> Peter was kind of helpless – putty in her hands. He would do anything she wanted. If she rang him up he would drop everything and go to her. But he was a fairly weak character – an angel, a darling man, no evil in him – but

> he was content to just love life and eating and drinking and sleeping with lovely ladies. She could do anything with him.[5]

Finch maintained that the affair only began in Ceylon, and Trader Faulkner has said that Vivien was "the greatest influence"[6] in his life, that when the situation became really grave he threatened suicide in order to "blot out the whole bloody business once and for all,"[7] and that after Vivien his life began to spiral downwards.

Vivien flew to Ceylon at the end of January. *Elephant Walk* was loosely based on a novel by Robert Standish. The story concerned a tea planter, John Wiley, who took his bride to Ceylon to his mansion, Elephant Walk, built across the traditional marching route of the elephants. The bride found the house ruled by the memory of 'the Guvnor,' John Wiley's father. She objected to the scrounging cronies who came round each evening to get drunk at her husband's expense and she contemplating eloping with the only sympathetic member of the community, Dick Carver. She remained to do her duty when an epidemic of typhoid broke out and she was finally reunited with her husband after the elephants had trumpeted their stolid way through the Wiley home.

The attraction of the film for Vivien was Peter Finch. Ironically he played the unsympathetic husband from whom the disenchanted bride sought freedom. Halfway across the world together, they were free to do as they pleased. Finch began well, eating sparingly to ensure what Yolande Finch called "that hollow look that his audiences interpreted as emotion."[8]

Vivien was entering another exhausting phase of her illness, drawn to any lighted candle or tribal gathering at impossibly late hours of the night. She wrote to Leigh: "This is the most fascinating country. I have seen the most extraordinary and beautiful things. Sitting in a tea field at the moment."[9] Finch was hardly a restraining factor. He drank heavily, as Vivien did only when in such a phase, and the pair of them were pushing themselves and each other to the limit. However, Vivien being Vivien, she found time to teach one young boy, Keith Bentley, how to swim and sought out a Sri Lankan artist, George Keyt, buying some of his works (a soundly judged investment). Vivien's health deteriorated in February and Olivier was contacted by the producer, Irving Asher, who feared she had suffered a breakdown. Olivier, who had been staying with the Waltons in Ischia, departed at once for Ceylon where Vivien met him. At first she appeared deceptively normal, but flew into a rage when he asked her if she should not be back at work. Olivier soon discerned what was going on but could not blame Finch: "Was he not simply doing what I had done to her first husband seventeen years ago?"[10] But there remained a feeling of resentment combined with the horror of the situation in which they all found themselves. Olivier left and early in March the crew set off for Hollywood, with some location shots safely filmed, consisting mainly of long shots of the car journey from the airport to Elephant Walk (the only scenes with Vivien herself that survived in the final film).

The seventy-two hour flight was difficult. In Hollywood matters became worse. Sunny met Vivien at the airport: "I could see that she was exhausted."[11] Vivien announced that she did not wish to go to the room reserved for her at the Beverly Hills Hotel, but would be staying at Spencer Tracy's house in his absence. Nobody seemed to know about this, but Tracy's brother was happy to surrender the key. "I took her there," said Sunny, "all that lovely, beautiful house, all alone."[12] Vivien wanted Sunny to stay, but she had young children to look after. Urging Vivien to take care, she left her. "Next day I leased a house right away."[13] In due course Vivien was sharing her dwelling with Peter Finch, his wife, Tamara, and their daughter, Anita. She arranged a great party for the Finches but then could not face it. One evening Tamara went up to see her while she was bathing and, in Trader Faulkner's words, Vivien "tried to seduce Tamara or, truer to say, she tried to shock her."[14] Matters became worse when Vivien employed every caprice to lure Finch from his wife, even demanding that he leave Tamara's bed for hers.

Vivien's breakdown manifested itself when she began to recount passages from *Streetcar*. She was seen by the company physician and by 12 March the studio realized it was impossible to keep her in the film. Vivien was put into the care of nurses round the clock. Her close friends did their best to help though Peter Finch himself was by this time conspicuously not around. David Niven became involved in the final denouement. This he described in detail in *Bring on the Empty Horses*.[15] In effect Vivien was found wandering around naked and distraught in her house, veering from shaking fear to terrifying bouts of aggression. Her old ally, John Buckmaster, had joined her in various escapades round George Cukor's swimming pool. Now he was back at the house, dressed in nothing but a towel. He and Vivien enjoyed tearing up money, but she drew the line at his suggestion that they should fly out of an upper window together.

Buckmaster had spent three spells in mental institutions. The previous year he had suffered a serious nervous breakdown after a successful run in *St. Joan* in New York. Accused of molesting women on the corner of Madison Avenue and 67th Street at 7 a.m., he was chased by the police to Park Avenue and 75th Street and arrested for felonious assault and the possession of two kitchen-type knives, which he brandished at his captors. When the judge sent him to Bellevue Hospital for a psychiatric check, he said: "Well, I must say I can't blame you, judge, considering everything."[16] He was later transferred to the State Hospital for the mentally ill at King's Park, Long Island. Here he was rescued by his step-brother, John Merivale, and allowed to go to London on condition that he entered a psychiatric hospital and never returned to New York State again. He spent a few weeks at St. Andrew's, Northampton, but he escaped and proved that for two weeks he could look after himself. Thus he became free. He then slipped off to Ireland. And John Merivale was concerned to receive an in-flight postcard from him indicating his return to "the land of milk and money."[17] In due course he gravitated to Hollywood, where he found Vivien.

At the house, in the middle of the night Niven summoned Stewart Granger's help. Buckmaster told Granger that he had been sent by a higher power to protect Vivien, but Granger assured him that he was a higher power still and succeeded in stering him home to the Garden of Allah. The joint attempts of Niven and Granger to sedate Vivien she foiled adroitly, managing to engineer a situation in which Niven ate some drugged scrambled eggs prepared for her. Already a "hollow-eyed zombie,"[18] 'Niv' presently dozed off. Vivien continued to master the situation until Granger summoned a doctor and two large nurses. He carried her into the bedroom, fell on top of her and pinned her down. The nurse wielded the needle, at which point Vivien stared at him with a look of total betrayal and said, "I thought you were my friend."[19] It was a look he never forgot. Similarly Niven, a loyal and simple friend, confessed, "I found I had come to hate her."[20]

Vivien's part in *Elephant Walk* was taken over by Elizabeth Taylor (loaned by MGM). She was a glamorous addition to the film but, in the scenes when the tea-planter is cavorting about downstairs with his mates, Vivien would have been a more commanding presence on the upper landing.

The Ceylon scenes had already cost a million dollars. The film went through more problems before its release, including the breaking seven ribs of Abraham Sofaer, the actor playing Appuhamy, who hated real elephants and was lifted into the air by a mechanical elephant's trunk which unfortunately got out of control.

Vivien's plight was overseen, not entirely unselfishly, by Danny Kaye until Olivier and Cecil Tennant arrived. Olivier has also described the scene at length in his memoirs: "the encounter with Vivien, more dreaded than any other in my life."[21] Since Vivien was in a manic mood, it was decided that it was better if she did not see Olivier. On the other hand, she always trusted Cecil Tennant as a faithful friend. Thus Tennant went into the house while at first Olivier hid in the bushes. It was vital to get Vivien out of America because the doctors were obliged by law to report her behavior and had she been incarcerated in an asylum it would have been hard to secure her release. On the positive side, she would obviously recover quicker in the peace of Notley. More sedation was needed before the journey home. The first injection failed, and Vivien found it hard to forgive the cold inflection in Olivier's voice as she heard him say, "Give her another."[22]

The journey back to England was fraught with further problems. With Vivien heavily sedated and safely at rest in a special compartment of the airplane, Cecil Tennant felt he could allow himself to doze off. Not surprisingly he was worn out after dealing not only with Vivien, but also with the contractural details of her withdrawal from the film. But Vivien's constitution was so strong that she got up in spite of the heavy sedation, and the next thing he knew she was sitting beside him saying: "Cecil, you look exhausted. Are you all right?"[23] The long-suffering agent dreaded that she might cause a scene on board. He suggested a game of gin rummy and in this manner the long and wearing flight passed without further incident.

Unfortunately the press were alert to Vivien's plight. The *Daily Sketch* showed a stretcher being carried onto the flight at Los Angeles and a very drawn Vivien walking down the airplane steps at New York. When told that cameras and Danny Kaye were on the tarmac, Vivien attended to her make-up and made as professional an arrival as possible. But once in the car she hid on the floor and refused to move.

The last lap of the journey was just as difficult. Vivien's attitude was that she still had work to do in Hollywood and she wished to return there forthwith. She therefore refused to board the London flight. The *Daily Sketch* stated that Vivien arrived at New York airport with Olivier and Danny Kaye, "wrapped in a blanket across the laps of the two men."[24]She sat in the car, continually rubbing her hand across her forehead. Eventually she was forced to board the plane. She turned to reporters, waved and apparently said, "So terribly sorry, folks."[25] Olivier pleaded for no pictures and the group went into the front compartment, having taken over an area normally occupied by eighteen people.

By the time they arrived in London Vivien was more composed. Looking puffy and worn out, she was nevertheless able to smile as she walked calmly down the steps. Again there was a crowd of spectators and reporters. A voice called out "Welcome home, my lady," and Vivien turned nervously to Olivier and said: "We really are home, aren't we?"[26] Vivien was then put in the care of Dr. Freudenberg, who had agreed to treat her on condition that she became an inmate at his hospital. She was driven to Netherne Hospital at Coulsdon, Surrey, which was unmistakably a mental hospital and not a private clinic. Freudenberg sedated her heavily, putting her to sleep for about three weeks. She also received shock treatment.

Oswald Frewen was horrified at the press reports and wrote at once, inviting Olivier and Vivien for ten days of total peace at The Sheephouse. His letter got lost in all the fan mail and he recorded sadly: "She has gravitated out of normal life."[27] On 10 April, three weeks after Vivien's dramatic return, Frewen went to stay with Leigh at Woodlands, where he heard the full story:

> [Leigh] tells us he visited Vivling Thursday in her mental hospital, boss Freudenberg, whom she called 'Rosenkavalier,' She WON'T stay there. Leigh says she has the strongest will of anyone in the world, and when she won't, she won't, but she "can never be left alone" and needs 3 nurses. Larry was in Italy, address alledgedly unknown and her father and mother on holiday in Paris! so Leigh was sent for. Viv had been drugged to sleep ever since her return to England – say 14 to 20 days. Now, awake, she talks sense and remembers old things, but nothing of her voyage from Hollywood, or the recent past. Freudenberg

> didn't want *anyone* to see her, only got Leigh down to induce her to stay on there, and said he needn't stay, as he offered, in a nearby hotel in case he were needed. They can't keep her without her consent unless they certify her but it is a luny-bin [*sic*], and she knows it, and it must be shattering to her morale, poor pet, and *of course* she should have been allowed to see (selected and primed) friends. Next day, Saturday [11 April], the phone rang, Leigh answered it, and Viv's secretary told him she *had,* now, left Freudenberg, and arrived a'taunto at University College Hospital, to a private Ward with a telephone at her bedstead!! (which she immediately used to command her beauty-specialist's attendance and her leg-depilator!!!). We suspect her general practitioner, Dr. Childe, had had it up his sleeve the whole time, it's all on the National Health! And *Larry* arrived dramatically to see her: obviously his whereabouts *were* known. What a world of memory-losers and liars![28]

Olivier had returned to Ischia once Vivien was safely installed at the asylum. The Waltons tried to divert him, taking him to Southern Italy, but the press pursued him relentlessly. When Vivien was on the point of emerging from her drugged sleep and first program of shock treatments Cecil Tennant cabled Olivier and he returned. Meanwhile the Tennants oversaw her transfer to University College Hospital as a better alternative than returning at once to Notley. Nor was this easy, since Vivien sent specific instructions about the dress and belt she needed. The maid packed the wrong belt and Irina Tennant had to return to Durham Cottage from Surrey for the right one before she would dress.

Vivien was upset that Olivier had not been present at her bedside for her awakening. And she blamed him for putting her in an asylum without appreciating that this was the only way to secure Freudenberg's treatment. In his memoirs, Olivier confessed to lasting guilt at "not being more alive" to his duties, "no matter how painful or how mortally sick of them[29] he was. Instead, it was Noël Coward who lovingly ensured that flowers and scent were at her bedside to greet her. Vivien never forgot his kindness. She carried

Noël's card in her handbag and described his gesture as "all I had to hang on to at that dreadful time."[30] Vivien called Noël from University College Hospital. It was, he wrote, "a heart-breaking conversation. She started in floods of tears and then made a gallant effort to be gay and ordinary, but the strain showed through and she didn't make sense every now and then."[31]

Olivier found Vivien a changed personality after her treatment. He could not love her as before and was aghast that his feelings had changed in this way: "She was now more of a stranger to me than I could ever have imagined possible.[32] He discussed his plight with Noël Coward:

> Apparently things had been bad and getting worse since 1948 or thereabouts. It is really discouraging to reflect how needlessly unhappy people make themselves and each other. They are now going to start afresh down at Notley, which may work or may not. I shall be surprised if it does…[33]

Vivien recuperated slowly at Notley, her mother recording on 24 April: "Viv looking wonderful."[34] Gertrude could never accept that Vivien was ill. This annoyed Olivier but meant that Gertrude was forever optimistic and always forgave her daughter's behavior, however misguided.

Kenneth Clark and his wife, Jane, visited Vivien at Notley finding her pale and quiet, wrapped up on a chaise longue in the early spring sunshine:

> She spoke about her illness quite simply, without style or artifice. She knew quite well what had happened to her. But there seemed to be no way of breaking these cycles, because as she got better she became confident again and impatient of interference.[35]

As matters deteriorated Clark would mutter to friends: "She's killing our greatest actor."[36] He saw her wanting to be a great actress and a great social figure. He wrote:

> She would sit up till all hours in pursuit of that aim. That is what wore her out, and it also wore out Larry, who said to me, "I just want to act well. Nothing else." It led to the

great tragedy of her life.[37]

Vivien made an excellent recovery, though all was not well at home and even the *Hollywood Reporter* speculated that the Oliviers' marriage was now like that of the Windsors, "a marriage in name – and face – only."[38] From then on there were persistent rumors that the Oliviers were going to split, a line which was pursued relentlessly over the ensuing years.

The Queen's Coronation was a diversion for the other members of Vivien's family, who were able to watch the procession from St. James's Street. Leigh took part in it, riding postillion on one of the carriages, being a friend of Captain Frank Gilbey, the coach driver.

Vivien's recovery was not helped by two burglaries. While in hospital her *Streetcar* Oscar and £200 worth of clothes were stolen from Durham Cottage. Then in July burglars came to Notley, where the Waltons and Richardsons were staying. They stole Vivien's mink cape, a blue fox cape and a stole, and all her jewelry. Regrettably their Pekinese, Bosco, let the side down. "It barks only at me," said Olivier, "and made no noise during the raid."[39] A fortnight later, Vivien was well enough to emerge in public to see Noël Coward play King Magnus in Shaw's *The Apple Cart*. Noël thought her "papery and rather frail but there was no sign of there ever having been a mental breakdown."[40] After the show Binkie Beaumont gave a party and Vivien handled all press enquiries with her habitual tact. She had over-worked. *Streetcar* had been too grueling, the Cleopatras "hardly a rest cure,"[41] Ceylon too hot, Larry and the doctors had been wonderful. She had rested, gardened, read, sewn a Queen Anne cushion. She wished Elizabeth Taylor well in the film and indeed she hoped to film in Hollywood in the future. Vivien then went to stay with Leigh at Woodlands, describing her visit as "such a carefree peaceful time for me."[42]

Because it was Coronation Year, Olivier had intended that he and Vivien should co-star in Terence Rattigan's play, *The Sleeping Prince*. When Vivien was first ill, he told the press he would be delaying it by four weeks. However, it finally opened at the Phoenix Theatre on Vivien's fortieth birthday.

The Sleeping Prince was an intentionally light confection. Set at the time of George V's Coronation in 1911 it was an "occasional fairy tale"[43] concerning a business-like Prince who liked to fit an hour of philandering into his schedule of public duties. A chorus girl was found for him but she had notions of a more perfect, lasting love. Rattigan explained:

> His frenzied attempts to disentangle himself from this imbroglio thereafter make the whole play, together with his genuine transformation from Prince Un-charming, if not into Prince Charming, at least into Prince Half-Way Human.[44]

Olivier was determined to undertake it, despite Rattigan's fear that Vivien, "one of nature's grand-duchesses," could hardly play "a chorus girl thrilled to her Brooklynese death at the prospect of meeting a real grand duke in the flesh.[45] Rattigan was never convinced that she succeeded. Nor were the critics, Milton Shulman judging: "It seems a pity that in these spare times so much talent should have gone into so little."[46] Tynan snarled once more – condemning Olivier for taking part in such a "quilted cushion of a play"[47] and dismissing Vivien in a throw-away mention:

> There is also Miss Leigh, looking (I must say) very well indeed in a white dress and a strawberry-blonde wig. Admirers of her art will recognize this as her 'American-type' performance complete with sing-song accept à la Katharine Hepburn. I found her beautiful without being attractive, technically competent without being emotionally convincing. It is a strangely bloodless display.[48]

The Queen, Prince Philip, and Princess Margaret came to one of the performances. Much of the press attention was devoted to Vivien's miraculous recovery. In the *Daily Express* John Barber thought that on her fortieth birthday she looked barely half her age. "The phenomenal kitten is back,"[49] he wrote.

The early months of 1954 caused no further alarms, and the summer was punctuated by visits to The Frog (the society charity play directed by Judy Montagu and Princess Margaret). Marlene Dietrich's sensational opening at the Café de Paris, and one of Charles Russell's 'Night of 100 Stars" at the Palladium, where Vivien, Olivier, and Jill Esmond were amongst the galaxy of "guests" in a cabaret compéred by Douglas Fairbanks Jr. On 31 May Vivien repeated her Lady Teazle in the screen scene of *The School for Scandal* opposite Alec Guinness and James Donald (the latter pair uncomfortably cast) at an all-star matinée in the presence of the Queen Mother and Princess Margaret to honor Dame Sybil Thorndike's golden jubilee on stage and that of RADA.

The press continued to look for any further signs of Vivien's ill-health during a longish run (the play closed on 3 July 1954). One night Vivien missed a performance due to a broken wrist. While she wound a piece of wispy scarf the same color as her dress around the white plaster cast and made it yet more elgant with a brooch, the press flashed the missed evening as headline news, in the hope, no doubt, that more serious problems were afoot.

Hardly had she finished *The Sleeping Prince* than Vivien began filming Rattigan's *The Deep Blue Sea.* First, though, there was a holiday in Italy. The Oliviers went from the Père Bise restaurant at Talloires to San Vigilio, the beautiful locanda on Lake Garda so favored by the Duff Coopers and Winston Churchill. Here there was nothing to do but eat delicious food and row on the lake. They moved south to Portofino to stay with Rex Harrison and Lilli Palmer, in their hilltop villa. "It is heavenly here and I'd like always to be on holiday,"[50] wrote Vivien to Leigh. These were difficult days in the Harrison houschold, since "Sexy Rexy" had recently met Kay Kendall, the beautiful but ill-fated filmstar by whom he had been quite bowled over."[51] Jean-Pierre Aumont was there, and the Duke and Duchess of Windsor were on board Daisy Fellowes's yacht, the *Sister Anne*, in the harbor. Harrison rceivd a surprise visit from Kay Kendall during the holiday, which confirmed what Lilli Palmer had already deduced. Not long afterwards he and Miss Kendall eloped.[52] Aumont recalled an evening when Olivier and Harrison joined him for a late drink in the harbor and returned to hear Vivien's voice raised on high, Olivier stopped in his tracks and said: "My God, it's starting up again."[53] However, from Ventimiglia on the way home, Vivien wrote to her parents: "It has been such a glorious holiday. We arc both so well, if extremely large!"[54] In September Noël Coward summed it all us: "Rex Harrison has fallen in love with Kay Kendall and is breaking Lilli's heart… Larry and Vivien are fine.'[55]

In September Vivien filmed *The Deep Blue Sea.* She played Hester Collyer, the High Court Judge's wife with whom a young pilot, played by Kenneth More, had fallen in love. Hester was meant to be somewhat unattractive. People did not fall in love with her. She left the safe affection of her conservative marriage for an initially passionate affair with the pilot. But this went wrong and she made a suicide attempt. The plot involved discovering what had driven her to this act, and then whether or not it was likely to happen again.

Kenneth More, at that time an impecunious actor, disliked the script, feeling that there was too much of the director, Anatole Litvak, and not enough of Terence Rattigan. He said so loudly at the time and he said so again in his memoirs. Everyone agreed that Vivien was badly miscast as the unadmired wife because of her undoubted beauty. More alienated Vivien because she knew he thought this. He judged that the chemistry was wrong between them and noticed that, off-stage, her personality "completely smothered Olivier's."[56] More contributed the only spikey comments in Alan Dent's posthumous *Bouquet* to Vivien, and his postbag proved the unpopularity of his views:

> Of all the women I have ever met, she was the *most* sure of herself! But I could never really trust her and I suspected her almost overwhelming friendliness. I thought she was petulant, spoilt, overpraised, and overloved…[57]

Moira Lister played Dawn Maxwell in the film. She agreed that Vivien was miscast: "She was too beautiful. It was played originally by Peggy Ashcroft in the theatre and it needed that plain, earthy quality and sadness that Peggy Ashcroft displayed so beautifully…With Vivien you thought he would be mad if he ever walked out on her."[58]

Moira Lister also thought Litvak "a horrifying director."[59] She explained:

> He had this theory that you have to destroy somebody first to get a good performance out of them and he used to – systematically – every day – destroy Vivien until he got her to cry, and he said "Right. Now you're in a mood to do the scene. We'll do the scene." He was really very harsh with her. She used to arrive on the set every morning

> looking so beautiful and so fresh with those amazing eyes of hers, and I used to think how can she get up at 6 o'clock in the morning and look so absolutely ravishing? We all knew that she only slept two or three hours a night...She was a strong character and tried not to show that she was ill and so overcame it with a sort of brash harshness and a viper tongue, which, I think, came out of fighting something that nobody was helping her with.[60]

While Vivien filmed the Rattigan (some of it in Switzerland), Olivier was busy with *Richard III* (jokingly dubbed Richard Three Eyes). Just as this had been one of his greatest triumphs on the stage, so it proved a remarkable film. A competitive actor, Olivier must have enjyed the opportunity to have John Gielgud (or his double) tipped head-first into a butt of malmsey wine, and oblige Ralph Richardson to kneel and kiss his ring. Again, Vivien was disappointed not to be involved, the part of Lady Anne going to Claire Bloom. For this film Olivier won another Oscar. However, *Richard III* was not at first a financial success, so little so that Olivier found it impossible to raise money for a joint *Macbeth* and it appeared that his days of filming Shakespeare were over.

Christmas at Notley was an occasion of strained relationships. The Waltons were there and the Harrisons, now uncomfortably matched in *Bell, Book and Candle*. So too was Peter Finch, who had failed to be resolute about giving Vivien up. She continued to dominate him and, while on the one hand he was still stimulated by her glamour and sharp intelligence, on the other he was worn out by her demands on his time and energy. Trader Faulkner, who knew all the protagonists, has given the most satisfactory explanation of Vivien's affair with Finch:

> It was a dynamic union in which, according to Peter, Vivien became very possessive and tiresome but, out of physical attraction, real friendship and rapport developed at a much higher level than the purely sexual aspect which adverse publicity so magnified and distorted...Vivien told me she would never have broken her marriage for Peter. She understood him, but the problem at the beginning of their

> affair, apart from her illness, which was a major factor in its disruption, was that she was accustomed to having her own way, and Peter, being a past master at evading any issue, very often avoided a confrontation by simply opting out.[61]

That Christmas at Notley Lady Walton was able to assess the scene:

> I had the distinct feeling that Larry, while setting off the Christmas fireworks, was pointing a rocket directly at Peter, but reluctantly changed his aim at the last minute and shot the rocket up into the evening air.[62]

Chapter 18

Look! No Hands!

Beautiful and sinuous, her Lady Macbeth was like a dangerous snake gliding about the stage.

Fabia Drake, *Blind Fortune*

The year 1954 had been a disappointing year at Stratford. To celebrate Glen Byam Shaw's phase as a director, it was announced that the Oliviers were to undertake the 1955 season. At once there was the normal rush to the box-office. There were 600,000 applications in the first week and every seat was taken. The schedule was grueling. For example, *Twelfth Night* (directed by John Gielgud) opened on the twelfth night of April (with Prince Rainier of Monaco in the audience). There were five evening performances and two matinées. The play was performed on a daily basis at first, then joined by *All's Well That Ends Well* (without the Oliviers) on 26 April, *Macbeth* on 17 June, *The Merry Wives of Windsor* (again without them) on 12 July, and *Titus Andronicus* in the nineteenth week. Thus in the twentieth week (22 to 27 August), Vivien performed in *Twelfth Night* on Tuesday evening, *Macbeth* twice on Wednesday, and *Titus Andronicus* on Friday night and twice on Saturday.

Olivier was more interested in the last play than in the other two (which he had already taken part in, though Vivien had not). The situation was not unlike 1944 again. With *Richard III*'s release as a film, and three major Shakespeares on stage, Olivier was reassuring himself that his victor's crown was securely in place.

Stratford became the center of the Olivier's lives for the next thirty-three weeks. They took a house at Alveston called Avoncliffe, preferring as always to settle in a home than reside in the transitory atmosphere of a hotel. Olivier had not played at Stratford since 1922. Nor had he been directed by John Gielgud for twenty years. This was inevitably a difficult meeting of two disparate views. John Gielgud believed that *Twelfth Night*, though a favorite play of his, was very hard to direct:

> It is so difficult to combine the romance of the play with the cruelty of the jokes against Malvolio, jokes which are in any case archaic and difficult. The different elements in the play are hard to balance properly.[1]

Michael Denison, who received glowing notices as Sir Andrew Aguecheek, wrote of an element of indecisiveness in Gielgud's direction. Sir John addressed them on the first day: "Now I'm not sure what I shall have to offer you in this lovely play, so let's see first of all what you've got to offer me."[2] Gielgud's vision of the play as "a quiet romantic piece" rather than "an Elizabethan romp"[3] owed much to Granville-Barker's preface and a recent interpretation by Leslie Hotson.

Gentle, discreet direction, with ideas tried and rejected, left room for insurrection and Olivier was not slow in imposing his will. He feared that Gielgud was confusing the company. He wrote: "Noël Coward once said that the only real use of a director was to stop the actors from bumping into each other; at the rate our *Twelfth Night* was going our first performance would have been more like a game of Blind Man's Buff than anything else."[4] In due course, "at the risk of hurting his feelings,"[5] Olivier asked Gielgud to leave the company to rehearse on their own. According to Olivier this rescued the production from disaster.

Gielgud wrote of the problems that Vivien endured – "she was torn between what I was trying to make her do and what Olivier thought she should do."[6] Olivier's performance he thought "extravagant"[7]:

> He was extremely moving at the end, but he played the earlier scenes like a Jewish hairdresser, with a lisp and an extraordinary accent, and he insisted on falling backwards

> off a bench in the garden scene, though I begged him not to do it.[8]

Although *Twelfth Night* was greeted as an elegant, dignified, and poetic production, many first-nighters and reviewers were left with a haunting feeling of disappointment. W.A. Darlington felt that neither Olivier, Vivien, nor Gielgud's direction "had taken wing."[9] The evening was "a big occasion, agreed; but there had been the possibility of a great one if our highest hopes had been realized."[10]

Malcolm Pride's set was a further disappointment since the formal gardens with the palace at the back meant that not everyone could see it in its entirety, and the comedy scenes were played so far upstage that the audience felt left out. Other reviews refer to Vivien's "wealth of eloquent and tender expression,"[11] "carefully restrained, yet spontaneous, fresh and human study,"[12] and "most bewitching boyishness."[13] She was praised for in no way upstaging Maxine Audley's Olivia. Peter Fleming wrote in the *Spectator*:

> Miss Vivien Leigh's Viola is trim, pretty, poised and resourceful; but to the qualities which distinguish an air-hostess something must be added – warmth, uncertainty, a capacity for being embarrassed – if she is to lead this improbable dance through Illyria in the way it should be led, and Miss Leigh's performance, though talented and charming, has too strong a bias towards what politicians call non-involvement.[14]

This did not prevent the habitual Olivier crowds from thronging the theatre. Olivier's main annoyance was that, despite Vivien's earlier triumph as Cleopatra, the critics were still saying that she could not act Shakespeare.

Macbeth opened under Glen Byam Shaw's direction on a night of thunder and lightning on 7 June. Nearly every actor and actress who expressed their opinion judged Vivien the best Lady Macbeth they ever saw. The photographer Angus McBean wrote that Vivien was the only Lady Macbeth he wanted to see and Olivier the only Macbeth who cold sustain the play after she had gone. However, once again the critics were lukewarm and Kenneth Tynan's dismissive line is often quoted:

> Vivien Leigh's Lady Macbeth is more niminy-piminy than thundery-blundery, more viper than anaconda, but still quite competent in its small way.[15]

This was also the review in which Tynan opined: "Last Tuesday Sir Laurence shook hands with greatness."[16] Later Tynan confessed to John Russell Taylor that his condemnation of Vivien was "one of the worst errors of judgement he had ever made."[17]

Praise has been poured on her performances in recent years. Olivier wrote: "the best [Lady Macbeth] in my seriously considered opinion was Vivien Leigh."[18] In later life he would judge Vivien was ill-treated by the critics for two reasons – first, her beauty, and secondly, being matched against him. Gielgud said: "Her Lady Macbeth…showed an astonishing vocal power and poignancy of feeling – and it is a thousand pities that the project of filming her performance was abandoned.[19] Glen Byam Shaw wrote: "I consider her Lady Macbeth the finest of all the performances I saw her give."[20] And Alan Dent: "I thought she was superlative, and even transcendent."[21] Fabia Drake quoted from the play in a telegram she sent Vivien: "Look like the innocent flower but be the serpent under't and we will have another *Mask of Virtue*."[22] Maxine Audley, who played Lady Macduff, explained:

> She was wonderful, because of the changes in the mood. Just as you believe they were in love in *Antony and Cleopatra* you absolutely believed that they had been in love in *Macbeth* and it was beginning to crumble. Most Macbeths and Lady Macbeths don't seem to behave like a married couple. I never believe they actually lived together. But Larry and Vivien at the banquet scene, when he sees the ghost of Banquo and she's trying to keep control, they were like any married couple with awkward guests. I thought she was marvelous and of course her mental disintegration. The whole thing about Macbeth is that he starts off rather quietly and gets madder and madder the more murders he commits, and she starts off on a high note and gradually

> crumbles, after the first murder. She goes to pieces and he gets stronger – madder but stronger. They change places. And that was very clear – wonderful.[23]

Noël Coward saw *Macbeth* in August. He was another who believed that Vivien's performance achieved greatness: "She had a sort of viperish determination and a physical seductiveness which clearly explained her hold over Macbeth."[24] Invariably a victim of the critics himself, Coward was again enraged by the *Macbeth* reviews not just for their content, but also for their tone. John Barber, a scourge appointed by Beaverbrook to "make a star or break a star,"[25] went so far as to describe Vivien's Lady Macbeth as "the most monumental piece of miscasting since Arthur Askey appeard as Shakespeare."[26] Barber combined this with a more general attack on the Oliviers entitled "Have the Oliviers lived on too little for too long?"[27] His line was that Olivier had achieved nothing of lasting merit for a decade: "Olivier was a great actor…Now, at 48, he is an ageing matinée idol, desperately fighting to win back his old reputation."[28] As for Vivien: "She is a great beauty – still, at 42. As an actress, excellent in a dainty, waspish way that seldom touches the heart."[29] Noël Coward marveled at "one of those rare magical evenings at the theatre when the throat contracts,"[30] but when he went back to Avoncliffe with the Oliviers he was seriously alarmed to discover Vivien on the verge of another breakdown:

> She talked at supper wildly. She is obsessed, poor darling, by the persecutions of the Press; her voice became high and shrill and her eyes strange. This morning when she had gone to a fitting, Larry came and talked to me. He is distraught and deeply unhappy. Apparently this relapse has been on the way for some time. She has begun to lose sleep again and makes scenes and invites more and more people to Notley until there is no longer any possibility of peace. Their life together is really hideous and here they are trapped in public acclaim, scrabbling about in the cold ashes of a physical passion that burnt itself out years ago. I am desperately sorry because I love them both and I am truly fearful of what may happen. The cruelty of fifth-rate

> journalists has contributed a lot to the situation but the core of the trouble lies deeper, where in fact, it always lies, in sex. She, exacerbated by incipient TB, needs more and more sexual satisfaction. They are eminent, successful, envied and adored, and most wretchedly unhappy.[31]

Coward discussed the matter at length with Lilli Palmer (who had now recovered from her sorrows over Rex Harrison in the arms of a good-looking Argentine actor, Carlos Thompson, whom she later married). They thought the Oliviers should live and sleep apart, while maintaining a public front, and that Vivien should give up tragic parts and aim to become a top-rate witty comedienne.

Coward was back at Stratford on 16 August for the opening night of *Titus Andronicus*, where he found the Olivier situation "worsening by the hour."[32] Despite Peter Brook's excellent production, he was left unimpressed. He found Vivien "in a vile temper and perfectly idiotic,"[33] while Olivier was in despair. Discussing the matter with Tarquin, Olivier's son, a few days later, he discovered that he too was desperately worried. Coward concluded that Vivien was spoiled and egocentric, that she suffered from an inability to match Olivier on stage and thought that "if Larry had turned sharply on Vivien years ago and given her a clip in the chops, he would have been spared a mint of trouble."[34]

Titus Andronicus is Shakespeare's bloodiest play and could easily have been run as a horror-comic Grand Guignol farce. T.S. Eliot described it as "one of the stupidest and most uninspiring plays ever written."[35] As the audience mingled in the foyer on the first night there was an air of nervous gaity as though there might be some good laughs to be had. But they counted without Peter Brook, whose ingenuity soon held them in the grip of something more coldly terrifying. The staging of *Titus* was an historic event since it was the only one of Shakespeare's plays never to have been performed at Stratford. Indeed it had only been staged twice in the twentieth century. There was a prevailing view that even twice was excessive. The reviewers called it a "dramatized abattoir"[36] and Philip Hope-Wallace began his review: "Look! No hands!"[37] It was not everyone who wanted to see "two chaps chopped up into pudding for their mother to eat,"[38] as Milton Shulman pointed out. Bernard Levin was one of several reviewers to produce a "head count" of the various tragedies:

> The play opens with a dead march for three coffins. This is immediately followed by a human sacrifice, which is in turn scarcely over when a father stabs his son for disobedience; the horrors thereafter come thick and fast, including a rape, five stabbings, a strangling, an immolation, two cut throats, several horrible mutilations, a spectacular piece of involuntary cannibalism, and, shortly before the interval, what sounded remarkably like someone on the left-hand side of the stalls being violently sick.[39]

Twenty-seven year-old Brook wisely eschewed the traditional "Kensington Gore." Had he not done so the stage would have been awash with blood by the first curtain. Instead he implied severed hands with flowing chiffon scarves and, as the heads rolled, so the stage was bathed in a warm red light. "At Stratford last night corpses fell like autumn leaves and blood spilled like wine."[40] He reserved one particularly shocking moment, the severing of Titus's hand by Aaron's axe, made more ghastly by Olivier's moment of restrained silence before he emitted one of his celebrated cries of pain. Vivien had a less challenging role, being tongueless and handless throughout most of the play. She claimed that while acting she thought of Clarissa Churchill (then Lady Eden, the Prime Minister's wife), who had worked for Korda at the time of *Anna Karenina.* The reviewers thought Vivien's Lavinia a serene sufferer expressing statuesque pathos. Maxine Audley had a better part and better reviews. Kenneth Tynan, who had but lately savaged Vivien's Lady Macbeth, went ten steps further in his victimization:

> As Lavinia, Miss Vivien Leigh receives the news that she is about to be ravished by her husband's corpse with little more than mild annoyance of one who would have preferred foam rubber; otherwise the minor parts are played up to the hilt.[41]

Evelyn Waugh took his children to see *Titus* on 19 August, noting: "Sir

Laurence soldiered manfully through his part. Lady Olivier played hers with delicious nonchalance, full of wit in the dumb show, demure as an early Victorian bride when attending the murder of her ravishers."[42] He went round to see her, finding her "friendly but wary."[43] The following week he wrote an essay on *Titus* for the *Spectator:*

> When she was dragged off to her horrible fate she ventured a tiny, impudent, barely perceptible roll of the eyes, as who would say, "My word! What next?" She established complete confidence between the audience and the production. "We aren't trying to take you in," she seemed to say. "You're too clever and we are too clever. Just enjoy yourselves." It was the grain of salt which gave savour to the whole rich stew.[44]

Waugh meant this as "a fan letter to Lady Olivier."[45] Later he worried that it might upset her: "It appears she is morbidly sensitive to criticism."[46]

Olivier grew increasingly nervous about Vivien's condition. Once again she was entertaining wildly, and yet rising at 5 a.m. Olivier, struggling to remember the large part of Titus, was deprived of sleep, and made more anxious by the fear of tragedy. He believed that Tynan was "directly responsible for at least one of Vivien's nervous breakdowns."[47] One day he took her to Dr. Freudenberg but she summoned every skill in her thespian repertoire and convinced him that she was quite well. Maxine Audley explained what happened to Vivien:

> She started going a bit mad during *Titus*. She started to go strange in the spring and thorugh the summer months and by autumn she seemed to have recovered. Not only did she behave violently to everybody – probably worse to the people she loved and who were closest to her, but she physically swelled up. It was really weird. Her whole body swelled, particularly round the neck and face and shoulders. That would last two days and then she would go back to normal again.[48]

Maxine Audley also remembered that towards the end of the Stratford season, Tynan suddenly appeared on the scene:

> I think Vivien was absolutely determined to win him over, which she did. Absolutely. And he became a sort of devoted slave in a way. He adored her. He fell in love with her when he met her, having said all those nasty things about her…I don't think he wrote anything nasty after that.*[49]

The Deep Blue Sea was released on 24 August and shown at the local cinema at Stratford. One afternoon Michael Denison went to see it:

> I thought she was most frightfully good. So I went to tell her that evening in her dressing-room and tears came into her eyes and she said "Oh thank you Michael." She said "You know if you read what they've written about my performance in that you would think I'm a woman who has never experienced love or anything else."[50]

In October he and Dulcie Gray went to Notley and after an excellent supper endured one of those evenings when nobody was allowed to go to bed until 3 a.m. The next morning Denison found Olivier looking anxious. He announced that Vivien had pleurisy and that he had called the doctor. She did not appear at the lunch party at which Danny Kaye was a guest. Michael Denison recalled:

> It was a lovely autumn day and Larry, who was looking exhausted, said "Would you two like to come for a walk over the fields?" So we pottered off together – Viv was apparently sleeping – and as we came back every light was blazing and there was a sort of hum. It sounded like the Duchess of Richmond's ball on the eve of Waterloo. And there she was, having had a great telephoning marathon, got all possible friends in for a party which went on till four

*Tynan mentioned *Look After Lulu* in a summary of the theatre in 1959, but avoided expressing any opinion about Vivien.

> the next morning – in radiant form, pleurisy forgotten.[51]

The next morning the Denisons were worn out and Olivier was yet more exhausted. They asked after Vivien:

> He said 'I think she's all right," and there appeared at the end of the long gallery a girl of eighteen in the most beautiful narrow grey and white striped dress with an enormous bunch of scarlet roses in her arms. All the fit people had been demolished and she was the belle of the ball. And she played that night.[52]

The Stratford season ended in November. On 14 December there was a royal premiere of *Richard III* attended by the Queen, "radiant in pink and diamonds."[53] Vivien was present, elegant, almost regal herself. Olivier picked up yet more rave notices, all richly earned.

The three productions at Stratford are the more memorable for the circumstances in which they were achieved. Olivier was harassed in his private life by the fear that Vivien was about to suffer another nervous collapse. Additionally there was the discreet but hovering presence of Peter Finch, at times a relief, at times a threat. Hamish Hamilton remembered Olivier telling him "what it did to him to go into her dressing-room and see the photograph of that god-damned Finch on her dressing-table."[54] During these Stratford months Finch had moved into Notley, where, during the week, he lived alone, contentedly recovering from an illness. To many it seemed that Vivien was conducting her affair with Finch right under Olivier's nose, and that he did not mind. When Finch appeared at Stratford the other members of the cast dreaded being caught in the interplay between Vivien, Finch, and Olivier. At Notley Vivien inspired an uncomfortable discussion, describing Finch as "an old soul" and Olivier as "a brand new soul with a plastic Karma and a marital deficit balance."[55] When she became especially difficult, Finch quickly disappeared from view. With all his responsibilities it is not surprising that Olivier became tired. The situation was not helped when Vivien took to telephoning him at strategic intervals during his brief hours of rest between performances.

Despite all this, Olivier achieved yet more triumphant peaks and glorious acclaim, while Vivien's position was steadily undermined. Maxine Audley pinpointed one of the problems:

> I think it was terribly unfair. People would say to Larry: "You are the greatest actor in the world" and they would turn to Vivien and say: You are the most beautiful woman in the world." They never said those words she longed to hear: "You are the greaest actress in the world." She wasn't *the greatest* actress in the world but it's very difficult to nominate a person who is. She was stupendous in her way – as well as being beautiful. She had the temperament. She didn't always have the vocal power to reach the back of the gallery. But she did develop her voice and she had intelligence. Larry has always had an actor's intelligence. He could go to the heart of the play, the heart of a part and dig it out. She had to work much harder at it…Vivien didn't have that instinct. She had to acquire it.
>
> Larry was always tunnel visioned: how would *that* affect his performance, or that color would be a wonderful color for a costume. She would look at a work of art as a work of art. That was the big difference. He was much more straight line. Acting was it. The theatre was his entire life. Other things didn't matter. But I remember her talking about Maria Callas, Dietrich. She thought they were tremendous in their particular spheres. She was interested in cows and trees and gardening and buildings and clothes.
>
> The saddest thing is that we didn't realize that she had an illness. We all thought she was just behaving badly.[56]

Equally Vivien took a professional interest in the way her health was deteriorating. She read Scott Fitzgerald's essay *The Crack Up*, which appeared with other autobiographical fragments at this time. She gave copies to Peter Finch and to Trader Faulkner, then a member of the Company. *The Crack Up* described the general way man disintegrates with external blows that show their effect later and internal ones that happen imperceptibly and yet have an immediate result. A fellow-sufferer from tuberculosis, Scott

Fitzgerald turned on his own plight the same objectivity that emerged in his novels, concluding that he was like an old plate that cracked, but was kept in the household for minor service. It is not hard to determine the essay's appeal for Vivien.

In December Vivien set off to Paris, where she stayed with Ginette Spanier at 70 avenue Marceau. Vivien was expecting Peter Finch to arrive and Ginette made it clear that there was no question of his also staying in their apartment. Vivien's plan was to steal a few days in France with him and Alan Webb (who had also been in the Stratford company). Vivien prevailed upon Paul-Louis Weiller, and he offered them sanctuary at his magnificent property near Hyères.

Commandant Paul-Louis Weiller got to know Vivien through the Duff Coopers. A rich industrialist and a noted collector, he lived to 100, and was still wind-surfing within a month of his ninety-ninth birthday. He had been director of the Societé Gnôme et Rhône before the war, and formed an aircraft company which was later nationalized and became Air France. During a difficult war he had been imprisoned, but escaped and re-emerged in Cuba, rallying the cause of the Free French. He dug a well-positioned hole from which oil pouted and returned to France in 1947 with a new fortune. In Paris, Vivien and Ginette dined with him at the Grand Vefour. During dinner the discussion turned to the sum of money Noël Coward was receiving for three television films in America. Weiller was disbelieving and Vivien consequently irate: "Are actors and actresses not allowed to be paid properly? For businessmen it's all right. Are we just vagabonds?"[57] In due course Vivien stormed off, announcing: "I have to meet one of my friends."[58] The next morning the bathroom at avenue Marceau was filled with men's clothes and a razor. Presently Finch ambled in wearing Vivien's dressing-gown. They then left for the South of France.

They went to the Weiller villa, La Reine Jeanne, built in 1930 between two private beaches at Bormes-les-Mimosas. The drive is over half a kilometer from the small road, some five miles from Bormes itself. And the building is so well-laced that it merges into the Provencal landscape of trees and rocks, the perfect haven, as it so often proved, for celebrities who sought peace. The villa flourished in the month of August when it was filled with royalty, stars such as Douglas Fairbanks, Charlie Chaplin, and Merle Oberon, a successful blending of the old and distinguished with the young and energetic. Occasionally, however, the Commandant loaned it to friends off-season. After the hectic Stratford season Vivien was delighted to spend peaceful days with Finch and Webb, be served delicious meals, and to wander in the woods and along the empty beaches. On one such walk Vivien found a piece of gnarled wood, which, when mounted, resembled a primeval horse of great beauty. The three signed it and this piece of natural sculpture occupied a place of honor in the villa's drawing-room for years to come.

Vivien's hideaway was no secret from Olivier, who flew to Paris on 20 December and presently arrived with Ginette Spanier and Paul-Emile Seidmann for moral support. The Seidmanns and Alan Webb tactfully retired to bed soon after dinner, leaving Olivier, Finch, and Vivien to their discussions. However, late in the night, they heard raised voices and went down to investigate. Far from encountering an ugly scene, they saw Olivier and Finch tearing off their ties: "Dear boy, I forgot to get you a Christmas present..."[59] Vivien was to be seen observing these exchanges, grinning as contentedly as a kitten. On Christmas Eve, afer eight days at the villa, Vivien, Olivier, and the Seidmanns set off to San Vigilio.

They stayed again in their favorite hotel, the lakeside Locanda, enjoying the more temperamental hospitality of Leonard Walsh.* Vivien relaxed under one of Gertrude's Vitacel treatments. They were joined by the Waltons, and Vivien urged the party to enjoy watching Ginette Spanier getting lost each evening coming from her room. Inevitably the question of Finch arose and the point was put to Vivien: "You cannot do this to him. He is Sir Laurence Olivier, our greatest actor." But Vivien was unmoved. Perhaps she thought of her mother and Tommy. The example she cited was an unfair one: "Why not? Diana always had two men."[60] There was a considerable difference between Diana Cooper's innocent literary friendship with Conrad Russell, and Vivien's affair with Peter Finch.

Vivien returned to London on 23 January.

*Of him John Julius Norwich wrote: "Leonardo shuffling about in his braces, no belt could have encompassd that girth – expressing sentiments of a kind and in a manner that no other hotelier could ever have got away with, in that rambling rasp of a voice that his liberal intake of Italian brandy seemed powerless to lubricate." [*The Times*, 2 June 1971]

Chapter 19
Ruritanian Escapades

Why, er, yeah, how do I er... O gee, I've gone.
Marilyn Monroe on the set of *The Price and the Showgirl,*
Recalled by Esmond Knight

Olivier had sold Durham Cottage to Baroness Ravensdale in 1956, because it was too small to contain the retinue of two secretaries and cooks. Whereas it had been a perfect love nest in 1937, they now needed a larger dwelling. They leased a not dissimilar house, Lowndes Cottage,* in Lowndes Place from the Waltons, who were now living permanently in Italy. Similarly, Leigh Holman put Woodlands Manor on the market (in January 1955 and again that December), though he remained there another four years, moving into Woodlands Cottage in 1959, and then to Manor Farm House, Zeals later that year. In 1955 there had been a crisis in his 120-year-old law firm in which another partner had spotted a technical irregularity and called for Leigh's resignation. A partner's meeting was convened and a resolution passed that he be no longer a member of the firm. Leigh told the story to Oswald Frewen, who observed him "rather like a dismasted rudderless ship; with her compass overboard."[1] It was a situation which caused him some anxiety for several years to come. Just as Leigh had stood by Vivien in so many crises, she now stood by him, offering to help "in any way at all *ever*."[2]

*Lowndes Cottage was bequeathed to Sir William Walton by Alice, Viscountess Wimborne, with whom he had enjoyed a prolonged affair. Lady Wimborne had put in white marble mantelpieces and mahogany doors. There was also a roof terrace.

Oswald Frewen continued to take an interest in the Oliviers, albeit not so intimately as before. The New Year had scarcely begun when he became a Marilyn Monroe fan, driving into Rye to see Billy Wilder's "exercise in titillation and double entendre,"[3] *The Seven Year Itch*, because he had heard that Olivier was to make *The Prince and the Showgirl* with her. His interest was combined with a certain amount of concern: "she's a noted glamour girl, and we were, frankly, a little anxious at his knocking off acting with Viv to go screening with *her.*"[4] Sir David Cunynghame, on the board of various film companies, assured him that it was nothing more than a combination between the classical premier and the commercial premiere. Frewen kept a close eye on developments: Marilyn's film *Niagara* had shocked the League of Virtue. Sir David Cunynghame said of *The Seven Year Itch*: "It goes to the edge of vulgarity but never goes over it."[5] Clare Sheridan began to voice fears over the safety of the Olivier marriage. Frewen scrutinized an article in *Paris Match* showing the celebrated signing ceremony between Olivier and Marilyn at the Plaza Hotel in New York on 9 February: "*Match*'s account and pictures of it cruelly depict a posing vulgar American and a rather grim-faced Englishman."[6] Olivier was quoted as saying: "No more photos of legs. From now on she is too ethereal."[7]

On a second trip to New York in March, Olivier invited Cecil Beaton to design the costumes for the film. Beaton wrote to his secretary: "It would be a nice thing to do this summer, as (famous last words) it *should* not take me a terrific amount of time. There aren't all that number of costumes!! And Roger Furse will do the scenery. I was impressed by L.O., his solidity and maturity, seriousness. He is sad, is aged, but faces reality."[8] However, Beaton asked too much money, and the costumes were realized by Bumble Dawson. Leigh provided some more news later in the month:

> Leigh has seen Larry since his return from New York and reports Larry as saying that Marilyn Monroe has the brains of a *poussin* and *one* dress for day and evening; black and cut low.[9]

Frewen concluded that Olivier was denigrating her for fear of people thinking him attracted to her.

Vivien was not to take part in the film. Instead, she had agreed with enthusiasm to go into Noël Coward's slight play, *South Sea Bubble,* rehearsing in February, touring in March and opening at the Lyric in London on 25 April. This was quite a turn-about for, in 1949, she and Olivier had judged the play "old fashioned Noël Coward,"[10] which would do him considerable harm. Coward was delighted and hoped "it might conceivably set her on her emotional base again."[11]

At one point Peter Finch was to be in the play, but this plan was suddenly dropped. Olivier had a show-down with Finch at Notley early in the New Year. As a result of this, Finch agreed not to continue seeing Vivien. He did this for sensible reasons. Trader Faulkner explaind: "Olivier had a position to uphold, and Peter and Vivien were liable to bring him into the limelight of the press in a way that could only be detrimental to all three."[12] On 19 February Coward noted: "Larry and Vivien have decided to present a united front to a deeply concerned world, and so Peter Finch is *not* going to be her leading man in my play or out of it."[13] As rehearsals progressed, so Vivien's health seemed to stabilize.

Vivien's part was originally written for Gertrude Lawrence, the play set on a Pacific island under British rule. Vivien played the Governor's wife, the victim of an amorous pass from a drunk native politician. Her part included a tipsy rendering of the Roedean song, "Oh, the Cricket First Eleven is the best in all the land." William Chappell directed it, but found Vivien nervous during the pre-London tour. Once again Olivier was redirecting her part back at the hotel. *South Sea Bubble* opened in Manchester, and Coward heard it was "quite definitely a roaring success."[14] Vivien had "a comedy triumph."[15] From Edinburgh Vivien wrote to Maxine Audley: "The play is going quite wonderfully well."[16] The same was not said for the first night at the Lyric. "We had a most frigid audience, but since then all has gone well."[17] This time Vivien's notices were quite good, though the play underwent the customary treatment meted out to Coward in the 1950s. There is no doubt that Vivien was the draw and consequently *South Sea Bubble* was sold out for months. "Without Vivien the play wouldn't have lasted a week!'[18] recalled William Chappell. Oswald Frewen came to London to see it and thought it "v. good & amusing,"[19] though he now suffered from growing deafness and had left his long-distance spectacles in the car. He went round to the dressing room:

> Larry, there also, truth to tell looking rather fat and middle-aged. I asked him: "What are you doing with Marilyn Monroe?" and he made a gesture of annoyance and said "Oh! there's nothing in *that*,' leaving me to wonder whether he has, as Pussy [Lena Frewen] says, been ragged about his association with her and is annoyed at being twitted with it, or whether the "Sleeping Prince" film he was to make with her is all off.[20]

In the summer of 1956 Sue and Tarquin were invited to Notley to be told some momentous news: Vivien was expecting a baby. There have been many theories about this pregnancy. Several people believe that Vivien was not pregnant, that it was all a publicity stunt or a ruse to break her contract in *South Sea Bubble*. Sir David Cunynghame told Oswald Frewen "that Viv has tuberculosis and can't *have* a baby!"[21] However, the word of her daughter and certain references in her mother's diaries confirm that it was so. And there was further evidence from an equally conclusive quarter. Charles Russell organized his annual "Night of 100 Stars" in aid of the Actors' Orphanage on 28 June. His fitter at Bermans and Nathans ran his tape measure around Vivien's waist and reported that without question Vivien was pregnant.

At the Palladium Vivien performed with John Mills and Olivier in an energetic rendering of Irving Berlin's "Top Hat, White Tie and Tails." All three were identically dressed. She wrote to Noël Coward in Bermuda informing him that she was pregnant. He began by sending loving congratulations despite the conviction that it was 'fairly unforgivable"[22] of the Oliviers not to have let him know sooner. He hoped that a baby might make Vivien more tranquil and save the marriage. He also worried about finding a replacement, eventually settling on Elizabeth Sellars (Olivier's co-star in *Voyage Round My Father* in 1982). Coward had his suspicions about the pregnancy. He remained on a short fuse: "I shall be hopping mad if, as I unworthily suspect, the whole business comes to nothing."[23]

Vivien then made a late-night announcement of her pregnancy and the papers were full of it on 13 July. The prospective parents were photographed at Lowndes Cottage, and asked the normal questions that emerge on such occasions. The baby was expected on 22 December and they hoped it would be a girl, called Katherine. Vivien was asked what Noël thought and replied,

"He's delighted. He wrote me that in some strange way he was entirely responsible for the whole thing."[24] Someone asked if Marily Monroe (due in London two days later) would be a godmother. "That's an interesting idea," said Olivier. Vivien added, "But, darling they've already been chosen."[25] When asked to kiss for the cameras, Olivier demurred: "We're too old for that sort of thing."[26] The press was predictable in their reaction to the news, the *Daily Sketch* running an article entitled "The Great Lover to be a Daddy at 49."[27] Osbert Lancaster linked the event to recurrent spy stories. He showed Maudie Littlehampton passing a poster which announced: "GUY BURGESS MOTHER SURPRISE," captioned "Don't say he's having a baby too!!"[28] Vivien was bombarded with letters of congratulation. Maxine Audley sent a present from her daughter, Deborah. Vivien replied: "Please give Deborah a huge kiss from me. I know the beautiful pink 'Baba-Bear' will be adored and admired."[29]

Marilyn Monroe flew into London on 14 July, bringing with her Arthur Miller (her new husband), Paula Strasberg (her morale-booster), a great number of suitcases and every possible frustration and problem for Olivier. The Oliviers and Terence Rattigan gave a huge party for her at Rattigan's Ascot home so that she could meet the great stars of the stage and friends such as Margot Fonteyn, the Duke and Duchess of Buccleuch, and Diana Cooper. Dinah Sheridan recalled that Vivien never appeared, claiming that she could not fit into her dress due to her pregnancy.[30] Marilyn's dress was described to Fleur Cowles as being "as tight as the curves will allow – with seams reinforced."[31] There was a press conference at which, according to Radie Harris, Marilyn was asked the question "What do you wear when you go to bed?" and made her legendary reply "Chanel No. 5."[32] In the early days of filming Vivien used to come down to the set and talk to Maxine Audley, who found her reluctant to put her feet up as instructed by her doctors.

Vivien left *South Sea Bubble* on Saturday 11 August after 276 performances (one of which was seen by Marilyn Monroe). There was a farewell party. The next day at Notley she lost her baby. "Very sad poor little Pet,"[33] recorded her mother. Suzanne wrote to her grandmother from Sirmione: "I was terribly sorry to hear about Mummy's baby. I do hope they aren't too upset and that Mummy is recovering."[34]

While sympathetic, Noël Coward unleashed a burst of rage in his diary, not unlike that of Cecil Beaton after *School for Scandal*. Noël concluded:

> Altogether I'm sick to death of them both at the moment. I've been bored and involved with their domestic problems for years and done all I could to help, and as they haven't even troubled to write me they can bloody well get on with it.[35]

Hamish Hamilton summed up this pregnancy: "Our great friend Alan "Jock" Dent was to be a godfather. Alas, poor V. was in one of her feverish moods, incapable of quiet, and the result was a miscarriage. What her relations with Larry were at this time I don't know."[36]

A fortnight later Vivien was back in London, house-hunting. Then, because Olivier was busy filming the Profumos took her to join Binkie Beaumont for a holiday in Portofino where she relaxed, swam and slept. "Binkie was a dear companion,"[37] she wrote to Maxine Audley, "but I missed Larryboy so much and was quite delighted to be back."[38] In October Vivien and Binkie Beaumont flew to Dublin where Noël Coward, now a tax exile forbidden to set foot in London, had gone to see his play *Nude with Violin.* Late that night Noël, Vivien, and Binkie were in his dressing-room and Binkie revealed that he had known about the baby ages before and had sworn to Olivier that he would not tell Coward. Noël was livid:

> This really made me lose my temper and I let them both have it. The scene lasted until 3:30 a.m., but it finished amiably enough. I at least had the satisfaction of saying what [was] in my mind for a long time. Vivien was really very sweet and I think and hope the air is now cleared.[39]

Later Coward apologized to Olivier for his "unbecoming outburst."[40]

Marilyn's lateness, her stupidity, her aggravating behavior, her lack of respect for Olivier and her complete unconcern about studio-time and studio-money have been described at length by Olivier and by her biographers. Vivien was horrified by her, particularly when at a dinner Marilyn disappeared to the bathroom with her glass of champagne. Vivien had to go and find her. Esmond Knight played Hoffman in the film. He remembered it well:

> I was around when it was decided that he and Marilyn Monroe should do *The Prince and the Showgirl.* What a

> marvelous idea! Larry Olivier, the great classical actor of our time playing a picture with a great sex symbol – Marilyn Monroe. By God what a marvelous idea! Probably an idea conceived at Notley I should think. And then of course Terry Rattigan said "You know what to do – you know the subject: *The Prince and the Showgirl…*" It was a disaster! Ghastly failure! It was taken off the road. He had an *awful* time with her, Marilyn – stupid, stupid woman that she was – she was an absolute cretin – she couldn't remember the simplest line –
>
> TAKE 32. TAKE. "Now darling, you understand: I say 'Will you have dinner with me tomorrow night?' and you say 'Yes I'll meet you at 7:30'– all right?"
>
> TAKE 73. "Will you have dinner with me tomorrow night?" "Why, yeah. I'll come at – gosh – I'll come…"
>
> But nevertheless, she was superbly photogenic and Vivien realized that Marilyn, stupid woman though she was, idiot, could do no wrong in front of a camera. Whatever the angle was, everything about her face was marvelous so that one always had to print the take that *she* was all right in…
>
> She'd just married Arthur Miller and this sort of tall weird man use to come onto the set just looking on, and then she would run over and jump into his arms and wrap herself around him and they would disappear into the dressing-room for about ten minutes – Ahem! – and then she would reappear again "refreshed" – and they would go on with the shooting.[41]

One day, she didn't appear at all. Tony Bushell finally trackd her down and all she would say was "Aw shucks, I've got the curse. Don't you English know about that?"[42]

Leigh Holman and Oswald Frewen had a chat about the development of the film after Leigh had been down to Notley. He told Oswald that the Oliviers had been obliged to accompany the Millers to the theatre in order to silence rumors of a rift (an evening recalled by Sue as a particularly sticky dinner). Oswald dutifully recorded the latest news:

> Larry says of [Marilyn] that she has the "brains of a *poussin*" and teaching her acting is like teaching urdo to a marmoset, that she is incapable of learning 5 lines by heart, but she has "something" between lens and screen which may come out *perfect*, or just nothing at all…She disapproved of the rushes…and just didn't return to the studio for 3 days, incurring losss, therefore of some £6,000 to £7,000. "Pretty hard on Larry," commented Pussy. "Oh, no, this is a Marilyn Monroe Inc. film: the losses are *hers*, but mean nothing to her," said Leigh.[43]

In November Marilyn finished the film and was kissed a formal and public farewell by Olivier and Vivien simultaneously. With sighs of relief all around, the Oliviers were free to depart for Spain on 22 December for a three-week holiday.

The early months of 1957 were uneventful for Vivien with weekends at Notley and visits to Leigh at Mere. Little did she show there were changes afoot that would have grave consequences. On 25 April Gertrude wrote simple but significant words: "Larry's show. *The Entertainer*."[44]

Without realizing the long-term consequences of a wish to explore all that was new in the theatre, Vivien had taken Olivier to see *Look Back in Anger*. John Osborne's play had opened at the Royal Court on 8 May 1956. Legend now has it that the play was uniformly disliked by all critics except Kenneth Tynan. The general consensus was that Osborne was "a dramatist to watch and that this was just the sort of thing required to justify the new company's existence."[45] Kenneth Tynan was certainly the most enthusiastic in the *Observer*: "that rarest of dramatic phenomena, the act of original creation, has taken place…a minor miracle…I doubt if I could love anyone who did not wish to see *Look Back in Anger*. It is the best young play of the its decade.[46] Olivier was disappointed on his first visit, but he went again with Arthur Miller and Marilyn Monroe. It was Miller who forced him to concentrate and to recognize a significant new theatrical trend. Michael Denison pointed out that, in *Look Back in Anger,* Kenneth Tynan had found the alternative theatre he had been seeking when he attacked the earlier drawing-room comedies. He chose to glorify the kitchen sink as opposed to the French window. Presently Olivier asked John Osborne if he would ever consider writing a play for him: “I was feeling frustrated by the boredom of my own career, and my personal life was a tiresome tease to me.”[47] The result was *The Entertainer*.

Olivier has written of various excursions intro extra-marital affairs during these years. In one of the more candid passages in his *Confessions,* he justified these with references to menopause, to seeking comfort and finally “an equable detachment from the obstinate grasp of the single, if tattered, standard I held for Vivien, as I believed for ever.”[48]

Olivier opened in *The Entertainer* on 10 April and ran for four weeks. He was supported by his old friend George Relph (who played Archie Rice’s father) Brenda de Banzie (as Phoebe) and Dorothy Tutin (one of the actresses with whom he had an affair). He was widely praised, Harold Hobson writing in the *Sunday Times:* “I doubt if anyone who sees it will ever forget it.”[49] Olivier was happy during his excursion into the new theatre, but he was already committed to a Shakespeare Memorial Theatre Company Tour of Europe with Vivien.

The company played *Titus Andronicus* in six cities before London: Paris (15 to 25 May), Venice (28 to 30 May), Belgrade (2 to 4 June), Zagreb (7 and 8 June), and then London from 1 July to 3 August. The company included Maxine Audley, Alan Webb, Anthony Quayle in important roles and future stars such as Ian Holm and John Standing in minor roles. Floy Bell was the administrator working with her husband Patrick Donnell. Kenneth Clark’s son, Colin, was Olivier’s assistant. Most of the company traveled by train though Quayle expressed his independence by driving everywhere in a brand new Aston Martin (which he wrote off on the road to Zagreb). This was a significant tour because the company were the first to go behind the Iron Curtain.

It was a memorably difficult time. Olivier would no doubt much have preferred to stay at home with *The Entertainer* rather than cope with Vivien, particularly in the close circumstances of a touring company.

Any apprehensions he may have felt were presently more than justified as it became clear that her illness was returning. She stayed up late, exhausting those around her, and, as the tour progressed, so her illness rose to a new climax. This notwithstanding, Vivien was as considerate as ever to the need for unity within the company. She and Olivier were often issued with grand invitations. She insisted that it was everybvody or nobody. Olivier had made the whole cast buy dinner-jackets and he was determined they were going to get good value out of them. David Conville, the Second Goth (who went on to run the Regent's Park Open Air Theatre), recalled:

> She was adored and people were also rather frightened of her. They weren't frightened because she could be nasty, but she was so erratic. But she was a terrific company girl, so in all entertainments the company all had to be together and all had to be entertained.[50]

Thus an invitation from Marie Bell, the former leading lady of the Comédie Française, to dine on a bateau-mouche was converted by Vivien into a buffet for fifty-five, and David Conville recalled that while Vivien joined the young and drank vin rosé, he, John Standing, and Colin Clark found the smart end deserted and enjoyed a selection of clarets, champagne, and fine delicacies. Vivien finally took over at the helm and steered the boat home, a somewhat precarious operation.

Titus Andronicus opened at the Sarah Bernhardt Théatre des Nations on 15 May. Reactions to the play were not dissimilar to those at Stratford two years earlier. Harold Hobson wrote that the French were "keyed up to a pitch of great expectation by the prospect of seeing not only Olivier but also Vivien Leigh, of whose transcendent beauty and talent uninhibited reports had crossed the Channel.[51] In Olivier they were not disappointed but Vivien perplexed them. Edwige Feuillère, whom Hobson had hailed as "the greatest actress in the world"[52] when she appeared in a season at the St. James's Theatre, enquired, "What can the English see in her?"[53] Hobson continued:

> Where was her talent? What sort of part was she good in? Was there any kind of part in which, with such resources as she had displayed in *Titus Andronicus*, it was possible for her to be good? Paris had in fact been as disappointed – and subsequent inquiry confirmed this – in the wife as it had been elated by the husband. Even Vivien Leigh's legendary

beauty seemed to have passed unnoticed by the French.[54]

Olivier has also written: "From now on [1955] for the next five years, it was as if she had just lost touch with her craft."[55] This can be explained by her illness and unhappiness, and, of course, Lavinia in *Titus* was by no means a part that offered scope for excellence.

Behind the scenes it was Colin Clark who had charge of stage effects:

> Olivier put his hand down and Quayle chops it off and as he lowered the axe I was right beside the stage with a great big awful piece of sort of squashy bone stuff. And I went skwww…and it made the most awful, sickening noise. I was the only person Larry would trust to get the noise absolutely synchronized.[56]

Floy Bell confirmed this: "It did make the most marvelous crunch you've ever heard."[57] And Paddy Donnell explained:

> Both Tony [Quayle] and Larry, who were great technical actors, did it brilliantly. Tony brought the axe down but he did it as he if he'd pressed on it so that the crunch coincided…On the first night in Paris there was a girl sitting at the end of the row two rows in front of us and at that incident she suddenly rushed out![58]

Similarly David Lewin reported:

> Douglas Fairbanks swallowed his chewing-gum in excitement, Jean Marais bit his tongue quite badly, and Françoise Rosay swore she would become a vegetarian immediately.[59]

Floy Bell concluded:

> When we were at Stolls [at the end of the tour] a man rushed down for St. John's Ambulance and he shouted at Paddy:

> "One on every floor tonight, Guv!" But it was the hand crunch that somehow affected people more than the heads baked in a pie or whatever. I think because they actually saw it and heard it.[60]

David Conville recalled that after one show they were queuing to take off their make-up when someone summoned them back to the stage. The cast reassembled in the hope of a party:

> So there we all were, half made-up, dripping, putting towels round us and all thinking: "What's happening? Vivien's having a surprise party." We arrived almost naked, asking "Where's the drink?" behaving like all ghastly actors and there was Vivien in the most wonderful dress, looking radiant. We didn't know what was up. Vivien said "Wait and see." Then the Minister for Cultural Relations [Roger Seydoux] stepped forward and gave her the Legion of Honour. Vivien made a charming speech in fluent French.[61]

It was Commandant Paul-Louis Weiller who arranged this honor for her. During the Barraults' London season, he had done the same for Olivier, but, Weiller recalled: "Well, he only agreed to accept it on condition that Vivien did not receive it at the same time. She said that she did not mind."[62] Now Vivien accepted it, looking "like a lovely girl receiving her prize" wrote Frank Thring (Saturninus). "The tears were streaming down her face and ours too."[63] The motley crew of spear-holders formed an impromptu guard of honor around the new Chevalier.

Vivien's friendship with Paul-Louis Weiller was another considerable asset to the company's enjoyment of Paris. It fell to Floy Bell to convert an invitation for ten or twelve members of the company into an invitation for all of them. Colin Clark, who was lodging in a Weiller apartment at the Ambassade d'Hollande in the Marais quarter, recalled what then happened:

> The last night he invited everyone to this enormous banquet in his house. I got told about it and said, "But the house is just a ruin. There's nothing there." And about five days before

> the party 400 people came and they banged about and they put gold leaf everywhere, put down carpets. By the time of the party it was a kind of fantastic chateau inside. And Vivien and Larry said, "What a beautiful house," and he said, "Yes, it's just almost as it was, an eighteenth-century house. It's been restored." And it had been done in four days. He did do it beautifully.[64]

David Conville remembered:

> There was a private room where Vivien dined with about twelve people. There were gold and white flowers – absolutely superb. We all sat in lots of other little rooms. I sat at a table of four with Charles Boyer. One was blasé by then. All the pretty little starlets were there and I remember John Standing saying "Come on. We'll ask them to dance" and they all said "non," as they were there with their millionaires.[65]

Maxine Audley kept the oak-leaf traditionally used as a name-card, and menu for the party on 18 May. It was signed by Maurice Chevalier, Jean Marais and Marcel Achard amongst others. A few days later they celebrated Olivier's birthday though the new half-centenarian was depressed at his age and the simultaneous announcement of Donald Wolfit's knighthood, described by Olivier as "the biggest ham in the business."[66] And they took a trip into Touraine with Jean-Pierre Aumont and his new wife, Marisa Pavan. Aumont recalled that Olivier was very sleepy, but Vivien could recall the names of people in shops she had seen perhaps once before.

From Paris the company entrained to Venice but Vivien persuaded Olivier and Frank Thring to break the journey to lunch with the ninety-one-year-old Bernard Berenson at I Tatti. The first show in Venice went badly. Peter Brook called all the cast onto the stage and complained that their performance lacked authority. On the way to Belgrade by train, Vivien was energetic and determined that the cast should miss nothing. She aroused the post-prandial slumberers lest they miss the coast view. Then she sent Colin Clark to buy chocolate. He saw the train begin to move off and leapt into the baggage department at the back. He could not get through to the main part of the train until it stopped, by which time Vivien was explaining in fluent Italian to the frontier guards that a man had been lost.

Paddy Donnell advised the company to be careful about what they said in the Communist countries. "Tito is above criticism," he said and he warned them never to discuss politics at table in Poland lest the waiter was a party agent.[67] They arrived in Belgrade, "a grey concrete city with badly dressed people walking the streets and no signs of a prosperous middle class."[68] At the theatre they were just as impressed by the simple bouquets of field flowers and the giant baskets of flowers eight feet high that the audiences sent to the stage. One night President Tito gave a party for them in the private room behind their box at the Croatian National Theatre.

Olivier was already feeling the strain of leading a large company, playing a demanding role, and coping with Vivien (who had an undemanding part) at the end of the day. She would invite anyone she could find back to the hotel for champagne late at night despite Olivier's longing for sleep. In the daytime she was the ideal companion, visiting the art school studios and talking with genuine interest to the students. She climbed into obscure attics, drank a glass of slivovitz, and seldom left without buying a picture. In public there was never a sign of any problem between the Oliviers,though at picnics they were perhaps too over-emphatically loving to one another.

Vivien's health began to deteriorate in Belgrade and got worse in Zagreb. Her handwriting became energetic and disorganized. Maxine Audley recalled that in Zagreb, Vivien discovered that she had been given the biggest dressing-room:

> We were unpacking our stuff and she came in. I said "Darling, take this one" and as I touched her she leapt away as if I was burning her skin or something. It really was quite frightening sometimes.[69]

David Conville remembered:

> When we got to Zagreb there was a terrible man who was put in charge of her called Otto. We called him "Otto the agent." He worked for the British Council. He was a kind

> of Hollywood gunman. He didn't have a revolver but he looked as if he did. After four days he was always saying "Vivien, I love you." He fell madly in love with her. But she wrangled the man so much. he must have lost two stones. He was a gibbering wreck. He came out with us every night and it was serious. People used to ask Vivien to dance and he had one man taken away by the police. She got the fellow back. She used to do that very embarassing thing saying "We must all go up to the bedroom and play cards till dawn." We used to go up and poor old Olivier was lying there, groaning.[70]

One night Vivien attended an academic dinner wearing her Legion of Honour and became bored because nobody spoke English. Presently she gathered the members of the company to sit near her. After interminable speeches in Yugoslav, Vivien rose with an angelic smile and, in the knowledge and hope that they did not understand, recited her speech in a lyrical voice. However, far from delivering the polite reply they were expecting, out came a string of four letter words to the effect that she was having the most boring evening of her life, all said with a smile and greeted by cries of "Ya. Ya."[71]

Late one night Vivien broke a window in her hotel room. Maxine Audley remembered that it was her chauffeur, Bernard Gilman, who finally got her to the station in the morning:

> She sat up all night with him somewhere on a park bench... Of course one of the troubles was that, in Yugoslavia particularly, the whole population would crowd round the theatre and yell for Scarlett O'Hara. And there she was playing this tiny part in which she had fifteen lines and then had her tongue cut out. It was rather frustrating.[72]

Otto, the police chief, was at the station. Colin Clark recalled:

> Vivien wouldn't get onto the train. Finally Larry said, "I can't stand it." Then the train began to move and Vivien stood her ground on the platform. And the police chief, still

> very much in attendance, simply picked her up and put her on the train. And she gave him such a shiner, such a smack in the eye.[73]

The ensuing journey to Vienna in scorching heat was a prolonged nightmare. At one point in the mountains the train stopped in a cutting with a tunnel at either end, and a sheer drop below. Vivien again got off the train, so Clark got off with her. The train drew away while they sat looking at the magnificent view. Then after fifteen minutes the train slowly reversed a little, they got back on, and continued on their way.

Olivier was keeping a low profile, in a different carriage, unable to cope, while Vivien pursued Maxine Audley, throwing bits of bread at her. Finally, as she calmed down, she went to sleep with her head on Maxine's shoulder.

In Vienna Peter Brook persuaded Vivien to go to the doctor for sedation to knock her out for two or three days. Moira Redmond, the understudy, was rehearsed in secret and the long-suffering Cecil Tennant flew out. David Conville remembered:

> We were then called together by the company manager and given this lecture saying Miss Leigh had been given a heavy sedation and she won't be playing in Vienna. No one was to accept any invitations from her if she did appear. About three of us went up to the swimming pool and were having this conversation about poor Vivien when through the gardens came a caravan. I've never seen such a caravan. There was Vivien in a huge hat, dark glasses, Peter Brook looking a bit sheepish and people carrying wine and picnics. No way were sedatives going to do anything to her. She was up and about to Whoopee![74]

Later she did collapse and rest. When she was better, Colin Clark recalled her saying: "Oh Colin, it's so nice when it's over."[75]

Meanwhile *Titus* was staged at the magnificent Burgtheater which had many revolves in the stage and sumptuous dressing-rooms. There was a seated dinner in the foyer. The lights were lowered, liveried flunkies brought in flickering candelabra while an orchestra, dressed in period costume, completed the scene.

The long journey from Vienna to Warsaw (crossing Czechoslovakia) involved a marked change in culture. The Czech border was manned by armed guards bearing tommy guns, and there was a profusion of barbed wire. None of the travelers was allowed to descend onto Czech soil. Those who took photographs had their film confiscated. The Polish border was reached at midnight and Warsaw itself at 8:30 the following morning.

Arriving rather wearily at the hotel, the actors steered towards a vast table draped with a Union Jack and served an unappetizing concoction consisting of a slice of ham floating amidst two lukewarm raw eggs.

By now Vivien appeared to be over the worst of her illness. As usual, she insisted on extracting every possible experience from the trip, insisting that the company visit Cracow, one of Poland's oldest and most cultured cities. Twenty-one members of the company gathered to fly there for the day in a specially chartered plane under the surveillance of a ferocious lady member of the Communist party, described as the interpreter. There was one seat too few and it was suggested that lots be drawn. Vivien said, "Oh that's quite easy," and the woman said, "I'm so relieved that you've taken it like that. Now who's going to get off?" "You are," said Vivien. "But I'm the representative." "You are getting off. GET OFF!" Her voice was so icy and determined that the disliked guide departed in tears, leaving Vivien triumphant: "I'm not letting the Polish Government muck up my actors."[76] In Cracow itself Vivien decided exactly what they would see regardless of Government planning. It fell to Colin Clark to ensure that the company were back in time for their last evening performance:

> We all got completely lost. We had no idea where we were. We had by now attracted a crowd of about 200 Poles. It was actually getting quite alarming because on that tour Vivien was infinitely more famous than Olivier. I was getting into quite a state. But Vivien was saying "Why are you fussing and shouting, Colin?" Then, all of a sudden through this crowd at about a quarter to four a Rolls-Royce appeared, stopped right by Vivien. We got in. The chauffeur didn't speak any English, drove us to the airport and that was it. It never crossed her mind that anything untoward would happen.[77]

The actors boarded their plane an hour late, laden down with gifts and vodka.

On 22 June the company flew home. Olivier was worn out, as David Conville confirmed:

> He was absolutely exhausted. I think that while in everyday life she adored him, she was happier with Helpmann and Binkie Beaumont and all the witty chat. She was always worried about him. She petted him in the aeroplane and looked after him and in Poland Alan Webb had got very drunk and gone staggering off into Warsaw. I'd packed all his clothes for him and kept a place for him on the plane. He came in: "I don't sit next to fucking spear carriers. I'm a star." Olivier was sitting with Vivien and said, "Don't worry. I'll go and sit next to David. You go and sit next to Vivien." There were little things like that. I was very surprised when it all went crash. I think in many ways she took him for granted. She couldn't believe it when he met a younger girl who he thought was the cat's whiskers.[78]

Colin Clark concluded:

> The trouble with Vivien was she absolutely adored Olivier. She simply worshipped him. But, when she was with him, she couldn't resist needling him like a bullfighter with a bull. She couldn't resist trying to keep him up to her scratch and Larry couldn't do it.[79]

Chapter 20
The Ermine and the Stoll

The death, or more correctly, the murder of the St. James's Theatre must be seen in the wider context of the ruin spread throughout the West End in the years since the First World War. One more building of historical and architectural importance is gone, one more place devoted to entertainment and the arts shut down.

Vivien's introduction to *St. James's Theatre of Distinction,* by W. Macqueen-Pope

Olivier had financed his losses at the St. James's Theatre with the money that he and Vivien earned in films. He never made anything out of the little theatre but some of his happiest hours in the 1950s were spent in the office, which had been Sir George Alexander's in Victorian times. For most of 1952 he had let the St. James's Theatre. In the intervening years he had enjoyed various successes, particularly *Anastasia* and *Pygmalion* and Terence Rattigan's *Separate Tables* in 1954, which ran with an excellent cast until the end of June 1956. During the run, there was a threat that the theatre itself was to be sold, pulled down and replaced by shops and offices. By some mischance the St. James's had not been scheduled for preservation. There was an outcry with written questions in Parliament and other protests. For a while the matter died down.

However, while Vivien was playing *Titus* at the Stoll Theatre in London, news came that the London County Council had granted appoval for the demolition of the St. James's Theatre. In many ways the theatre was old fashioned and inconvenient to work in. It only sat 800 people, it had become a fire hazard, and it needed £250,000 spent to make it workable. St. John Ervine supported the campaign in *The Times*, and T.C. Worsley became incensed in the *New Statesman*, describing the proposed demolition as an act of barbarism. Vivien then joined the crusade. Her efforts were dubbed by Olivier a "ludicrous farce."[1]

Vivien was still in an over-energized state. Since her return to England her mother had become more closely involved with her plight. The normally optimistic Gertrude recorded on 23 June: "spent the day and night with Vivien. Very sad indeed. Got to bed at 4:30 a.m.."[2] The following week Olivier had confided his recent agonies to Noël Coward before emerging in public with Vivien for a charity gala of *The Prince and the Showgirl*. A few days later Vivien and Olivier enjoyed themselves at Mike Todd's famous Battresea Fun Fair party after the premiere of *Around the World in 80 Days*. It was a rain-sodden night. Vivien escaped the queue by climbing a five-foot wall with Patrick Leigh Fermor and Ann Fleming, the latter observing: "Vivien climbs like a small exquisite cat."[3]

The Oliviers had now bought a flat at 54 Eaton Square, which was to be Vivien's last London home, but they remained a few months at Lowndes Cottage while the new flat was gutted and decorated. Gertrude went to Notley again on 6 July and recorded: "Vivien very upset."[4]

Incensed by the threat to the St. James's Theatre, Vivien prevailed upon her old colleague, the critic Alan Dent, and the veteran comedy actress, Athene Seyler, to form a trimuvirate and march along Fleet Street and the Strand, bearing a placard and a bell. At the age of ninety-seven Athene Seyler recalled:

> We set out boldy togther to walk and she was ringing a bell to attract attention, and nobody paid the *slightest* attention to us! And she said to me: It's extraordinary. If I go into a restaurant, quite quietly, everybody turns and looks. Now I walk down the Strand, ringing a bell and nobody pays any attention at all." It's very funny![5]

On the same evening, 9 July, the socialist peer and town-planner, Lord

Silkin, rose in the House of Lords to ask "whether the Government are prepared to take all possible steps to save the St. James's Theatre?"[6] He pointed out that the St. James's was one of two remaining Georgian theatres in London, that eight London theatres had been lost since the war, and he asked for "sufficient time and opportunity to see what can be done by those who are lovers of the theatre and anxious to preserve it."[7] He was supported by certain peers and opposed by others, notably Lord Blackford, who described the St. James's as "simply an obsolete, inconvenient, uncomfortable old playhouse."[8]

Vivien read the report of this debate the following morning. She was not pleased by what Lord Blackford had said. Clearly sterner action was called for.

Two days later Lord Silkin proposed a motion drawing attention to increased state assistance to the arts. Olivier and Vivien went to the House of Lords to hear the debate as guests of their friend, Lord Bessborough. Arriving at 3 o'clock she and Olivier enjoyed a tea party with seven peers, before taking their place in Black Rod's box on seats traditionally reserved for distinguished visitors. The debate began at 3:45 p.m. with a long speech from Lord Silkin. Other peers, distinguished and undistinguished, spoke at length. Olivier left the House at 6:20 and four minutes later Lord Blackford rose to speak.

Vivien listened to his speech with growing impatience. As before he addressed the House "from a somewhat different standpoint."[9] Lord Blackford called for the introduction of museum charges and concluded: "In the present state of national financial emergency I feel that any help should be on a voluntary basis."[10] He ended his speech on a personal note:

> My Lords, that is all I have to say except to apologize to the noble Lord, Lord Mancroft, for the fact that I have to dine at a quarter to eight, and therefore I am afraid it will be impossible for me to enjoy the very admirable speech which he will certainly make about that hour.[11]

At this point Vivien could bear it no longer. She rose to her feet and in what she described as "a loud voice throwing it as I do in a large theatre,"[12] she called out: "My Lords, I wish to protest against the St. James's Theatre being demolished."[13] There were cries of 'Hush' from a Chamber which in those days never heard a female voice other than the Sovereign's speech from the Throne. Black Rod, General Sir Brian Horrocks, escorted her away with the words, "Now you have to go." Vivien replied, "Certainly – I have to get to the theatre."[14] Lord Bessborough rushed from his seat and drove Vivien to the Stoll. The peers resumed their debate and not a mention of the incident was made in Hansard, the official record of Parliament. Horrocks wrote later that Vivien had said "it was the worst audience to which she had ever played, as no one took the slightest notice."[15] He was surprised and a little hurt by the incident, but enjoyed an American newspaper which reported him turning to Vivien after the last Lord sat down and saying: "Now you have a go."[16]

In Russia where Vivien's films had made her a legend and where some film-goers were secretly convinced that she was a Russian, the incident was misunderstood. It was interpreted as Vivien making a spirited demand for better conditions for "the Workers of Westminister."[17] Reporters gathered swiftly at the Stoll. Vivien told them that she had spoken on impulse:

> We have just come home from a tour of Europe where they are building theatres as hard as they can go. Yet here in London I saw British workmen pulling down the Gaiety on Sunday…I will tell you this. If the St. James's Theatre is pulled down, I will consider leaving the country. It may interest you to know that I can act in French, German, Italian and even Serbian.[18]

She justifield her action, having become "angrier and angrier"[19] as Lord Blackford spoke. Olivier was more reserved. His comment was "I think it was a very sweet and gallant thing to do. But I did not know she was going to do it."[20]

The protest made front page news in most newspapers, with headlines such as 'VIVIEN LEIGH SHOCKS PEERS"[21] and "PEERS THROW OUT VIVIEN LEIGH."[22] There were enjoyable cartoons from Giles and Osbert Lancaster. By and large her action was commended, Olga Franklin writing in the *Daily Mail*: "Vivien Leigh hit on the only way to get things done."[23]

The matter did not end there. Vivien had discussions with the bearded Felix Fenston, Chairman of the Mayflower Foundation, who had bought the site. She appeared on Granada Television's *People and Places* but was blacked out after two and a half minutes, and complained: "I won't go on that nasty machine for a long time to come."[24] There was a leader in *The Times* which judged: "The sincerely of Miss Vivien Leigh's feelings is as beyond question as is the charm of her photographs."[25] She then arranged a march from the theatre to St. Martin's-in-the-Fields from where Felix Aylmer, John Clements, Olivier and she addressed a rally, Olivier having reluctantly walked with the crowd. Rain drizzled down on the marchers, who included Alan Webb (in G.K. Chesterton's hat), Michael Redgrave, Richard Attenborough, Bryan Forbes, Anna Massey, and Peter Cushing. Dame Edith Evans was heard to boom: "Don't we actors look ordinary, all in a heap?"[26] Olivier said the Government should buy the theatre. In public he joked: "I'm going to change my name to Mr. Pankhurst."[27] In private he bemoaned: "This is the most expensive menopause in history."[28]

Nor was all the stage sympathetic. Judy Campbell remembered one actor declaring: "I'm damned if I'm going to tramp through London to save Vivien Leigh's change of life."[29] Maxine Audley was another absentee. That night at *Titus* Vivien riled her before the curtain rose. Finally Maxine said, "I'm not standing for this rubbish," and turned to walk off stage. Vivien planted her foot on Maxine's dress and there was a dramatic rip. "It was the only time I have seen the foot on the dress gag,"[30] recalled David Conville.

Sir Winston Churchill came to see *Titus Andronicus* on the day that he received a letter from Vivien. She was too nervous to lobby him in person, but he wrote her offering £500 to the fighting fund:

> I hope you will succeed in your defence of St. James's Theatre, though as a parliamentarian I cannot approve your disorderly method…I shall be definitely committed to the cause. [31]

The Minister of Housing, Henry Brooke, agreed to meet a Parliamentary deputation and Vivien announced that two American millionaires had volunteered substantial funds. On Saturday 27 July the curtain fell at the St. James's Theatre for the last time (on *It's the Geography that Counts).* John Gregson, the leading man, declared:

> There has been a lot of talk, but now grim reality takes its place. We are in at the death of a theatre…this must never be allowed to happen again.[32]

While all this was taking place publicly, Vivien's private life was in considerable disarray. On Sunday, 21 July the Oliviers gave a party at Notley for the *Titus Andronicus* company. There were plans for tennis, bowling, fishing, and punting on the river, but rain drove them inside. Olivier strode the lawn in a tweed sports jacket and beige muffler, very much the country squire. Lady Diana Cooper was dressed in chain mail (originally worn by Sybil Thordike in Shaw's *Saint Joan* in 1924), and Vivien kept changing her outfit. David Conville recalled:

> It was an amazing party. It must have cost a lot of money. Vivien went a bit odd during this party and stood in the hall glaring: "This is going to be the greatest party of all times. No one is going to leave." And she wouldn't let anyone out. Someone did have to go back to their children, and Olivier pushed us all out through the kitchen.[33]

On 27 July Vivien sent Berenson a type-written letter, apologizing:

> Since speaking to some of those Lords the other day I have really been deluged with things that had to be done and letters to be answered. I still have high hopes of saving Saint James's Theatre, and I know you would wish me well.[34]

The St. James's Theatre debate took place in the House of Lords on 30 July. Lord Silkin again opened, naming two potential millionaire benefactors as Mr. Huntington Hartford and Mr. Cort. In between several digs at Lord Blackford, he asked for a postponement of the demolition. He raised the matter of Olivier's constant complaints about "the bad seating arrangements and inconvenience of the theatre."[35] Peers failed to secure a Government promise of intervention but the Resolution that no action should be taken to demolish the theatre or otherwise prejudice its continued use was agreed to (twenty-two versus eighteen),

The last week of July was a bad one. On the night of the debate, Gertrude Hartley recorded: "Called to Viv's at 3 a.m. Dreadful tragedy. Sent for Dr. Altman. Spent the night at Lowndes Cottage."[36] Olivier was more forthcoming about this incident in his book. He wrote that Vivien had discovered he was having a romance, that she slashed him across the eyes with a wet face-cloth and, that when he retreated to another room, she hammered constantly on the locked door. He then confessed that he lost control, came out and seized Vivien, aiming to hurl her onto the bed. She hit a marble bedside table-top, causing a gash just above her left eye, "I realized with horror that each of us was quite capable of murdering or causing death to the other."[37] Olivier retreated to a hidaway room in a nearby mews.

The following day the Oliviers were together to lead an Equity deputation to see The Minister of Housing, Henry Brooke. Press photographs show Vivien wearing a black eye patch, which she explained was the result of an insect bite. She looked puffed around the face, and Olivier looked drawn and tired. Brooke explained that it was his impression that the St. James's Theatre had "slipped through the net."[38] However, he also said that there would be an amendment to LCC dvelopment plans in the future to ensure that such a situation did not recur.

In the end the campaign failed, and on 11 January 1958 the St. James's Theatre was demolished. While it is simple for Olivier to dismiss Vivien's mission as "futile"[39] there was at least one positive result. Legislation was passed to the effect that, if a London theatre was pulled down, a new one must be built in its place.

The cut-eye evening weighed heavily on Olivier. Irina Tennant recalled that at this point the doctors stepped in and warned Olivier of the danger of such a situation recurring. It was for that reason that he veered away from Vivien. He had not then become involved with Joan Plowright.

Titus Andronicus closed on 3 August and with it the Stoll Theatre also shut down, and the long shared acting career of the Oliviers came to an end. Gertrude noted: "Very distressed about V. The saddest night of my life."[40] On the following Bank Holiday Monday, Olivier and Tarquin went to Scotland, combining their holiday with a search for *Macbeth* locations for the film that would never be made, due to the recent death of Korda. On Thursday, 8 August Vivien set off with Suzanne and Leigh for a European holiday. Oswald Frewen came over to Lydd airport to see them fly off in a special aeroplane. He described it as a "terrific press stunt."[41]

It was a much-needed break. Suzanne, having given up any attempts to act, had been working with her grandmother in her successful beauty business. She was proficient at full-scale beauty treatment. Though they had known each other slightly for about two years, she had recently fallen in love with Robin Farrington, a handsome Lloyds underwriter, who had won the MC in Palestine. He had come down to Notley to meet Vivien two Saturdays before, awaiting her habitually late arrival after *Titus.* "I was very nervous," he said, "and as she came into the drawing-room I walked forward to shake her hand. Unfortunately the cat inserted itself onto my toe and I have never done such a good rugger conversion. The cat flew across the room. It was a bad beginning."[42]

Robin and Suzanne had become engaged secretly just before the trip. The news was broken to both parents simultaneously at San Vigilio. At this point an irate Socialist MP, Mrs. Jean Mann, happened to make publicity about Vivien being on holiday with her former husband. Speaking on the BBC programme *Tonight*, she proved far from understanding:

> When a woman finds her ex-husband so easy to get on with that she can spend a holiday with him she should have thought a little longer before she cut the knot.[43]

Cliff Michelmore, the interviewer, was more to the point when he asked if she was not raising this matter because it was the closed season for politics. The press remained persistent. One American headline read: "Vivien Leigh Holiday with ex-mate flayed."[44] From San Vigilio Vivien would say no more than "no comment,"[45] but she cabled the press: "Criticism ill-considered and unmannerly. Presence our daughter gives explanation to any reasonable person."[46] Gertrude was also questioned by the press. She explained that the Oliviers had taken holidays in Europe before. "But Larry didn't have much fun. Vivien is fluent in French, German and Italian. He doesn't speak any of them. Larry likes a quiet time. Vivien's idea of a rest-cure is a change of scene and a bit of excitement."[47] On 19 August Leigh flew home.

Vivien traveled with Suzanne to Yugoslavia and later to the South of France, ending their stay at Paul-Louis Weiller's villa. Here Vivien attempted to water-ski, gamely assisted by the Commandant. The villa was packed with cosmopolitan house-guests, with whom Vivien coped very well. Roger Furse came over for dinner. He was then working on designs for Otto Preminger's film, *Bonjour Tristesse,* which was being filmed nearby with Jean Seberg, Deborah Kerr, and David Niven.

While Vivien was away, Gertrude went down to Notley with Jeanne de Casalis and a long talk with her son-in-law, then back to Scotland. Leigh had also been to see him, and reported to Gertrude on 25 August:

> I think he really wanted to explain to me why the marriage had broken down. I do hope when Vivien gets back that they will agree to part for the present and I think it would be much better if Vivien suggested it. She could have the flat and he Notley. If Peter [Hiley] told the Press at some convenient time that they were living apart at present but that no question of a divorce was being considered by either of them — and nothing more – surely there would be an end to publicity and idle speculation. I am not writing this to Vivien, but if you wish to tell her what I think, here it is. As you think the same I believe that the two people in the world who treasure her welfare most must have an influence on her. I cannot believe it is at all certain that her life with Larry has ended irretrievably. Her present idea of living alone is only a variant on the theme of taking another husband, but we know the truth is "When you're out keep hold of nurse for fear of finding something worse."[48]

On 30 August Vivien and Suzanne flew back to Lydd airport and Olivier (then rehearsing a revival of *The Entertainer* at the Palace Theatre) came down with Colin Clark to meet them in order to assuage the rumors of separation. Their arrival was the cause of a telling incident which Clark, still working as Olivier's assistant, related:

> Everyone was waiting at Lydd airport to see whether Larry would meet her or not because there were rumours of a breakdown. I drove down very fast and we got there about

> a quarter of an hour early and we didn't want to go to the airport too early because all the reporters were going to be there. So we went into a pub to have a drink and the whole pub was full of reporters. They all saw me and they all recognized me as Olivier's assistant and said, "Oh, Colin, what's going on? Is Larry coming?" I thought Crikey, where's Larry? I can't dare look around. And I said, "No, Larry's not coming. I've come down to meet Vivien. I don't know if Larry's coming to meet Vivien or not. Maybe he will. Maybe he won't."
>
> I thought: Where is he? Did he manage to back out or what? I turned round and Larry was standing right at my shoulders. Not one reporter, who were all there just to see if Larry turned up, could recognize him. His face dropped and sagged. He just turned into another person. They did not recognize him, nor could I hardly. And they said, "Who's this?" I said, "He's just someone come down with me to meet Vivien." Of course later on when we got to the airport they're all there again and they recognized him. They said "Why didn't you tell us he was coming?" I said "He was standing right with me." They couldn't believe me. They just thought I was kidding. But he was. That's really acting. Just incredible the way he could act.[49]

Vivien was immensely relieved to see Olivier, but in due course they went their separate ways. She had promised to call in at the Sheephouse for forty minutes. Later she took Suzanne to stay with Kenneth Clark at Saltwood.

On 10 September *The Entertainer* reopened, this time with Joan Plowright in Dorothy Tutin's role as the daughter. There had been talk of Vivien playing Phoebe, the wife; and a bizarre idea that she would wear a rubber mask to disguise her beauty. Even if Olivier did not recognize it consciously, his decision to become involved with *The Entertainer* was another step in his separation from Vivien. They played for eight weeks at the Palace and then went on tour. Olivier was much taken with George Devine's ideas for the new theatre. His jacket and tie came off and his pullover went on. He took on a new lease of life. And in this phase he fell in love with Joan Plowwright, the girl he had first seen in *The Country Wife* earlier in the year.

Vivien traveled again, this time with her father in Ireland, revisiting old haunts. She stayed with Leigh in November, pleased that Oswald Frewen was there. Leigh wrote to Oswald: "Vivien is, I regret to say, more enthusiastic about her weekend now she knows you will be here too."[50]

In November Vivien visited the tour of *The Entertainer* in Glasgow to celebrate her forty-fourth birthday. Colin Clark recalled:

> That was a complete and total nightmare. She wasn't very welcome. We had a dinner party in a hotel in Glasgow. There was old George Relph and Brenda de Banzie, I suppose. The waiter had been told it was Vivien's birthday and had prepared a whole menu to celebrate what Vivien had done. So it was like – as it were – soupe Blanche Du Bois – meringues Scarlett O'Hara. That did not go down well with Vivien, that sort of joke. She was just frightfully bored to be reminded of all this stuff. Larry was having an affair with Joan Plowright. Vivien stayed the night and then she went back to London. I suppose she came up to see what was going on. That must have hastened things.[51]

Needless to say, Vivien was the last to find out about the affair. Others had known but she never blamed them. But she did blame Olivier for moral cowardice in not owning up. No doubt her recent behavior justified his reluctance to cause further scenes by such an admission. Suzanne's wedding to Robin Farrington took place at Holy Trinity, Brompton on 6 December 1957. A few days before Suzanne wrote to Gertrude to thank her for undertaking the role of surrogate mother:

> You have done so much for me, starting before I remember and coming into memory with Canada. I didn't realize your sacrifice then, but I do now. You know that I love and admire you, but it's nice being told that, and thanked. You have done all that a mother could do and more bringing me up and loving me…

> P.S. Please go on praying for us, darling. I am sure it helps and so many people won't be concentrating on anything else but hats at the service.[52]

Appropriately Oswald Frewen was at the wedding: "I joined in on the Lord's Prayer and Doxology."[53] Gertrude noted: "Glorious day. Radiant bride. I didn't cry."[54] The night before the ceremony Vivien wrote to Suzanne:

> I am thinking of you so much and cannot go to sleep without telling you how much I love you and how I hope with all my heart that today will be the beginning of a most wonderful and happy life. You have a rare and radiant nature and I know you will help to carve a full and close future together with Robin. Take care of yourself and him my darling and if you ever need me I shall feel it a joy and blessing to be of any help or comfort I can.[55]

Leigh and Vivien were hosts at the reception at the Hyde Park Hotel. The press concentrated on the fact that Suzanne had "*two* dads"[56] at her wedding. Olivier was in the background. The *Daily Mail* diarist, Paul Tanfield, found him nursing a glass of champagne behind a huge pillar at the reception. "I supposed you could say I'm standing to one side,"[57] he said. William Hickey quoted him as saying: "I must say this seems to be rather an awkward situation. I feel like the uninvited guest."[58] Both diarists relished the scene when Leigh and Vivien drove from the church together and Olivier was left in the cold amidst press, police, and crowds to give them a sad, lonely wave.

Though this sad wave did not signify the actual last parting of the Oliviers, the diarists were right in one sense. Olivier had gone. He was in a new orbit. Certainly he would come and go for another year or so, but spiritually they were now apart. Just as in 1937 the happiness that Vivien and Olivier found with each other was tinged with guilt for the sorrow they caused Leigh and Jill, so there were new sadnesses to cope with. Olivier was about to embark on a new adventure of career, of love, and in due course of fatherhood. Vivien was already the victim of her illness. She was not at a good age or in a good condition for life to hold much hope of further happiness. Comfort, companionship and interest she would find, but nothing could replace Olivier. Tragically, as so often, Olivier proved easier to love in absentia. From now on he was invariably away, and Vivien missed him bitterly. Gradually her love of him became obsessive. In consequence the next years were easy for nobody.

Chapter 21
A Devilish Angel

Archie Rice: *"What would you say to a man of my age marrying a girl of about your age?"*
Jean: *"Oh, Dad. You're not serious. Oh you couldn't. You couldn't do a thing like that to Phoebe."*

The Entertainer

Olivier left London for a run of *The Entertainer* in America in February 1958. He was away until June. The role of his daughter, Jean, was taken by Joan Plowright during the tour. Here they were still more free to indulge their love affair. Miss Plowright, "this brassy girl from Lincolnshire,"[1]* was a relative newcomer to the New York scene, whereas Olivier was an experienced old-timer with plenty of cronies of the ilk of Douglas Fairbanks Jr. Vivien remained in London, rehearsing for *Duel of Angels.* Gertrude was very much about, busily moving her beauty business into new offices at 46 Dover Street. Ernest was occasionally there but more often in Ireland. Robin Farrington had gone to work in Berne, and Leigh took Suzanne over on 2 February to join him. Vivien admitted in interviews that she had only got to know her daughter properly in the past three years. She sent a letter to greet her in Berne, adding:

> For my part I am missing Larry terribly but thank goodness very occupied with rehearsals, which are going well. *The*

*She was born at Grigg, near Scunthorpe.

> *Entertainer* has broken all records in Boston and the NY season is sold out, so *that* is very nice.[2]

Duel of Angels, originally *Pour Lucrèce*, by Jean Giraudoux, had been translated by Christopher Fry. Vivien asked Jean-Louis Barrault to come from Paris to direct it. Barrault was surprised to find Vivien hating the character she played.

> She assailed her. She was constantly on the lookout for reasons for not loving her. This forced me to plead for Paola. She attacked her by provoking antipathy. It was only when she had exhausted all the reasons for hating her that she assumed her. In the part she was not merely a cat, she had become a panther.[3]

Alan Dent claimed this play was "the last of [Vivien]'s great, unquestioned successes."[4] Cecil Wilson described it as "a battle between vice and virtue, contested in a strange but immaculately written mixture of mythical tragedy and Victorian melodrama with a tang of French bedroom farce, all rather overloaded with philosophy."[5] He commended Vivien for having "abandoned her old archness for an authoritative new poise and a wider range of feline mischief," concluding that she had "never commanded a stage more surely."[6] Vivien played the faithless wife and Claire Bloom the virtuous one. Claire Bloom claimed to be greatly influenced by Vivien:

> Over other women, and certainly over men, she cast an extraordinary spell. I don't know that I ever heard her say anything profound or knew her to read anything demanding. I also thought she was a social snob, though I now realize that she was simply interested in interesting people and they were people generally who were well known…She was breakable, that was very much a part of her – that terror and anxiety and delicacy and fear…In *Duel of Angels* she gave the same performance on the last night as she did at the first rehearsal. It was all worked out and so without real spontaneity.[7]

Claire Bloom had an easier time than her replacement angel, Ann Todd, for whom Vivien developed an intense dislike and jealousy. Ann Todd came to dread going to the theatre each night for fear of "what was going to happen next, on or off the stage."[8] Jack Nimmo remembered that as Vivien handed her the cup of poison, she would say under her breath: "You'll never know if it's real..."[9]

Vivien's leading man in the play was Peter Wyngarde, soon a close ally. He first met the Oliviers in the autumn of 1956, when he was playing an intrepid Chinese pilot in the Brecht play, *The Good Woman of Setzuan*, at the Royal Court. At that time he favored an early attempt at method acting and used to sit in a rubbish bin outside the theatre in order to immerse himself in his part. When he was introduced to Vivien, a stickler for cleanliness, she could hardly come near him. Nevertheless, he was selected for *Duel.* He soon found in Vivien that rare combination, an "extremely beautiful and also wildly intelligent woman with a brain as quick as quicksilver and an ability to send herself up rotten." He fell in love with her there and then. He thought her "one of the best actresses" he had ever worked with, "including Edith Evans, who was acclaimed as the greatest actress in the English-speaking world."[10]

Wyngarde became an intimate friend. There is a cryptic reference to him in Olivier's *Confessions*: "My diaries bear evidence of determined encroachments on my resolve: Vivien departs, Vivien back; Peter away, Peter back (this was evidence of another encroachment from another quarter)."[11] During this period Vivien told Wyngarde: "I had a choice. Either to be an actress or to be Larry's wife. If I had decided just to be Larry's wife, I'm sure I'd still be married to him."[12] She continued to worship him as the greatest living actor and Wyngarde remembered that, before every performance, "in the wings and just before her entrance she would pause and there was that little gasp of breath as if to say: 'This one is for you.'"[13] Wyngarde said:

> One of my greatest joys playing with her was the fun of playing on two levels. Being completely *in* the play and at the same time being able to comment in a language of our own like two ventriloquists. It was telepathic. It achieved two things – the alpha state (the state in which athletes achieve records) and an effervescence which was infectious

> to the audience. The essence of high comedy.[14]

Wyngarde loved Vivien's "wicked" humor as when she related the course of her day to him, blithely sandwiching the purchase of a Renoir between lunch at Prunier's and tea at Fortnums. There were difficult times too:

> I went through hell. I came to know when her illness was coming on. One night at Eaton Square she suddenly said, "I've got to go and talk to the chauffeur." She went downstairs. I knew the chauffeur had left hours before. So I went out and found her running around the garden with nothing on. It was bitterly cold. I came down after her with a blanket and managed to cover her with it. There she was with a policeman. He of course recognized Scarlett O'Hara. This was before any treatment was prescribed. One night at Notley I found her, after a perfectly wonderful night, sobbing uncontrollably on the bathroom floor at four in the morning.[15]

When times became fraught in the theatre, Binkie Beaumont urged Alan Dent to come round and see Vivien "as a steadying influence."[16]

Duel of Angels toured in places such as Newcastle, Edinburgh, and Glasgow in March. In Newcastle Vivien heard bad news:

> All is well with Larry but we have had a horrid blow because he feels he *must* go on with the play for another 4 weeks! He *is* coming back on 6th as arranged but only for 4 days. That will be so wonderful but I just try not to think of him going away again. It seems silly to be making such a fuss about it, but I am missing him most dreadfully.[17]

Duel of Angels was an L.O.P. production. Olivier came to see the play in Oxford during rehearsals and thought Barrault's direction too stylized for English audiences and, as so often, he redirected the play, changing Vivien's performance, and removing from it a certain strength she did not find again until the play opened in New York.

In New York in May Noël Coward attended *The Entertainer* and he and Olivier dined later at Sardi's. Olivier made it clear that "he couldn't really take living with Vivien any longer."[18] However, Coward did not think either of them was "willing to face the contumely and publicity of a divorce."[19] While in New York Olivier was host at a party aboard *SS Knickerbocker VII* with guests ranging from Greer Garson and Douglas Fairbanks to Truman Capote and the Lunts. Joan Plowright was there and soon afterwards rumors appeared in the *Hollywood Reporter* that Olivier wanted to marry her. Around 20 May Olivier came home. Vivien wrote to Suzanne:

> It is absolutely heavenly to have Larry back. He is very well indeed, though looks rather odd as he is in the process of growing his beard for *Macbeth.* It is emerging in the strangest colours. We think the film is definitely on… Meanwhile he is in Scotland pinpointing locations for the picture. The play continues to do wonderfully well and I am even enjoying it occasionally.[20]

The hope of filming *Macbeth* had been fraught with disappointment. None of the early backers had been willing to go in after the initially disiappointing returns on *Richard III*. Mike Todd, however, told Olivier that money was no problem as long as it was filmed in his new and dramatic Todd-Ao. But Todd was killed on 22 March. The Oliviers then tried the Rank Organization but early in July they backed out; the film was permanently shelved and the beard shaved off.

Olivier was in England for some weeks in the summer. His son, Tarquin, then at Christ Church, Oxford, set off with two friends on an exciting adventure to find Dr. Livingstone's sunken steam launch, Ma Robert, in the Zambesi. Weekends at Notley resumed. Gertrude found Peter Finch there early in July, now accepted as a friend. The Oliviers attended Robert Donat's memorial service. There was another "Night of 100 Stars" (which Olivier refused to allow to be televised), in which Vivien appeared as a clown with John Mills and William Chappell (replacing Olivier at the last moment). Then, in August, Ernest and Gertrude stayed at Notley. Diana Cooper was there "looking most glamorous at 1 a.m."[21] The next day there was a lunch party with Michael and Lady Pamela Berry, Lord Dudley, Geordie

Ward (then Secretary of State for Air) and his seventeen-year-old daughter, Gerorgina, who gave a vivid account of the meeting:

> My uncle Eric Dudley took me to Notley to meet the Oliviers. I met Larry first, charming, remote. Vivien came into the garden and, even as she was greeting everyone, stared at me. When we were introduced she really stared, holding my hand, and then she kissed me. She continued to hold my hand as she offered me drinks. She talked to me sideways "Good voice, needs training – lighter eyes with green in them." At lunch she rearranged the table so that I sat next to her. It seemed as if she never spoke to anyone else…she was flirting with me – flirting I discovered later was natural – and magic-ing me. It was as if I'd lit her up. Frankly I thought she was bats and so I noticed did Larry. (My doting father thought it perfectly normal!) I was of course totally flattered, amazed. It was heady stuff. I tried to figure out out why and came to the correct conclusion. She thought I looked like her.[22]

Georgina worked out that Vivien saw in her a surrogate daughter, Suzanne having rejected any attempt to be like her mother:

> Vivien felt that she could soak me in her magic so that by osmosis I'd absorb it and become a STAR – her STAR – her continuation, her posterity. She was petrified of death as she was of being alone, the two going together. A substitute daughter to carry the legend, her legend, her glory.[23]

Vivien was never slow to match her thoughts with action. Despite protests from Olivier, she announced that Georgina would be admirable for Dodie Smith's play *These People – These Books,* which they were backing. Her father hesitated momentarily and agreed. Georgina discovered she had acquired a fairy godmother whom she loved "with the passionate adoration of a child as well as with the critical eye of a teenager."[24]

The audition was fixed for the following Tuesday. Georgina auditioned at four and got the part (the play was staged in Edinburgh and Leeds). The same night she dined with Vivien in a party that included Ken Tynan and his wife, Elaine Dundy, and which continued until 7:30 a.m.:

> Dinner was very surprising. Larry wasn't there but he might as well have been. His absence heavily pervaded the atmosphere. Vivien was somewhat hectic (in retrospect – manic) pulling gaiety out of the air. One of her great charms was a sort of tartness like crab-apples, which sliced through the saccharine, was always amusing sometimes very funny indeed. She never told anecdotes but was very good at one-liners. She kept the night going successfully except for one thing. She constantly referred to Larry as if they were at the glorious height of romantic love. Even I had seen that Larry had had her in a big way. The Tynans knew he was desperately trying to get out from under. I caught Ken's eye once. He shrugged very, very sadly.[25]

Gertrude was the person upon whom the next burst of hysteria fell, and the phase which lasted a month was well-documented in her diary. She found Vivien 'very ill' on the weekend of 13 Sepember, when the Tynans came to Notley and Peter Finch's mother had to be sent home. Olivier was in Spain with his dying brother, Dickie, and Dickie's wife, Hester. Elaine Dundy has described this weekend – Ken Tynan putting on the chain mail, Vivien accusing her mother of having tried to stop her playing in *Streetcar*, and finally, Olivier returning from Spain*. Gertrude recorded "upsetting scene with Vivien."[26] Further difficult days followed and Vivien saw various doctors. A nurse moved in. The following Friday she calmed down and slept for eight hours. Vivien's parents remained with her the whole time. On 22 September Leigh came for an overnight stay and the next day Vivien was well enough to go to *Romeo and Juliet* at Stratford. In her over-energized state Vivien suddenly decided to clean the whole of Notley, leaving it spotless for Olivier. She scrubbed until 3:45 a.m. The next day she was rude to Olivier, and then Gertrude and Vivien flew to Milan in the hope of a soothing break.

*See *Olivier in Celebration*, pp. 167-73.

In due course they settled at San Vigilio, still under the patronage of the splendid Leonard Walsh. One 'happy' day was followed by an 'unhappy' night, during which Vivien threw a glass of water in her mother's face in Leonardo's kitchen. Presently Leonardo asked Vivien to leave the locanda because she had invited a fisherman in for a drink (he had rescued them when their car ran out of petrol). Finally the police were called at 2 a.m. and Vivien bit two fingers of one of them. Gertrude then took her to the Gardesana Hotel at Torri del Banco, where once again the situation assumed an element of calm. Banned from San Vigilio, Vivien bought some land on Lake Garda where she hoped to build her own house one day. They left their car in Florence and finally flew home from Rome on 8 October, "Viv not charming to anyone, very cross looking."[27] The next night Vivien returned to *Duel of Angels* and "was wonderful as usual."[28] Bumble Dawson, Cecil and Irina Tennant and Kay Kendall were in the audience to give moral support. The play ran until 29 November without further upset.

In October Olivier went to Ischia and then to Florence, to fetch the deserted car. He made his way back through Paris. He stayed with the Seidmanns, from whose apartment in the avenue Marceau he wrote Vivien a fourteen page letter of farewell (which did little good, but caused a lengthy rift between Vivien and Ginette Spanier, only resolved some years later in New York). On her forty-fifth birthday, Vivien dined with Olivier. He gave her a Rolls-Royce, reputedly costing £7,000, and explained that they must part. On 7 November she and Olivier gave a magnificent star-studded dance at Les Ambassadeurs for Lauren Bacall. In the press they were praised as excellent hosts because they made each guest feel that the night would not be complete without him or her. But privately Vivien's mother complained: "Viv didn't take any notice of us. Got home at 4:30 a.m.[29] Meanwhile Olivier branched into television in ATV's production of Ibsen's *John Gabriel Borkman*. Peter Wyngarde had been at Eaton Square while Olivier read the script:

> We all had to be very quiet. At six o'clock he came storming in and threw it across the room. He stood fuming: "What's the matter with you, Vivien. I don't come on until fucking Act II!" Vivien then pointed at a page and said, "Larry, darling, it says here: all through Act I we can hear

> his footsteps above, and, darling, the play is called *John Gabriel Borkman*, and you'll be wonderful in it."[30]

After seeing it, Vivien said: "Wonderful, I was thrilled."[31] The critics did not agree and Olivier avoided television for some years to come.

December was a month of beginnings and endings. Olivier was back in New York at the end of November telling Noël Coward that he had "firmly left Vivien after terrible dramas–how long for nobody knows."[32] Then, having thought he had safely escaped, he was obliged to return home because his brother Dickie died. A week later Coward reported that Olivier had endured "several more ghastly scenes with Vivien."[33] Dickie was buried at sea and, while Vivien stayed at Notley, he spent the night at Hester's cottage, Notley Mead. The death of Dickie (on 28 November) heralded the end of Notley Abbey days.

Looking back, Dickie's widow, Hester, recalled that the last five years at Notley, invariably described as so awful, were often very happy. Both Olivier and Vivien derived great pleasure from their garden, from his steadily growing avenue of trees, and there was much laughter over simple word-play and descriptions of friends. Despite the dreadful end to the marriage, Olivier told his sister-in-law: "I'll miss Vivien every day of my life.[34] Irina Tennant commented:

> There was so much love between the two of them. If it wasn't for the illness those two would have remained together for the rest of their lives. But his nerves started to go. At first Larry refused to go, saying, "I can't abandon a person when she needs me." But he had to do it.[35]

Suzanne gave birth to her first-born son, Neville, on 4 December. Vivien, who had expressed some anguish at the concept of being a grandmother, nevertheless became fond of him and of the two brothers that followed. The next night Leigh and Vivien gave a party at the Savoy to celebrate Gertrude's seventieth birthday.

Another old friend was waning. Oswald Frewen had suffered a series of black-outs in recent months. In March he had "prayed for life after July."[38] Leigh had stayed with him twice and Oswald had been to Leigh in May. His breathing became bad in late November and he was taken to London to the King Edward VII Hospital. Leigh went to visit his old friend: "The last time I saw him he had just the strength to open his eyes and say: 'How is Sue?' Concern for himself was the least of the cares of this much loved man."[37] He died on 7 December 1958.

Leigh wrote to Hester about Dickie and Vivien wrote to Leigh:

> Hester showed me your letter to her. She said it was the most beautiful and helpful she had had. I wish to goodness I could write to you like that of dearest Oswald. I know how deeply distressed and sad it will have made you. I shall miss him very much too, but not in the way you will. I am so sorry darling. He was very much part of our lives and even though I have not seen him so much of latter years it was good just to know he was there. It has been a dreadful year, hasn't it? But little Suzie has certainly done a lot to brighten it.[38]

For Christmas, Vivien loaned Bernard and the Rolls to drive Ernest and Gertrude and Sue's nurse down to Woodlands. But Vivien did not join them, preferring to go to Notley to be with her sister-in-law. The Hartleys, Sue, and her baby joined her for New Year's Eve.

Just before Christmas Vivien had helped Noël Coward celebrate his fifty-ninth birthday, attending the first night of *Who's Your Father?* And then a party given by Gladys Calthrop in Cadogan Place. Coward found her "in a bad way, drinking far, far too much and attacking everyone right and left."[39] He was about to stage *Look After Lulu* in America and Vivien was angry that she could not be in it,* mainly because Olivier was to be in the States for six months (undertaking *The Moon and Sixpence* for NBC Television and filming *Spartacus* in Hollywood). Coward was bored with the situation and unsympathetic to her plight. He now believed that Olivier would be lucky to break away, having endured years of torment. However, he was also aware that, despite the inevitable chaos of working with her, she remained "the biggest draw in the business."[40]

Seeing her again in February, Coward noted Vivien's despair, but thought

*Tammy Grimes was the star.

that Olivier's departure "may have done her a power of good."[41] Noël joined Vivien's party with Lauren Bacall and Kay Kendall to see Celia Johnson in *The Grass is Greener.* The four were photographed together in the bar of the Ivy during the interval.

Vivien was struggling bravely to create a new life, while never surrendering her love for Olivier. There are numerous examples of her kindness to others at this time. She continued to promote Georgina Ward, presently finding a film for her directed by Carol Reed (from which Georgina extricated herself in favor of the stage). When Jean Dawnay, the top model, suffered unwelcome publicity in the *Daily Express*, she took her at once to lunch at the Caprice and then very publicly to a John Cavanagh fashion show. She even went round to see Cecil Beaton in Pelham Place to present him with a beautiful edition of Piero della Francesca paintings, but Cecil was still reluctant to respond to her olive branch. Her friends were enormously concerned in the protective way that fellow stars are mutually supportive – not always to the bitter end, perhaps, but certainly while box-office ratings are high. The press made much of Vivien's friendship with Kay Kendall and Lauren Bacall, the *Woman's Mirror* going so far as to air brush Noël Coward out of the photograph for a headline: "The Gay Trio who are the Talk of the Town."[42] The three were undoubtedly friends, heading off night after night for some new excitement. To the press they were a dream, three beauties whose combined ages made 110, three very feminine ladies driving mighty Rolls-Royces, one widow and two grass widows. Lauren Bacall had returned to London to create a life following the death of Humphrey Bogart in January 1957, Vivien had been deserted by Olivier and was about to do *Skin of Our Teeth* for television (shown on 17 March and described by her later as "a most remarkable failure)[43], and Kay Kendall had time on her hands since the failure of her play, *The Bright One* (written by Judy Campbell). Her husband, Rex Harrison, was playing Higgins each night in the sensational musical, *My Fair Lady*. David Lewin, a trusted journalist on the *Daily Express* (who had accompanied the *Titus Andronicus* tour in 1957), invited all three to dinner in a Jermyn Street wine-cellar restaurant. Vivien told him: "We just like being together and seeing plays and doing jig-saws, anything in fact."[44] Kay Kendall said: "We don't bitch about people and we don't talk about clothes. What do we talk about?"[45] And Lauren Bacall concluded aptly: "When they made the three of us they sure broke the molds and threw them away. They don't come like us any more."[46]

Sadly, however, the group was soon dissolved, Lauren Bacall flying to India to film *North West Frontier*, and Kay Kendall leaving for Paris to make *Once More With Feeling.* The English press was kind to Vivien. Not so the *New York Enquirer*, which reported that she was "living it up in London with a young artist who sports a beard and wears sunglasses in nightclubs"[47] and that she had been pursued by a Sussex businessman in the plastic business, that she had been furious to find him at a party, "kicked the Casanova" and "followed her kick with a downward slash against his cheek with her fingernail that drew blood."[48] It should be added that Vivien fared quite well compared to the other stars whose antics, true or false, were the subject for such speculative reporting.

In February 1959 Suzanne wrote to her step-father, then in Hollywood, filming *Spartacus*, and residing at the Chateau Marmont. The gist of her letter was to report that her mother was much better in health and in attitude to Olivier and to ask him whether he would not give the marriage another try. Olivier's reply expressed panic and desperation, a wish to retreat even further – to the South Seas if necessary. He explained that he no longer wished to share his life with Vivien, that in the past decade she had become a different person to him, as he himself had done. He could not face a relationship that was only façade. He acted enough on stage without attempting to act in reality too, he claimed. He wanted to be alone – presumably alone with Joan Plowright.

In daily letters Olivier and Joan Plowright remained resolute in their determination to find happiness together, their optimism ringed by the real fear that Vivien might take her own life. Olivier was convinced that she would be deserted by their friends when they separated and was surprised when she was not. Vivien remained optimistic, while Gertrude wrote to Leigh and he replied:

> Vivien will get no peace of mind until she recognizes that this break with Larry is final…Let Vivien accept that what she did to me Larry is doing to her. It must be faced. She owes it to her relations, her friends and herself not to let this destroy that lovely and exquisite personality that we adore and cherish.[49]

In June Olivier returned to London. Vivien greeted him at the airport with a kiss somehow not quite smack on the mouth. All too soon afterwards he set off for Stratford to rehearse *Coriolanus*. He also filmed *The Entertainer* with Joan Plowright as his daughter. The enterprise included some weeks on location in the seaside resort of Morecambe. At this point Joan Plowright split up with her husband, Roger Gage.

Vivien was present at the opening night of *Coriolanus*. At Stratford Olivier stayed in a hotel, giving Notley a wide berth. Vivien was often alone there, though friends visited her and Tarquin came over for weekends from Christ Church. On such occasions Vivien would talk through the night. Breakfast would merge with lunch, the same thing would recur the next evening and yet on Monday night she would be back in the theatre. Godfrey Winn was another who stayed. As they walked in the garden, she said: "We must stay near the house, Larry has promised to telephone as soon as the curtain is down."[50] Winn then launched into a tedious précis of Comptom Mackenzie's novel *Guy and Pauline* (a most unsympathetic subject, as he later admitted), while Vivien "sat indoors frozen into immobility,"[51] surrounded by lovingly collected treasures, which seemed now "objects in a cold impersonal museum, as she went on waiting, with dying hope for the telephone to ring."[52] Presently it was decided to put Notley on the market. With Dickie dead and Olivier away a lot, Vivien had found herself lonely there. Its going was another step in the inevitable collapse of the marriage. Notley appeared in *Country Life* on 13 August, and offers soon began to come in: "I feel just overwhelmed at the thought of Notley going,"[53] Vivien wrote to Leigh (who had likewise sold Woodlands.) Driving to Stratford one day, Olivier told Harry Andrews: "Well, now my baronial period is just about over. I'm not sure what comes next."[54]

After some prevarication, Vivien agreed to play in Noël Coward's *Look After Lulu,* which arrived from New York in July. Originally a Feydeau farce entitled *Occupe-toi d'Amélie*, Coward had adapted it the previous year. The play toured in Newcastle and then opened at the Royal Court, an unusual choice of venue. According to KennethTynan, John Osborne wandered in "and found it full of Miss Leigh, Mr. Coward, and Hugh Beaumont, the most powerful of West End producers. He wondered for a second if he had come to the wrong place."[55] The notices were poor but, as Coward had predicted, the presence of Vivien ensured splendid takings at the box office. Harold Hobson of the *Sunday Times* judged: "The trouble is that Mr. Noël Coward is too witty and Miss Vivien Leigh too beautiful. For the kind of play that *Look After Lulu* is, beauty and wit are as unnecessary as a peach melba at the North Pole."[56] Godfrey Winn wrote: "She galvanized the predictable, artificial farce into life."[57] The play moved to the New Theatre on 8 September, where again it did well, and might have continued beyond Christmas but the management decided to close it on 12 December.

Meriel Forbes (Lady Richardson) was in the play. She knew that Vivien was unhappy. Between matinée and evening shows they would sit in the dressing-room:

> She would talk and talk, but cry all the time. And then would come the voice on the tannoy saying "half an hour." She opened the play and I came on very soon after. She was as if nothing had touched her at all. No emotion. She went straight into the play, with her beautiful head held so proudly on that long neck. Her stance was very rare. You would never know that half an hour before she'd been weeping. Immense control.[58]

At about this time Rosemary Kirby (later Mrs. Geddes) came to work for Vivien. She had worked in the box office at Stratford and for Peter Hiley in his office at L.O.P. She recalled: "I was very thrilled when she picked me to be her new secretary but I felt rather young and inexperienced."[59] She found Vivien very organized, meticulousy answering all her personal letters by hand. And she soon learned how to deal with the unscrupulous enquiries of the press.

More tragedy was afoot. On 6 September Vivien's great friend Kay Kendall died at the London Clinic. The vivacious star, best known today for her roles in *Genevieve* (1953) and *The Reluctant Debutante* (1958) had come to know Vivien well following her pseudo-spontaneous arrival in Portofino in the quest for Rex Harrison in 1955. Her myeloid leukemia had been diagnosed in the autumn of 1956 and confided to Harrison in January 1957. A great number of friends such as Lilli Palmer, Noël Coward, and Terence Rattigan were in on the secret, but despite the story being leaked to sensational Italian newspapers, Kay Kendall herself never knew.* On her way to the Clinic, she told reporters: "Don't think I'm coming here to die. I'm not."[60] Her death was a further cruel blow for Vivien, who attended the sad funeral with a dark-spectacled Noël Coward. She was laid to rest in the shade of a cedar tree in the actors' corner in the additional churchyard of St. John-at-Hampstead. Noël wrote later:

> There were no mobs and shaming demonstrations, only a few scruffy newspaper photographers clambering about on the cemetery railings and snapping the coffin being lowered into the ground.[61]

Vivien spoke words written for her by Terence Rattigan at the memorial service at St. Martin's-in-the-Fields on 22 September:

> We are giving thanks for the love and happiness, comfort and joy that Kay Kendall brought into this world so short a time ago, lavished on so many of us, and has left behind her for our memories to take delight in.
>
> It was as if she had a premonition that the gift of life which she relished so greatly would not be hers for very long – with such intensity and gaiety and fervour did she pack every minute of her stay on earth. Rest and peace were two things that in life Kay hardly knew. They would have seemed a waste of time."[62]

Vivien could, of course, have been talking of her own life.

There was more trouble on the horizon. At the end of November, a German magazine stated that the Oliviers were no longer living together. This was picked up by the *Daily Sketch* which claimed that Olivier had admitted that 'neither of them knows what the outcome may be."[63] Gertrude was quoted in the *Daily Mail*: "I'm sure the trouble in my daughter's marriage is not serious and that it will soon blow over."[64] Vivien and Olivier were then pictured leaving the theatre together; they were also photographed

*Terence Rattigan's *In Praise of Love* was based on this dilemma. Rex Harrison played it in 1974. By then, he had married and divorced Rachel Roberts, and was married to Elizabeth Harris.

rehearsing for a midnight show in aid of the Frejus disaster victims, and then Olivier sailed for America. Vivien had no excuse for not going too, other than that she was not welcome. Noël Coward took pity on his star and invited her to Les Avants for Christmas. *Look After Lulu* closed on 12 December. Cecil Brock, who played Emile, recalled:

> She was so kind to everyone and considerate, industrious and professional with her talent, and gay and warm and charming, I remember her buying presents for us on the last day of the run – and that, on a day of sorrow for her.[65]

Vivien's father had been taken to hospital for an operation the day before. On Sunday, after mass at the Brompton Oratory, Gertrude and Vivien went to see him. Ernest remained very ill, weakened on Thursday, and died at about 7 a.m. on Friday, 18 December, at the age of seventy-six. The surgeon wrote to Gertrude that he was sorry he had not managed to be more successful with her husband. However, a leg would have had to go and Ernest would not have relished life anchored to a chair.

Somehow, the jocular, powerful figure that Ernest had been in India had been transformed in recent years into a more mute, shuffling figure, sometimes (though by no means always) to be found in a flat in which Gertrude was the ruler. There were many tributes to his cheerful disposition and to his kindness. Evidently Ernest's last action at Page and Gwyther was to take a bag of old clothes down to the old woman who sold newspapers at Monument tube station.

Gertrude and Vivien went to see Ernest's body laid out, "looking very beautiful and so peaceful."[66] On Monday he was cremated at Golders Green. There were forty-nine wreaths, one of them unmarked. Gertrude sent all the flowers to the hospital. Suzanne took her sad grandmother to Leigh's sister, Dorothy, at Topsham, while Vivien flew as planned to stay with Noël Coward. On Christmas Day: "Vivien rang us up from Geneva. Noël was very sweet and sympathetic."[67] Reporters did not make Vivien's time there any easier. But Noël and Cole Lesley decided to invite them in for a drink. Vivien put on a brave face. There were no hard questions. Vivien saw in the New Year "with deep sadness in her heart and for one fleeting moment tears in her eyes," but "never for one instant allowed her unhappiness to spill over."[68]

Early in the New Year Gertrude and Sue flew to Ireland and Gertrude scattered Ernest's ashes in the River Moy at Ballina, County Mayo, "between the 4th and 5th tree on the right of the little gate. Agonizing moment."[69]

Olivier, aboard the *United States*, wrote of Ernest's optimism and indomitable spirit, and of Gertrude's strength; he wished that he could report that all would be well between himself and Vivien. But he could not. Then the inevitable reporters gathered impatiently outside his cabin door and he had to go. Olivier went to spend Christmas with Stewart Granger and Jean Simmons, pouring out his heart to what he believed was a happily united couple. At the end of his stay he declared that he must file for divorce. Granger wrote:

> He then said something I'll never forget. "It was really nice seeing you two together, how much you loved each other, that made me decide I wanted that kind of happiness too."[70]

The Grangers and the Oliviers were both divorced in 1960.

Chapter 22
Starting Life Anew

Streetgirl: *"And then?"*
Lady Hamilton: *"And then what?"*
Streetgirl: *"What happened after?"*
Lady Hamilton: *"There is no then. There is no after."*
Lady Hamilton

The Olivier marriage was over in all but name. Olivier had faced the problems as long as he could. He had tried and eventually failed. A weaker man would have thrown in the sponge a decade earlier. However, when Vivien's problems began to affect his work and his career, it was time to go. He made a thorough and effective escape. There was a considerable element of "slumming it" in his life from now on. One actor recalled that his suits were by no means as elegant in the 1960s as when Vivien oversaw such matters. He bade farewell to his baronial life and to Vivien's taste and style, which had become oppressive to him. In a sense it did not matter whom he found. As one friend said: "Any young actress would have done."[1] From his point of view he happened to choose a highly talented one, thus opening up a new career for himself in the theatre, and later in films and television. As the 1960s progressed so there were photographs of the proud father collecting his young children from school. There was a bounty of happiness and fulfillment in store for him, before his health collapsed. He used to say that his decision was between staying to be a nurse to Vivien or going to run the National Theatre. He also uttered the plaintive cry: "I just have to get some sleep."[2] There was an element of compromise too. In 1964 Richard Burton deserted his first wife, Sybil, in favor of Elizabeth Taylor. In so doing he sacrificed a sensible, stable agent (who later ran a highly successful night club in New York) and began a front-page, diamond-invested life with a glamorous mega-star. Thinking back on his own life, Olivier issued a stern warning. Richard Burton told David Lewin:

> Larry Olivier really didn't approve of my marrying Elizabeth. What Larry said to me was this: "I went from Vivien Leigh to Joan Plowright and you have gone from a Joan Plowright in Sybil to a Vivien Leigh with Elizabeth. And that is the wrong way round."[3]

There was guilt too. When Olivier left Jill Esmond with her baby son to bring up alone, he could justify this on the pretext that he and Vivien were predestined to be the golden couple of the stage. There was guilt then, and inevitably there was double guilt when the second marriage eventually failed. Michael Denison said:

> The marriage to Vivien had to be justified in every possible way. They had to have total success so that the world could say "it's so wonderful." I believe Larry wanted to justify it as far as he could to appease his own conscience and took whatever Vivien threw at him in her extremis with the most fantastic forebearance. It was only when she had really gone that he turned to the total contrast – from champagne to "Guinness, from mink to mackintosh and to youth of course. Also, very much, to have another family.[4]

Maxine Audley recalled one theory prevalent in the mid-1950s:

> Tony Quayle had this wonderful theory that they had made a pact with the devil. He said "You can have everything, all the riches, and you will be King and Queen of the theatre but there's only one condition: You must stay together for

> the rest of your lives." That was the kind of feeling there was – that they were bound together irrevocably because it was *the* great love affair. Like the Windsors they could not part.[5]

For Vivien the parting was more wounding. She had lost the love of her life and she must have realized that it was her fault. She had abused and mistreated him, no doubt thinking he would never go. She was used to getting her own way. Certainly there had been the occasional part that had eluded her – and the film of *Macbeth* – but this was the first time she had truly lost.

The choice of Miss Plowright caused her particular distress. She was heard to say, "When you think I am often cited as one of the great beauties of the century…"[6] She soon coined a semi-alliterative sobriquet for Olivier's bride that caused ripples of laughter among certain elements in the theatre world. Moira Lister recalled:

> I think it was a huge shock for her. Not only because he'd gone off with someone who wasn't particularly beautiful but the fact that she was a terribly good actress. I think Vivien, all her life, struggled to get on the same level as Larry and didn't quite make it. That was a terrible challenge that she wasn't quite able to fulfil. So I think it was a double-edged sword when he went off with her.[7]

Vivien returned to London early in 1960 and Olivier returned in March. About nine days later Vivien herself set off to the United States to take part in a production of *Duel of Angels* directed by Robert Helpmann with Mary Ure as her opposite angel.

During the days before her departure Vivien paid daily visits to the bedside of George Relph, one of her oldest friends, and companion to the Oliviers with his wife, Mercia Swinburne on the 1948 Australian tour. She was in America when George died on 24 April at the age of seventy-two, severing another vital link with the happiness of the past. Vivien wrote at once to his widow:

> We have walked our different paths of such deep unhappiness

> together for so long now that I feel so very cloe to you and there is nothing in the world I wouldn't do to try and help even if it is a little. So many memories of happiness come to my mind. So many joys shared to be grateful for I think most of all, my darling, the way you and Georgie took me for your friend at the very difficult beginning of Larry and my life together. Since then what wonderful times we have had – to be treasured for ever. I loved Georgie so deeply and shall miss him the rest of my life, more than my own father, you know…[8]

Meanwhile, Olivier stayed with Noël Coward at Les Avants. Coward found him "happier than I have seen him for years,'[9] hoped he would not divorce Vivien for Joan Plowright, but feared he would. As for Vivien, he thought: "She will have to face up to the truth sooner or later and the sooner the better. She will inevitably suffer less as time goes by, but she's still at the stage when she doesn't wish to believe this."[10] In America Vivien was lucky to be surrounded by staunch friends. Peter Wyngarde was again her leading man:

> When Vivien asked me to join her in New York I refused because I felt I had done the play for nearly a year in London and couldn't bring anything new to it. But she knew instinctively that the one quality I possessed was to complement her unconditionally on stage. She said she would not go unless I came with her. At least that is what I, in my vanity, thought. It was, however, for a different reason. Vivien needed moral support. It was my debut on Broadway and Bobby [Helpmann] insisted I have a new costume – a pair of *very* tight riding breeches, which I wore at a costume parade. When I came on Vivien asked me what I thought I was doing. Bobby screamed, "Isn't it perfect? So much more revealing than those baggy numbers you wore in London." Vivien said very firmly: "Peter dear, if you come on in that on the first night, the audience will not only not be looking at your face but they won't be looking at mine either. Take them off at once.'[11]

The part of Armand in the play was taken by John Merivale, whom Vivien had only seen fleetingly over the years.

John Merivale, always called Jack by his friends, was one of the four children of the actor Philip Merivale, by his first wife, Viva Birkett, and thus the stepson of Gladys Cooper. Jack was good-looking, in the Anthony Eden mold, well-read, a lover of the English language. He was the step-brother of John Buckmaster (by now residing in the Priory, the well-known psychiatric hospital*) and Joan Morley, Robert Morley's wife, and also of Sally Pearson, Robert Hardy's wife. Born in 1917, he was educated at Rugby and New College, Oxford, though by tradition he came from a Harrovian family. His ancestor, Joseph Drury, had been Harrow's headmaster for twenty years in the late eighteenth century (when Byron was there), as well as helping to establish Edmund Kean at Drury Lane Theatre. The Merivales came from Middleton Cheney, near Banbury and "emerged from the peasantry 250 years ago (at Naseby we were 'digging for victory')."[12] They went on to achieve distinction as men of letters and learning, in the law, on the stage, and in the Church. One ancestor started the Oxford and Cambridge Boat Race, and a cousin succeeded in getting Sir Henry Irving elected to the Garrick Club after a previous blackballing. The sons of John Herman Merivale included Herman, the Under-Secretary for India, and Charles, Dean of Ely, the Roman historian, Jack's great-grandfather. His father, Philip, "the most romantic and poetic of men,"[13] in Jack's words, was born in India, was the first ever Colonel Pickering in Tree's production of Shaw's *Pygmalion* and graduated to playing Higgins to Mrs. Patrick Campbell's Liza in New York. He married Gladys Cooper in 1937 and loved her till his death in 1946. Jack himself went on stage in 1938, beginning, in Sheridan Morley's words, "a stage career which had started better than it could possibly hope to go on."[14] In 1941 he married the actress Jan Sterling, joined the Canadian Air Force and won his wings. After the war he took part in the California and Broadway productions of *Lady Windermere's Fan* (which Cecil Beaton designed and in which he made his only professional stage appearance). He was divorced in 1947.

Jack had first met Vivien when he was an understudy in *A Midsummer Night's Dream* in 1937. She had wished him good luck when he went on stage and he had been struck by her beauty. He was in the ill-fated 1940 production of *Romeo and Juliet* and had been surprised to be accused

* He committed suicide there on 1 April 1983.

by Vivien of cheating at Chinese checkers. He had departed at 9:10 the following morning, and had scarcely seen her since.

Jack had continued on the stage as a supporting actor. Binkie Beaumont used to find parts for him. When in the cast of *Duel of Angels* in New York, Jack liked to go out drinking on Saturday evenings. One particular Sunday morning he made his way to the oak room of the Plaza for a vodka and tonic to clear his hangover. However, he inadvertently attracted the attention of a homosexual who liked beards. Therefore he repaired to the Sherry-Netherland Hotel where Vivien was lunching with Bobby Helpmann. They fell into conversation, Jack told some ribald stories, and subsequently he accompanied Vivien to the theatre on several occasions.

Duel of Angels opened in New Haven. It was there that Vivien turned to him one evening as though she wanted to be kissed. Jack was reluctant to go further, however, since he was not certain of the state of the Olivier's marriage. Vivien said, "You know what he's doing," and in due course invitied him to make love "properly."[15] Later she told him he was only the third man she had ever woken up with.[16] At first the affair was secret. Walking with her in New Haven, Jack told her: "It's terrible to have fallen in love with the most famous woman in the world."[17] Their journey from New Haven to New York was made irksome by the unshakable presence of another suitor, Jones Harris, the son of Jed Harris and Ruth Gordon.

Duel of Angels opened at the Helen Hayes Theater in New York on 19 April to a rave review from Brooks Atkinson: "Not since [Peter Shaffer's] *Five Finger Exercise* has a play been expressed so thoroughly and beautifully."[18] He continued:

> As the duelists, one for vice, the other for virtue, Miss Leigh and Miss Ure give an amazing performance in an artificial style. Since nothing gross is ever said or done, the duel is performed in terms of attitudes and inflections. Although the hatred is bitter, the style is cool. From each encounter both ladies emerge like cameos, not a detail bruised or battered. Their acting is a splendid demonstration of high style sustained through the vicissitudes of a contentious evening.[19]

Frank Aston wrote: "Miss Leigh grows into someone viperishly desirable;"[20] and Walter Kerr: "For my modest money, this is Miss Leigh's most controlled and captivating performance."[21]

What the reviewers did not know was that there had been a crisis behind stage on the first night. Peter Wyngarde went round to see Helpmann in his dressing-room:

> The room was bright yellow and Bobby, normally deeply bronzed, matched the color of the dressing-room perfectly. He said, "Vivien's not going on and the whole bloody world's out there." Vivien had received a telegam, timed to arrive a few days later, but delivered all too efficiently by Western Union. It was Olivier asking for a divorce. It was as if we both knew why I was there. I had to persuade Vivien to go on. I don't believe she ever recovered from the impact of that telegram, and throughout the performance I had to watch and gently guide her through. I had to be not only in character but also to let her know I was there if she wavered for a second. She never did. It was why I consider her to be such a great actress. Without a shadow of a doubt it was her best performance in *Duel*. She was devastating. It was as if she realized she was on her own from now on. She completely won with her talent and overwhelming courage.[22]

Vivien became the toast of New York once more with great crowds of fans waiting at the stage door. Inevitably she was asked to compare her role as the wicked angel with previous better-known successes. She said: "Paola has depth. Scarlett was much, much simpler. And Cleopatra had much more poetry."[23] Vivien was unmoved by her success except on one point. Her old friend, Charles Russell, the organizer of the 'Nights of 100 Stars,' called on her in her dressing room. When he praised her, she besought him: "Do tell Larry."[24] One afternoon, between matinee and evening performance, she was determined to see Ruth Gordon and Garson Kanin. The latter recalled:

> Vivien called up Ruth and me. Ruth never gave up on her. She loved her to pieces. She came over and said, "You've

> got to help me. Talk to Larry. Tell him he mustn't do this. He'll kill me if he does this." She believed in her heart and mind and soul that Larry would come back to her in time.[25]

Both Kanins did as bidden and posted their letters without showing each other the contents.

> A while later Ruth received a wild, hysterical, furious blister of a letter, telling her to mind her own god-damn business. Later Larry sent Ruth a letter of apology Her letter had troubled him so much that he had reacted in a rather furious way.[26]

Jack's new role as Vivien's protector meant that he bore a considerable share of the burden of any incipient problems. Peter Wyngarde took him aside and advised him to watch out for signs of nervous temperament and late night parties, which invariably heralded serious problems. Jack's old friend, Rex Harrison, was in town, and judged: "You seem to be doing all right."[27] Jack used to take Vivien to the Little Club on East 56th Street, which was also a favorite of the Harrisons. Later Wyngarde said:

> I have nothing but the greatest admiration for Jack. After that cathartic first night Vivien knew instinctively where to turn. I was involved elsewhere. She didn't want the insecurity of a restless energy but the solace of sweet and gentle maturity. Jack never dreamed in a million years this would happen. I said to him: "*You've* got to do it, now." He said ruefully, "I know…" He started as her supporting actor and became marvelous with her, gaining strength through her and soon he became her leading man. A very rare person.[28]

Early in May Vivien began to become increasingly energetic. One day Jack mentioned casually that he thought white Thunderbirds upholstered in black leather were the ultimate chic in cars. To Cecil Tennant's considerable annoyance, Vivien promptly purchased one. On Thursday, 12 May Vivien's mother flew into New York. There was a party after the show and Gertrude noted: "I'm not happy about my Pet."[29] Gertrude stayed in New York for three bumpy weeks. She was certainly impressed with Vivien's "beautiful new car."[30] Most nights there were parties. On Monday the sixteenth, Vivien suffered "a most unhappy breakdown just before the play."[31] During this time, Vivien was giving Jack little presents, thanking him for his "kindness and goodness to me"[32] and assuring him, "I love you every day of the year."[33]

During the weekend of 21-22 May Vivien received a letter from Olivier specifically asking her to allow him to divorce her. He explained that he was anxious that Joan Plowright's father should not be appraised of the exact nature of his relationship with Joan. This letter caused Vivien considerable distress. On the Sunday evening, late at night, when she was neither well nor particularly sober, she was encouraged by the Mephistophelian Helpmann to make the following announcement:

> Lady Olivier wishes to say that Sir Laurence has asked for a divorce in order to marry Miss Joan Plowright. She will naturally do whatever he wishes.[34]

The announcement arrived on Olivier's fifty-third birthday. Its effects were far-reaching. Unquestionably Olivier wanted to escape from the marriage but he was uncertain how to do it. Evidently Vivien had written to him about her affair with Jack. Jack was then living at a hotel on the West Side, dubbed "The Strangler's Arms' by Robert Coote, because a guest had been murdered there. One night Olivier telephoned him and asked, "Any chance of a union?"[35] But Jack was still unsure of how much he could commit himself, having suffered the endless problems of poor John Buckmaster. His reserved reply was met by "a deep sigh over the Atlantic."[36]

Vivien's statement gave Olivier the release he prayed for, but it almost ruined his hope of a divorce, appearing, in legal eyes, to be an act of collusion. At Eaton Square he was greeted by a barrage of reporters. Joan Plowright at once withdrew from the cast of *Rhinoceros*, in which they were both playing. Peter Hiley was quoted: "Miss Leigh's announcement creates a new and somewhat embarrassing situation for everybody."[37] Banner headlines in the tabloids proclaimed "The Hazard to Love,"[38] "Sir Larry and the Girl from Scunthorpe,"[39] and worse. Angus Hall became almost poetical on the subject of Olivier and Vivien in the *Daily Sketch*; "They decided to live apart in peace rather than together in pieces…it is going to sadden everyone who hoped that, despite every danger, this was one stardust marriage that wouldn't just end up as dust of the stars."[40] Even the *Daily Mail* commented: "A legend crumbles. The magic turns to myth."[41]

Back in New York, it was quickly realized that the situation was out of hand. Bobby Helpmann told Jack ominously, "Better watch it or you'll have the men with the white coats."[42] However, at this moment, when Helpmann could have given Jack moral support, he disappeared for three days. Irene Selznick advised Gertrude and Jack of a good doctor to give Vivien shock treatment. This Vivien accepted "with equanimity."[43] Jack recalled waiting with Irene in the waiting room, hearing "a strange noise like a cat outside," at which he jumped "with anxiety and horror":

> Then Vivien came out, complained of an awful headache – I saw burn marks on the temples. But she played that night with the headache and the burnmarks.[44]

Jack had to take Vivien for a second treatment a few days later:

> In my anxiety I got her there ten minutes too early. One of her rules was that to be ahead of time for any appointment was a social solecism. At the doctor's door she said "I'm not going to have it." My heart absolutely sank.[45]

They telephoned Dr. Arthur Conachy in London. He gave Vivien a reprieve. On 28 May Vivien's mother noted: "Viv very nasty to me at the Theatre. Came home and cried, feeling miserable."[46] Just before Gertrude left, Vivien made this up wth a party for her. Back in London Gertrude went to see *The Entertainer* and had supper with Olivier at Eaton Square to discuss the recent developments: "Very sad evening for me,"[47] she wrote.

In May a long-running dispute between Actors' Equity and the New York Theater Managers came to a head. The insurrectionists hit on the ingenious notion of closing down one theatre a night an hour before curtain-up without prior notice. This proved an impossible situation so at the beginning at June all the New York theatres were closed for ten days. Several plays were lost in the course of this action, one of which was *Duel of Angels*. Thus, on 10 June, Vivien was free to fly to London for ten days in the hope of resolving her marital problems and her health.

Vivien flew with Bobby Helpmann, aptly described as a "Iago" [48] figure by Virginia Fairweather and Peter Wyngarde. Jack stayed in New York. The official reason for the trip was to prepare a second Old Vic tour. This necessitated discussions with Michael Benthall.

Vivien had her first two shock treatments soon after arrival. Gertrude was in and out of Eaton Square, and Bumble Dawson stayed in order to deal with the unceasing pressure of reporters. Fifteen of them followed her car on one excursion. Vivien lunched with Lady Alexandra Metcalfe at Little Haseley and went to see her gardener, Mr. Cook, at Notley, now the property of a Canadian writer called Arnold Swanson. To Jack she wrote: "They have made it so awful as to be amusing almost – and the garden untouched which is the important thing."[49] Vivien saw Alec Guinness in *Ross* at the Haymarket but fell asleep; "I was too distraught and tired to concentrate."[50] She also wrote: "This is being an unpleasant time, but I am feeling very, very much better."[51] On 17 June Gertrude and Vivien lunched with Valerie Hobson, wife of John Profumo, the Minister of War. Gertrude then drove her to Welbeck Street, followed by two carloads of reporters and another two on motorbicycles.

Whenever she called Jack he detected "the considerable noise of parties going on."[52] Vivien asked to see Noël Coward alone, but when he arrived the flat was packed. He concluded that a great many of her problems stemmed from "the demon alcohol."[53] When she rang him the next day he told her he did not wish to see her until she pulled herself together. She hung up on him.

Evidently Olivier did go to see her but remained unmoved by her pleas. During her stay she had further treatments with Dr. Conachy. A while after this, on 20 June 1961, Conachy wrote a report on her psychiatric condition which she carried around with her lest she need to show it to a doctor abroad. Conachy pointed out that Vivien was "a person of very high intelligence and education, nimble wit and extremely good judgement and reasoning power."[54] She had the necessary determination, even ruthlessness, to reach the top of her profession. She was in no way suffering from a psychoneurotic illness. However, between 1949 and 1960 she suffered from "fairly regular cyclic periods of manic and depressive phases."[55] These had been diagnosed in various different ways by different doctors in America. He concluded: "I feel that there can be no doubt that she has a cyclic manic-depressive psychosis." In the depressive phase she becomes "increasingly depressed, finds it difficult to think or concentrate, loses appetite and weight, and sleeps rather poorly without help."[56] Suicide did not seem to be a practical risk, however. Dr. Conachy deemed February 1959 to June 1960 to be such a phase, aggravated by "her most reluctant separation from her husband."[57] What he did was to give her sedation and supportive psychotherapy. The other part of her illness was the manic phase:

> This is of a sudden onset. Within twenty-four hours there is marked elevation of mood and general activity. She rapidly loses her natural restraint and normal reserve, talks freely, and during this period loses judgement, reasoning power and insight. She adopts lost causes, will parade in the streets in procession, invade the House of Lords, and talk freely to the Press. It was during the manic phase of June 1960 that she announced to the Press that Sir Laurence Olivier wished to marry Joan Plowright. She also gave the nurse I used to help me in her treatment a valuable diamond ring. In addition, she develops marked increase in libido and indiscriminate sexual activity. These illustrations are her symptoms, particularly her overt sexuality, loss of judgement, and persistent overdrive makes me feel, that for a person in her position, from the social and publicity consequences that arise from this, that her manic phase is much more undesirable than the depressed phase. Last June she flew to London from New York. I had explained the position to her, and she had enough insight at the onset of her condition, to go to a psychiatrist in New York and ask for E.C.T. to be given. She had one treatment, but unfortunately the technique used was not satisfactory, and she refused to have further treatment there. During the period June 11-18th, 1960, I administered five electroconvulsive treatments under general anesthesia of sodium penthothal and with scoline as a muscle relaxant given by an anasthetist. I

> used a Shotter-Rich electronarcosis machine to avoid memory loss, but any good E.C.T. machine, providing it is certain that a convulsion has been triggered off, would be adequate.[58]

He concluded that Vivien had responded well to this treatment and remained well for the year that followed. At the end of her London stay Vivien spent the weekend with Helpmann. The next Monday he drove her to the airport. On board her flight she wrote to Jack:

> I am feeing so very well. It seems like a sort of miracle, indeed I believe it is. This has been a very extraordinary week. I think the most extraordinary of my life. Alone, and yet so infinitely so close to you. Friends have been most remarkable and I have every reason to be very grateful. I seem to have seen everyone I meant to and there have even been some hilarious moments…[59]

Jack was not aware that while on the flight, Vivien had also written to Olivier:

> Whatever may happen let us be friends, my dearest one. Conachy has done a very marvelous thing for me—and I am feeling as I have not felt for many years. Perhaps all the interim mistakes have made just too much difference for our life together – I do not know – and you must leave it to me to do what I think best for the future and in my own time. It will take a little time to decide…one does not let twenty-five years go lightly. I feel very deeply in love with Jack and very dearly grateful to him but it does not alter the fact that I shall love you all my life and with a tenderness and respect that is all embracing. [60]

Jack was at the airport, feeling not unlike Frank Aston's description of his recent portrayal of Armand "as a man, seeing the light, [who] senses the doom awaiting him."[61] But he need not have worried: "Down the steps came that entrancing figure, light as a feather. She looked so wonderful. My fate was sealed."[62] The next day Jack wrote to Gertrude:

> Your daughter arrived yesterday not only safe and sound, but looking, if possible, even younger than you. I am overjoyed to report that you can be as calm in your mind about her as I am and – more important – as she is.[63]

To this Vivien added: "I am feeling very well and so terribly happy."[64]

Meanwhile, in London, before Olivier could have received Vivien's letters, his solicitors wrote to Vivien making it clear that she must be under no misapprehensions. The marriage was over and Olivier wanted a divorce at the earliest moment possible in order that he could marry Joan Plowright.

Vivien met Ginette Spanier in Emlyn Williams's dressing-room, and they resumed the friendship lost on account of Olivier's avenue Marceau letter in 1958. "She was looking quite beautiful in a Balmain outfit named 'Paris,' a straightish sheath with one of those wide frills at the hemline."[65]

In July *Duel of Angels* went on tour. Vivien took herself in hand, drinking considerably less. She and Jack were amused by the black steward's name. "We just ring for Larry,"[66] became their refrain. Also on board the train was David Lewin, her favorite feature writer, with whom she had agreed to cooperate for a series of interviews in the *Daily Express*. Jack put his foot down, agreeing only to two hours on record each morning. Lewin proved a good friend, discreetly not mentioning Jack's role in Vivien's life. "Everything is fine," Vivien wrote to her secretary, Rosemary Kirby. "The opening night was terribly exciting and the reaction to the play very good indeed and it's simply heavenly being back here again."[67]

There was now a general reshuffling of the various relationships. Vivien resumed contact with Leigh. She did not mention Jack. Indeed, her passing reference to Olivier was as though she wanted Leigh to believe nothing had changed:

> My plans are of the vaguest but the film in Rome [*The Roman Spring of Mrs. Stone]* now looks fairly set. I had hoped so much to finally getting the house on Lake Garda started but now Larry writes and tells me he doesn't think the Bank of England will allow it even now. I thought

> doing an American film being paid in dollars in Italy would help.[68]

Vivien longed to find a new house but insisted that it had to be near water. Meanwhile, Jack had written to Olivier to tell him of his love for Vivien, a letter greeted with relief and gratitude by Olivier for it meant that Vivien had agreed to a divorce. In one of his florid epistles, Olivier wrote that he had guessed that some such thing had taken place. He now felt released from the torture of guilt and could enjoy with a clear conscience the prospect of happiness that (we now know) he was in fact already enjoying. Thoughtfully he warned Jack of the tell-tale signs that heralded an impending manic phase. He suggested that if she became inconsiderate it was the moment for medical attention, in other words, shock treatment. Thus, Olivier relieved himself of any further responsibility in the matter.

Both Vivien and Jack were on home ground in Hollywood. In her suite at the Chateau Marmont, Vivien hung her Impressionist pictures. She shared the suite with Jack, and with Poo Jones, her much loved Siamese cat with violet eyes. Her old ally, George Cukor, was nearby. She often rested by his pool, once wearing Constance Collier's somewhat oversized bathing costume. Cukor wandered about in pajamas and Helpmann pulled in his well-tanned stomach when Jack wielded Vivien's cameras. Sunny Lash came to see the play and judged:

> She had lost her little fragile actress quality. She was more mature, more of a Lynn Fontanne. She was absolutely in command in *Duel of Angels*.[69]

They lunched together and Vivien showed her letters from Olivier saying he would always help her if she needed him.

At San Francisco, their next port of call, they stayed at the Huntingdon Hotel. Vivien was on the third floor and Jack on the twenty-third. Vivien insisted he move nearer. The very military English manager rang Jack and informed him: "I run this pub. I had you down for the twenty-third floor. Understand you want to be closer to Headquarters?" Then he added, "I don't blame you."[70] Vivien wrote to Leigh:

> This morning I was up at 5:30 for deep sea fishing. I caught a very nice 9lb salmon and played two others. It was most exciting. It is a really ravishing city, beautiful surrounding country, charming people, full and good audiences.[71]

Whereas in Hollywood the audiences were polite but unresponsive, in San Francisco they were lively and full of laughter. There was a farewell party for Mary Ure (then married to John Osborne, who came out to join her), and there were evenings when Helpmann danced in Vivien's suite, a carnation in his buttonhole, and a pink handkerchief in his pocket. Jack and Vivien went up to Lake Tahoe, so tired on one occasion that on arrival they asked their hosts for a room and collapsed asleep at once. The company made their way to Denver (where they played in an unpleasantly large auditorium in September), then to Kansas and at length to Chicago. By now Vivien was happy enough to joke to the press that she might be sending Joan Plowright her visiting cards. She wrote to Leigh:

> I like this city so much. My apartment looks straight over the great lake and there are trees everywhere, and of course the Art Gallery is one of the finest in the world so I am happy wandering about there. The audiences are awful, slow and stupid but the theatre charming.[72]

Wherever Vivien played or stayed Olivier's photograph went with her. On 17 October, they returned to New York, where Olivier and Joan Plowright were both playing, he in Anouilh's *Beckett* and she in Shelagh Delaney's *A Taste of Honey*. Then they sailed home in *Queen Elizabeth*. Jack was not entirely pleased when Peter Wyngarde decided to accompany them. However, they enjoyed at least one entertaining evening judging a bizarre beauty contest. There were some initial problems with the Purser over the presence of Poo Jones, but Vivien's cat proceeded to suit himself, savoring daily walks on the boat deck.

At Cherbourg, where the *Queen Elizabeth* docked, Vivien and Jack experienced their first onslaught from the press. Evidently "the attentiveness of 6ft.5in. bearded Mr. Merivale" had been "a main topic among the passengers"[73] on the crossing. At least they were able to report that Vivien looked ten years younger. Vivien's Renoir (then worth a mere £5,000) was impounded by the Customs despite her insistence: "I never travel without it. I like to have something pretty to look at when I'm on tour."[74]

Vivien's next project was to film *The Roman Spring of Mrs. Stone* by Tennessee Williams. She and Jack drove to Paris in her new Rolls-Royce so that she could have fittings at Balmain with Ginette Spanier. Elspeth March was in Paris and Vivien invited her to stay in part of her enormous suite. She found Vivien very upset because the Olivier divorce papers had just been served on her. One day Louis de Rochemont, the producer of *The Roman Spring of Mrs. Stone*, came to see Vivien. Elspeth March let him in without saying who she was. She made him comfortable. The bell rang again and a pageboy delivered a box from Balmain, which she unpacked, hanging up the dress. Elspeth March said:

> Then Vivien came in and she said, "Oh, you've got the new script. I can't wait to read it. And now then what about a part for Elspeth?" His jaw absolutely dropped because I think he thought I was the housekeeper.[75]+

Elspeth March thought Vivien and Jack were lucky to have found each other:

> He was quite remarkable in his whole relationship with her. I think she was a very lucky girl. At the same time Vivien absolutely changed him. He became sunny and warm and a much lighter character.[76]

After Paris, Vivien and Jack toured France and in mid-November they went to Les Avants, where Noël Coward joined them from London, relieved to find Vivien in considerably better form than the previous June. Noël noted: "Inwardly she is still hankering after Larry. However, she is putting up a gallant performance and seems very fond of Jack, who is constantly fulfilling a long-felt want."[77]

While Vivien had been able to ensure first-class travel for Poo Jones on

+Elspeth March played Mrs.Barrow, a rich American lady seen in a café in Rome giving her gigolo a cigarette case. The boy who played the gigolo claimed to recognize her and then revealed he had been a waiter at the Caprice.

the tour, her well-mannered Siamese had to endure six months of quarantine in England. Jack was impressed that, on their fortnightly visits to the kennels, Poo eschewed his favorite recipe of shrimps in brine in order to be with Vivien, but as soon as she left, his head was buried in his dinner. For the first time Jack appreciated how it is possible to love a cat. Vivien, of course, had a lifelong rapport with them.

In London soon after her return, Vivien was obliged to go to court to face the divorce. She wrote to Hermione Baddeley: "I have been made unhappy for so long but once Puss makes up his mind there seems to be nothing to do but let him have his way. God knows I have been fiercely reluctant, but now it seems inevitable."[78] There was intense press interest. One evening Jack took Vivien and Bumble to Buck's Club for dinner. The press followed the car until the chauffeur, Bernard Gilman, asked: "Do you want me to lose them, your ladyship?"[79] Given the nod, he disappeared at speed.

The hearing took place on 2 December just after Roger Gage was freed from Joan Plowright. Cecil Tennant and Peter Hiley went to court with Vivien. She was cited by Olivier and admitted adultery with unnamed men in Ceylon, London, New York, and elsewhere. Thus Vivien's marriage to Olivier was finally dissolved.

Vivien coped better than might be expected, thanks to Jack's presence. She was soon busy making plans with Jack, Cecil Tennant, Bobby Helpmann, and Peter Hiley, and even attending midnight mass on Christmas Eve. At the end of the year she wrote to Rosemary Kirby:

> I am working on this film. Jose Quintero is an adorable person and a marvelous director and we are a wonderfully happy unit…Xmas was very gay with party after party.[80]

Chapter 23
Tennessee to São Paulo

> Paolo to Mrs. Stone: *Even when you smile you are not really happy. You are frightened of your feelings.*
>
> The Roman Spring of Mrs. Stone

New Year's Even 1960 was celebrated at 54 Eaton Square. Vivien and Jack gave a party at which the guests included Bumble, Michael Benthall, and Bobby Helpmann. Gertrude also noted the presence of others whose names were of no consequence to her: "An American singer, v. charming. Viv's leading man, his girlfriend, V's film director."[1] These were, variously, Lotte Lenya, Warren Beatty, Joan Collins, and Jose Quintero.

The idea that Tennessee Williams wrote *The Roman Spring of Mrs. Stone* for Vivien or with Vivien in mind is granted little credence by the experts, the accepted line being that Williams always wrote about Williams. Nevertheless, he published his novella in 1950, by which time Vivien had proved a success in *A Streetcar Named Desire*. The story concerned an actress advancing in years and failing in reputation, who forsakes the stage to care for her ailing husband. He dies on a flight (a weak moment in the film), and Mrs. Stone finds herself a lonely if elegant widow in Rome. Below the steps of her palazzo, there lurks a disagreeable youth who declines all advances from strangers, "for when a man has an appointment with grandeur, he dares not stoop to comfort…"[2] Mrs. Stone is seen as good prey for the wicked Contessa who brings round Paolo, a smooth gigolo of studied Italian accent, greased hair and shiny grey suit. As they dine alone together for the first time (at her expense), the serenaders surround her menacingly and his proffered Negroni cocktail becomes a forerunner of ensuing doom. From then on she is marked. She relies increasingly on Paolo, who takes full advantage. So too does the Contessa. Eventually Paolo moves on, lured by the chance of new romance and a career in films. In despair, Mrs. Stone throws her keys to the ever-lurking youth (the angel of death) and awaits her doom.

For Vivien it was another brave part to undertake, and one she took in her stride, suffering only the habitual criticism that she was too beautiful to suffer the neglect of Mrs. Stone, who, in Vivien's embodiment, could logically have picked any man of her choosing. For the part she wore a grey-blonde wig and Balmain clothes. Alan Dent, still a familiar on the studio set, was impressed by her portrayal of the character "as it ought to be shown… the crow's feet that were added to her complexion, the eyelashes that were so over-mascara'd* that Karen sheds black disfiguring tears on receiving Paolo's insults just before he finally quits her."[3] Vivien was assisted by an able cast: Warren Beatty, who had been determined to get the role; Coral Browne, who had loved the book and took part because Vivien wanted her there as a friend;[4] Lotte Lenya+ as the wicked procuring Contessa; Jeremy Spenser as the youth, familiar to Vivien in many productions since his boyhood appearance in the film of *Anna Karenina*; Jill St. John (then married to Lance Reventlow, Barbara Hutton's son); Ernest Thesiger (who died during filming on 14 January); Bessie Love (the former D.W. Griffith silent star), Elspeth March; and Cleo Laine as the jazz singer. Roger Furse recreated Rome at Estree Studios and Bumble Dawson supervised the costumes.

The film had many memorable scenes, not least when after a disastrous party, the Contessa turns to Mrs. Stone, mutters "Wunderbar" and disappears from the apartment with a nonchalant slam of the door. And there are sad lines from Mrs. Stone: "Shall I never know if you love me unless you hurt me?"[5] and "Three or four years is all I need. After that a cut throat will be a convenience."[6] Seeing the film later, Tennessee Williams wrote: "I just sat

*One of Gertrude Hartley's particular beauty products was tear-proof mascara, which would have assisted Mrs. Stone, but not the plot of the film.

+Lotte Lenya (1900-1981). Austrian singer and actress, famous for her role in *The Threepenny Opera,* worked with Kurt Weill, whom she married, and Bertholt Brecht. Possessed a voice describved as "one octave below laryngitis" (Desmond Shawe-Taylor, *Sunday Times*, 29 November 1981).

and watched the grace and tragic style of Vivien Leigh. I think this film is a poem. It was the last important work of both Miss Leigh and of the director, Jose Quintero, a man who is as dear to my heart as Miss Leigh is."[7]

Warren Beatty sought out Tennessee Williams and put himself forward for the part. Vivien also had to be convinced. Beatty went to see her in New York with his dark make-up on, looking and sounding as much like the part as possible. Jack Merivale recalled:

> What impressed Vivien most was that when he offered her a light for her cigarette, his hand was shaking and she thought that was the sign of a true actor. He wanted this part so much.[8]

Alain Delon was an alternative suggestion but Vivien said: "He's much too pretty. He's prettier than I am."[9] Jack was there on the day that Vivien's horse bolted. The scene was filmed on a lawn and there were various paths symbolizing which one she would take with her own life. The mare[++] had been used by Olivier in *Richard III* and when it heard the clapperboard, it charged. Charles Castle, then Jose Quintero's assistant, recalled:

> She had the presence of mind to duck and fortunately she had Stanley [Hall's] wig on, and as she ducked, the branch ripped the wig off. Had she not had the wig on, it would have ripped her scalp. But I must say she was courageous because when the horse came back she got right back on it and she redid the take. Otherwise she would have lost her nerve.[10]

After lunch Beatty would not return to film, Jack recalled:

> He just sat there drinking his coffee and I said "That was your call," and he said "They'll wait," and that steamed me up a bit. Then he was called again and he made no move

++This mare's eventful film career included an unfortunate incident in *Richard III* when Esmond Knight's stallion attempted, somewhat clumsily, to cover her. Both Olivier and Knight were in their respective saddles and Olivier turned round irately and and shouted: "Get off, Ned, you stupid twit." (Esmond Knight manuscript, p. 210)

> and I got really cross. I said "Vivien has just had a nasty accident and she's professional enough to go early to make-up, have a small lunch and be there on time." In a rather sulky way he went back.[11]

Evidently Beatty felt that, by being late, he would be noticed. Joan Collins remembered that Vivien criticized her extravagance on clothes and urged her to buy jewelry as an investment instead. "She did not take kindly to me, Miss Leigh," she wrote, "but she certainly did to Warren."[12] For Vivien, the best part of the film was working with Jose Quintero, who knew exactly what he wanted and how to get it, even if he was so shy and gentle that the first time he called "Action," he said it so quietly that nobody heard.

The Roman Spring of Mrs. Stone was released in London on 15 February 1962. Vivien was pleased with its reception: "I am getting all sorts of lovely letters and cables about *Mrs. Stone* and am pretty pleased and relieved."[13] Arthur Schlesinger Jr. wrote:

> Vivien does Karen Stone with an immense grace and restraint; it is a lovely performance, and the only tolerable thing in the film.[14]

The following Sunday Vivien, Gertrude, and Jack drove to see a house near Uckfield, recommended by Dirk Bogarde. They had a picnic lunch and Vivien loved the house instantly. "We came to a certain point in the drive and we saw the house and saw a glimpse of the water beyond it and she let out a sort of sigh."[15] This was Tickerage Mill, Vivien's last country home, which filled her requirements of garden and proximity to water. Tickerage had some interesting links. The Armstrong-Joneses had lived there and their son, Tony, had his first dark-room there. Barbara Skelton has recorded that it was owned later by Major Dick Wyndham, and Natalie Newhouse had shared it as a love nest with the bibulous actor, Robert Newton, who starred in Olivier's *Henry V*.

Before filming was over, Vivien was given a few days' leave from the studio to fly to America to be present at a Civil War Centenary of *Gone With the Wind* in Atlanta. David O. Selznick was there, looking worn and ill, though only fifty-nine. Olivia de Havilland was there, too. With Vivien, she was the only major survivor (Clark Gable had died of a heart attack the year before). Vivien wore a low-cut gown specially made for the occasion. She took part gallantly in the celebrations, reporting to Jack: "We are on our way to 'Aunt Fanny's Cabin' (if you please for a brunch) – then somewhere for mint juleps – then bed."[16] But when a cub reporter asked her which part she had played in the film she told him that the interview had just come to an end. In New York she stayed at the Plaza and insisted on seeing Olivier, who would only agree to the confrontation at Sardi's and in the presence of Joan Plowright. Whatever she hoped the meeting would achieve was to no avail, and she left soon afterwards. Indeed, stepping off the airplane in London, she was greeted with the news that Olivier and Joan Plowright were man and wife.

The next day she went to St. Michael's, Chester Square, to attend the wedding of her chauffeur, Bernard. Her mother was there too: "My sweet Vivien was marvelous. She kept a smiling face although her poor little heart was agonized. I know it broke my heart to see her valiant effort."[17]

A week later Vivien took Jack on holiday with her. She had £3,000 in a Canadian bank left over from a bonus given her by Korda. She insisted on paying for Jack and would not have gone without him. She even offered to have a bout of shock treatment before the trip to ensure that all went well. Binkie Beaumont recommended Tobago. They began with six "rather hectic"[18] days in Jamaica. Noël Coward was relieved to find Vivien so cheerful and happy and noted: "Jack is good with her and a gentle, nice creature," but added, "I wouldn't care to change places with him."[19] Tobago was more peaceful. They stayed at the Beach House of the ArnosVale Hotel, and Jack reported to Gertrude: "Your daughter is wonderfully well and relaxed and rested. She is learning to use the underwater mask to watch the fish which are glorious in color and variety."[20] Vivien herself thought it "a most heavenly island, peaceful and comfortable."[21]

There were two untoward incidents. The first was their discovery by the press, who at once predicted marriage between Vivien and Jack, noting in that romantic vein so often adopted by hard-hearted journalists: "Yesterday, the love-birds lolled in the sun on the same secluded beach in Tobago, where Princess Margaret and Tony Armstrong-Jones spent part of their honeymoon."[22] The second was a robbery in which her purse was stolen. Vivien was home in time for the birth of her second grandson, Jonathan, on

13 May. Vivien thought about it for a while and then wrote to Suzanne: "I think I would like the children to call me 'Grandmother'!! when they can manage it."[23]

Vivien was due to lead the second Old Vic tour to Australia, departing in June 1961 and not returning until May 1962. She only just had time to set John Fowler's assistant, Paul Anstee, to work on Tickerage and have a few friends down. In London there were rehearsals for the tour at the Finsbury Park Empire, and on 21 June *The Valiant Years*, a life of Winston Churchill, in which Vivien appeared, was shown. Unfortunately, her best lines were cut. She recalled a meeting with Sir Winston at Chartwell during which she enquired about a bull. He said, "Though he leads a life of uparalleled boredom, *remember* it is punctuated by moments of extreme, emotional excitement."[24]

The company flew to Australia, via California, leaving on 26 June. They took three plays, *Twelfth Night* and *Duel of Angels*, both of which Vivien knew well, and *The Lady of the Camellias*, a dramatization of which Arnold Weissberger, Vivien's New York agent, found for her. This last play Jack read, and Vivien was surprised to come in and find him reading with tears in his eyes. "Oh, is it that good?"[25] she asked.

Jack gave Vivien an inscribed Cartier cigarette lighter, to start the trip. She wrote: "It is a *flame*, which is what you have been and *are* to keep my heart and spirit going. I do *thank* you, dearest darling love – in the air and round the world. I love you, your Angelica."*[26] From California they flew via Hawaii, Honolulu and Fiji to Australia, Jack reporting to Gertrude: "She's sleeping like a lamb in the seat next to me, has been as good as gold, well 14 carat, in America."[27] Her maid, Trudie Flockert, and Bernard, the chauffeur (astutely given a world trip as a wedding gift) were also there to help and support Vivien.

Duel of Angels opened in Melbourne, but badly: "The audience was too busy looking at itself and being sensible of its own importance to pay full attention to the play,"[28] reported Jack to Gertrude. Vivien was incensed by the late curtain due to "people who wanted their dreadful dresses photographed in the foyer. I thought a pack of huskies had been let into the stalls, there were so many off-white white fox stoles!"[29] The notices were bad, but business was good.

* Since *Duel of Angels*, Jack and Vivien called each other 'Angel' and 'Angelica.'

Whatever the company thought at the time, there was a considerable element of putting on a brave face. By the time they reached New Zealand they were happy to concede that Australia had been pretty gloomy. Jack wrote to Gertrude of the "tremendous difference" the audiences were making, storming and stamping for Vivien at the end of each show, and queuing for tickets, whereas before they had become almost melancholic – "in a rough sort of way, that is what happened for one reason or the other all through that fiendish Australia – though you had better not say so publicly!"[30] Jack further bemoaned the Australian critics who "used to delve into their Thesauruses to find new words of abuse to describe the horror and revulsion with which my work filled them."[31]

One of the problems was that Vivien was alone. The last Old Vic Tour had been such a resounding success, and the lack of Olivier deprived the romantic colonials of the chance to see the pair still united. They resented Jack (who appeared from time to time in newspapers as Vivien's companion), nor was he as powerful a leading man, as he himself pointed out: "I wasn't Laurence Olivier. I was not star quality. I was not very good as Armand in *The Lady of the Camellias* either."[32]

In late July Helpmann and Vivien broadcast on television. Jack recalled:

> One of the questions was "What do you think of Australian audiences?" and Bobby hastily said "Very fine, most understanding." So Vivien then chipped in with "Not in Melbourne. I never spent a gloomier night than I did in Melbourne." Well, that phrase followed her all around Australia. There were headlines the next morning: Vivien hits out at first-nighters" and "Actress raps theatre-goers." As hard as she tried to make them remember that she had said only *that* audience, the papers had got onto a good thing.[33]

Nevertheless, Vivien wrote to her mother: "The T.V. interview did nothing but good and letters pour in full of congratulation and the audiences are much better."[34] She also reported that she had drunk no martinis for a month. When not playing, Vivien was as energetic as ever, setting out at 4 a.m. in quest of a lyre bird.

On 28 August they opened in Brisbane. "We are mad about Brisbane!" wrote Jack. "It's a charming, sunny, pretty warm place after old Melbourne."[35] Vivien organized a beach-barbecue picnic at Surfers' Paradise and watched "while the rest of us tried with indifferent success to ride the waves."[36] Luckily, *Lady of the Camellias* proved 'the smashingest success."[37]

After Brisbane, Bobby Helpmann, Jack, and Vivien snatched a week's holiday on Orpheus Island off the Barrier Reef, where they lazed in the sun, swam, and hunted for shells. "Those were the most idyllic times we had," recalled Jack. "It was a matter of simply relaxing, enjoying the sun and the water. It was exactly what Vivien needed. If it hadn't been for that I don't think she would have lasted the tour."[38]

In Sydney *Twelfth Night* opened to an audience that cheered Vivien, received rave notices but low bookings, and Helpmann was informed he had been "laid off the booze FOREVER, because of his recent attacks of hepatitis."[39] Meanwhile, Vivien spent "a fearful lot of time opening things and shaking hands."[40]

They moved from the glass-plated Chevron to the Fernleigh Castle Hotel on Rose Bay, overlooking Sydney Harbor. "Pip" Barnard and Hugh Stewart, from the 1948 tour, came to see her in her suite:

> We expected to find her very much the grand lady when, granted an audience, we were ushered into her presence by her devoted maid. Actually she was still fixing the day's make-up, sitting at her dressing table. Though she was most charming and warm on the surface to us both, enquiring after our Sydney lifestyles, I immediately sensed a deep sadness and a restlessness. I was convinced she was not a happy lady and my heart went out to her. I had not seen her on stage since 1948. She moved one utterly. She *was* the *Lady of the Camellias*. It was the most truthful performance I had experienced from her, not having witnessed her stage Blanche of *Streetcar.* Yet even as I rejoiced that she had joined the ranks of the great ones, I also felt a sense of foreboding.[41]

One unfortunate incident concerned a weekend party about 120 miles from Sydney with some friends, Mr. and Mrs. John Thompson. Vivien and Jack got lost, suffered a puncture, and arrived for lunch at about 5:30 p.m. Vivien was too tired to attend the actual party given by some neighbors. Jack recalled:

> The hostess had a bad evening because there were people from miles around to see Scarlett O'Hara and she wasn't there. Then a chap who had been at the party left and went and blew his brains out all over the lawn. He was the best friend of Mr. Thompson.[42]

Then came Vivien's forty-eighth birthday. David Dodimead recalled:

> We loved her so much, man, woman and child, that we rehearsed a special show for her – unknown to her, of course – and the plan was we crept out of the theatre after the night of her birthday, and it was outrageous to run away from Vivien on her birthday – I mean she was furious. And we rushed to this house and hid ourselves – put all the lights out – and Jack brought Vivien, who was furious – she was swearing like a trooper: "Where in the hell do you think we're going?..." All this was going on, and we listened to it in the dark with great amusement. And then suddenly we switched all the lights on – there was Basil Henson dressed as Eamonn Andrews with a red book saying "Vivien Leigh, This is Your Life." We had made up a totally fictitious story of her life. I was standing with her favorite drink in my hand, a large glass, gin – a lot of gin – a lot of water, a lot of ice and half a lemon cut across the slip down the side so that the zest would come out. She adored it. And of course forty years fell off her face the moment she realized.
>
> We had the most wonderful evening. It was a short show for her, so we then had a party and at about three o'clock in the morning, the drink ran out. So I went up to Vivien and I said "Darling, I'm so sorry, it's the end of the

> party, the drink's run out." "Oh, has it?" she said. "Where's the telephone?" And she rang her hotel and just said "Send champagne round to this address till dawn. There are fifty of us by the way." She was the most generous person in the world.[43]

On 11 December they moved to Adelaide until the end of the year. They spent New Year's Eve between Adelaide and Perth. While Britain froze throughout the early months of 1962 in the worst winter on record, Vivien and her troupe of actors boiled merrily in temperatures somewhat over 96 degrees. Vivien compared Britain's 'freeze-up' with their 'burn-up.'[44]

After a snatched holiday in Rotarua, they opened in Auckland: "Best audience so far and great stamping for V at the end,"[45] reported Jack. At the end of January Queen Salote of Tonga came especially to Auckland to fulfill a long-standing wish to meet Vivien. Later, Jack described the opening of *The Lady of the Camellias*:

> You could have heard a pin drop throughout, except when there was laughter (and except when someone fainted in the gallery during the death scene) and there was no question but that they were with us all the way. The audience was so good and appreciative that Vivien felt impelled to make a charming curtain speech of thanks to them – a thing she normally does only on the very first and last nights of the season in a city.[46]

Jack also reported on Vivien's condition:

> Her behaviour on this exacting tour has been an object-lesson in deportment in every department. But even more important than that she has remained calm and relaxed and well. I won't say there haven't been flashes of gunfire you wouldn't expect me to, or believe me if I said there hadn't – but she's never brought up the big artillery, and I think she's forgotten how to make the H bomb! You need not worry about her in any way.[47]

To which Vivien added: "Doesn't Jack write the BEST letters?"[48]

Vivien, Jack, and David Dodimead shared a house with a large lemon tree in the garden. Dodimead was a good cook, and this gave Vivien the chance to learn the rudiments of cooking. David Dodimead recalled:

> The most marvelous evening I ever had with Vivien was when we were staying in this bungalow in Auckland, and I went to her room after the show and she said: "Where's the party, Dodders?" I said, "There isn't one tonight." So she said, "All right, we'll make our own. Bring a couple of the boys back and we'll have some games," which often happened. We played silly games and drank and so forth until late. And the boys said, "Oh, we must go." It wasn't a riotous party or anything like that, and Vivien said, "Dodders, run them back in the car." So I ran them back in *the* Rolls-Royce. It was still dark and I thought: "It's matinée day, so I'd better go to bed." Not a bit of it. At the end of the driveway Vivien was standing, in her bathing costume, a bundle under her arm which was my bathing costume and a towel and wrap – and she said "Remember that marvelous little place we saw about seven miles up the coast?" So we went up to this place and we'd taken the car onto the beach, and she said, "Keep the lights on and head out to sea." So we did that, and I got out of the car, Vivien stayed in, and I changed into my bathing costume. And she suddenly looked round and said, "Nobody can see us from here," and I looked round and couldn't see a house or anything, and she said, "I dare you!" And I knew exactly what she meant. I said, "Oh, all right." So we stripped off, and went into the sea and she then did this terrifying, terrifying, thing of swimming straight out – out and out and out, for a long, long way. And I, although I am a very good swimmer, I wasn't going out that far. I waited, and I waited, twenty minutes, twenty-five minutes, which is an awful long time – it seemed like three hours. And then she came in, bright as a button. I had her wrap ready, and

> she wrapped up and we drove home. And as we got to the house she said, "Bacon and eggs!" It was not full daylight. But that's a story of the madness of her – the best madness – and the joy of being with her. She was so alive. The most alive person.[49]

David Dodimead recalled another incident at the bungalow. Vivien was opening her mail and he noticed that she paused a long time with one particular letter. Vivien handed it to him:

> She said, "See what I have to put up with." And it was a sheet of paper, and pinned to it was a photograph cut out of a newspaper of Joan Plowright and Olivier baptizing their first child. And written beneath it the word: "Jealous?"*[50]

Vivien was not expecting such a good reception in New Zealand. Nor was she expecting a proposal of marriage. However, one came and from an unlikely quarter. "We all loved Auckland," she wrote to her sister-in-law, Hester, "In particularly because a sprightly nonagenarian took a shine to me and spoilt me greatly which I thoroughly enjoyed."[51] She was yet more forthcoming to Leigh:

> He seems to own Auckland and is unceasingly kind. Sends lots of gin (which he distills), hams (owns pigs of course), grapefruit (flown from Tahiti), chickens (cooked because he seems to think one's sort of incapable), And calls me "The Girl!"[52]

The nonagenarian was a celebrated figure in Auckland, indeed its mayor from 1935 to 1941, a craggy old multi-millionaire called Sir Ernest Davis. Born 17 February 1872 he joined his father's distilling business, Hancock & Company, straight after leaving school. This he greatly expanded, becoming over the years a celebrated philanthropist, civic administrator, and sportsman. His business activities were wide-ranging and he made numerous extravagant gifts to Auckland, the last of which was a marine light,

*Richard Olivier had been born 1 December 1961.

costing about £30,000, intalled at the entrance to Hauraki Gulf to "enhance the prestige of the port, contribute to maritime safety, and assist the little ships of Auckland, for whom Tiritiri makrs the edge of sanctuary."[53] One New Zealander, Julian Faigan, recalled with horror his Trevor Moss Davis Fountain at Mission Bay: "A most hideous fountain with hidden colored lights. When I was last there the fountain was still in place, and the horrible colors had not changed."[54]

Davis was, in the words of his biographer, "colorful in the sunlight and sinister in the shadows." In the end he was more villain than hero.

He was something of a ladies' man, and in his youth had played hard and loose with many young girls who worked for him. When he died, a Catholic paper wrote that he had surely been received into Abraham's bosom, which many people thought a penance "considering the number of more delicate bosoms from which in younger days he had been reputed to rise."[55]

A noted yachtsman (he owned a yacht called *Alert*), he became New Zealand's leading racehorse owner, his *Arawa* winning the Auckland Cup in 1954. A few years later, in February 1958, his black gelding Bali H'ai III won the St. James's Cup at Trentham, north of Wellington. Queen Elizabeth the Queen Mother was present at the race and, while presenting Sir Ernest his cup, was somewhat taken aback when he seized the microphone and to resounding cheers presented his winner to the Queen Mother, "the greatest lady in the world."[56] On the way down the Queen Mother could hear him muttering: "Shall I?...Can I? No, I can't…I'd better not…perhaps I will..."[57] Bali H'ai came to England in a crate, traveling with a plentiful supply of peppermints. He was Queen Elizabeth's first runner on the flat and won her the Coombe Stakes at Sandown and the Queen Alexandra Stakes at Ascot. In 1961 Bali H'ai retired from the Turf, re-entered his crate and went back to Sir Ernest in New Zealand. Vivien went to see Bali H'ai, feeding him gobstopper peppermints. She asked Sir Ernest how many he ate each day. "Oh, about a bushel,"[58] was the reply.

Davis's generosity, though a tonic to Vivien, was somewhat irksome to Jack. He recalled various expeditions wth Sir Ernest:

> He said he was as blind as a bat, but he could see Vivien all right. He rather annoyed me by ordering me about. Of course he was immensely flattering to Vivien and she rather

> ate it up. We went to have dinner with him one Sunday at some hotel. He said, "Be there at 6:30." Of course Vivien was never very punctual except in her professional life. She was practically always late. We arrived at about three minutes to seven and old Davis was sitting there. He said "Come in quickly. The bar closes at seven and we can't get another drink." Very serious news on a Sunday evening. And he owned the place![59]

On 11 February Vivien reported to Leigh: "My nonagenarian has proposed tho' I think it was a little vague."[60] Vivien did not accept nor, following her departure from New Zealand, did she ever see Sir Ernest again. This was certainly not through neglect on his part. There exist sixteen long letters from Sir Ernest to Gertrude written between March and September in which he made it quite clear that he adored Vivien, that he was aware of a sadness in her soul (the loss of Olivier), and the hint that Jack might be somewhat jealous. Gertrude had suffered her heart attack and Sir Ernest was at once solicitous, recommending anginine tablets. He had had experience with hearts, he wrote. He told Gertrude that his friends had often besought him to write a book but he had no wish to go to jail, he said. He continued to adore Vivien not as an actress but for her womanly qualities. He sent Gertrude two dozen tins of toheroa soup. Then he sent £20 for Suzanne's expected baby. Gertrude said she thought there might be twins. Sir Ernest sent another £20. He sent a case of whisky and gin to Eaton Square, and then a rug for Vivien to take to New York.

Vivien sent him a ring which he cherished. While he continued to love Vivien and this love occupied his thoughts considerably, he was always at pains not to be possessive. He recognized that she had many friends, even sweethearts, and this, he said, he would tolerate – though, frankly, he would prefer to shoot them. In July he almost set sail for Britain. However, the morning that the steamer was due to leave he was suffering from bronchitis and had not heard from Vivien, so he cried off. In the afternoon her letter arrived but he had missed the steamer by six hours and there was not another until October. However, by then he was dead. The vigorous old character died on 16 September, leaving Vivien some valuable shares, to the annoyance of his family.[61]

While Sir Ernest was left with his thoughts of love, Vivien and the company continued their tour to Palmerston North and Wellington before making their way to South America.

They opened in Mexico City, where Vivien had a particular success with her recital, *An Evening of Shakespeare,* introduced into the repertoire by Helpmann to replace *Duel of Angels.* On the first and last nights, Vivien addressed the audiences in Spanish, always a success. They flew via Guatemala to Caracas, where Vivien celebrated the second anniversary of their relationship on 8 April by giving Jack a further gift "in remembrance of a day that changed my whole life. A change for the very best…You have taught me more than you imagine."[62]

From Caracas they progressed to Lima: "We had a most thrilling opening here and tonight is the 'recital' which *kills* me it is so exhausting."[63] After Santiago they took an Easter break at Punta del Este in Uruguay, before facing Buenos Aires. Jack warned Gertrude:

> Tomorrow we go back to work – horrid thought, especially as Buenos Aires is under military law at the moment and the inhabitants of the city are glaring at each other with mutual hostility over barricades in the streets.[64]

In Buenos Aires Vivien had to face a particularly awkward press conference. She was becoming wound up once more, Jack detected the signs, most notably irascibility towards him. One evening after the show, she became angry and threw a precious clock from a fourteenth-floor window. Luckily nobody was hurt but she said later: "That's the worst thing I've ever done."[65]

The first night was no easy matter. Vivien wrote to Leigh:

> All night long during the play rumours reached us that there was fighting in the streets and that the political situation was deteriorating minute by minute…I am utterly stupid about such matters, as you know, and only worry about where the "quick-change room" is and how Trudie is feeling for on such depends the performance.[66]

They then went on to Montevideo and São Paulo, ending the tour in Rio, which Vivien thought "the most wondrous beautiful city."[67] They returned to London via New York on 25 May.

Chapter 24
Tovarich

> *I am really much too old to embark on a musical comedy and it is quite clear to me now that such a thing would never have happened had I not been in the Antipodes and therefore upside down.*
>
> Vivien to Leigh Holman, 19 March 1963

Vivien was only able to enjoy Tickerage life, reunion with family and friends, and with Poo Jones for a period of six months. Jack was constantly with her. Mercia Relph said of him: "He wasn't the host, but he was a very charming host."[1]

A new challenge confronted Vivien as she explained to Barry Norman:

> I only do the things that really interest me, the worthwhile things. The musical, *Tovarich*, which I shall be doing in New York early next year, comes into that category. It may be a terrible disaster. Who knows? Who cares? The only thing that matters to me is that it's worth doing.[2]

Vivien proceeded to take singing and dancing lessons and practiced the guitar. From Tickerage she wrote to Leigh: "The roses are quite wonderful now and I dread November more each day."[3] Olivier was appointed head of the National Theatre, causing an eruption of jealousy from Cecil Beaton in his rose-encrusted bower at Broadchalke. Beaton wrote in his diary:

> The news fills me with resentment and anger…I know perfectly well that Olivier is the most suitable person for the job – any of the other runners up are homosexuals who might at any moment bring shame on the holy shrine and Olivier is in many ways a worthy creature. He adores the theatre and is dedicated to it. Little matter if deep down he is not a very nice person. What does matter is that perhaps he has little intellect and is likely to flounder if he should try to do something in the modern idiom or something experimental.[4]

Marilyn Monroe committed suicide (or so it was thought at the time), inspiring Noël Coward to observe:

> It is sad comment on contemporary values that a beautiful, famous and wealthy young woman of thirty-six should capriciously kill herself for want of a little self-discipline and horse-sense. Judy [Garland]* and Vivien in their different ways are in the same plight. Too much too soon and too little too often.[5]

But, lunching with Vivien at Tickerage soon after, he was reassured: "She was at her tiptop best, calm and wise and pretty and *off* the bottle."[6] Vivien's third grandson, Rupert, was born on 31 August.

In October she was left alone for a short while because Jack flew to California to film *The List of Adrian Messenger*. Jean-Pierre Aumont was a regular visitor, reading the script of *Tovarich* with her. Invariably, he found her stretched out on a chaise-longue, her mood constantly changing. On 12 November Vivien flew to New York, settlng at the Hotel Dorset on West 54th Street.

Vivien's star-role in Tovarich meant a long separation from Jack. From the airplane she wrote: "I do dread all this time without you."[7] A cohort of loving friends awaited her at the airport. Meanwhile, Leigh reassured Gertrude:

*Judy Garland survived suicide attempts before succumbing to an overdose in June 1969.

> Vivien rang me up the day before she left. Although she is anxious about the musical and miserable at leaving it seems to me that she is very well and collected about everything. It can hardly be a greater trial than her tour with the Old Vic. You and she are great ones for doing the impossible.[8]

Tovarich was based on a comedy by Jacques Deval, translated into English by Robert E. Sherwood. Vivien played an exiled Russian Grand Duchess reduced to earning her living as a maid in Paris. Abel Farman, the producer, had been so keen to get her that he had visited her in several places during her world tour to persuade her to take it on. Vivien found the rehearsals difficult and frightening. A musical was a new medium in which she felt she lacked experience. She had to undertake singing practice on certain days, and dancing practice on others. She missed Jack (who presently moved to Sloane Gardens) and she resorted to sleeping pills at night. In constant touch with him by letter and telephone, she wished him to believe that she was not being naughty: "not in the very least, a little bit is the answer, just very late (no drinking – I really am behaving beyond belief, well – you know!)"[9]

From early on there were problems between Vivien and Jean-Pierre Aumont, many of which stemmed from her keeping him up too late at night. He thought her performance too mechanical and unchanging, and in due course he became thoroughly exhausted. But he did his best to cope with his difficult co-star. As time went on Vivien grew lonelier, as she wrote to Jack:

> I do not know which time of the day is the worst without you. Now [after dinner] is just dreadful and waking without you is fearsome and then all during the hours in between life does not seem worth living. I love you and need you.[10]

Rehearsals moved to the Broadway Theater, and Vivien read the script to a genuine Russian Princess "so we can listen to her accent."[11]

Just before Christmas, Trudie Flockert, Vivien's maid, gave Gertrude a report on how Vivien spent her time. She thought her breathtakingly beautiful, working hard, singing and dancing well:

> Today the proper rehearsals started and everybody was a bit tense and nervous, but that is only natural. From now on it is 8 hours of hard work, seven days a week for the next five weeks. But don't worry, your daughter will make it. She is terribly good, restrains herself from doing lots of things she was used to but will help her to tackle this venture. She has cut down on her cigarette consumption by at least 50%. She drinks very very little indeed and she goes to bed early. She sleeps at least eight hours every night and quite often more than that. So you see, she herself is doing everything she possibly can to make this a 100% success.[12]

As 1962 drew to a close, the rehearsals and the conflicting advice were beginning to exhaust Vivien. On Christmas Eve she declared she would not take part in the play. Jean-Pierre Aumont believed that this was because his lines got more laughs than hers. She disliked many aspects of the production, especially a scene in which she was obliged to confess she had been raped by her Russian jailers. She began to become depressed and found it "difficult to get an overall picture."[13] She told Jack: "They keep saying Philadelphia and Boston do not matter but they *do* to me."[14]

Early in 1963 Vivien moved to the Barclay Hotel in Philadelphia, where the musical opened at the Erlanger Theater on 2 January. Vivien enjoyed good reviews and a multitude of enthusiastic curtain calls. Noël Coward came to see it, cabling Jack: "Vivien triumphant. Perfectly enchanting throughout. Book needs fixing. Leading man dicey. First night on the whole enormously successful."[15] In his diary he added, "When she did attempt to sing, in a deep bass-baritone, she got away with it brilliantly. The same cannot be said for the wretched Jean-Pierre Aumont who can't even attempt to sing…[16] Aumont was aghast when Noël proceeded to tell Vivien that on no account must she prostitute herself on Broadway in such a show. He was obliged to invest many hours of reassurance to undo Noël's unsettling verdict.

Vivien's secretary, Kathy Jones, reported to Gertrude:

> Miss Leigh has got thin, but otherwise seems to be standing up to this strenuous work, although I do think she should be

> relieved of a lot she does in the show as she seems to carry the whole thing herself…All the men in the company are in love with Miss Leigh, and all the women with Mr. Aumont, so you can see we have a wonderful company which is completely devoted to both of them, and would lie down and let them walk on them if they wanted to.[17]

At this point Peter Glenville took over as director because Delbert Mann was considered to lack theatrical experience. Glenville effected a great number of changes, which included some upsetting dismissals from the cast. Aumont spent many nocturnal hours discussing aspects of the play with Vivien and wrote later:

> No wonder people who saw me leaving her suite, exhausted, at dawn, assumed that we were having an affair. Certainly we were both in love: she still and forever with Laurence Olivier, and I with Marisa.[18]

Vivien wrote to Jack:

> You know my voice is just *not* up to it. The notices are quite right about that. Neither may I say is J.P.'s. Indeed Noël says his is very much worse!! So you see it is hardly fair on our dear composer! While on the subject of J.P. I assure you there will be absolutely no question of your having to do any separating my beloved. That ludicrous rumour has made me *so* angry. Nothing in the world could be further from the truth.[19]

Vivien longed for Jack to come over but he had to have work and this proved a problem. *Tovarich* broke box office records, taking more than $72,000 in Philadelphia, with audiences fighting for standing room. However, those involved remained convinced that the show was not working. Vivien began to express warning notes: "I am assailed by fear of what would happen if it should turn out to be a failure."[20]

Vivien dreaded the opening in New York, and due to a newspaper strike it was impossible to gauge the general reaction.

Arnold Weissberger, Milton Goldman, and Radie Harris conceived the idea of flying Gertrude over for Vivien's first night in New York as a surprise. Lucinda Ballard Dietz was alarmed by this plan, because Gertrude's presence, particularly at such a difficult musical, was sure to make Vivien additionally nervous. "She is well and comes to the play *every night* and is just as silly and sweet as can be,"[21] reported Vivien. Presently Vivien focused her problems on acting with Aumont: "It is nightmarish acting with dear old J.P. He must be the slowest actor on earth. That, combined with a pseudo Russian-French accent, makes it all v. difficult and much harder work than it need be. I keep hearing myself groan and wonder whether the mikes are picking it up![22]

While America remained silent because of the strike, Vivien received triumphant notices in the English press with front page coverage in the *Evening Standard* and *Evening News*. In April, after Gertrude left and life returned to normal, Vivien took an apartment, 223 East 52nd Street, by which time Jack had secured the part of Algy in *The Importance of Being Earnest* (he was presently promoted to be Ernest opposite the teenaged Mia Farrow). Hearing news of Vivien's Broadway life from Gertrude, Leigh commented: "This is perhaps her last lesson in the art of how not to live."[23]

Having heard all about the incipient problems, Jack was most impressed when he saw *Tovarich*, which made him cry:

> It was something about her quality which was so appealing in its charm, beauty and extraordinary grace. Her movements were always absolutely lovely. The authority and this sense of vulnerability all came from this onc little person.[24]

Jack was soon aware of the exhaustion of her performance:

> She danced and she sang and she was on practically non-stop. She did that showstopper, her dance, of which she was inordinately proud, but at the same time she used to come off absolsutely streaming and had to be toweled down by Trudie before her next number.[25]

Sir David Webster, who ran Covent Garden, confirmed this:

> I've never known an audience so completely at her feet, or more in the hollow of her hand. She had a marvelous and quite electrical animation all the way through that show.[26]

On 28 April Vivien received a Tony for best musical comedy performance by an actress, beating Georgia Brown for Nancy in Lionel Bart's *Oliver:* "I was mighty surprised and delighted."[27] Sam McGredy named a rose after her, declaring, "You are just about the strongest fresh red rose I know and you have a very nice fragrance."[28]

Vivien invariably weekended with the Dietzes. Lucinda Dietz recalled:

> Vivien was the perfect house-guest. I felt she was family, and at the same time she never did any of the basically ghastly things that family members do when they're staying with you. She had trouble sleeping very early in the morning. At Sands Point I would sometimes be having breakfast by the pool at eleven o'clock and Vivien had been all over the place gardening, picking flowers and arranging them.[29]

On 6 August Vivien was in the audience to hear *Fool Britannia*, a brilliant satire on the Profumo scandal, recorded. She wrote to Leigh:

> I am sending you shortly a record that those wicked boys, Anthony Newley, Peter Sellers, and Leslie Bricusse, have made about the present goings on at home. We heard them record it last night, and I have rarely laughed so much in all my life.[30]

Because the play was so well booked, Vivien took no summer holiday. Seeing her early in September, Noël Coward thought her getting near the edge. Jean-Pierre Aumont said: "I suffered by day and Jack suffered by night."[31]

Jack used to observe Vivien's mood changing and could not be sure if she was approaching another high or just drinking too much. The latter he was able to control, talking to Vivien about it and then lacing her Bloody Marys with many sauces but the minimum of vodka (not that she was fooled by this). In due course the promised week's holiday took place and Jack bore her off to stay with Katharine Cornell. When she reopened she began to behave badly on stage, culminating with a matinée on 28 September when, during a love scene with Jean-Pierre Aumont, she stamped on his foot and walked off the stage. Unfortunately, this performance was being watched by Ismail Merchant and James Ivory, who wanted to cast Vivien in a film, but they lost heart when they realized she was ill.

Aumont wrote an account of this episode:

> She began to claw me, slap me in the face, and kick me in the balls. Since it was a quarrel scene I tried to make the audience believe that this boxing exhibition had been planned. It was a bit excessive for a domestic quarrel, but at least the little old ladies who filled the theatre on Saturday afternoon might not find the outburst entirely out of keeping.[32]

Jack took Vivien home. She was restless, and suddenly conceived the notion that, if her New York apartment did not have a garden, her maid Trudie should not have one either. Jack recalled:

> She took a glass and a bottle of brandy and said: "I'm going to see." At that moment I knew absolutely that she couldn't go back. I don't think she actually did any damage to Trudie's flat but she pushed things around. It was a way she had when she wasn't well. Things on the mantelpiece would be moved around with no apparent object in mind.[33]

Jack was unable to get to a telephone to alert the stage manager of these developments and, alas, Vivien was determined to play that night. Back at the theater he told them to put the understudy on half an hour before the curtain. There ensued a horrible scene in which Jack and Kathy restrained her in the dressing-room, while Vivien became increasingly wild and angry.

The Hamish Hamiltons were at the show that night, disappointed not to see Vivien. Hamilton recalled:

> When we went round, Jack said it had been hell, "but for God's sake help me by coming to her flat at eleven." This we did and after keeping us waiting an hour V. turned up with a maid carrying huge bunches of flowers. At first we were treated as if we were non-existent. Drink helped to dispel this and for a short while she was her amusing self. Then the devil took over and she started to pick imaginary dirt from the carpet. Poor Jack said, "It's hopeless now. You had better leave me to it." So reluctantly we left them…[34]

Eventually Dr. Henry Ross came round to sedate her, a situation which worried Jack because of the echoes of California in 1953. It was deemed wise that Vivien should return to England for shock treatment with Dr. Conachy and there was no reason to suppose that after a week Vivien might not be back in the show. Jack continued:

> At some point, when she knew that was going to be done, she said to me, "Are you coming too?" and I said, "No. It doesn't seem worthwhile to pay two air fares." I really thought that Conachy would do the trick. And she went on and said, "Please come back with me," and she really did plead and she said, "If you come back with me, we'll be married at Tickerage on Thursday." I said, "Darling, I would marry you at absolutely any time except at present because you are really not yourself." I suppose I was wrong. But when she was ill like that she wanted somebody close with her – if only to be beastly to them. She used to send for her mother when she felt these things coming on.[35]

Vivien also worried whether Olivier knew about her having to have the injections. A nurse was hired to accompany her home and Jack went to see her off:

> I'm ashamed to say that a feeling of terrible relief came over me. Apart from the fact that if you lose contact with someone you love it's really indescribably difficult. You've got someone physically there whom you adore and yet it's not the same person. It's horrible.[36]

However, Jack felt that she would be in safe hands in London with Dr. Conachy, her mother, Bumble, Cal Darnell (her American secretary), and others. Jack was exhausted. He seized the chance of a few days' respite with Bert McCall, former drama editor of the *New York Herald Tribune*. Then he returned to New York awaiting an appointent with a specialist for his back.

Vivien flew home, again waking on the flight and causing considerable anguish to her custodians. It was another flight home that attracted press interest about her "mystery illness." She arrived at Heathrow, wrapped in blankets, her head covered with a gauze hood. In London Vivien was put into the Avenue Nursing Home in St. John's Wood. She arrived there almost unconscious.

During the first three days Vivien hallucinated, even reliving scenes from *Gone With the Wind* for the benefit of her housekeeper, Mrs. Mac. Vivien's clothes were taken away from her so that she could not run away. The press hung like vultures outside the nursing home, even securing a grim photograph of Vivien when she ran out onto a balcony.

In the time when Vivien had been planning her week in London, she had written to invite Lady Diana Cooper to a buffet lunch at Eaton Square. Diana Cooper related the story to Cecil Beaton:

> Following week there were grizzly accounts of her arrival by stretcher – nobbled and unconscious. The party was called off, and the fresh American male secretary told me she was in a 'home' and suffering from nervous exhaustion. "Where?" I asked, "I must write and send her flowers." "She's not allowed letters, and for the Lord's sake no more flowers. The place is full of them and they're all dying." "In which case," I said, "I'll be round and grab a few for my lunch party."
>
> When I got there they were all hanging their heads past

> reviving but I found a bath full and gathered 2-3 dozen roses. Consciously stealing from the sick, I was uncomfortably surprised by the sec. saying, "Lady Olivier on the phone," and there she was bright as a button saying the nursing home had stolen all her jewels, that she was packed and ready to leave, and they wouldn't let her out and talked of committing her. Calm and coherent she seemed but with fearsome things to tell. A sort of housekeeper there arrived fresh from the bedside to say she couldn't be let out, perhaps the next day with 2 nurses she might return to the flat, but more treatment was essential. "Where are you lunching?" she asked. "At home. That's why I'm pinching yr. roses." "I'll come," she said. My blood froze but I made a noise of welcome. The little round lunch table was already tightly seated and I dreaded Ophelia's entrance, straw in hair. Only the telephone rang with a nurse asking me to speak to her. I persuaded her to say she had spoken to the maid, who'd said there was no lunch here.
>
> Next day I went to see her in the flat. She looked 28, dressed like a little powder-blue velvet pussy cat toy, slim as a sugar plum, trousers and pull-over and becoming Alice in Wonderland hair. She talked of her shock treatments as we talk of an osteopath's manhandling. She told me stories that I didn't believe ascribing them to hallucination. But since then I have proved them all true – how she slapped Jean-Pierre Aumont on the open stage and *walked off,* addressed the audience, told all the cast how abominably they acted. She tells me she will bring that shaming play *Tovarich* to London. It should be a disaster.[37]

At Eaton Square Vivien had a day and night nurse. Dr. Conachy treated her on arrival and again at Eaton Square, but then died suddenly in his Harley Street surgery on 12 November, a serious blow to Vivien's chances of a quick recovery. There were endless telephone calls from friends. Leigh and Suzanne were in attendance. Vivien came to trust and like her new nurse. Because she was an Australian, she called her 'Adelaide.'

Quiet days followed at Tickerage. Adelaide was there to monitor her progress, to see that she did not become too depressed, and to be at hand when Vivien had more ECT at home. Vivien and Adelaide used to go down on odd evenings to the pub, where Vivien would drink a pink gin. Vivien used to say, "Adelaide, if you drink half then I won't feel bad in the morning."[38] On some evenings Vivien would be unable to sleep, so they would walk in the woods or row on the lake in the small hours of the night.

Another who showed concern was Olivier. Adelaide remembered that he used to telephone a lot in the early days and one day he arrived at Tickerage:

> His car pulled up in front of the house and we were up on the first floor bedroom and I said to her: "Oh, he's here. Quick. You'd better go down." And she said, "Oh, no! I can't." And she was like a little schoolgirl and here I was, old enough to be her daughter and I was saying, "Miss Leigh you must go down." And then his voice came up the stairs: "Vivien, are you coming down, or am I coming up?" I nearly ran straight down into his arms – the voice alone. She just took off like a little schoolgirl meeting her boyfriend. Oh, it was beautiful, and they walked by the lake together.[39]

Hester Olivier (now Mrs. St. John Ives) was there on the day when Olivier called. She remembered them sitting together on the sofa as in the times gone by. Only a sharp telephone call from Joan Plowright broke the mood and caused him to return to London. There then came the return of the man described by Adelaide as "the fellow with the camel hair coats."[40]

Jack had remained in America for a week, awaiting the appointment with a doctor for his back. In New York, Bumble Dawson telephoned, summoning him back. Despite his appointment, she said, "You've got to fly home on Monday. Everything is at sixes and sevens here. Vivien's not well and there's nobody here at all. You must fly."[41]

> So I flew back. And Bumble met me at the airport. She said "Oh, you can have my car. It will take you straight

> down there. It's a studio car." I thought that meant it was all paid for. And a chauffeur-driven car was only £10. Well £10 in 1963 was about £50, and I'd only just got it. I mean it emptied my pocket. So I arrived at Tickerage and there were Mrs. Mac, and Cal, two nurses staying there and down in the gardener's cottage was Mrs. Cook. Six people. I was really very cross with Bumble. And Vivien received me coolly because Bumble had told her she had to winkle me out of New York to get me home, which stuck in Vivien's mind for the rest of her life. It was a very, very nasty thing to say to V. In those periods, it was quite extraordinary, she was able to recall distinctly and verbatim. So she never quite forgave me. The combination of that and my not marrying her when she wanted me to. Bumble was dying to drive me away. She wanted to be the boss.[42]

Jack mistrusted Bumble. When he asked Vivien who was coming for the weekend, she invariably replied: "Only Bumble," and on one particularly difficult weekend when Vivien was far from well, Bumble went so far as to say: "And I had a better invitation too."[43]

Vivien continued to run the house during her convalescence. There was a robbery in which some jewelry was stolen. "Things went on," as Jack put it, "in a dull, exciting, dreadful way."[44] Mrs. Mac got tipsy from time to time, Vivien and Jack listened to *Fool Britannia* and tapped out a dymo-tape to Adelaide with a line from it: "We love you more 'an Mandy." Vivien, Jack, Gertrude, and Bumble stayed with Leigh and then he and Daisy came over to Tickerage. Vivien was well enough to take her mother to the theater on 5 December. Vivien told Adelaide how much she admired Joan Collins: "She thought Joan Collins was one of the best things that had ever happened."[45] They spent Christmas and a further weekend with Leigh at Zeals, the latter described by Vivien as "a peaceful respite after all the hurly-burly."[46]

One evening Vivien provoked Jack while he was washing up. He knew he must be restrained but she went too far and he reacted by hitting her over the head with the soapy dish-cloth, so that she was soaked with liquid and shocked into silence:

> Within three days she was sitting on one side of the fireplace with Gertrude and I was sitting on the other side and suddenly and quite miraculously the awful look behind the eyes cleared and I looked at her and she looked at me and I said "Hallo" and she said "Hallo" and I said to Gertrude, "I'm going to church on Sunday." And she said, "Why?" And I said, "Because a miracle has just happened."[47]

Soon after the end of this manic cycle, Jack and Vivien took a happy holiday at the Arnos Vale Beach Hotel in Tobago, returning home on 6 February.

Early in May, Terence Rattigan took Jack and Vivien to see Joe Orton's play, *Entertaining Mr. Sloane,* which Vivien saw as "a funny, rather camp play."[48] In due course she invested in Orton's play, *Loot.*

Soon afterwards, on 12 June, Vivien set off for California to take part in the film, *Ship of Fools.* To Leigh she wrote:

> California fills me with such dread but perhaps it is salutary to do things one does not like![49]

Chapter 25
Ship of Fools

Mary Treadwell (Vivien): Oh, we put up a wonderful front in public. We were everybody's favorite couple. In private it was something else again.

Ship of Fools

Ship of Fools was based on the novel by the American writer Katherine Anne Porter, and was the story of a group of doomed refugees returning to Bremerhaven from Vera Cruz in Mexico in 1933. Katherine Anne Porter had struggled with the novel for over twenty years. When she finally published it in 1962, it attracted considerable acclaim and controversy, not least because as one reviewer put it, the novel had been "awaited through an entire literary generation."[1] The poet Robert Lowell judged: "It is one of the very few American novels (almost unique in this lately) that deserves to be long; the writing is always alert, modest and honest. As for its gloom and grayness, I find them in their way glorious."[2] The book did well, earning about a million dollars from hard-cover sales, and from film and paperback rights. United Artists paid $400,000, outbidding David O. Selznick in April 1962 (a month after the novel came out).

Katherine Anne Porter took considerable interest in the casting. Stanley Kramer would only consider Katharine Hepburn or Vivien. Porter's biographer thought Vivien portrayed Mrs. Treadwell very much as her creator would have been in earlier days, and Kramer was happy to give Vivien latitude in her interpretation.

As depicted in the film, the sea voyage consisted of a series of vignettes, some enjoyable and others a little tedious. For this last film, Vivien attempted to read the book but did not feel that it was vital to her portrayal of the ageing American divorcee, who was placed at table opposite a former baseball player (well played by Lee Marvin) and eventually assaulted by him. Simone Signoret was also in the film and enjoyed many candlelit dinners with Jack and Vivien during their time in Hollywood.

Vivien's voice in the film was in such a low register that it contrasted sharply with her earlier work. Her performance was restrained. Her eyes and lips heavily made-up, she often wore dark glasses or lit a slow cigarette. And then there were the sudden dramatic scenes when she danced – to the Spanish dancers, or alone on the way to her cabin, a drunken Charleston. In the assault scene, Vivien took on the fire of her Scarlett again, defending herself against Lee Marvin with energetic slaps with a slipper. Vivien's lines were as poignant as ever. Asked what Mary Treadwell had wanted in life, she said, "A useful life. Someone to love forever." Of her marriage she said, "I made life hell for him." And Lee Marvin told her: "Behind those old eyes you hide a sixteen-year-old heart."[3]

Vivien flew to Los Angeles on 12 June, sitting next to Ringo Starr. "Miss Leigh wore a floppy hat and Ringo his usual floppy hair-do,"[4] noted the *Los Angeles Times*. Vivien was quoted: "Ringo and I had a marvelous trip together. He is absolutely enchanting. He told me he was on his way to Australia to meet his fellow Beatles," she laughed. "I just can't get used to that name."[5] Jack arrived a little later and they settled at 8918 Thrasher Avenue, off Doheny Drive, a house with a sensational view over Los Angeles. George Cukor and Katharine Hepburn filled it with personal things to make Vivien feel at home. She wrote to Leigh:

> I was wrong as usual! It is perfectly delightful here. Everyone is so very kind and considerate (so there is something to be said for being an elderly actress!). The work is fascinating. I like the director [Stanley Kramer] and the writer [Abby Mann] enormously. My clothes are going to be ravishing and I am enjoying studying the Virginian accent.[6]

Peter S. Feibleman, the American novelist, was an early visitor. He found Vivien looking a bit lost on her terrace:

> "I suppose I'm here," she said, "are you?" I said I wasn't sure. Vivien nodded. "It's hard to tell in Hollywood," she said, "whether you're here or not. Do you think *they're* here?"
>
> She was looking past the terrace at the tiny glittering cars moving through the city below…[7]

Vivien appeared to be upset by something. It transpired that the bright red camellia blooms were all plastic and had been stuck on by hand. "I *know* I'm here now," she said. "I feel lots better. It takes a while to be able to see in a place like this." Feibleman concluded: "She was never quite a part of the landscape she walked through."[8]

From the moment of his arrival, Jack had "a bit of foreboding"[9] about Vivien's health. In July be came alarmed by new "signs of a developing high."[10] He noted that Vivien had only truly emerged from her long period of depression six weeks before. Vivien was giving parties again – for the Jose Greco troupe one night, for the propmen at Columbia the next. The director, Stanley Kramer, thought she was afraid of loneliness and that "alone meant not having fifty people there."[11] Nevertheless, Vivien remained highly professional, learning her lines somehow (Jack never saw her learn them at home) and delivering them faultlessly on the set.

Stanley Kramer was impressed that, like Katharine Hepburn, Vivien could cry exactly on cue nine or ten times if necessary, a rare talent much appreciated by directors. Kramer began by being unsympathetic because Vivien was participating in every aspect of the film, down to wanting an entire set reversed because she had visualized it the other way. Though Kramer agreed, he was irritated to lose three hours of filming. He was also nonplussed when, in the midst of the upheaval, Vivien said very quietly: "Stanley, I can tell you're getting a little irritable, but if you think this kind of modified bitchery is difficult, wait until you hit Katie Hepburn."[12] One day Vivien was taking an undue time with the make-up department, over two-and-a-half hours. Kramer came in and she looked at him piercingly and said, "I…Stanley, I can't do it today."[13] Kramer continued:

> And I knew from the best friend she ever had for a limited

> period, Katharine Hepburn, that she was ill and that she couldn't do it. I'll never forget that look…She was ill, and the courage to go ahead, the courage to make the film – was almost unbelievable.[14]

Katharine Hepburn took Vivien to Dr. Karl von Hagan for two shock treatments in July. Then Gertrude arrived in Hollywood for a fortnight. On 13 August Vivien went reluctantly for a third shock treatment. There were visits to Disneyland and dinner with a great number of stars, "many film actors and actresses I didn't know,"[15] noted Gertrude. After Gertrude returned home, Jack reported:

> Vivien really seems so much better that I don't believe any further treatment will be necessary. One never *quite* knows whether the thing has totally subsided or not but I believe I detect certain signs that it has. It was such a pity that you should have arrived just when she was at her worst and I felt so sorry that after making the long journey to see her you couldn't, as the Americans say "enjoy" her more.[16]

Stanley Kramer brought the film to London for a private showing on 2 May 1965, but Vivien was upset that a vital scene had been cut. At the first preview in New York, Noël Coward said to Radie Harris: "Why does Vivien keep choosing roles that cast her as a rejected, fading beauty?"[17] When the film was released, Dilys Powell wrote that only Vivien relieved its sluggishness: "It is a demonstration of the power of true action."[18] Nor did Alan Dent spare it much toleration, judging that Vivien had too few good lines. Vivien's former scourge, Kenneth Tynan, described *Ship of Fools* as "not *Grand Hotel* afloat, but rather *Grand Hotel* aground in the shallows of Mr. Kramer's imagination."[19] He continued:

> Vivien Leigh, as a waspish American divorcee, has no one to pair off with: deflecting amorous passes with sleek, misanthropic aplomb, she is eventually reduced to addressing herself in the mirror. Within its Shaftesbury Avenue limits, this is a glittering and not over-glamorized

> performance. The most effective pairing, winning by a neck from Miss Leigh and her mirror, is that of Oskar Werner and Simone Signoret.[20]

Vivien and Jack arrived home on 22 September. Jack was feeling a little disconsolate when Vivien celebrated her fifty-first birthday at Zeals:

> A poor present I'm afraid – but comes at a poor time. It is given with my love, in which you seem not to believe, although I promise you it's there. I just wish that it were more commensurate: that it would justify my saying what I want to say, which is that I pray fervently that you will again rejoin me and others who truly love you…I am here when you want me.[21]

While thanking Leigh for a weekend that "seemed to surpass them all," she added, "Jack has now been told he must be in California this Wednesday! Goodness, it is *not* a tranquil existence."[22]

Jack was finally filming *King Rat*, which he had hoped to undertake while Vivien was at work on *Ship of Fools.* Vivien stayed in England for a further eleven days and planning the last minute details for a trip to Nepal and India with the Hamish Hamiltons, ending in Corfu with Roger and Ines Furse. Vivien went to India because she wanted to see the land of her birth. Her doctor sent drugs with her, including libraxin, seconal, seranace, and marplan in case she fell ill. He described her as having been "reasonably well" since her return from Hollywood.

"The first sight of the Himalayas is unfogettable," she wrote to Jack. "Peaks of blue white you think *must* be clouds."[23] She marveled at the sights she saw but was often sleepy as a result of the injections. "This is being a very healthy holiday,"[24] she reported to Jack. At Gwalior they stayed in the Maharanee's Palace, in Delhi they rode on elephants. "The dust is positively Australian and Jamie and Yvonne travel looking like Bobby's Arabian lady! It does not bother me though."[25] Hamish Hamilton recalled the trip:

> In Kathmandu Vivien suffered from the lack of alcohol (her hosts having been warned) and Yvonne found her

> wandering in the small hours lamenting "Is there no booze in this place?", and ending up drinking witch hazel. In Kathmandu no one had heard of *Gone With the Wind*, so no fuss was made. Quite the reverse in Bombay, where the over-weight, seldom-moving hostesses were treated with great courtesy, however boring. Indeed V's manners throughout the Indian trip were excellent. I only saw her irritated once, in Mahabalipuram, when the children were too pressing. Thence to Trivandrum in the south, where we separated. Yvonne said Vivien always preferred to sleep *à trois,* and we felt very unenterprising.[26]

After Vivien died, Hamish Hamilton wrote to Jack:

> I keep thinking with sickening remorse of times when I was short with her, particularly on our Indian trip, and comparing my behavior with Yvonne's saintliness and compassionate understanding. If only one could make amends.[27]

Vivien ended her trip in Corfu with the Furses. She hoped that Jack would join her, but he could not get to Corfu:

> We were supposed to meet there but I discovered that, after federal taxes, my pay-check was about half. I really didn't have enough money to go to Corfu for a few days. Vivien rang Roger's and asked where the hell I was.[28]

On 8 January 1965 Tarquin was married to Riddelle Gibson. The event attracted much press interest due to the presence of Olivier with Jill Esmond, and Vivien with Jack. Joan Plowright stayed in Brighton with her young children. Jack said: "Vivien insisted on going, and Larry begged her not to. He said, "I can't sit in a pew with three wives!!" At the reception I shook his hand and said, "Nearly over, Larry!," and he said, "Oh, God!"[29]

Vivien's next project was the play *La Contessa* by Paul Osborn, based on Maurice Druon's novel *The Film of Memory*. Bobby Helpmann directed and Bumble Dawson designed the costumes. The novel was originally translated by Moura Budberg, who had known the Marchesa Casati* on whom the story was based. Vivien played the Marchesa, disguised in a bright red wig. There were high hopes for this. Leland Hayward wanted to produce it in New York.

The play opened in Newcastle on 6 April, went to Liverpool and Manchester, but no further. Jack was filming, so Vivien was on tour alone. From Newcastle she wrote to Suzanne: "I wish I could tell you that all is well with the play, but it is far from it…It is horrid and lonely up here."[30] Following a mixed reception, there was considerable rewriting. Vivien's eternal problem of looking youthful and beautiful left her miscast as the eccentric septuagenarian Contessa and thus unacceptable to the audience. In Liverpool on 1 May Vivien wrote to Leigh:

> It is indeed extremely depressing about the play and it has been a horrid time but I am sure the decision not to bring it to London is the right one. It is not John Osborne darling…I think J.O. would be very surprised if this particular play were attributed to him.[31]

The summer was spent calmly in London. On 20 October *Ship of Fools* was released. There were worries about Gertrude, who suffered a heart attack on 29 October.

In the New Year of 1966 Vivien and Jack returned to America to play together in *Ivanov,* produced by Alexander H. Cohen. Jack recalled Cohen sinking lower and lower into his chair as the terms required by Vivien's agent were listed and approved:

> Finally he said, "And of course she would like a chauffeur-driven limousine from the time she lands." And Alex said, "I suppose it would be the best thing if she had the same car and same chauffeur," which was very generous. "Now we come to Jack's contract," and Alex said, "Does he want a chauffeur- driven limousine too?"[32]

*A legendary figure in Venice who lived at the Palazzo dei Leoni on the Grand Canal. She once walked through the Piazza with a leopard on a chain. Understandably the crowds parted to let her through.

Vivien played Anna Petrovna. John Gielgud was not only Vivien's co-star (Ivanov); he adapted the play and directed it as well. Jack played Lvov. Gielgud was particularly taken by "the play's changing moods, the cross-currents of farce and drama, the strange assortment of contrasted characters, touching and ridiculous at the same time."[33] The *Boston Herald* recognized this: "What Sir John Gielgud and his company of artists have created is a wonderful evening of vivid comic and character invention. Their ensemble is brilliant."[34]

Roland Culver (Lebedev) recalled that Vivien was 'quite relaxed and well"[35] in all but one of the cities they toured between March and April – New Haven, Boston, Philadelphia, Toronto, and Washington – before opening on Broadway in May. He recalled an evening in Toronto when the hotel caught fire. Though they all greeted this with a certain nonchalance at first, they found that the corridors were full of smoke. The fire was dealt with the same evening, but Vivien and Jack's clothes smelled of smoke for weeks after.

In New Haven Vivien found the audiences enthusiastic. In Washington she relished the multitude of magnolias and the cherry blossoms.

From Vivien's point of view, the play was a sad forerunner to her actual fate, that of the consumptive who dies (to the disappointment of critics and public alike) after Act II. The *Hartford Times* in Connecticut was especially poignant:

> Vivien Leigh, in the role of the Jewish wife who gave up everything for the man she loved, and who now, dying of tuberculosis, watches him fritter away what little love he has left on a young girl, is giving far and away her finest and most mature performance…[36]

The draw of Vivien was followed by the let-down of her short time on stage. In New York the audiences grew gradually smaller, but the play survived its limited two-month season.

While Vivien was in New York, Joan Fontaine was in London. On Milton Goldman's advice, an unfortunate plan was conceived that the two ladies should swap apartments. Both Jack and Radie Harris warned against the wisdom of this, but Vivien was resolute. Her mistake was in thinking that, because Joan Fontaine was Olivia de Havilland's sister, she would be as sweet. Rosemary Kirby (now Mrs. Geddes) was again working for Vivien as secretary (Cal Darnell having gone to Noël Coward). From Toronto Vivien instructed her to count the dresses and suits, list the small ornaments, leave the books in the bedroom, and the dining room and bedroom ornaments. Vivien wrote a card for Joan Fontaine, asked Rosemary to get flowers and to give them to Mrs. Mac to put them in a previously selected case. This good beginning was soon followed by trouble.

Joan Fontaine was particularly sensitve to cats and took a deep dislike to the presence of Poo Jones, whose 'feline proximity' permeated the flat. Contrary to Vivien's express wishes, she sent Mrs. Mac and Poo away. Then she telephoned Vivien to ask if she could use the garage, but Vivien forbade it. Then, when Joan Fontaine returned to New York, she found Vivien still in her apartment, though *Ivanov* had finished. The last straw, according to Miss Fontaine, was when some valuabe watches were found to have been stolen from Eaton Square and she was accused of the theft.[37] Jack was proved right in his forebodings:

> I felt I was being crushed by a nutcracker by these two powerful ladies. When we got back to the flat, it was in a mess and the porter there said that he and Mrs. Mac had spent three days cleaning it up. She had had a party the night before she left…I also remember there was a desk in la Fontaine's apartment on which had been put a vase of flowers that had leaked, and Vivien said, "Oh God, we'll hear about that." I think it just ended with them both hating each other.[38]

After a holiday in St. Vincent and nearby Young Island, Vivien and Jack returned home via New York. They went to the Persian Room of the Plaza to see Vivien's old sparring partner Jean-Pierre Aumont and Marisa Pavan perform their cabaret act. Jack recalled:

> Jean-Pierre introduced her, thinking that Vivien would just stand up and bow. But to my horror she went up to Jean-Pierre and said "How lovely to see you again. Shall we

> do one of our numbers?" And Vivien didn't remember the words at all. Most embarrassing.[39]

On their last night Vivien stayed out very late dancing at the nightclub run by Sybil Christopher (Richard Burton's first wife). The next day there was a dreadful rush to the airport. "You thought I wasn't going to make it, didn't you?"[40] asked Vivien, when they were safely on the airplane. In the summer Leigh sent Vivien a check. She put it on a horse at Goodwood, which won handsomely. Then in August she went to Cap Ferrat in the South of France to stay with her friend Bill More (Kenneth More's ex-wife) and on to Greece without Jack. From Athens she went to Spetses, which she found extremely hot, and then on to Corfu, where she contemplated building a house. Jack said:

> I think she recognized the permanence in our relationship. I remember her announcing at the table at Tickerage: "When I am sixty, Jack and I are going to go and live in Corfu," just like that.[41]

On this holiday, Vivien was alone, but she was looked after by Lady Alexandra Metcalfe and later by the Furses. One day she went onto the Heinzes' yacht where she encountered Lord Lambton. He found her in a slightly pathetic state, drinking too much and foolishly flirtatious.[42] *The Evening News* reported that Vivien had "suddenly fallen ill after attending a party in the Melos district."[43] The overall impression was the sad decline of a lonely, beautiful woman. Jack was alarmed by Vivien's appearance when she came home and summoned the doctor to give her etc. On 8 September Gertrude noted, "Dr. says V. is very ill."[44]

Vivien was awarded the Étoile Crystale, a French 'Oscar,' for her performance in *Ship of Fools* and received it in Paris. Ginette Spanier went to the ceremony with her. She felt that Vivien was alone and neglected and asked Brigitte Bardot, surrounded by admirers, to go over and greet her, but in vain.

Chapter 26
The End

Misha (Ronald Radd): "*Tell me doctor, is Anna Petrovna so ill that she needs to go to the Crimea?*"
Lvov (Jack): "*Yes, tuberculosis.*"
Misha: "Oh, that's bad."

Chekov, *Ivanov*

The year 1967 offered little promise. Vivien was beginning to find difficulty in selecting a suitable part. She read scripts constantly but was disinclined to accept anything that was not worthy of her. She explained to John Gruen:

> What's happening is that roles come few and far between when an actress gets older. In the past and particularly in London, producers, playwrights and directors would think nothing of casting a woman in her 40s or 50s to portray a heroine in her 20s. These days age has become such a factor.[1]

Sometime before she had rejected Edward Albee's *Tiny Alice* as "too obscure,"[2] but she was now prepared to attempt his *A Delicate Balance*, though she told Jack she did not understand it, either. She said to Albee: "Frankly, I don't know what your plays mean." He replied: "In my plays symbols are really cymbals."[3] Vivien thanked him and decided to find her own meanings.

The play was being produced by Toby Rowland, whom she had known since 1949. He and his wife had often sat up late into the night with her when she was enduring her separation from Olivier. He recalled:

> We started to plan the play in December [1966]. We had our first meeting with Vivien and John Dexter and Carl Toms and Bumble. Vivien used to come and talk about the play. Then she got sick and she called me and said, "You won't recast?" And I said, "Of course we won't. We'll postpone." And I really do believe that she thought she was going to get well."[4]

On 8 April Vivien did not forget her seventh 'anniversary' with Jack, writing, "My love for all our years together and all our years to come."[5] For some months there was the additional hope of making Dimitri Tiomkin's film about the life of Tchaikovsky in which Vivien might play his friend, Nadezhda von Meck, with whom he had a long correspondence not unlike that between Shaw and Ellen Terry.

In May Vivien went to Oxford to undertake a reading of *Hazlitt in Florence* in aid of serious flood damage in Florence. The *Oxford Times* wrote that her reading "brought back to the stage after far too long an absence, a sensitve actress."[6] It was her last pubic appearance.

At the end of May Vivien fell ill with what everyone thought was influenza. Rosemary Geddes, her secretary, was at the flat most days. Nobody knew how ill Vivien was and in retrospect it would have been safer if she gone to hospital. This she refused to do and her doctors were anxious to spare her anything that would upset her. Rosemary Geddes recalled:

> She got dreadfully thin and she had this cough and I can remember saying a few times: "Now do you think your old trouble's starting up again?" And she said, "Oh, no, no," because she was terrified of illness. Of course it was and she was ill for quite a while before anybody cottoned on. Until she literally collapsed they thought it was 'flu. Even then she had to get dressed to go down for her chest X-ray

> in Harley Street. Of course when they saw the X-rays and how ill she was, that's when she should have gone to hospital.[7]

Jack recalled:

> She was coughing and she said, "That hurts," so we got Dr. Linnett who came round one day. He diagnosed return of tuberculosis. I didn't take it desperately seriously because I knew she had had it before and she'd been cured before. Or did they tell me quie how bad this was. She really had a patch on her lung the size of my fist.[8]

Jack collected specially prescribed medicine from the chemist, which Vivien did her best to avoid taking. She was ordered to rest in bed, but Jack caught her going about the flat, watering her flowers. "She firmly said: 'I'm allowed to water my plants for an hour every day.' And as she said it I had the feeling that she had made it up. But it was marvelously well done, and it shut me up."[9]

Every other afternoon Vivien rehearsed her Albee play with Michael Redgrave in her room. Toby Rowland came round regularly. He recalled:

> Those last months when we were doing the play were very exciting ones for me, and very sad ones for Vivien. The room was always full of flowers and she always looked beautiful, but there were too many people. She drank and smoked. She had a lot people smoking in her bedroom. She didn't try to get well.[10]

The news of Vivien's illness broke in the press on 9 June. It was announced that the opening of the play would be postponed.

Twelve days later Noël Coward was describing the recurrence of her tuberculosis as "apparently very mild and curable."[11] Vivien was more worried about Olivier, who had been taken to St. Thomas's Hospital with cancer of the prostate. She made frequent enquiries about him, while Gertrude sent him pink carnations. Visitors continued to arrive, as Jack noted:

> As time went on and she got weaker, I tried to ration them. She still went on smoking. I simply couldn't stop her. I had no notion she was going to die. I thought she got weaker because she had been so long in bed. When friends popped in to see her, I said, "Try not to stay longer than ten minutes, quarter of an hour." On the whole they were very good about limiting their time. She had Poo Jones with her, of course.[12]

Lady Richardson commented that many people considered themselves to be Vivien's best friend, without perhaps choosing to recognize that others felt that distinction belonged to them. Similarly many considered that they were the last, or almost the last, person to have seen her alive. Rosemary Geddes cited Coral Browne as one of those who still came to see her. "She used to sit on the bed and talk to her."[13] Coral Browne recalled:

> I saw Vivien the Friday before she died. She complained, "These new drugs are making me feel so ill." I was going to see her again on Monday…You don't expect people to die of consumption these days.[14]

There was a time when Vivien seemed to have re-adopted the role of the *Lady of the Camellias*, drinking, smoking, and entertaining when rest and peace were what she truly needed. On 27 June Noël Coward found her "pale but lovely, and smoking, which she shouldn't have been doing."[15] When Brian and Eleanor Aherne came to see her, Jack urged them to stay only twenty minutes. They were on the point of leaving when the Douglas Fairbankses arrived. "Drinks were called for, and gaiety filled the room," wrote Brian Aherne. "Suddenly she seemed to wilt like a fading flower and quickly we left."[16]

Vivien once told Radie Harris: "I would rather have lived a short life with Larry than face a long one without him."[17] It almost seemed as though she was allowing herself to weaken to a state in which death could take her. Lucinda Dietz was told by her doctor that Vivien suffered from a mild diabetic complaint. Given that Vivien never showed any signs of illness when staying either with them or with Leigh, where regular meals were served, she wondered if a large part of her condition might be attributable to diet. Vivien used to say to Jack, "Why can't I have a nice respectable illness like cancer?"[18] And yet in her last days the telephone calls did not cease, nor the thoughtful cards or gifts she sent out, nor her concern for her friends or her wish for news of them. René, the well-known Mayfair hairdresser, cut her hair short, George Cukor called on her on his visit to London. Gradually her condition worsened.

Gertrude attended a beauty congress in Monaco early in June, noting wryly: "Delia Collins asks me to speak up for her!!!"[19] Returning on 11 June she found Vivien not at all well. She lunched with her on 4 July and departed for St. Andrew's, not unduly concerned, planning to remain in Scotland until 17 July. The end was sudden, as Jack related:

> Then I got a job in a production of *The Last of Mrs. Cheyney* with George Benson, Peter Graves and Vanessa Lee. I got two very good notices in *The Times* and the *Telegraph* and Vivien was overjoyed. She was thrilled that I seemed to have made a success. After every performance I used to ring up Vivien at once after the curtain was down. On the last night, Friday 7 July, her voice by now was rather weak, but she seemed happy, and she was comfortable. I wasn't that worried. I said I'll be home in whatever time it took – at that time of night about 45 minutes. And I belted home and looked in the bedroom and there she was, asleep, with Poo Jones curled up beside her. And I went into the kitchen to make myself some soup out of a tin. I had that, and I went back into the bedroom, and she was lying on the floor. So I tried to wake her, with no result, and then she wasn't breathing so I tried mouth to mouth resuscitation, what I knew of it, and no result whatsoever. Then I was pretty sure she was dead.[20]

Jack rang the doctor, then Bumble and Alan Webb. At about 3 a.m. he called Peter Hiley: "He said he'd be there at nine o'clock. And, being Peter Hiley, he was there at nine o'clock."[21] They finally located Gertrude in Scotland, reaching her at 11:45 a.m.They also telephoned Olivier, who at once checked out of St. Thomas's Hospital and came round. Olivier was still at the flat when Jack was obliged to leave for his matinée at Guildford.

Olivier left an account of his visit in his *Confessions*, which detract considerably from the respect in which he is held. Other statements made by him at this time, which fortunately he had forgotten by 1982, are recorded in private papers and are best left unrepeated. He ended his account: "[Jack] undertook to see to all the funeral and other arrangements as I obviously wasn't in any condition to do much in that line."[22]

Gertrude flew down from Scotland and went to the morgue with Suzanne to see Vivien on Sunday evening. Following a post-mortem, the cause of death was certified as "chronic pulmonary tuberculosis."[23] There was no inquest. The private Catholic funeral was on the following Wednesday at St. Mary's, Cadogan Street. Jack was upset because there was a congregation of strangers who received communion in the middle of the service. The mourners then went to Golders Green at 11 o'clock. Jack told them not to press the button that removes the coffin during the service. "I was the last to leave. I remember standing by the coffin. There were masses and masses of flowers,"[24] he said.

Vivien's death received considerable press coverage. She was described as the eternal Scarlett O'Hara, a legend of stage and screen, the greatest beauty of her time. *The Times* concluded, anonymously:

> Somerset Maugham had hoped to see her play his favorite feminine character, the charming, promiscuous and kind-hearted Rosie Driffield of his own *Cakes and Ale,* and had encouraged her to play Bathsheba Everdene, the innocently vain and unstable heroine of Hardy's *Far from the Madding Crowd*, but in fact neither of those promising projects for films was carried out. It might almost be said that the roles she did not play and the opportunities that now lay behind her gathered about her lately to form an aura peculiarly her own; but if so, it was an aura surrounding a beautiful woman whose strong character, humour and wit, love of works of art and delight in their collection, had all been proved and were well-known.[25]

On the Saturday evening, London's theaters paid Vivien their highest tribute by switching off their outside lights for an hour at 10 p.m. A fan wrote on the pillar of 54 Eaton Square: "Great actress for ever and ever. We vote you the young at heart and a true beauty."[26]

Then there was another death, that of Cecil Tennant, Vivien's agent. He died when his E-type Jaguar crashed at Chertsey, returning from the funeral. Irina Tennant recalled that once, many years before, he had complained of Vivien's overspeeding and she had replied: "Cecil, I will take you with me when I go."[27] After Vivien's death he told the press: "She was a marvelous actress and a marvelous friend."[28]

Many wrote to Gertrude, foremost among them John Gielgud:

> You know how I loved Vivien. Her passing is unbelievable and tragic, and she will leave an irreplaceable gap amongst the very small circle of my intimate friends besides the hundreds of devoted admirers who adored her both as an actress and a woman.[29]

Mills Martin, her childhood friend, thought: "Her life was extraordinarily rich and varied. She lived in her fifty years what other people might in ten lives."[30] Leigh's sister, Dorothy, gave her opinion: "I thought she was much the loveliest and must uncommon actress on the stage. All others seemed so common and ordinary beside her."[31] Jeanne de Casalis's widower, Steve, shared Gertrude's sorrow: "Please believe that I not only sympathize, I also suffer with you at your great loss."[32]

Requiem masses were arranged in New York by Paula Laurence (Lebedev's wife in *Ivanov*) and on Staten Island by Radie Harris and Ted Tenley. Gertrude attended another arranged by Christopher and Camilla Sykes, when staying with Leigh at Zeals.

Later, one of her fans, Ivy Pugh, a more reasoned fan than most, sent a long letter to Gertrude, which ended: "We kept in touch with her wherever she went in the world, for more than twenty years…though the rest of the world may forget, we never shall, we loved her."[33]

Others wrote to Jack. Tennessee Williams judged: "She was a definition of loveliness as a woman and artist."[34] Rachel Kempson wrote to Jack:

> Thank heaven she has had you all these years and during

> this illness. I don't know what to say except that she keeps appearing in my mind and the picture is young and beautiful and always will be.[35]

David Niven had suffered a similar loss in the 1940s. "I am so terribly sorry for you…I know only too well that there is nothing to say."[36] So, later had Rex Harrison: "You have at least a tiny compensation, as I had with Kate, that it was a guardianship of great worth, in the Eliot sense."[37] John Gliddon reminded Jack: "It was 23 years ago when I first met Vivien and was able to help her to become a star in record time."[38] Cathleen Nesbitt was staying with the Dietzes: "I think it would have been Vivien's choice to go quickly, while life looked good."[39]

Katharine Hepburn's letter was one savored by Jack:

> Devotion is a rare quality and even I personally used to rest more easily about Viv because she had you. I knew that you would stick. I think she bothered all her friends, but you were the one who delivered the goods – and really enabled her to go on as long as she did.[40]

So too, that of Simone Signoret:

> I will miss her, her laughs and her screams, her humour and her toughness and her tenderness.[41]

Lady Diana Cooper applied her customary perception:

> Condolence is sent for comfort, but there is no comfort to be sought when something so exquisite and brilliant and unique as Vivien is torn away from you. I think of all her demanding roles that the most difficult was her own life's part and but for you and yr. love and dedication and yr. goodness she would not, these last years, have been able to play it with such strength, courage and gaity…Poor valiant little heroine.[42]

Sunny Lash, Vivien's American secretary, considered:

> She was delicate but she was also dynamic…For Vivien to have left us while she was still young and beautiful I'm sure must have been the way she wanted it. I remember when she was ill how much she disliked "old ladies" as she would call them jokingly…When I first learned of her death I went to the little house on Crescent Drive where we first lived together. I sat their quietly in my car from 9 until 10 p.m. in silent prayer and with tears of both joy and sorrow.[43]

Jack had opened in *The Last of Mrs. Cheyney* at the Phoenix Theatre on Saturday 13 July. He replied to the three hundred or so letters: "I shed no tears for, I think, about three months. I answered all the letters, but I could do no more than about five a day because it got rather wearing."[44]

In an interview Peter Finch was quoted:

> I remember her most now – walking like an eager boy through temples in Ceylon – walking in the wind near Notley. I always see her hurrying through life. I miss the fact that she is not somewhere in London or Greece or New York, among her friends, talking volumes – with those bright eyes always in laughter.[45]

A Memorial Service was held at St. Martin's-in-the-Fields on 14 August, and attended by numerous stars and old friends. John Clements read the lesson, there were readings by Emlyn Williams and Rachel Kempson. Sir John Gielgud gave the address:

> To talk of Vivien Leigh in public so soon after her death is almost unbearably difficult for me…What seems to me most remarkable, as far as her career was concerned, was her steady determination to be a fine stage actress, to make her career in the living theatre, when, with her natural beauty, skill, and grace of movement, gifts which were of course

> invaluable in helping to create the magic of her personality, she could so easily have stayed aloof and supreme in her unique position as a screen actress.[46]

Jack said: "Johnny's very close to tears at anything sentimental, and I was afraid he wasn't going to get through it, he got so moved. But, being a great actor, he could carry it.[47]

The congregation was led by Gertrude, and by Suzanne and Robin with their three boys. Jack was there, so too was Leigh, and Olivier arrived quietly with Ginette Spanier. Jill Esmond also attended the service, unrecognized at first by Olivier. Of all the accounts of the service, Gertrude especially liked the *South Wales Echo,* which wrote:

> Tears mingled with the rain as great names of stage and screen gathered to say their final goodbyes to one of the loveliest and most talented actresses of our time.[48]

Postscript

Vivien's ashes were scattered on the lake at Tickerage on Sunday, 8 October 1967. In due course Gertrude presented a memorial bench to the gardens at Eaton Square and a plaque was placed in the actor's church, St. Paul's, Covent Garden. Seeing it proved one of the most spontaneously moving moments for Helen Hanff on her pilgrimage to London to visit 84 Charing Cross Road: "Just inside the door as I was leaving I came upon the most recent plaque, VIVIEN LEIGH D.1967, and was suddenly moved to tears."[1]

Not long after Vivien's death, Gertrude and Jack received letters from Consuelo Langton-Lockton, Tony Bushell's friend, who had cast Vivien's horoscope as early as 1938. She was anxious to "expose herself" as a channel for any message that Vivien's spirit might wish to convey from across the divide. 'Martha' therefore contacted a medium on the coast near Bexhill, where she lived. Evidently a number of friendly spirits wished to make their presence known before Vivien came through. The medium reported:

> She is very indistinct – She is very tired – *very* tired – she is absolutely *exhausted* – she tries to wake, but cannot – she floats as on a river which bears her up – *very, very* tired.[2]

The medium said that the spirit is anxious that nobody should think that she committed suicide. She was upset about this, and equally upset to find herself cut off from those she loved. As she "passed through the veil," she had felt a great weight on her chest and then a sharp and piercing pain near her heart and the end had come. Jack and Leigh, at Tickerage together, thought it very like Vivien to mind being isolated.

Two weeks later there was another session, during which 'the spirit' again returned, recalling a terrible party at Tickerage at which 'Martha' had arranged a surprise by having a village band come out to play for her. Vivien evidently thought that the surprise was going to be Olivier, and burst into sobs while the band crept away. 'Martha' experimented with another medium, and Vivien again returned to her. This proved a highly emotional session during which she continually asked how Larry was. 'Martha' realized that it was Olivier who was drawing her back to earth. She was begging for forgiveness and wanted Olivier to know she loved him still. 'Martha' concluded:

> If he should 'go,' she will be waiting. Love is stronger than death – and things get sorted out on that side. Thank God.[3]

On 17 March 1968 there was a lengthy memorial evening at the University of Southern California in downtown Los Angeles, entitled "An Appreciation of Vivien Leigh." Numerous stars took part, including Dame Judith Anderson, Dame Gladys Cooper, Greer Garson, and Wilfrid Hyde White. George Cukor wrote to Gertrude describing it as "a most moving and impressive occasion…an outpouring of love."[4] He continued:

> An added thrill for the audience was when it was announced that they were to see the tests for *Gone with the Wind* that I'd made in 1938. I hadn't seen them myself since then. They were electrifying. It was quite obvious why this accomplished, exciting and beautiful creature got the part – it couldn't have been otherwise.[5]

Hollywood being Hollywood, the proceeding required a touch of levity. Cukor added:

> I was busy giving instructions and signals when, much to my surprise, my chair slipped from under me and with a great clatter and noise, I landed on the floor. There was a moment of concern for my well being – a rather short one. When it was established that I hadn't broken any bones,

> there were many ribald and disrespectful remarks from my colleagues and from certain parts of the audience. Somehow I had a feeling that Vivien joined in the laughter.[6]

In due course a booklet was produced. Vivien was often described in Charmian's words from *Antony and Cleopatra*, "A lass unparallel'd."[7]

Tickerage was burgled soon after Vivien's death. The Farringtons were down there from time to time with Gertrude and the children, and then the Mill was sold. Poo Jones stayed with Mrs. Mac, who went back to her former employer, Peter Hiley. Poo outlived Mrs. Mac, ending his days with the Hileys.

Gertrude was heart-broken by Vivien's death. She was seventy-eight when Vivien died and had sold her beauty business in January 1964. Her sister, Aggie, died later in 1967, severing another link. Gertrude remained close to Suzanne and to Leigh, always spending Christmas with them at Zeals. She derived great pleasure from her three great-grandchildren and was considerably fortified by frequent attendance at Mass. She continued to travel and to be interested in anything connected with her daughter. "Watched my Vivien in *Waterloo Bridge,*" she recorded in February 1968. "Felt so heartbroken."[8] Gertrude celebrated her eightieth birthday in December 1968. She suffered occasional mild heart attacks as the years passed and a bout of pneumonia at the beginning of 1972. Elegant to the last, she outlived Vivien by five years, dying in hospital on 9 August 1972 in her eighty-fourth year.

Noël Coward died in Jamaica on 26 March 1973, and Bumble Dawson died suddenly while staying with George Howard at Castle Howard on Good Friday, 16 April 1976. Peter Finch died in the lobby of the Beverly Hills Hotel on 14 Janaury 1977.

Leigh Holman lived on at Zeals for some years. For a long time he was able to enjoy a round of golf and a game of croquet. Towards the end of his life he was visited by Hugh Roberts, then a representative of Christie's, who happened to notice a photograph of Vivien Leigh in his drawing-room. He thought it surprising that the old gentleman should be a fan of this star. He was still more surprised when Leigh said he had once been married to her. In 1980 Leigh moved to Highfield, a smaller house, in Mere. Daisy, faithful to the end, moved with him. Having kept cancer at bay for many years, he died there at the age of eighty-one on 8 February 1982. Zeals was taken on by Suzanne and Robin.

Jack remained at Eaton Square until October, sleeping on the long sofa in the drawing-room. One day Peter Hiley telephoned and said that Vivien had left him £6,000 in her will. "I was so moved I couldn't talk to him. I put the phone down."[9] Jack then went to house-sit for his stepmother, Gladys Cooper, at Barn Elms. He used to drive her to the Phoenix Theatre, where she was playing in *Let's All Go Down the Strand*. While waiting he would often take a drink with Hugh Williams. Here he met Dinah Sheridan:

> Sometimes, round the corner, behind the door, there would be Dinah. And she later confessed that this was because she thought I was some sort of zombie. Sometimes I would say hallo and sometimes I would ignore her.[10]

Jack and Dinah acted together at Guildford in *Robert's Wife* in May 1968. Like Jack, she had recently lost a lover. They were both in somewhat the same predicament. Dinah Sheridan found that the presence of Vivien lay heavily on Jack at first, almost threatening the relationship, not helped in the early days by the re-release of *Gone With the Wind* and the frequent renderings on radio of the film's theme. Gradually, however, this mattered less. They shared their lives and in 1986 she became Jack's wife. They remained happily married until Jack's death on 6 February 1990.

Olivier went from strength to strength, exploring several new careers, delighting in his growing family. He became a Life Peer in 1970 and a member of the Order of Merit in 1981. He undertook notable televison roles, crowning a long Shakespearian career with *King Lear* for Granada in 1983. He fought off illness in the most remarkable way. He was once so ill that a friend said, "It was almost as though he was a dead man, acting being alive."[11] Olivier portrayed Lord Marchmain in *Brideshead Revisited* and John Mortimer's father in *A Voyage Round My Father*. In both of these he played dying men, and said that he hoped that when the real moment of death came, he would carry off the scene as proficiently.

A visitor to Olivier's Steyning home in 1986, found the old actor watching a Vivien Leigh movie on televisioin. He sat there with tears in his eyes, saying: "This, this was love. This was the real thing."[12]

Lord Olivier died, aged eighty-two, on 11 July 1989 and his ashes were placed in Westminster Abbey.

Notes

SFP = Suzanne Farrington Papers
CBP = Cecil Beaton Papers

CHAPTER ONE

1. Vivien Leigh interview, *What Success has Taught Me* (1950s article)
2. John Merivale to author, 30 November 1986
3. Selznick, *Memo from: David O. Selznick*. D.O.S. to E.S., 7 January 1939, 186
4. *Bridlington Free Press,* 30 November 1929
5. Mrs. Sykes to author, October 1987
6. *The King's England, Yorkshire*, ed. Arthur Mee, 108
7. A. E. Kibblewhite to Mrs. Hartley, 20 December 1959 (SFP)
8. *Ibid.*
9. Mrs. Frances Martin to author, 19 October 1987
10. Rumer Godden to author, 10 June 1987
11. Mrs. J. Tayler to Mrs. Hartley, 4 April 1963 (SFP)
12. Mrs. Frances Martin to author, 19 October 1987
13. Hugh Martin to author, 9 November 1987
14. Lord Hardinge of Penshurst, *My Indian Years 1910-16*, 37
15. *The Hill of Devi*, E.M. Forster, ed. Elizabeth Heine, 181
16. Hardinge, *My Indian Years,* 77
17. Hardinge, *My Indian Years*, 88
18. John & Rumer Godden, *Two Under the Indian Sun*, 161
19. Rumer Godden to author, 10 June 1987
20. V.L. interview, *What Success has Taught Me*

CHAPTER TWO

1. Late Ian Thomson to author, 10 June 1987
2. *Ibid.*, 15 June 1987
3. Elizabeth Thomson to author, 9 June 1987

4. Mrs. Frances Martin to author, 19 October 1987
5. *Ibid.*
6. Late Ian Thomson to author, 10 June 1987
7. *Ibid.*, 15 June 1987
8. Mrs. Frances Martin to author, 19 October 1987
9. Mrs. Hartley diary, 26 September 1920 (SFP)
10. Dulcie Gray to author, 2 February 1987
11. Sir Alec Guinness to author, 18 March 1987
12. Antonia White, *Frost in May*, 86
13. White, *Frost in May*, (Introduction by Elizabeth Bowen, p. vii)
14. *Ibid.,* 100
15. *Ibid.*, 99
16. *Ibid.,* Introduction, x
17. Anne Edwards*, Vivien Leigh,* 24-25
18. V.L. To Leigh Holman (L.H.), 24 January 1944 (SFP)
19. V.L. interview, *What Success has Taught Me*
20. Desert Island Discs (Castaway no. 152) 9 September 1952, *Desert Island Lists*, Roy Plomley (Hutchinson, 1984)
21. Mrs. Hartley diary, 17 March 1925 (SFP)
22. *Ibid.*, 30 March 1925 (SFP)
23. I*bid.*
24. *Ibid.*, 24 May 1925 (SFP)
25. Alan Dent*, Vivien Leigh: A Bouquet*, 43
26. *Ibid.*
27. *Ibid.*, 45
28. V.L. to L.H., 16 August 1932 (SFP)
29. V.L. interview, *What Success has Taught Me*
30. Mrs. Hartley diary, 10 September 1926 (SFP)
31. Dent, *Bouquet*, 48
32. Mrs. Davis Glass to author
33. Lady Lambert to author, 6 April 1988
34. Thomas Kiernan*, Larry Olivier,* 119
35. Mrs. Frances Martin to author, 19 October 1987

CHAPTER THREE

1. Guthrie Watson-Williams to Mrs. Hartley, 30 November 1922 (SFP)
2. G. E. Kingston to Mrs. Hartley, 14 August 1924 (SFP)
3. Henry Musgrave to Mrs. Hartley, 4 February 1923 (SFP)
4. *Ibid.*, 5 February 1923 (SFP)
5. *Ibid.*, 2 February 1924 (SFP)
6. Laurence Olivier (L.O.) to Mrs. Hartley, 22 December 1959 (SFP)
7. Lady Lambert to author, 6 April 1988
8. Late Ian Thomson to author, 15 June 1987

9. *Bridlington Free Press*, 30 November 1929
10. Mrs. John Hodges to author, 25 May 1987
11. V.L. interview, *What Success has Taught Me*
12. John Merivale to author, 4 May 1988
13. Radie Harris, *Radie's World*, 176
14. V.L. to L.H., 10 March 1932 (SFP)

CHAPTER FOUR

1. Kiernan, *Sir Larry,* 121
2. V.L. to Jane Glass, 12 January 1932
3. Mrs. Frances Martin to author, 19 October 1987
4. Oswald Frewen, *Sailor's Soliloquy*, Concluding Note by Leigh Holman, 245
5. *The Times*, 9 December 1958
6. Oswald Frewen diary, 20 October 1924
7. *Sailor's Soliloquy*, 246
8. Oswald Frewen diary, 28 May 1925
9. *Ibid.*, 4 August 1925
10. *Ibid.*, 9 August 1925
11. *Ibid.*, 6 December 1925
12. Anita Leslie, *Cousin Clare*, 227
13. Oswald Frewen diary, 25 May 1927
14. *Ibid.*, 17 March 1929
15. *Ibid.,* 26 April 1927
16. Late Hamish Hamilton to author, 2 November 1986
17. *Ibid.*, 19 October 1986
18. *Ibid.*
19. Mrs. John Hodges to author, 25 May 1987
20. V.L. to L.H., 4 March 1932 (SFP)
21. V.L. to Jane Glass, 9 February 1932 (SFP)
22. V.L. to L.H., 13 March 1932 (SFP)
23. *Ibid.*, 27 February 1932 (SFP)
24. *Ibid.,* 4 March 1932 (SFP)
25. *Ibid.*, 13 March 1932 (SFP)
26. *Ibid.*, 28 March 1932 (SFP)
27. *Ibid.,* 20 April 1932 (SFP)
28. *Ibid.*
29. *Ibid.,* 19 August 1932 (SFP)
30. *Ibid.*
31. Oswald Frewen diary, 3 February 1949
32. *Ibid.*
33. V.L. to Jane Glass, 7 July 1932
34. *Ibid.*, 6 August 1932 (SFP)

35. *Ibid.*
36. *Ibid.,* 25 August 1932 (SFP)
37. *Ibid.,* 19 August 1932 (SFP)
38. *Ibid.*
39. V.L. to Jane Glass, 3 December 1932
40. Miscellaneous press cutting in album (SFP)
41. Gwen Robyns, *Light of a Star*, 22
42. *Ibid.*, 23
43. Mrs. Hartley diary, 20 December 1932 (SFP)
44. Mrs. Hartley, note in album (SFP)
45. V.L. to Mr. and Mrs. Hartley, December 1932
46. V.L. to Jane Glass, 12 January 1933
47. Oswald Frewen diary, 3 February 1949
48. V.L. to L.H., 2 February 1933 (SFP)
49. *Ibid.*, 3 February 1933 (SFP)
50. *Ibid.*, (Tuesday), postmarked 16 August 1933 (SFP)
51. *Ibid.*
52. *Ibid.*
53. Xan Fielding to author, 8 June 1987
54. *Good Housekeeping Magazine,* undated
55. Mrs. Hartley diary, 12 October 1933 (SFP)
56. V.L. to Jane Glass, October 1933
57. Jack Thomson to Gertrude Hartley, 15 October 1933 (SFP)
58. Mrs. Hartley diary, 31 December 1933 (SFP)
59. V.L. interview, *What Success has Taught Me*

CHAPTER FIVE

1. Mrs. Frances Martin to author, 19 October 1987
2. Fabia Drake to author, 10 February 1987
3. L.H. to V.L., 11 August 1934 (SFP)
4. *Ibid.*, 15 August 1934
5. V.L. to L.H., (Monday) postmarked 13 August 1934 (SFP)
6. *Ibid.,* (Wednesday) postmarked 15 August 1934 (SFP)
7. *Ibid.*, The Little House, Monday 20 August) postmarked 21 August 1934 (SFP)
8. Anne Edwards, *Vivien Leigh,* 40
9. Dent, *Bouquet*, 108
10. John Gliddon, unpublished manuscript, *A Tribute to a Legend*
11. *Ibid.*
12. H.W. Austin to author, 24 November 1986
13. Oswald Frewen diary, 26 September 1944
14. Coral Browne to author, 30 January 1986
15. John Cottrell, *Laurence Olivier*, 109

16. Oswald Frewen diary, 12 December 1934
17. Gliddon, *Tribute*
18. *The Times*, 26 February 1935
19. V.L. Interview, *What Success has Taught Me*
20. *The Times*, 26 February 1935
21. Oswald Frewen diary, 27 February 1935
22. Kiernan, *Sir Larry,* p. 125 (*London Evening News*, 13 May 1947)
23. Diana Churchill to author, 27 February 1988
24. Oswald Frewen diary, 27 March 1935
25. Late Hamish Hamilton to author, 19 October 1986
26. Gliddon, *Tribute*
27. Oswald Frewen diary, 19 Marcy 1935
28. Basil Dean, *Mind's Eye*, 207
29. Gracie Fields, *Sing As We Go* (Frederick Muller, 1960), 101
30. Robyns, *Light of a Star*, 33
31. Gliddon, *Tribute*
32. *Ibid.*
33. *Ibid.*
34. Robyns, *Light of a Star,* 43
35. V.L. interview, *What Success has Taught Me*
36. V.L. to David Lewin, *Daily Express*, 17 August 1960
37. V.L. interview, *What Success has Taught Me*

CHAPTER SIX

1. Dent, *Bouquet,* 95
2. Felix Barker, *The Oliviers,* 100
3. *Ibid.*, 102
4. *The Times*, 16 May 1935, Alan Dent, 144
5. Barker, *The Oliviers,* 102
6. *Daily Telegraph*, 23 May 1935
7. Dollie to Mr. & Mrs. Hartley, Sunday 19 May 1935 (SFP)
8. Gliddon, *Tribute*
9. Late Hamish Hamilton to author, 19 October 1986
10. Gliddon, *Tribute*
11. *Ibid.*
12. Oswald Frewen diary, 19 May 1935
13. John Gliddon to author, 16 April 1986
14. Oswald Frewen diary, 10 June 1935, Alan Dent, 25
15. *Ibid.,* 19 and 26 May 1935
16. *Ibid.*
17. *Ibid.*, 10 June 1935
18. Fabia Drake to author, 10 February 1987
19. Dent, *Bouquet*, 60

20. *Ibid.*, 55
21. *Ibid.*, 62
22. Robyns, *Light of a Star,* 34
23. *Ibid.*
24. *Daily Express*, 27 August 1957
25. Jeanne de Casalis, *Things I Don't Remember*, 26-7
26. V.L. To L.H., Saturday or Sunday (postmarked 1 August 1935) (SFP)
27. *Ibid.*, Monday, (postmarked 1 August 1935) (SFP)
28. *Vivien Leigh, An Appreciation*, University of Southern California, 17 March 1968, Friends of the Libraries, 1969
29. Daisy Goguel to author, 7 April 1988
30. V.L. to L.H., 15 August 1935 (SFP)
31. Mrs. Sally Hardy to author, 8 December 1987
32. V.L. to L.H., p.m. 15 August 1935 (SFP)
33. Oswald Frewen diary, 19 August 1935
34. John Gliddon to author, 15 April 1986
35. Laurence Olivier, *Confessions of an Actor*, 77
36. Cottrell, *Olivier,* 115
37. Olivier, *Confessions,* 77-8
38. Fabia Drake to author, 10 February 1987
39. Dent, *Bouquet,* 88-9
40. Barker, *The Oliviers,* 107
41. Dent, *Bouquet,* 96
42. John Gielgud, *Distinguished Company,* Memorial Service address, August 1967, 70
43. Dent, *Bouquet,* 96
44. *The Times*, 18 February 1936
45. Michael Denison to author, 2 February 1987
46. V.L. to L.H., 11 February 1936 (SFP)
47. *The Times,* 18 February 1936
48. David Cecil, *Max*, 150
49. V.L. to L.H., 10 March 1936 (SFP)
50. *Ibid.*
51. *Ibid.*, 27 March 1936 (SFP)
52. *Ibid.*
53. *Ibid.,* 26 March 1936 (SFP)
54. *Ibid.*
55. *Ibid.,* Manchester 1 April 1936 (SFP)
56. Dent, *Bouquet,* 74
57. John Merivale to author, 14 November 1987
58. Cecil, *Max,* 436
59. Barker, *The Oliviers,* 109
60. Dent, *Bouquet,* 12-13
61. W. Macqueen-Pope, *Ivor, The Story of an Achievement*, 355
62. Barker, *The Oliviers,* 109
63. *Ibid.*

CHAPTER SEVEN

1. Late Esmond Knight to author, 11 February 1988
2. Olivier, *Confessions,* 50
3. *Ibid.*, 61
4. *Harold Nicolson Diaries & Letters, 1930*-39, 10 July 1930, 52
5. Fairbanks to Melvyn Bragg, South Bank Show Profile of Olivier
6. Irene Mayer Selznick, *A Private View*, 180
7. Late Esmond Knight to author, 11 February 1987
8. Olivier, *Confessions,* 78
9. *Ibid.*
10. *Ibid.*
11. *Ibid.*
12. *Ibid.*
13. Janet Dunbar, *Flora Robson*, 193-9
14. Frank Evans column, miscellaneous press cutting (SFP)
15. V.L. to L.H., 10 August 1936 (SFP)
16. *Ibid.*
17. *Ibid.*
18. Cottrell, *Laurence Olivier,* 117
19. V.L. to L.H., postmarked 17 August 1936 (SFP)
20. *Ibid.*, 19 August 1936 (SFP)
21. *Ibid.*, 21 August 1936 (SFP)
22. *Ibid.,* 26 August 1936 (SFP)
23. Kiernan, *Sir Larry,* 137
24. Godfrey Winn, *The Positive Hour*, 397
25. V.L. to L.H., 31 August 1936 (SFP)
26. Oswald Frewen diary, 31 August 1936
27. *Ibid.*
28. *Ibid.*
29. *Ibid.*
30. V.L. to L.H., 1 September 1926 (SFP)
31. Godfrey Winn, *The Positive Hour,* 82
32. *Ibid.*
33. *News Chronicle*, 27 March 1937
34. V.L. to Frank Evans – miscellaneous cutting (SFP)
35. *Sunday Times*, 28 March 1937
36. Oswald Frewen diary, 25 October 1936 (written 17 December 1936)
37. *Ibid.*
38. V.L. to L.H., Taormina 29 October 1936 (SFP)
39. *Ibid.,* 27 October 1936 (SFP)
40. Oswald Frewen diary, 31 October 1936 (written 12 January 1937)
41. V.L. to L.H., Quisisana et Grand Hotel, Capri 2 November 1936 (SFP)
42. Oswald Frewen diary, 25 October 1936 (written 17 December 1936)
43. *Ibid.*

44. *Ibid.*, 3 November 1936 (written 13 January 1937)
45. *Ibid.*, 28 June 1937
46. Rex Harrison, *Rex, An Autobiography,* 52
47. *Ibid.,* p. 51
48. Oswald Frewen diary, 19 January 1937
49. *Ibid.*, 23 March 1937
50. *Ibid.,* 19 January 1937
51. *Ibid.*, 27 January 1937
52. *Ibid.,* 29 January 1937
53. *Evening Standard*, 27 February 1937
54. Miscellaneous press cutting, February 1937 (SFP)
55. Miscellaneous press cutting, March/April 1937 (SFP)
56. *Manchester Evening News*, 5 February 1937
57. *Observer*, 6 June 1937
58. Oswald Frewen diary, 11 February 1937
59. V.L. to L.H. (then in Exeter), 31 March 1937 (SFP)
60. Oswald Frewen diary, postscript to 3 March 1937 (written 5 September 1937)
61. *Memo from: David O. Selznick,* op. cit., D.S. to Katharine Brown 3 February 1937, 149
62. Basil Dean, *Mind's Eye,* 251
63. Oswald Frewen diary, 12 April 1937
64. *Ibid.,* 28 June 1937

CHAPTER EIGHT

1. Kiernan, *Sir Larry,* 139
2. *Ibid.*
3. *Ibid.,* p. 144
4. *Ibid.*
5. V.L. to L.H., 30 May 1937 (SFP)
6. Cottrell, *Laurence Olivier*, 131
7. Lady Diana Cooper, *The Light of Common Day* 194
8. Georgiana Blakiston, *Letters of Conrad Russell*, 147
9. Lady Diana Cooper anecdote, recalled by Artemis Cooper, 6 October 1987
10. Dent, *Bouquet*, 84
11. Barker, *The Oliviers,* 130
12. Olivier, *Confessions,* 78
13. Sir Alec Guinness to author, 18 March 1986
14. Kiernan, *Sir Larry,* 151
15. Daisy Goguel to author, 7 April 1988
16. L.H. to Mrs. Hartley, 20 May 1959 (SFP)
17. V.L. to L.H., 19 July 1937 (SFP)

18. Oswald Frewen diary (coded), 27 June 1937
19. *Ibid.* (uncoded), 28 June 1937
20. *Ibid.*
21. C.A. Lejeune, *Thank You for Having Me*
22. *Evening News*, 12 July 1937
23. V.L. to L.H., 2 November 1938 (SFP)
24. Oswald Frewen diary, 20 November 1937
25. *Ibid.*
26. *Ibid.*
27. *Ibid.*, 6 December 1937
28. Mrs. Frances Martin to author, 19 October 1987
29. *Ibid*
30. Dent, *Bouquet*, 69
31. *Ibid.,* 158
32. *Ibid.*, 156
33. Private Information, 16 March 1987
34. *Ibid.*
35. Lady Richardson to author, 4 February 1987
36. Gliddon, *Tribute*
37. *Ibid.*
38. *Ibid.*
39. Basil Wright, *Spectator*, April 1938
40. *Ibid.*
41. *Daily Mail*, February 1938
42. John Gliddon to author, April 1986
43. Olivier, *Confessions,* 81
44. *Ibid.*
45. *The Times,* 28 December 1937
46. Oswald Frewen diary, 27 December 1937
47. *The Times*, 28 December 1937
48. Ninette de Valois, *Come Dance With Me* (Hamish Hamilton, 1959), p. 82
49. Oswald Frewen diary, 27 December 1937
50. *The Times*, 28 December 1937
51. V.L. to L.H., 2 January 1938 (SFP)

CHAPTER NINE

1. V.L. to L.H., 2 March 1938 (SFP)
2. Kiernan, *Sir Larry*, 162
3. *Film Weekly*, 1938
4. Oswald Frewen diary, 12 May 1938
5. *Ibid.*
6. *Ibid.*

7. Olivier, *Confessions,* 80
8. V.L. to Mr. and Mrs. Hartley, 5 June 1938 (SFP)
9. *Ibid.*, 28 June 1938 (SFP)
10. Oswald Frewen diary, 30 July 1938
11. *Ibid.,* 26 September 1938
12. *Ibid.*
13. Stewart Granger, *Sparks Fly Upward,* 44
14. Elspeth March to author, 16 February 1987
15. *The Times,* 14 September 1938
16. V.L. to L.H., 18 September 1938 (SFP)
17. Oswald Frewen diary, 26 September 1938
18. *Ibid.*
19. *Ibid*, 29 September 1938
20. *Ibid.,* 28 November 1938
21. Details of Tommy's will, dated 1 October 1937, and the codicil (ref. SC70/4/747 F416) are published with the approval of the Keeper of the Records of Scotland.
22. L.O. to Mrs. Hartley, 2 October, 1938 (SFP)
23. L.H. to Mrs. Hartley, 14 October 1938
24. V.L. to L.H., 3 October 1938 (SFP)
25. *Ibid.*, 2 November 1938 (SFP)
26. L.O. to Mrs. Hartley, November 1938
27. Gliddon, *Tribute*
28. V.L. to L.H., 25 November 1938 (SFP)
29. *Ibid.*
30. Late Hamish Hamilton to author, 19 October 1986
31. *Ibid.*

CHAPTER TEN

1. Muriel Spark, *Daughter of the Soil*, *Observer*, c. 1956
2. *Ibid.*
3. V.L. interview, *What Success has Taught Me*
4. *Ibid.*
5. Irene Selznick, *A Private View* , 205
6. *Ibid.,* p. 208
7. *Ibid.,* p. 212
8. Quoted *Los Angeles Herald Examiner*, 16 September 1971
9. Selznick, *Memo,* D.S. to J.H. Whitney, 24 December 1936, 143
10. *Ibid.,* D.S. to Katharine Brown & Oscar Berlin, 3 February 1937, 149
11. *Ibid.,* D.S. to Richard Wallace, 17 February 1938, 154
12. *Picturegoer Weekly,* 9 April 1938
13. Selznick, *Memo,* D.S. to Ed Sullivan, 20 September 1938, 161-2

14. Bette Davis, *The Lonely Life: An Autobiography,* (Macdonald & Co., 1963)
15. Selznick,*Memo,* D.S. to Marcella Rabwin, 12 November 1938, 170
16. Interview in *Hollywood, The Selznick Years*, November 1969 © MPC Productions 1969
17. Selznick,*Memo,* D.S. to Katharine Brown, 6 December 1938, 178
18. *Ibid.* D.S. to J. H. Whitney, 10 December 1938, 179
19. *Ibid.,* D.S. to Irene Selznick, 12 December 1938, 180
20. Selznick, *Memo*, "Discovering the New Ones, 180
21. Irene Selznick, *A Private View*, 214-15
22. Fabia Drake, *Blind Fortune*, 96
23. Olivier, *On Acting*, 178
24. Irene Selznick to author, 15 April 1988
25. *Gone with the Wind, Making of a classic,* produced by A.V. Westin © ABC News, 1987
26. *Ibid.*
27. Beverly Hills Hotel notepaper (1988)
28. V.L. to L.H., 16 December 1938 (SFP)
29. Barker, *The Oliviers,* 152
30. Selznick, *Memo,* Selznick to Jock Whitney, 4 January 1939, 183
31. V.L. to Mr. and Mrs. Hartley, 26 January 1939 (SFP)
32. *Ibid.*
33. Bob Thomas, *Selznick*, 149-50
34. V.L. to L.H., cable 15 January 1939 (SFP)
35. V.L. to Mrs. Hartley, January 1939 (SFP)
36. V.L. to L.H., 24 January 1939 (SFP)
37. V.L. to Mrs. Hartley, 26 January 1939 (SFP)
38. V.L. to L.H., 24 January 1939 (SFP)
39. *Ibid.*
40. *Margaret Mitchell's Gone with the Wind Letters*, Susan Myrick to Margaret Mitchell, 11 January 1939, 239
41. *Ibid.,* Margaret Mitchell to D.S., 14 January 1939, 240
42. *Ibid.,* Quoted *Atlanta Constitution* 14 January 1939, 245
43. *Ibid.,* Margaret Mitchell to V.L., 30 January 1939, 245-6
44. *Ibid.,* Margaret Mitchell to D.S. 13 March 1939, 260
45. *Ibid.*, 262
46. *Ibid.*, 268
47. Selznick, *Memo,* confidential memo, D.S. to M. Ginsberg, 6 January 1939, 183
48. V.L. to Mrs. Hartley, 29 January 1939 (SFP)
49. V.L. to L.H., 24 January 1939 (SFP)
50. V.L. to Mrs. Hartley, 8 March 1939 (SFP)
51. Gavin Lambert, *On Cukor*, 149
52. Selznick, *Memo,* D.S. to Mr. Klune, Mr. Menzies, 9 March 1939, 195
53. *Ibid.*, D.S. to Will Price, 13 March 1939, 199

54. Olivier, *On Acting,* 181
55. V.L. to L.H., 13 March 1939 (SFP)
56. Olivier, *Confessions,* 70
57. V.L. to Mrs. Hartley, 8 March 1939 (SFP)
58. L.O. to Mrs. Hartley from the Barclay Hotel, N.Y., 21 March 1939
59. *Ibid.*
60. *Ibid.*
61. V.L. to Sunny Alexander, 22 July 1939
62. Sunny Lash to author, 22 April 1988
63. L.O. to Mrs. Hartley, 21 March 1939
64. Olivier, *Confessions,* 85
65. V.L. to L.H., 3 April 1939 (SFP)
66. *Ibid.*
67. *Ibid.*
68. V.L. to L.H., 14 May 1939 (SFP)
69. *Ibid.*
70. Vivien Leigh, "My Scarlett Days," *Movie Mirror*, December 1939
71. *Ibid.*
72. V.L. to L.H., 14 May 1939 (SFP)
73. Selznick, *Memo,* 138
74. *Ibid.*
75. Evelyn Keyes, *Scarlett O'Hara's Younger Sister*, 175
76. *Ibid.,* 31
77. Gavin Lambert, *On Cukor,* 149
78. Sunny Lash to author, 22 April 1988
79. Selznick, *Memo,* D.S. letter (unsent) 20 October 1939, 225

CHAPTER ELEVEN

1. Selznick, *Memo,* D.S. to J.H. Whitney, 27 June 1939, 264
2. Irene Selznick, *A Private View,* 223
3. Barker, *The Oliviers,* 158
4. *Ibid.*
5. Selznick, *Memo,* D.S. cable to L.O., 18 August 1939, 271
6. Kiernan, *Sir Larry,* 184
7. Logan Gourlay, *Olivier*, 83
8. Dent, *Bouquet,* 83
9. V.L. to L.H., 11 September 1939 (SFP)
10. Sunny Lash to author, 22 April 1988
11. Sunny Alexander to Mrs. Hartley, 19 October 1939 (SFP)
12. *Ibid.*
13. V.L. to Mrs. Hartley, 19 October 1939 (SFP)
14. Sunny Alexander to Mrs. Hartley, 19 October 1939 (SFP)
15. V.L. to Mrs. Hartley, 19 October (SFP)

16. Ruth Gordon, *An Open Book*, 161
17. V.L.to L.H., 23 October 1939 (FP)
18. *Ibid.*
19. *Ibid.,* 16 November 1939 (SFP)
20. Miscellaneous press cutting in album (SFP)
21. V.L. to Mrs. Hartley, 27 November 1939 (SFP)
22. *Ibid.*
23. Irene Selznick, *A Private View,* 220
24. V.L. to Mrs. Hartley, 31 December 1939 (SFP)
25. Sunny Alexander to Mrs. Hartley, 11 January 1940 (SFP)
26. L.H. to Mrs. Hartley, undated (but late 1939) (SFP)
27. V.L. to L.H., 17 January 1940 (SFP)
28. *Ibid.*, 23 October 1939 (SFP)
29. *Ibid.*, 17 January 1940 (SFP)
30. *Ibid.*
31. Foster Hirsch, *Laurence Olivier on Screen*, 39
32. *Los Angeles Examiner*, January 1940
33. V.L. to L.H. 18 February 1940 (SFP)
34. Sunny Lash to author, 22 April 1988
35. Lady Diana Cooper, *Trumpets from the Steep,* Lady Diana Cooper to Conrad Russell, p. 28
36. V.L. to Mrs. Hartley, from Hotel Ambassador East, Chicago, 19 April 1940 (SFP)
37. Sonia Lee, *Movie Guide*, 1940
38. *Ibid.*
39. *Ibid.*
40. *Ibid.*
41. *Ibid.*
42. *Ibid.*
43. V.L. contemporary film-clip
44. Miscellaneous press cutting in album (SFP)
45. Sir John Colville, *The Fringes of Power*, diary 15 December 1940, 319
46. Dent, Bouquet, 123
47. *Ibid.*
48. Script of *Lady Hamilton*
49. Mervyn LeRoy, *Take One*, 147
50. *New York Herald Tribune,* undated cutting but c. 17 May 1940
51. *Ibid*, 19 May 1940
52. *Ibid.*
53. *Ibid.*
54. *Ibid.*
55. Olivier, *Confessions,* 88
56. V.L. to the Hartleys, 19 April 1940 (SFP)
57. *Ibid.*
58. V.L. to L.H., Chicago, 29 April 1940 (SFP)

59. *Ibid.*
60. Sunny Alexander to Mrs. Hartley, 11 January 1940 (SFP)
61. Brooks Atkinson, *Broadway,* 389
62. *Ibid.*
63. Gordon, *An Open Book*, 162
64. Cottrell, *Laurence Olivier*, 171
65. Olivier, *Confessions,* 90
66. *Daily Express*, July 1940
67. V.L. to L.H., 5 July 1940 (SFP)
68. Sunny Lash to author, 22 April 1988
69. V.L. to L.H., postmarked 26 July 1940 (SFP)
70. *Ibid.*, 9 August 1940 (SFP)
71. Sunny Lash to author, 22 April 1988
72. *Daily Province*, 15 August 1940
73. V.L. to L.H., 16 August 1940 (SFP)
74. *Ibid.*, 4 September 1940 (SFP)
75. Michael Korda, *Charmed Lives*, 149

CHAPTER TWELVE

1. Garson Kanin, *Tracy & Hepburn*, 75
2. *Santa Barbara News-Press*, 3 May 1987
3. Garson Kanin to author, 22 January 1988
4. *Ibid.*
5. *Ibid.*
6. V.L. to L.H., 17 September 1940 (SFP)
7. *Ibid.*, 22 October 1940 (SFP)
8. Script of *Lady Hamilton*
9. V.L. to L.H., 17 September 1940 (SFP)
10. Script of *Lady Hamilton*
11. *Ibid.*
12. *Ibid.*
13. *Ibid.*
14. *Ibid.*
15. V.L. to L.H., 22 October 1940 (SFP)
16. Dent, *Bouquet,* 60
17. Kiernan, *Sir Larry,* 199-200
18. Cottrell, *Laurence Olivier*, 183
19. *Tatler and Bystander*, 6 August 1941
20. Ronald Tree, *When the Moon was High,* 131-132
21. *Diaries of Sir Alexander Cadogan*, 8 August 1941, 396-397
22. Roy Howells, *Simply Churchill*, 63-5
23. Script of *Lady Hamilton*
24. *Ibid.*

25. Mrs. Hartley to L.H., 10 September 1940 (SFP)
26. *News Herald*, Vancouver, 28 November 1940
27. L.H. to Mrs. Hartley, 3 January 1941 (SFP)
28. *Ibid.*
29. *Ibid.*, 8 February c. 1942 (SFP)
30. *Ibid.*
31. Oswald Frewen diary, 4 November 1940
32. *Ibid.*
33. *Ibid.*
34. Irene Selznick, *A Private View,* 237
35. Miscellaneous press cutting in album, 29 December 1940 (SFP)
36. *Daily Express,* 11 January 1941
37. *Sunday Dispatch*, 12 January 1941
38. Lady Richardson to author, 7 February 1987
39. L.H. to Mrs. Hartley, 24 January 1941 (SFP)
40. *Ibid.*, 9 February (SFP)
41. Kiernan, *Sir Larry,* 201
42. James Forsyth, *Tyrone Guthrie*, 183
43. *The Noël Coward Diaries,* 12 July 1941, 8
44. V.L. interview, *What Success has Taught Me*
45. Olivier, *Confessions,* 96
46. Lady Richardson to author, 7 February 1987
47. Oswald Frewen diary, 23 September 1941
48. *Ibid.*
49. *Ibid.*
50. V.L. to L.H., 14 October 1941 (SFP)
51. *Ibid.*, 5 November 1941 (SFP)
52. Cecil Beaton Unpublished Diary, 24 November 1941 (CBP)
53. *Ibid.*
54. *Ibid.*
55. V.L. to L.H., 29 December 1941 (SFP)
56. L.H. to Mrs. Hartley, 2 February 1942 (SFP)
57. *The Complete Plays of Bernard Shaw*, 516
58. Dent, *Bouquet,* 152-3
59. *Punch*, quoted in Dent, *Bouquet,* 153
60. Cecil Beaton, *The Theatre in Wartime* (CBP)
61. *Ibid.*
62. *Evening Standard*, 29 December 1942
63. Kitty Black, *Upper Circle* (Methuen, 1984), p. 61
64. *Ibid.*
65. Dent, *Bouquet,* 71
66. *Ibid.*
67. *Ibid.*, 38-9
68. Kenneth Clark, *The Other Half,* 59
69. Kenneth Clark, *Another Part of the World*, 214

70. *John O'London's Weekly*, 1942
71. *Ibid.*
72. *Ibid.*
73. Gourlay, *Olivier,* 95
74. Olivier, *Confessions,* 96
75. L.O. to Mrs. Hartley, 25 September 1942 (SFP)
76. *Ibid.*
77. Oswald Frewen diary, 2 September 1942 (SFP)
78. L.O. to Mrs Hartley, 25 September 1942 (SFP)
79. Selznick, *Memo,* D.S. to William Goetz, 10 December 1942, 314-5

CHAPTER THIRTEEN

1. Cottrell, *Laurence Olivier,* 193
2. Dent, *Bouquet,* 79
3. *Daily Sketch*, 6 May 1943
4. V.L. to Mrs. Hartley, 20 August 1943 (SFP)
5. Harold Macmillan, *War Diaries*, 9 June 1943
6. V.L. to Mrs. Hartley, 20 August 1943 (SFP)
7. Alec Guinness, *Blessings in Disguise*, 121-22
8. V.L. to Mrs. Hartley, 20 August 1943 (SFP)
9. *Ibid.*
10. *Ibid.*
11. Peter Daubeny, *Stage by Stage*, 31
12. V.L. to Mrs. Hartley, 1 September 1943 (SFP)
13. *Ibid.*
14. Marshal of the RAF Sir John Grandy to author, 28 March 1988
15. *Ibid.*
16. V.L. to Mrs. Hartley, 1 September 1943 (SFP)
17. *The Times*, 23 June 1943
18. Patrick, 3rd Baron Kinross to his mother, 9 July 1943 (Kinross Papers, National Library of Scotland)
19. Unpublished diary of Lord Killearn, 29 June 1943 (St. Anthony's College, Oxford)
20. *Ibid*, 2 July 1943
21. V.L. to Mrs. Hartley, 1 September 1943 (SFP)
22. Vice Admiral Eric Bradby to author, 22 January 1987
23. Commander John Rusher, RN (Ret.) to author, 24 January 1987
24. Graham Turner to author, 16 December 1986
25. Noël Coward, *Middle East Diary* (Heinemann, 1944), p. 13
26. *Ibid.*
27. *Ibid.,* p. 16
28. *Ibid.,* p. 17
29. *Ibid.*, p. 18

30. V.L. to Mrs. Hartley, 1 September 1943 (SFP)
31. Air Vice Marshal J.G. Elton to author, 30 December 1987
32. V.L. to Mrs. Hartley, 1 September 1943 (SFP)
33. *Ibid.*
34. Oswald Frewen diary, 4 October 1943
35. *Ibid.*
36. Dent, *Bouquet,* 61
37. Judy Campbell to author, 29 November 1986
38. *Ibid.*
39. *Ibid.*
40. David Niven, *The Moon's a Balloon*, 229
41. *The Hollywood Reporter*
42. V.L. to L.H., 6 March 1944 (SFP)
43. Kiernan, *Sir Larry,* 207
44. Marjorie Deans, *Meeting at the Sphinx,* Shaw's Foreword, vii
45. Deans, *Mind's Eye,* 28
46. Miscellaneous press cutting in album (SFP)
47. Deans, *Mind's Eye,* 65
48. *Ibid.*, 41
49. *Ibid.*
50. Quoted in *Tatler,* 19 December 1945
51. *Ibid.*
52. *Ibid.*
53. Stewart Granger, *Sparks Fly Upward,* 82
54. *Ibid.,* 83
55. *Ibid.*, 90
56. Stanley Holloway, *Wiv' a Little Bit of Luck*, 267
57. Pascal, Valerie, *The Disciple and His Devil,* from a Shaw letter to Pascal, 108
58. Kenneth Clark, *The Other Half*, 40
59. *Ibid.*
60. Dent, *Bouquet,* 39
61. *Ibid.,* 127
62. Miscellaneous press cutting in album (SFP)
63. Winn, *The Positive Hour,* 387
64. Deans, *Sphinx,* 66
65. V.L. to L.H., 16 August 1944 (SFP)
66. Dent, *Bouquet,* 18
67. Granger, *Sparks Fly Upward,* 83-4
68. Elspeth March to author, 16 February 1944
69. Oswald Frewen diary, 6 September 1944
70. Deans, *Sphinx,* 93
71. Robert Lowell quote (Caroline Blackwood to author).
72. Olivier, *On Acting*, 85
73. *Ego 7*, October 21, 1944, 224

74. *Ibid.*
75. *Ibid.,* Agate to Dent, 2 November 1944, 240
76. *Ibid.,*Agate to V.L., 1 November 1944, 235
77. Dent, *Bouquet,* 19

CHAPTER FOURTEEN

1. *Journals of Thornton Wilder*, 26
2. *Ibid.*, 37
3. Selznick, *Memo,* D.S. to Mr. O'Shea, 19 February 1945, 345
4. *Ibid.*
5. Olivier, *Confessions,* 112
6. Kenneth Tynan, *A View of the English Stage 1944-63*, 25-6
7. Quoted Alan Dent, *Boqet.* 154
8. V.L. interview, *What Success has Taught Me*
9. Dent, *Bouquet*. 101
10. *Ibid.,* 101-2
11. Barker, *The Oliviers,* 228
12. V.L. to Jane Glass, 9 December 1944
13. Olivier, *Confessions,*115
14. Olivier, *On Acting,* 142
15. *Kelly's Directory* 1907, Buckinghamshire, 127
16. *The Times*, 29 September 1986
17. Elizabeth Salter, *Helpmann,* 61
18. *Ibid.*, 63
19. *Ibid.*
20. *Ibid.,* 134
21. Late Hamish Hamilton to author, 19 October 1986
22. Barbara Ker-Seymer to author, 25 February 1988
23. John Merivale to author, 14 April 1987
24. Agate, *Ego 8*, V.L. to J.A., 30 October 1945, 245
25. *Ibid.*, J.A. to V.L., 1 November 1945, 246
26. Kiernan, *Sir Larry,* 208
27. *Ibid.,* 215
28. Late Esmond Knight to author, 11 February 1987
29. Kiernan, *Sir Larry,* 219
30. Garson Kanin, *Remembering Mr. Maugham*, quoted Alan Dent, 75
31. *Ibid.*, 76
32. *Ibid.*
33. *Ibid.*, 77
34. *Ibid.*, 78
35. Kiernan, *Sir Larry,* 224
36. *Hollywood Citizen News*, 19 July 1946
37. Kiernan, *Sir Larry,* p. 244

38. Lord Cottesloe to author, 10 November 1987
39. Susana Walton, *Behind the Façade*, 99
40. Niven, *The Moon's a Balloon,* 261
41. Winn, *The Positive Hour,* 387
42. *Ibid.*
43. Redgrave, *In My Mind's Eye,* 225-6
44. Cecil Beaton Unpublished Diary, February 1947 (CBP)
45. *The Noël Coward Diaries,*11 October 1946, 65
46. V.L. to L.H., 18 September 1946 (SFP)
47. *Ibid.*, 8 November 1946 (SFP)
48. Cecil Beaton Unpublished Diary, February 1947 (CBP)
49. *Ibid.*
50. *Ibid.*
51. *Ibid.*
52. V.L. to Bernard Berenson, 24 March 1947 (I Talti)
53. Late Esmond Knight to author, 11 February 1987
54. *Ibid.*
55. Nora Swinburne to author, 11 February 1987
56. *The Journals of Thornton Wilder*, 124
57. C.B. to Greta Garbo, written between 24 March and 9 April 1947 (CBP)
58. C.B. to Lady Diana Cooper, c. 22 April 1947 (Norwich papers)
59. Internal memo, London Film Productions, 5 May 1947 (Norwich Papers)
60. C.B. to G.G. 15 May 1947 (CBP)
61. Barker, *The Oliviers,* 260
62. C.B. Unpublished Diary, 7 June (?) 1947 (CBP)
63. *Ibid.,* May 1947 (CBP)
64. *Ibid.*
65. Late Hon. Stephen Tennant to C.B., 5 June 1947 (CBP)
66. Mary Kerridge to author, 16 December 1986
67. Quoted by C.B. in his diary, 11 May 1955 (CBP)
68. V.L. to B.B., 4 June 1947 (I Talti)
69. C.B. to G.G., 15 July 1947 (CBP)
70. *Leader Magazine,* 10 January 1948
71. Miscellaneous press cutting in album, 1948 (SFP)
72. Lady Richardson to author, 7 February 1987
73. *Ibid.*
74. C.B. to G.G., 17 May 1948 (CBP)

CHAPTER FIFTEEN

1. R.B. Sheridan, *The School for Scandal,* Intro. by Sir Laurence Olivier, 5
2. C.B. to G.G., 21 September 1947 (CBP)
3. Martin Battersby to C.B., 9 December 1947 (CBP)
4. *Ibid.*, 11 December 1947 (CBP)
5. *Ibid.*
6. *Ibid.,* 21 December 1947 (CB)
7. *Ibid.*, 25 December 1947 (CBP)
8. *Ibid.*
9. L.O. and John Burrell to C.B., cable 15 January 1948 (CBP)
10. M.B. to C.B. ,30 January 1948 (CBP)
11. Mrs. Emma Brash to author, 3 April 1987
12. Maud Nelson to C.B., 20 January 1948 (CBP)
13. Olivier, *Confessions,* 126
14. Gourlay, *Olivier,* 124
15. Mercia Swinburne to author, 25 February 1987
16. *Ibid.*
17. *West Australian*, 16 March 1948
18. *Argus,* Melbourne, 13 May 1948
19. *Sydney Morning Herald,* July 1948
20. *Ibid.*
21. John Barnard to Michael Redington, December 1986
22. *Ibid.*
23. Michael Redington to Jack and Winifred Hawkes, Perth, Western Australia, 21 March 1948
24. *Ibid.*, 27 March 1948
25. *Ibid.*
26. Garry O'Connor, *Darlings of the Gods*, 59
27. Georgina Jumel to author, 16 April 1987
28. O'Connor, *Darlings,* 65
29. Michael Redington to Jack and Winifred Hawkes, 3 April 1948
30. *Advertiser*, Adelaide, 14 April 1948
31. O'Connor, *Darlings,* 74
32. *Ibid.*, 100
33. Olivier, *Confessions,* 128
34. Terence Morgan to author, 16 April 1987
35. *Ibid.*
36. Floy Bell (Mrs. Paddy Donnell) to author, 17 March 1987
37. *Ibid.*
38. Mrs. Emma Brash to author, 3 April 1987
39. Michael Redington to Jack and Winifred Hawkes, 20 July 1948
40. V.L. to L.H., 24 July 1948 (SFP)
41. O'Connor, *Darlings,* 123

42. Miscellaneous press cutting, Sydney, August 1948 (SFP)
43. *Ibid.*
44. V.L. to L.H., 10 September 1948 (SFP)
45. *Ibid.*
46. O'Connor, *Darlings,* 145
47. L.O. to C.B., Hotel St. George, Wellington, New Zealand, 15 October 1948 (CBP)
48. Floy Bell to author, 17 March 1987
49. *Ibid.*
50. Michael Redington to author, 28 November 1986
51. Peter Hiley to Anne Edwards, 27 November 1975
52. *Ibid.*
53. Yolande Finch, *Finchy*, 28
54. Floy Bell to author, 17 March 1987
55. *Daily Express,* 21 January 1949
56. Leonard Mosley, *Daily Express*, 21 January 1949
57. *Ibid.*
58. Paul Boyle, *Daily Graphic*, 21 January 1949
59. *Daily Telegraph*, 21 January 1949
60. Cable Oliviers to C.B., 21 January 1949 (CBP)
61. Simon Fleet to C.B., 25 January 1949 (CBP)
62. Emma Brash to author, 3 April 1987
63. C.B. to G.G., 28 November 1948 (CBP)
64. *Ibid.*, 5 December 1948 (CBP)
65. *Ibid.*, 6 March 1949 (CBP)
66. Cecil Beaton, *The Strenuous Years*, 21
67. C.B. to G.G,. 16 May 1949 (CBP)
68. Miscellaneous press cutting in album, January 1949 (SFP)
69. *Ibid.*
70. *The Spectator*, 18 February 1949
71. Barker, *The Oliviers,* 286
72. Miscellaneous press cutting in album, February 1949 (SFP)
73. *The Times*, 11 February 1949
74. Beverley Baxter, M.P., *Evening Standard,* 11 February 1949
75. Alan Dent, "Is Vivien a Tragedienne," press cutting February 1949
76. Olivier, *Confessions,* 131
77. *Ibid.*
78. *Ibid.*, 136
79. Suzanne Holman to V.L, October 1949 (SFP)
80. V.L. to L.H., 3 November 1949 (SFP)

CHAPTER SIXTEEN

1. Donald Spoto, *The Kindness of Strangers*, 140
2. Benjamin Nelson, *Tennessee Williams:The Man and His Work*, 137
3. *Ibid.,* 139
4. Tennessee Williams, *Memoirs*, 136
5. Irene Selznick, *A Private View,* 302
6. V.L. interview, *What Success has Taught Me*
7. Irene Selznick, *A Private View,* 322
8. *Ibid.*, 323
9. Dent, *Bouquet,* 106
10. Irene Selznick, *A Private View,* 324
11. Irene Selznick to author, 15 April 1988
12. Irene Selznick, *A Private View,* 327
13. V.L. to L.H.,15 October 1949 (SFP)
14. Melvyn Bragg, *Laurence Olivier*, 80-82
15. Dent, *Bouquet,* 102
16. *Ibid.*, 103
17. *Time,* quoted by Sunny Lash, 22 April 1988
18. Dent, *Bouquet, 102*
19. *The Noël Coward Diaries,* 29 October 1949, 134
20. *The Times*, 13 October 1949
21. *Ibid.*
22. *Ibid.*
23. Kenneth Tynan, *He That Plays The King*, 142
24. *Ibid.,* 143
25. Irene Selznick, *A Private View*, 327
26. *Ibid.,* 328
27. Clark,*The Other Half,* 61
28. Lucinda Ballard Dietz to author, 17 April 1988
29. Sunny Lash to author, 22 April 1988
30. Suzanne Holman, M*y Mother is Vivien Leigh* (SFP)
31. Garson Kanin to author, 22 January 1988
32. Ron Offen, *Brando*, 63
33. Contemporary press cutting (SFP)
34. Warner Brothers Cutting Notes, 15 February 1951, (University of Southern California)
35. Elia Kazan, *A Life*, 387
36. Jeffrey Selznick to author, December 1987
37. Suzanne Holman to Mrs. Hartley, 17 August 1950 (SFP)
38. Mrs. Dietz to author, 17 April 1988
39. Suzanne Holman to Mrs. Hartley, 17 August 1950 (SFP)
40. *Los Angeles Times*, 1950
41. *Ibid.,* September 1950
42. Private information, 26 March 1987

43. Maxine Audley to author, 21 February 1987
44. *New York Times*, V.L. interview with Maurice Zolotow, 16 December 1951
45. Maxine Audley to author, 21 February 1987
46. Elspeth March to author, 16 February 1987
47. *Ibid.*
48. *Ibid.*
49. Esmond Knight manuscript, 131
50. Late Esmond Knight to author, 11 February 1987
51. *Ibid.*
52. Esmond Knight manuscript, 179
53. *Harold Nicolson, Diaries and Letters* 1945-62, 1 February 1956, 297
54. *Ibid.,* 29 August 1951, 208
55. Olivier*, On Acting*, 110
56. Kenneth Tynan, *A View of the English Stage, 1944-63*, 108
57. *Ibid.*
58. *Ibid.*
59. *Ibid.*
60. *Ibid*., 109
61. *Ibid.*
62. *Ibid*. 110
63. Gourlay, *Olivier,* 49
64. Sir John Gielgud address, August 1967
65. Maxine Audley to author, 12 February 1987
66. Martin Gilbert, *Never Despair*, 630
67. Miscellaneous press cutting, 26 June 1951 (SFP)
68. Jean-Louis Barrault, *Memories for Tomorrow*, 307
69. *Tatler and Bystander,* 10 October 1951
70. Jean-Louis Barrault, *Memories,* 307
71. *Daily Graphic*, 8 October 1951
72. Korda, *Charmed Lives,* 305
73. Interview with John Ralph, miscellaneous cutting, 1951 (SFP)
74. V.L. to Maxine Audley, undated, but October 1951
75. *Ibid.,* Liverpool, November 1951
76. Olivier, *Confessions,* 140
77. *New York Times*, 16 December 1951
78. *Ibid.*
79. *Ibid.*
80. *Ibid.*
81. Dent, *Bouquet,* 73
82. Diana Vreeland to author, 11 October 1986
83. V.L. to Suzanne Holman, 6 January 1952 9SFP)
84. C.B. to Lady Juliet Duff, 22 January 1952 (CBP)
85. *New York Times*, 30 December 1951
86. *Ibid*., c. 16 December 1951

87. Irene Selznick to author, 15 April 1988
88. Olivier, *Confessions,* 142
89. *The Noël Coward Diaries,* 22 April 1952, 191
90. Olivier, *Confessions,*148
91. Athene Seyler to author, 3 December 1986

CHAPTER SEVENTEEN

1. Oswald Frewen diary, 7 January 1953, written 5 May 1953
2. *Ibid.*
3. *Ibid.*
4. Trader Faulkner, *Peter Finch*, 181
5. Maxine Audley to author, 12 February 1987
6. Faulkner, *Peter Finch,* 224
7. *Ibid.*
8. Finch, *Finchy,* 36
9. V.L. to L.H.,13 February 1953 (SFP)
10. Olivier, *Confessions,* 153
11. Sunny Lash to author, 22 April 1988
12. *Ibid.*
13. *Ibid.*
14. Faulkner, *Peter Finch,* 182
15. David Niven, *Bring on the Empty Horses*, 309-321
16. *New York Times*, 8 February 1952
17. John Merivale to author, 23 March 1988
18. Niven, *Bring on the Empty Horses*, p. 319
19. Granger, *Sparks Fly Upward,* 293
20. Niven, *Empty Horses*, 319
21. Olivier, *Confessions,* 155
22. John Merivale to author 1987
23. Irina Tennant to author, 10 March 1988
24. *Daily Sketch*, 20 March 1953
25. *Ibid.*
26. *Daily Mirror*, 21 March 1953
27. Oswald Frewen diary, 22 March 1953,written 22 June 1953
28. *Ibid.,* 10-11 April 1953
29. Olivier, *Confessions,*159
30. Cole Lesley, *Remembered Laughter*, 365
31. *The Noël Coward Diaries*, 12 April 1953, 211
32. Olivier, *Confessions,* 160
33. *The Noël Coward Diaries,* 22 April 1953, 211
34. Mrs. Hartley diary, 24 April 1953 (SFP)
35. Dent, *Bouquet,* 40
36. Private information, 26 March 1987

37. Clark, *The Other Half,* 62
38. Marc Wannamaker, *The Hollywood Reporter*, 268
39. *Daily Telegraph*, 7 July 1953
40. *The Noël Coward Diaries,* 16 July 1953, 215
41. *Daily Mail,* 17 July 1953
42. V.L. to L.H., 22 July 1953 (SFP)
43. Gourlay, *Olivier,* 132
44. *Ibid.*, 131
45. *Ibid.,* 132
46. *Evening Standard*, 6 November 1953
47. *Daily Mail*, November 1953
48. *Ibid.*
49. *Daily Express*, 6 November 1953
50. V.L. to L.H., 19 July 1954 (SFP)
51. Harrison, *Rex,* 137
52. Ibid.
53. Jean-Pierre Aumont, *Dis-moi d'abord que tu m'aimes*, 171-2
54. V.L. to Mr. & Mrs. Hartley, 28 July 1954 (SFP)
55. *The Noël Coward Diaries,* 12 September 1954, 241
56. Kenneth More, *More or Less,*166
57. Dent, *Bouquet,* 82
58. Moira Lister to author, 26 March 1987
59. *Ibid.*
60. *Ibid.*
61. Faulkner, *Peter Finch,* 183-4
62. Susana Walton, *William Walton Behind the Façade,* 142

CHAPTER EIGHTEEN

1. John Gielgud, *An Actor and His Time*, 176
2. Michael Denison, *Double Act*, 55
3. Ronald Barker, *Plays and Players,* June 1955
4. Olivier, *Confessions,* 163-4
5. *Ibid.*
6. Gielgud, *An Actor and His Time,* 176
7. *Ibid.,* 177
8. *Ibid.*
9. *Daily Telegraph*, 21 April 1955
10. *Ibid.*
11. *Birmingham Mail*, 13 April 1955
12. *Stage*, 14 April 1955
13. *Morning Advertiser* (London), 2 June 1955
14. *Spectator*, 22 April 1955
15. *Observer,* 12 June 1955

16. *Ibid.*
17. John Russell Taylor, *Vivien Leigh*, 99
18. Olivier, *Confessions,* 26
19. John Gielgud, Memorial Service Address, August 1967, *Distinguished Company*, 71
20. Dent, *Bouquet,* 97
21. *Ibid.*, 162
22. Drake, *Blind Fortune*, 82-3
23. Maxine Audley to author, 12 February 1987
24. *The Noël Coward Diaries*, 7 August 1955, 278
25. Olivier, *Confessions,* 164
26. *Daily Express,* 8 June 1955
27. *Ibid.*
28. *Ibid.*
29. *Ibid.*
30. *The Noël Coward Diaries,* 7 August 1955, 278
31. *Ibid.*
32. *Ibid.*, 19 August 1955, 279
33. *Ibid.*, 280
34. *Ibid.*
35. J.C. Trewin, *Peter Brook*, 81
36. Cecil Wilson, *Daily Mail*, 17 August 1955
37. *Time and Tide,* 20 August 1955
38. *Evening Standard*, 17 August 1955
39. *Truth*, 26 August 1955
40. *Coventry Evening Telegraph*, 17 August 1955
41. *Observer,* 21 August 1955; Kenneth Tynan, *Curtains*, 104
42. Mark Amory, ed., *The Diaries of Evelyn Waugh,* 19 August 1955, 738-9
43. *Ibid.*
44. *Spectator,* 2 September 1955
45. Mark Amory, ed., *The Letters of Ann Fleming,* Evelyn Waugh to Ann Fleming, 12 September 1955, 160
46. Amory, *The Diaries of Evelyn Waugh,* 28 August 1955, 739
47. Olivier, *Confessions,* 166
48. Maxine Audley to author, 12 February 1987
49. *Ibid.*
50. Michael Denison to author, 12 February 1987
51. *Ibid.*
52. *Ibid.*
53. Nigel Nicolson, editor, *Harold Nicolson Diaries & Letters,1945-62*, 14 December 1955, 291
54. Late Hamish Hamilton to author, 2 November 1986
55. Faulkner, *Peter Finch,* 186-7
56. Maxine Audley to author, 12 February 1987
57. Private information, 16 February 1987

58. *Ibid.*
59. *Ibid.,* 6 October 1985
60. *Ibid.*

CHAPTER NINETEEN

1. Oswald Frewen diary, 10 August 1955
2. V.L. to L.H., 18 January 1956 (SFP)
3. Anthony Summers, *Goddess*, 101
4. Oswald Frewen diary, 25 February 1956
5. *Ibid.,* 9 March 1956
6. *Ibid.*
7. *Ibid.*
8. C.B. to Eileen Hose, 11 March 1956 (CBP)
9. Oswald Frewen diary, 25 March 1956
10. Lesley, *Remembered Laughter*, 287
11. *The Noël Coward Diaries,* 9 September 1955, 281
12. Faulkner, *Peter Finch,* 188
13. *The Noël Coward Diaries,*19 February 1956, 308
14. *Ibid*, 25 March 1956, 315
15. *Ibid.*
16. V.L. to Maxine Audley, 6 April 1956
17. V.L. to L.H., 2 May 1956 (SFP)
18. William Chappell to author, 8 February 1988
19. Oswald Frewen diary, 11 June 1956
20. *Ibid.*
21. *Ibid.*, 15 July 1956, written 4 August 1956
22. *The Noël Coward Diaries,* 11 July 1956, 327
23. *Ibid.*
24. *Daily Express*, 13 July 1956
25. *Ibid.*
26. *Daily Mail,* 13 July 1956
27. *Daily Sketch*, 13 July 1956
28. *Daily Express,* 13 July 1956
29. V.L. to Maxine Audley, 15 July 1956
30. Dinah Sheridan to author, 7 June 1988
31. Fleur Cowles, *Friends and Memories*, 194
32. Harris, *Radie's World*, 138
33. Mrs. Hartley diary, August 1956 (SFP)
34. Suzanne Holman to Gertrude Hartley, 17 August 1956 (SFP)
35. *The Noël Coward Diaries,* 14 August 1956, 331
36. Late Hamish Hamilton to author, 19 October 1986
37. V.L. to Maxine Audley, 1 October 1956
38. *Ibid.*

39. *The Noël Coward Diaries,* October 1956, 334
40. Lesley, *Remembered Laughter,* 366
41. Late Esmond Knight to author, 11 February 1987
42. Esmond Knight manuscript, 226
43. Oswald Frewen diary, 17 October 1956
44. Mrs. Hartley diary, 25 April 1957
45. John Russell Taylor, *Anger and After*, 31
46. Tynan, *Curtains,* 130-132
47. Olivier, *Confessions,* 180
48. *Ibid.,* 168
49. *Sunday Times*, 14 April 1957
50. David Conville to author, 24 November 1986
51. Harold Hobson, *Indirect Journey*, 245
52. *Ibid.,* 240
53. *Ibid.*, 245
54. *Ibid.*
55. Olivier, C*onfessions,* 168
56. Hon. Colin Clark to author, 22 February 1987
57. Mrs. Donnell to author, 17 March 1987
58. Paddy Donnell to author, 17 Mach 1987
59. *Daily Express*, 23 June 1987
60. Mrs. Donnell to author, 17 March 1987
61. David Conville to author, 24 November 1986
62. Paul-Louis Weiller to author, September 1985
63. Frank Thring article, August 1957 (SFP)
64. Hon. Colin Clark to author, 22 February 1987
65. David Conville to author, 24 November 1986
66. Hon. Colin Clark to author, 22 February 1987
67. *Daily Express*, 23 June 1957
68. Frank Thring article, August 1957 (SFP)
69. Maxine Audley to author, 12 February 1987
70. David Conville to author, 24 November 1986
71. *Ibid.*
72. Maxine Audley to author, 12 February 1987
73. Hon. Colin Clark to author, 22 February 1987
74. David Conville to author, 24 November 1986
75. Hon. Colin Clark to author, 22 February 1987
76. *Ibid.*
77. *Ibid.*
78. David Conville to author, 24 November 1986
79. Hon. Colin Clark to author, 22 February 1987

CHAPTER TWENTY

1. Olivier, *Confessions,* 182
2. Mrs. Hartley diary, 23 June 195 (SFP)
3. Amory, *The Letters of Ann Fleming,* 5 July 1957, 204
4. Mrs. Hartley diary, 6 July 1957 (SFP)
5. Athene Seyler to author, 3 December 1986
6. *Hansard* (traditional name for the printed transcripts of parliamentary debate in the Westminster system of government), 9 July 1957, 886
7. *Ibid.,* 890
8. *Ibid.,* 898
9. *Hansard* 11 July 1957, 1032
10. *Ibid.*
11. *Ibid.*
12. *Daily Mirror*, 12 July 1957
13. *The Times*, 12 July 1957
14. *Ibid.*
15. Sir Brian Horrocks, *A Full Life*, 260
16. *Ibid.*
17. Oliver Prince-White, "I lived in Leningrad," *Daily Mail*, 3 September 1957
18. *The Times,* 12 July 1957
19. *News Chronicle*, 12 July 1957
20. *Ibid.*
21. *Daily Express*, 12 July 1957
22. *Daily Herald*, 12 July 1957
23. *Daily Mail*, 13 July 1957
24. *Ibid.*, 17 July 1957
25. *The Times*, 20 July 1957
26. Miscellaneous press cutting in album, 21 July 1957 (SFP)
27. *Sunday Times*, 21 July 1957
28. Maxine Audley to author, 1986
29. Judy Campbell to author, 29 November 1986
30. David Conville to author, 24 November 1986
31. *The Times*, 22 July 1957
32. *Ibid.*, 29 July 1957
33. David Conville to author, 24 November 1986
34. V.L. to B.B., 27 July 1957 (I Talti)
35. *Hansard*, 30 July 1957
36. Mrs. Hartley diary, 30 July 1957 (SFP)
37. Olivier, *Confessions,* 183
38. *The Times*, 1 August 1957
39. Olivier, *Confessions,* 182
40. Mrs. Hartley diary, 4 August 1957 (SFP)
41. Oswald Frewen diary, 8 August 1957

42. Robin Farrington to author, 7 April 1988
43. *Daily Mail*, 15 August 1957
44. Contemporary Los Angeles news cutting
45. *Ibid.*
46. Edwards, *The Road to Tara,* 220
47. Miscellaneous press cutting in album, August 1957 (SFP)
48. L.H. to Mrs. Hartley, 25 August 1957 (SFP)
49. Hon. Colin Clark to author, 22 February 1987
50. L.H. to Oswald Frewen, 22 October 1957 (SFP)
51. Hon. Colin Clark to author, 22 February 1987
52. Suzanne Holman to Mrs. Hartley, 28 November 1957 (SFP)
53. Oswald Frewen diary, 6 December 1957
54. Mrs. Hartley diary, 6 December 1957 (SFP)
55. V.L. to Suzanne Holman, 6 December 1957 (SFP)
56. *Daily Mirror*, 7 December 1957
57. *Daily Mail,* 7 December 1957
58. *Daily Express,* 7 December 1957

CHAPTER TWENTY-ONE

1. Anthony Holden, *Olivier*, 314
2. V.L. to Suzanne Farrington, 5 February 1958 (SFP)
3. Barrault, *Memories,* 309
4. Dent, *Bouquet,* 170
5. Miscellaneous press cutting in album, April 1958)SFP)
6. *Ibid.*
7. Claire Bloom, *Limelight and After,* 149-50
8. Ann Todd, *The Eighth Veil*, 91
9. Derek Nimmo to author.
10. Peter Wyngarde to author, 3 May 1988
11. Olivier, *Confessions,* 185
12. Peter Wyngarde to author, 3 May 1988
13. *Ibid.*
14. *Ibid.*
15. *Ibid.*
16. Dent, *Bouquet,* 56
17. V.L. to Suzanne Farrington, 8 March 1958 (SFP)
18. *The Noël Coward Diaries,* 10 May 1958, 379
19. *Ibid.*
20. V.L. to Suzanne Farrington, 23 May 1958 (SFP)
21. Mrs. Hartley diary, 9 August 1958 (SFP)
22. Hon. Mrs. Tritton to author, 28 November 1986
23. *Ibid.*
24. *Ibid.*

25. *Ibid.*
26. Mrs. Hartley diary, 9 October 1958 (SFP)
27. *Ibid.,* 8 October 1958 (SFP)
28. *Ibid.*, 9 October 1958 (SFP)
29. *Ibid.,* 7-8 October 1958 (SFP)
30. Peter Wyngarde to author, 3 May 1988
31. *Daily Mail*, 20 November 1958
32. *The Noël Coward Diaries*, 30 November 1958, 391
33. *Ibid.*, 7 December 1958
34. Mrs. St. John Ives to author, 28 March 1987
35. Irina Baronova Tennant to author, January 1988
36. Oswald Frewen diary, 16 March 1959
37. Frewen, *Sailor's Soliloquy,* 248
38. V.L. to L.H., 9 December 1958 (SFP)
39. *The Noël Coward Diaries,* 21 December 1958, 392
40. *Ibid.*, 393
41. *Ibid.*, 8 February 1959, 401
42. *Woman's Mirror,* 6 March 1959
43. *Daily Mail*, 19 June 1962
44. *Daily Express,* March 1959
45. *Ibid.*
46. *Ibid.*
47. *New York Enquirer,* 15 March 1959
48. *Ibid.*
49. L.H. to Mrs. Hartley 20 May 1959
50. Winn, *Ordinary Seaman*, 393
51. *Ibid.*, 394
52. *Ibid.*
53. V.L. to L.H., 21 September 1959 (SFP)
54. Gourlay, *Olivier*, 81
55. Tynan, *Curtains*, 234
56. *Sunday Times*, 2 August 1959
57. Winn, *The Positive Hour,* 393
58. Lady Richardson to author, 7 February 1987
59. Rosemary Geddes to author, 9 February 1987
60. Harrison, *Rex,* 159
61. *The Noël Coward Diaries*, 19 September 1959, 416
62. *The Star,* 22 September 1959
63. *Daily Sketch*, 2 December 1959
64. *Daily Mail*, 3 December 1959
65. Cecil Brock to Suzanne Farrington, July 1967 (SFP)
66. Mrs. Hartley diary, 20 December 1959 (DFP)
67. *Ibid.*, 25 December 1959 (SFP)
68. *The Noël Coward Diaries*, 1 January 1960; Lesley, *Remembered Laughter,* 396

69. Mrs. Hartley diary, 10 January 1960 (SFP)
70. Granger, *Sparks Fly Upward,* 401

CHAPTER TWENTY-TWO

1. Private information, October 1987
2. Moira Lister to author, 26 March 1987
3. *Daily Mail*, 6 August 1984
4. Michael Denison to author, 2 February 1987
5. Maxine Audley to author, 12 February 1987
6. Private information, March 1987
7. Moira Lister to author, 26 March 1987
8. V.L. to Mercia Relph April 1960
9. *The Noël Coward Diaries,* 20 March 1960, 431
10. *Ibid.*
11. Peter Wyngarde to author, 3 May 1988
12. Stephen Merivale, C.B.E. to John Merivale, 8 February 1967
13. Sheridan Morley, *Gladys Cooper,* 213
14. *Ibid.*, 178
15. John Merivale to author, 30 November 1986
16. *Ibid.*, 29 April 1988
17. *Ibid.,* 3 May 1988
18. *New York Times*, 20 April 1960
19. *Ibid.*
20. *New York World Telegram and Sun*, 20 April 1960
21. *First Night Report,* April 1960
22. Peter Wyngarde to author, 3 May 1988
23. *New York Times*, 17 April 1960
24. Charles Russell to author, 21 January 1988
25. Garson Kanin to author, 22 January 1988
26. *Ibid.*
27. John Merivale to author, 30 November 1986
28. Peter Wyngarde to author, 3 May 1988
29. Mrs. Hartley diary, 12 May 1960 (SFP)
30. *Ibid.*, 13 May 1960
31. *Ibid.,* 16 May 1960
32. V.L. to J.M., 14 May 1960
33. *Ibid.*
34. *Daily Mirror*, 23 May 1960
35. John Merivale to author, 30 November 1986
36. *Ibid.*
37. *Los Angeles Times*, 29 April 1960
38. *Daily Sketch,* 23 May 1960
39. *The Star,* 23 May 1960

40. *Daily Sketch*, 23 May 1960
41. *Daily Mail*, 23 May 1960
42. John Merivale to author, 3 May 1988
43. *Ibid.,* 30 November 1986
44. *Ibid.*
45. *Ibid.*
46. Mrs. Hartley diary, 28 May 1960
47. *Ibid.*, 3 June 1960
48. Alexander Walker, *Vivien*, 252
49. V.L. to J.M., 15 June 1960
50. *Ibid.*
51. *Ibid.*
52. John Merivale to author, 30 November 1986
53. *The Noël Coward Diaries,* 19 June 1960, 441
54. Report by Dr. Arthur Conachy, 20 June 1961
55. *Ibid.*
56. *Ibid.*
57. *Ibid.*
58. *Ibid.*
59. V.L. to J.M., 20 June 1960
60. V.L. to L.O. 20 Jun 1960, in the aeroplane – British Library
61. *New York World Telegram and Sun,* 20 April 1960
62. John Merivale to author, 30 November 1986
63. J.M. to Mrs. Hartley, 21 June 1960 (SFP)
64. V.L. to Mrs. Hartley, 21 June 1960 (SFP)
65. *Housewife,* August 1960
66. John Merivale to author, 30 November 1986
67. V.L. to Rosemary Geddes, 14 July 1960
68. V.L. to L.H., 22 August 1960 (SFP)
69. Sunny Lash to author, 22 April 1988
70. John Merivale to author, 30 November 1986
71. V.L. to L.H., 22 August 1960 (SFP)
72. *Ibid.*, 20 September 1960 (SFP)
73. *Daily Express*, October 1960
74. John Merivale to author 5 February 1987
75. Elspeth March to author, 16 February 1987
76. *Ibid.*
77. *The Noël Coward Diaries,* 11 November 1960, 452
78. Hermione Baddeley, *The Unsinkable Hermione Baddeley* 185
79. John Merivale to author, 10 February 1987
80. V.L. to Rosemary Geddes, 30 December 1960

CHAPTER TWENTY-THREE

1. Mrs. Hartley diary, 1 January 1961 (SFP)
2. Tennessee Williams, *The Roman Spring of Mrs. Stone*, 12
3. Dent, *Bouquet,* 135
4. Coral Browne to author, 30 January 1986
5. Script of *The Roman Spring of Mrs. Stone*
6. *Ibid.*
7. Tennessee Williams, *Memoirs,* 226
8. John Merivale to author, 5 February 1987
9. Charles Russell to author, 21 January 1988
10. Charles Castle to author, 15 March 1987
11. John Merivale to author, 5 February 1987
12. Joan Collins, *Past Imperfect*, 191
13. V.L. to Rosemary Geddes, 21 February 1962
14. *Show*, February 1962
15. John Merivale to author, 10 February 1987
16. V.L. to J.M., 10 March 1961
17. Mrs. Hartley diary, 18 March 1961 (SFP)
18. J.M. to Mrs. Hartley, 5 April 1961
19. *The Noël Coward Diaries,* 3 April 1961, 468
20. J.M. to Mrs. Hartley, 5 April 1961 (SFP)
21. V.L. to Mrs. Hartley, 8 April 1961 (SFP)
22. *Daily Mirror*, 5April 1961
23. V.L. to Suzanne Farrington, 20 July 1961 (SFP)
24. John Merivale to author, 3 May 1988
25. *Ibid.*, 10 February 1987
26. V.L. to J.M., 26 June 1961
27. J.M. to Mrs. Hartley, 30 June 1961 (SFP)
28. *Ibid.,* 14 July 1961 (SFP)
29. V.L. to L.H., 14 July 1961 (SFP)
30. J.M. to Mrs. Hartley, January 1962 (SFP)
31. *Ibid.*
32. John Merivale to author, 10 February 1987
33. *Ibid.*
34. V.L. to Mrs. Hartley, 5 August 1962 (SFP)
35. J.M. to Mrs. Hartley, 30 August 1961 (SFP)
36. *Ibid.*
37. V.L. to L.H., 16 September 1961 (SFP)
38. John Merivale to author, 10 February 1987
39. V.L to L.H., 28 October 1961 (SFP)
40. *Ibid.*
41. John Barnard to Michael Redington, 1986
42. John Merivale to author, 17 February 1987
43. David Dodimead to author, 19 March 1988

44. V.L. to Mrs. Hartley, 8 January 1962
45. J.M. to Mrs. Hartley, 21 January 1962 (SFP)
46. *Ibid.*, 30 January 1962 (SFP)
47. *Ibid.*
48. V.L. to Mrs. Hartley, 30 January 1962 (SFP)
49. David Dodimead to author, 19 March 1988
50. *Ibid.*
51. V.L. to Hester St. John Ives, 30 March 1962
52. V.L. to L.H., 24 January 1962 (SFP)
53. *New Zealand Herald*, 18 July 1962
54. Julian Faigan to author, 8 May 1987
55. John A. Lee, *For Mine is the Kingdom,* 6 & 9
56. Ivor Herbert, *The Queen Mother's Horses*, 99
57. Queen Elizabeth The Queen Mother to Author, 2 April 1987
58. *Timaru Herald,* New Zealand, 14 February 1962
59. John Merivale to author, 17 February 1987
60. V.L. to L.H., 11 February 1962 (SFP)
61. Letters to Mrs. Hartley from Sir Ernest Davis, March-September 1962 (SFP)
62. V.L. to John Merivale, 8 April 1962
63. V.L. to Suzanne Farrington, 11 April 1962 (SFP)
64. John Merivale to Mrs. Hartley, 21 April 1962 (SFP)
65. John Merivale to author, 17 February 1987
66. V.L. to L.H., 23 April 1962 (SFP)
67. V.L. to Mrs. Hartley, 14 May 1962 (SFP)

CHAPTER TWENTY-FOUR

1. Mercia Relph to author, 25 February 1987
2. *Daily Mail*, 19 June 1962
3. V.L. to L.H., 6 August 1962 (SFP)
4. C.B. unpublished diary, August 1962 (CBP)
5. *The Noël Coward Diaries*, 6 August 1962, 511
6. *Ibid.,* 18 September 1962, 513
7. V.L. to J.M., 12 November 1962
8. L.H. to Mrs. Hartley, 14 November 1962 (SFP)
9. V.L. to J.M., 19 November 1962
10. *Ibid.,* 30 November 1962
11. V.L. to J.M., 14 December 1962
12. Trudie Flockert to Mrs. Hartley, 19 December 1962 (SFP)
13. V.L. to J.M., 28 December 1962
14. *Ibid.*
15. Noël Coward to J.M., cable, 22 January 1963
16. *The Noël Coward Diaries*, 27 January 1963, pp.526-7

17. Kathy Jones to Mrs. Hartley, 27 June 1963 (SFP)
18. Jean-Pierre Aumont, *Sun and Shadow*, 223
19. V.L. to J.M., 28 January 1963
20. *Ibid.,* 6 February 1963
21. *Ibid.,* 21 March 1963
22. *Ibid.,* 22 March 1963
23. L.H. to Mrs. Hartley, 3 April 1963 (SFP)
24. John Merivale to author, 14 April 1987
25. *Ibid.*
26. Dent, *Bouquet*, 100-101
27. V.L. to L.H., 29 April 1963 (SFP)
28. Quoted V.L. to L.H., 17 June 1963 (SFP)
29. Lucinda Ballard Dietz to author, 17 April 1988
30. V.L. to L.H., 7 August 1963 (SFP)
31. Jean-Pierre Aumont to author, 1 July 1988
32. Aumont, *Sun and Shadow*, 233
33. John Merivale to author, 14 April 1987
34. Late Hamish Hamilton to author, 19 October 1986
35. John Merivale to author, 14 April 1987
36. *Ibid.*
37. Lady Diana Cooper to C.B., 9-10 October 1963 (CBP)
38. Anne Tovey to Dick Wordley, 29 March 1987
39. *Ibid.*
40. *Ibid.*
41. John Merivale to author, 14 April 1987
42. *Ibid.*
43. *Ibid.*
44. *Ibid.*
45. Anne Tovey to Dick Wordley, 29 March 1987
46. V.L. to L.H., 2 January 1964 (SFP)
47. John Merivale to author, 14 April 1987
48. John Lahr, *Prick Up Your Ears*, 168
49. V.L. to L.H., 27 May 1964 (SFP)

CHAPTER TWENTY-FIVE

1. *New York Times*, 1 April 1962
2. Enrique Hank Lopez, *Conversations with Katherine Anne Porter*, 294
3. *Ship of Fools* filmscript
4. *Los Angeles Times*, 13 June 1965
5. *Ibid.*
6. V.L. to L.H., 21 June 1964 (SFP)
7. Dent, *Bouquet*, 67
8. *Ibid.*, 68

9. John Merivale to author, 21 April 1987
10. John Merivale medical note, July 1964
11. Vivien Leigh, *Two Letters, with An Appreciation by Charles H. Williamson,* 36
12. *Ibid.*
13. *Ibid.*
14. *Ibid.*
15. Mrs. Hartley diary, 23 August 1964 (SFP)
16. J.M. to Mrs. Hartley, August 1964 (SFP)
17. Harris, *Radie's World,* 188
18. *Sunday Times*, 24 October 1965
19. *Observer*, 24 October 1965
20. *Ibid.*
21. J.M. to V.L., 5 November 1964
22. V.L. to L.H., 7 November 1964 (SFP)
23. V.L. to J.M. 23, November 1964
24. *Ibid.*
25. *Ibid.*, 9 December 1964
26. Late Hamish Hamilton to author, 19 October 1986
27. Late Hamish Hamilton to J.M., July 1967
28. John Merivale to author, 21 April 1987
29. *Ibid.*, 23 April 1987
30. V.L. to Suzanne Farrington, Saturday (after or on 6) April 1965 (SFP)
31. V.L. to L.H., 1 May 1965
32. John Merivale to author, 21 April 1967
33. Gielgud, *Ivanov* record sleeve
34. *Ibid.*
35. Roland Culver, *Not Quite a Gentleman*, 166
36. Dent, *Bouquet,* 177
37. Joan Fontaine, *No Bed of Roses*, 280-4
38. John Merivale to author, 23 April 1987
39. *Ibid.*, 21 April 1987
40. *Ibid.*
41. *Ibid.*
42. Lord Lambton to author, March 1988
43. *Evening News*, 22 August 1966
44. Mrs. Hartley diary, 8 September 1966 (SFP)

CHAPTER TWENTY-SIX

1. *Status/Diplomat,* February 1967
2. *Ibid.*
3. *Baltimore and Morning Sun*, 21 July 1967
4. Toby Rowland to author, 8 December, 1986.

5. V.L. to J.M., 8 April 1967
6. *Oxford Times,* 5 May 1967
7. Rosemary Geddes to author, 9 February 1987
8. John Merivale to author, 4 May 1987
9. *Ibid.*
10. Toby Rowland to author, 8 December 1986
11. *The Noël Coward Diaries*, 22 June 1967, p. 651
12. John Merivale to author, 4 May 1987
13. Rosemary Geddes to author, 9 February 1987
14. Coral Browne to author, 9 February 1987
15. *The Noël Coward Diaries,* 2 July 1967, p. 651
16. Dent, *Bouquet,* 52
17. Harris, *Radie's World*, 189
18. Recalled by Sunny Lash, 22 April 1988
19. Mrs. Hartley diary, 5 June 1967 (SFP)
20. John Merivale to author, 4 May 1987
21. *Ibid.*
22. Olivier, *Confessions,* 230
23. Vivien Leigh death certificate
24. John Merivale to author, 4 May 1967
25. *The Times*, 10 July 1967
26. *Daily Telegraph*, 9 July 1967
27. Irina Baronova Tennant to author, 10 March 1988
28. *Evening Standard*, 14 July 1967
29. Sir John Gielgud to Mrs. Hartley, 12 July 1967 (SFP)
30. Mills Martin to Mrs. Hartley, 15 July 1967 (SFP)
31. Dorothy Holman to Mrs. Hartley, 13 July 1967 (SFP)
32. C.D. Stephenson to Mrs. Hartley, 9 July 1967 (SFP)
33. Ivy Pugh to Mrs. Hartley, 23 June 1967 (SFP)
34. Tennessee Williams to J.M., 8 July 1967
35. Rachel Kempson to J.M., 9 July 1967
36. David Niven to J.M., 11 July 1967
37. Rex Harrison to J.M., 13 July 1967
38. John Gliddon to J.M., 10 July 1967
39. Cathleen Nesbitt to J.M., July 1967
40. Katharine Hepburn to J.M., 10 July 1967
41. Simone Signoret to J.M., 9 July 1967
42. Lady Diana Cooper to J.M., 1967
43. Sunny Lash to J.M., 28 November 1967
44. John Merivale to author, 4 May 1987
45. Harris, *Radie's World*, 190
46. Gielgud, *Distinguished Company,* John Gielgud's address, 14 August 1967, 70
47. John Merivale to author, 4 May 1987
48. *South Wales Echo,* 15 August 1967

POSTSCRIPT

1. Helen Hanff, *84 Charing Cross Road*, 203
2. Consuelo Langton-Lockton to Mrs. Hartley, 16 December 1967 (SFP)
3. *Ibid.*
4. George Cukor to Mrs. Hartley, 21 March 1968 (SFP)
5. *Ibid.*
6. *Ibid.*
7. *An Appreciation of Vivien Leigh*, USC Friends of the Libraries, 1967
8. Mrs. Hartley diary, 25 February 1968
9. John Merivale to author, 4 May 1987
10. *Ibid.*
11. Private information
12. Holden, *Olivier*, 112

Chronology

1912	Ernest and Gertrude Hartley married
1913	Vivien Leigh born
1932	Vivien marries Leigh Holman
1933	Suzanne Holman born
1937	Vivien elopes with Laurence Olivier
1940	Vivien marries Olivier
1944	Vivien suffers miscarriage
1948	Old Vic Tour of Australia
1956	Vivien suffers second miscarriage
1957	*Titus Andronicus* European Tour
1958	Olivier leaves Vivien
1960	Vivien divorced by Olivier
1961-2	Old Vic Tour of Antipodes and South America
1967	Vivien dies at age 53

Theatre Chronology

1935	*The Green Sash*
	The Mask of Virtue
1936	*Richard II*
	The Happy Hypocrite
	Henry VIII
1937	*Because We Must*
	Bats in the Belfry
	Hamlet (Elsinore)
	A Midsummer Night's Dream
1938	*Serena Blandish*
1940	*Romeo and Juliet* (New York)
1942-3	*The Doctor's Dilemma*
1945	*The Skin of Our Teeth*
1945	*The Skin of Our Teeth*
1948	*The School for Scandal, The Skin of Our Teeth, and Richard III* (Australia and New Zealand)

1949 *Antigone*
The School for Scandal
Richard III
A Streetcar Named Desire
1951 *Caesar and Cleopatra* (London and New York)
Antony and Cleopatra (London and New York)
1953 *The Sleeping Prince*
1955 *Twelfth Night, Macbeth and Titus Andronicus*
1956 *South Sea Bubble*
1957 *Titus Andronicus* (European Tour)
1958 *Duel of Angels*
1959 *Look After Lulu*
1960 *Duel of Angels* (New York)
1961-2 *Duel of Angels, Twelfth Night, Lady of the Camellias* (Antipodean Tour)
1963 *Tovarich* (New York)
1965 *La Contessa*
1966 *Ivanov* (New York)

Film Chronology

1934 *Things are Looking Up*
1935 *The Village Squire*
Gentleman's Agreement
Look Up and Laugh
1937 *Fire Over England*
Dark Journey
Storm in a Teacup
1938 *A Yank at Oxford*
*St. Martin's Lane (*U.S. *Sidewalks of London)*
1939 *Twenty-One Days (*U.S. *Twenty-One Days Together* (filmed 1937)
Gone with the Wind
1940 *Waterloo Bridge*
1941 *Lady Hamilton (*U.S. *That Hamilton Woman)*
1945 *Caesar and Cleopatra*
1947 *Anna Karenina*
1951 *A Streetcar Named Desire*

1953 *(Elephant Walk)*
1955 *The Deep Blue Sea*
1961 *The Roman Spring of Mrs. Stone*
1965 *Ship of Fools*

Hugo Vickers was born in 1951 and educated at Eton and Strasbourg University. He has written the biographies *Cecil Beaton* and *Gladys, Duchess of Marlborough*. He lives in London.